CONTENTS

KV-636-058

When a woman renounces all claim to a voice in the selection of her abode, we may be sure that she will neither interfere much in her husband's political career, nor seek to shine in a salon of blue stockings.

J Holland Rose, *William Pitt and National Revival*, London 1911

PREFACE

This book is a testament to friendship. It attempts in the absence of a biography, to trace the daily life of a much loved woman through the letters she received from members of her family and from her friends.

As the wife of a famous statesman, William Pitt the Elder, first Earl of Chatham, and the mother of William Pitt the younger, the youngest and amongst the longest serving prime ministers in English parliamentary history, she could have been for nearly fifty years of her life the most powerful woman in the country. She was the repository of their plans and the confidante of both. But power, either in its public or private sense was not what she sought. Her husband and her son were men who abhorred patronage, and she will have shared this distaste. Only rarely do her correspondents request help to obtain posts or promotions for themselves or their relations and then only with many apologies for so doing. The correspondence is therefore mercifully free from tedious, though occasionally pitiful, submissions and the writers are free to give their views on social, domestic and, less frequently, on political matters, unhampered by the need to extol and to exaggerate the merits of those whose patronage they sought. Only towards the end of her life did Lady Chatham relax this self-imposed rule of no patronage: her letters to her son William from her home Burton Pynsent in Somerset, in the ten years before her death aged eighty-two on 3rd April 1803, contain requests for advancement for her local neighbours and their relations. Due in great part to Chatham's improvidence, his folie de grandeur, but also in the lack of method in the payment of government grants and pensions, the Pitts were always in debt and dependent on loans - and gifts - from family members and friends. Their son William, though content to live more simply than his father, was never free from debt; he would have understood the need for his mother to borrow freely to meet the expenses of a large estate, from friends, neighbours, tenants and employees, both mother and son having learnt from the adored husband and father to brush aside any trace of stigma which might be attached to such a way of life. But because in the last Somerset years Lady Chatham lived so close to her creditors and saw them frequently, often daily, her need to repay in patronage what she was unable to do in money became paramount and the last letters to her son reflect this need with some urgency.

The correspondence selected for inclusion, in whole or in part is from letters written to Lady Chatham and contained in the Chatham Papers in the Public Record Office. The emphasis has been placed on those letters which throw light upon social and family life in the second half of the eighteenth century. Hester Chatham was a home-loving, one might add a rather unsociable woman in the frivolous sense (though she enjoyed hearing about their party doings from her friends). Although steeped in politics all her life, she was essentially non-political; her own letters to her husband and son contain little reference to affairs of state other than rejoicings on a great naval or military victory.

This reluctance to take part in political discussion, on paper at any rate, was recognised by her correspondents; their letters with few exceptions contain only brief mention of public matters; where there is frequent reference to them as for example in the letters of Fanny Boscawen, these have been given fair weight in the extracts chosen.

The need to confine this book to giving a picture of the way people lived in Hester Chatham's time, and to embrace within this object the story of one woman has meant that the majority of the correspondents are women. Also included are letters from family members, of the Grenvilles though not of the Pitts, with whom Hester appears to have had little in common bar friendship and affection for, but no letters from, Pitt's youngest sister Mary, unmarried and for long periods resident at Hayes Place, Kent. There will of course be letters from Hester Chatham in other collections of family papers; it is however felt that there is sufficient material in the selection from this one source to illustrate the character of this endearing woman and those of her friends and relations, set against the background of their lives some two hundred years ago. The correspondence as a whole must inevitably limit the facts and observations contained therein to the lives led by a privileged class of people; but here and there, particularly in the last Somerset period, a welcome shaft of light falls upon those from a different milieu.

EDITOR'S NOTE

A problem with the editing of eighteenth century letters, especially those written by women, lies in the balance to be struck between retention of the customary spelling and phrasing of the time and the requirements of easy reading. The writers were not consistent either in their use of period spelling or in the use of shortened words, eg the words 'would' and 'should' though more frequently spelt 'woud' and 'shoud' were sometimes written in full. Similarly with all words ending in 'ed': the 'e' was omitted in most but not in all cases, some writers substituting an apostrophe, some not. The use of capital letters, although widespread, again was not consistent, varying from writer to writer, and by each writer.

In a publication devoted to letters from several people all living at the same time I have, after consideration, in the interest of uniformity and consistency, decided to keep the letters as written, with only an occasional silent amendment in the interest of clarity. This has meant:

(1) the retention of spelling which was in widespread use at the time, eg 'publick' for 'public'; all words ending in 'ful' spelt as then with double 'll', and so forth, and including the near phonetic spelling of some of the Somerset employees, but
(2) obviously careless spelling has been corrected,
(3) the individual use of capitals has been retained,
(4) the substitution of 'and' for the ampersand has been made throughout to keep uniformity.

Punctuation was universally haphazard, to say the least; it has been added and corrected where necessary to understand the meaning of the text.

Addresses and dates were sometimes placed at the end of letters, sometimes at the top. For appearance these have always been given at the top right hand side of the letter but the style of addressing and dating has been retained.

A feature of the letters is economy in the use of space (one correspondent apologises on grounds of tiredness for leaving a blank page). Consequently there is little attempt at paragraphing. Here also, in the interest of easy reading, indentations have been added to the text, always at the beginning of the letter or extract, less often in the middle.

The use of dots to indicate omissions has been confined to breaks in the main body of the text.

Beginnings and especially endings of the letters varied little and have been omitted in the main to save space, but in each individual correspondence they have been added from time to time to indicate changes, if any, in the styles used.

In order to keep the vast amount of material to form one volume of a reasonable size, it has been necessary to use only a fraction of the available correspondence and drastically to curtail most of the letters used. In this sorry necessity I have been guided by limited objectives:

(1)   to describe through their letters the domestic and social affairs, travels, hopes and fears of people who lived two or more hundred years ago;

(2)   to tell the story, as revealed in the letters to her, of one woman, Hester Chatham.

To these ends, comment on political affairs has been retained only insofar as it reflects the character of the writer and what he or she felt would be of interest to Lady Chatham. To keep the narrative in train, there has been some inclusion of letters written to William Pitt, husband of Hester, and a few extracts from her own letters to her husband and son.

The letters of some of the correspondents do not fall entirely within the outlines of the editorial scheme given in this note; to avoid separate notes preceding each chapter a short list of variations pertaining to the correspondence is given here:

The Brotherhood

All five of Hester's brothers received a good classical education and their letters reflect it. Very little silent amendment has been necessary. The most voluminous correspondence, which included many letters to William Pitt (Chatham) is that of the eldest brother:

Richard, Earl Temple. The early and the late letters begin 'Dear Sister', those of the mid-period more formally 'My dear Lady Hester' or after 1761 'Lady Chatham'. He was an emotional, excitable man and his letters mirror this aspect of his character. He signed himself mostly informally and generally affectionately, 'Temple' or 'T'.

George Grenville was a colder man than his elder brother, but equally devoted to his sister. His early letters are straightforward, written in a good clear hand with reasonable punctuation needing little amendment, and the use of capitals is restrained. Before Hester married the letters begin 'my dear Hetty', usually incorporated into the opening sentence and end simply 'Adieu' without signature. Later he wrote 'my dear Sister', the endings more formal and the letters signed.

James Grenville the third, and after Thomas, Hester's favourite brother, wrote well. The early letters were to 'Dr Hester' usually incorporated into the first sentence, later to 'My dear Sister' or 'My dear Lady Chatham' and with affectionate informal endings, some strangely modern - 'Ever Yours, JG'.

Thomas Grenville's letters were the earliest of all Hester's surviving correspondence and all were written before she married (he died in 1747). He addresses her as Hetty and his endings are informal and affectionate. The only amendment made to his letters has been to put the names of his ships in italics, thus to distinguish them from shore addresses.

Lifelong Friends

The epistolary styles, and probably the nature and degree of their education, varied considerably as would be expected, thus:

Hester Lyttelton, Mrs Fitzmaurice. Her letters are lively and easy to read, the punctuation superior to that of the other women correspondents and needing little amendment. Capitals are used in moderation, diminishing as the years went on (a feature of most of the correspondence). Beginning and endings were hardly changed and were mostly formal but with an affectionate turn. Although friends from childhood, the surviving correspondence begins only after Hester had been married several years which would account for the formalities.

Jane Hamilton, Lady Cathcart. Her letters begin when she was a young girl of twenty-one (thus far more immature than now) and cover the succeeding twenty years. The early letters in particular needed much added punctuation, but such stops have only been inserted when necessary to understanding her sometimes long-winded, even tortuous phrasing; at times she herself seems to lose the thread of what she was trying to convey, particularly when writing in her rather indifferent French. But always in mind was the need to keep intact the somewhat breathless flavour of her style, and her not very good spelling has been retained. The beginnings were formal throughout, the endings varying and affectionate.

Molly West, Mrs Hood. Significantly also a Lyttelton like her cousin Hester Fitzmaurice, Molly Hood's letters were well written and phrased and she was careful about punctuation, with prolific use of commas and full stops correctly placed. The beginnings of her letters were usually 'Dear - or Dearest - Madam' and the endings formal, with opportunity taken in each letter to include somewhere in them 'Your Ladyship'.

Elizabeth Wyndham, Mrs George Grenville. Hers are the earliest of the women's letters. Before Hester's marriage they begin 'Dear Miss Grenville'; the endings are formal with variations. But from 1746 there are no endings, not even a signature or initial, an unusual feature of the correspondence as a whole, until the last few letters written in the month or so before her death, which are ended and signed in the usual way for close friends. After her marriage in 1749 all Elizabeth's letters begin 'My dear Sister' and continue thus to the end. She was economic with punctuation and amendments have been made. Unfortunately a large number of her letters bear no date, but some attempt has been made to suggest a date arising from the contents of the letter.

Mrs Fanny Boscawen. This exceptional woman will have had many hours of letter writing almost every day and the style of her correspondence with Hester Chatham finds the sentences tumbling out one after the other, punctuation largely ignored. Some order has therefore had to be introduced into the letters and extracts chosen but it is hoped without loss of any of the essential characteristics of this noted letter writer. The beginnings of the letters are mainly incorporated in the opening sentence; where separated, Hester Chatham is addressed as 'My dear - or My Dearest - Madam'. Endings are in the prevailing style used for letters to a titled lady, but usually with the word 'affectionate' included.

Catherine Stapleton. The greatest number of letters written by any one correspondent to Lady Chatham is that of Catherine Stapleton, of which one third are undated. For punctuation she used only the ubiquitous comma. Construction of sentences was not Catherine's strong point and at times she gets herself tied up in knots; these have, when possible, been disentangled by the silent addition of other stops. The use of capitals is haphazard and widespread in the earlier letters, moderating somewhat as time went on. Catherine's mode of address and ending varies, becoming ever more affectionate as she grew older. There is little reference in the letters to political affairs though Catherine will constantly have heard such conversation. The selection reflects the omission and concentrates on the value and charm of someone who was essentially a domestic person.

Social Friends

Grace Trevor was the only spinster, other than Catherine Stapleton, among Hester Chatham's regular correspondents. She was a careful writer - all but eight of her letters are dated - but here too some punctuation has had to be amended. She used capitals with moderation. The beginnings and endings of her letters are formal; she was aware - it could be said in awe - of Hester Chatham's superior social status and 'Your Ladyship' appears in most of her letters. An unusual feature of the early letters is that they were written in the third person and included the name of her great friend Lady Lucy Stanhope; after the latter's death Grace Trevor reverts to the single person and the usual form of address.

Mrs Elizabeth Montagu. She was probably the most famous letter writer of all Hester Chatham's correspondents but it must be said that the letters of those less well known make far better reading. Mrs Montagu's grammar is however correct, as is her punctuation. The near total absence of dating, while tiresome, is not hampering, as her letters all belong to a short period - the early 1770s. She began and ended her letters in the strictly formal manner of her day.

Mrs William Beckford. Her letters were correctly written and punctuated. Beginnings and endings were formal but she occasionally began 'Dear Lady Chatham'. She was one rare correspondent who indented her paragraphs.

Professional Men

Canon Edward Wilson. His letters were a joy to edit. His handwriting is small, neat and legible. Punctuation is good and very few amendments have been necessary. His spelling, curiously modern, was excellent; the few characteristics of the period, eg 'stile' for 'style', have been retained. He was economic in the use of capital letters.

Edward Wilson began all the early letters 'Madam' which became 'My Dear Madam' occasionally 'My Good Madam' and continued thus to the end. His endings were always formal and were little changed throughout the long correspondence.

Dr Anthony Addington received a classical education and this is evident in his letters. Very little silent amendment has been necessary. His punctuation was good with only a slight superfluity of commas, and construction of his sentences admirable. Only fourteen of the near three-hundred letters are undated. The early letters begin 'Madam', becoming soon 'My Good Madam' or 'My Good Lady'. All the endings are formal.

Somerset People

This three-part chapter embraces extracts of letters from thirteen people as well as some from Lady Chatham and her son William Pitt. The correspondence covers a range of epistolary styles, degrees of education and facility of expression. The extracts have been left intact as written, including those of the lowly educated except where some silent punctuation has been added and minor grammatical faults corrected. Spelling, or rather misspelling has been left intact where the meaning of the misspelt word is perfectly clear. The auctioneers' survey of the Burton estate at the time of its sale in 1803 is included as an appendix.

William Pitt and his Mother

His letters, written as a child until his second entry to Cambridge in July 1773, all begin 'Dear Mama' and end (with minor variations) 'Your most dutiful and affectionate son, William Pitt'. Thereafter until the end of their correspondence, the letters begin 'My Dear Mother', the endings remaining the same but with the signature shortened to 'W Pitt'. It has not been found necessary to amend the spelling in the letters either of William or Lady Chatham; both were good spellers. Minor variations in spelling, eg 'tryal' for 'trial' have been left as written, and capital letters, of which William was fond have been retained; they were essentially a part of William's epistolary style.

Sources. All of the extracts from the letters, and quotations therefrom, have been taken from the Chatham Papers in the Public Record Office, PRO 30/8. The dates of the letters will indicate their positions in the chronological lists available in the Kew office of the PRO and from there lead to the folio numbers of the documents.

For background material I am indebted to a number of publications, quotations from which have received due credit in the end notes to chapters.

Vere Birdwood
Public Record Office
1993

ACKNOWLEDGEMENTS

My thanks must go first to John Walford, a principal assistant keeper of the Public Record Office, whose suggestion it was that I should attempt to put together a selection from the letters written to Lady Chatham in her own right, as distinct from the correspondence of her husband which I had been given earlier to edit.

I must also thank other members of the PRO staff: a number of senior officers for their enthusiasm and encouragement, and others for practical work on the project notably Wendy Goldsmith and members of the library staff at Kew and to Melvyn Stainton and Fiona Prothero of Publications Section at Chancery Lane. My gratitude rests heavily on Beryl Saddington and her assistants at Hayes for the skill and intelligence with which they have typed this most difficult manuscript. There can not be many typists who are required faithfully to reproduce faulty grammar and, in modern terms, spelling.

I owe much for help provided me from outside the office, especially to the County Record Offices and their archivists of Clwyd and Somerset and, in particular, Mr H.A. Hanley, county archivist of Buckinghamshire; to the Bath City Council and the archivist, Mr Colin Johnston; to the Huntington library of San Marino, California and its curator Mary L. Robertson. I am grateful to Lord Langford of Bodrhyddan for his interest and the provision of a picture of Catherine Stapleton, his collateral ancestor, and to Mr Tony Hoult for fieldwork locally on her life; to Peter Devlin, actuary, for providing comparative RPI figures for the period; to the late Mr John Schroder of Burton Pynsent, and to the late Mr A.O. Mounter for his fieldwork in Somerset; to Mr J.J. Mangan and his publishers for permission to quote from his book 'King's Favour'; and to my neighbour Mrs Lesley Lewis for the free use of her invaluable library and for her discovery of a portrait of Fanny Boscawen among its contents.

LIST OF ILLUSTRATIONS

LADY HESTER
GRENVILLE
1750

Hester Grenville aged 29
from the painting by Thomas Hudson

Hester Grenville
from the Pretyman portrait, engraved by Emery Walker

William Pitt, Earl of Chatham
studio of R Brompton, by permission of the National Portrait Gallery

William Pitt the Younger as Chancellor of the Exchequer
from the portrait by Gainsborough, engraved by Emery Walker

George Grenville
from the portrait by Joshua Reynolds

Richard Grenville, Earl Temple
from the portrait by Allan Ramsey

The East Front of Sr: Grenvill's house at Wotton
in Com: Bucks.

A View of Sr: Rich: Temple Bar: ...

Wootton Underwood [c 1720] from a drawing by Sir James Thornhill

Burton Pynsent from Collinson's History of Somerset (1791) engraved by T Bonner

Hayes Place, Kent by permission of Mary Evans Picture Library

The Circus, **Bath** by permission of the Victoria Art Gallery, Bath

Catherine Stapleton
by kind permission of Lord Langford of Bodrhyddan

Fanny Boscowen
from the painting at Bill Hill

Elizabeth Montagu
from the print by Joshua Reynolds, engraved by T Cheeseman by
permission of the National Portrait Gallery

Anthony Addington
from the portrait of John Romell, by permission of the National
Portrait Gallery

THE COUSINHOOD: Grenvilles, Pitts, Lytteltons

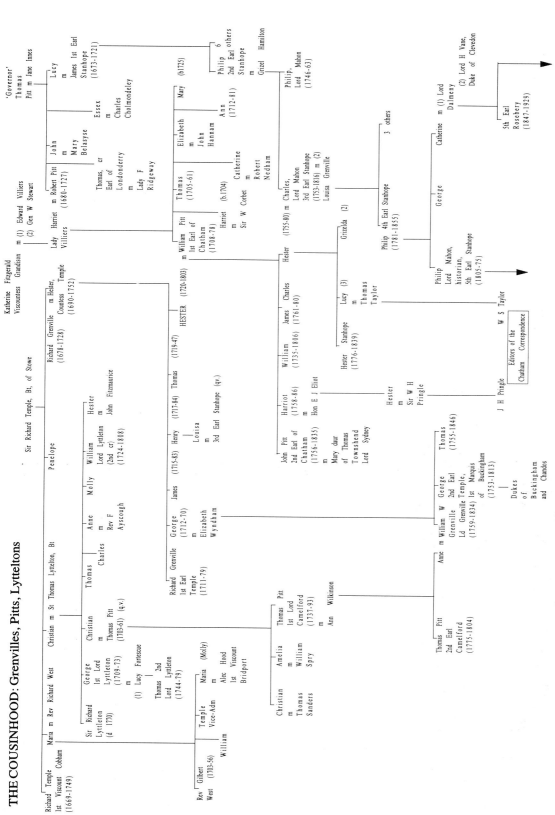

Hester Grenville's Family tree compiled by Melvyn Stainton

SO DEARLY LOVED, SO MUCH ADMIRED

Chapter 1

1720-1753

HESTER GRENVILLE

A chief talking point of her relations and their friends at the time of Hester Grenville's birth in London on 8th November 1720 would certainly have been the bursting of the South Sea Bubble two months earlier. The ensuing panic resulting from the fall in the South Sea Company's shares brought ruin to thousands. That this disaster, notable though it was, should have dominated national thought meant an absence of competition from the hitherto familiar episodes of war and revolution. 'Between 1714 and 1760, the English people, wearied with struggles and sated with glory, was content to stabilise the results of the Revolution, under a dynasty for which it had no love and accept an oligarchic system of government which for the time being was exactly suited to its needs. It was an age of stability in politics, in religion, in literature, and in social observances, a stability needed to enable the nation to recover its poise after more than a century of excitement.[1]

This baby girl, therefore, was born to peace but for most of the latter part of her adult life was to live with little else but war, albeit at a physical distance, and to know of, though not to experience, the greatest Revolution of them all, that in France in 1789. In fact, she never once left the shores of England or crossed the boundaries of Scotland or Wales in her long lifetime. She was the sixth and youngest child and the only daughter of Richard Grenville of Wotton Underwood in Buckinghamshire, nine miles north-west of Aylesbury. This house, Wotton, was admired and much loved by all the members of the family, and by George, the second son, and Elizabeth Grenville whose home it was after their marriage in 1749. Their letters abound in its praise: 'your poor old favourite Wotton [is] in its greatest beauty'. Long after Hester's death and that of all her generation and most of the next, the house they knew was burnt down. It was rebuilt in 1821 by her great nephew, Richard Grenville, first duke of Buckingham and Chandos in the style, according to the National Gazetteer of 1868 'of old Buckingham Palace, at Pimlico'. The Grenvilles of Wootten, as it was originally spelt, were an old family of landed gentry living in this house or possibly an earlier one on the same site, at least since the fourteenth century, distinguished locally but not in wider spheres until the marriage of Hester's parents. Her father was member of parliament for Andover, then for Buckingham; her mother was Hester, daughter of Sir Richard Temple of Stowe. The

Stowe connection transformed the fortunes of the family; Hester, wife of Richard, was the second and favourite sister of the fourth baronet, also Sir Richard Temple, better known as Viscount Cobham, a man not only of great wealth but also distinguished as a soldier, diplomat and politician. Dying in September 1749, he was succeeded in the peerage under special remainder by his sister Hester, who was created Countess Temple within six weeks of her brother's death. Cobham, on the death of his brother-in-law Richard Grenville in 1727 had 'virtually adopted his children, ultimately settling his whole estate on the eldest, Richard, thus uniting the estates of Wotton and Stowe'.[2]

So much for Hester Grenville's ancestry. For her appearance it is necessary to rely, as all the biographers of Pitt have done, on her portraits. Nowhere in the correspondence, whether in that between husband and wife, or in any of the letters from her friends and relations, is there mention of her physical appearance, or even of her dress, and we must assume that it was not *comme il faut* in her circles to commit to writing a lady's looks, even among women friends, though doubtless in intimate conversation between close friends of the same sex appearance and dress were often a subject of discussion. The portraits show a young woman (if any were painted in later life none survive) of good looks, not beautiful but infinitely attractive, with auburn hair and the tilted nose inherited by her second son, William Pitt of historic fame. Though essentially a countrywoman, she was at ease in a town setting and took care of her appearance. She writes in the early 1770s of being 'under the hands of Mitan', the fashionable hairdresser of the day. Much earlier, in an undated letter, Elizabeth Grenville, her sister-in-law, is surprised at hearing of Hester's party to Ranelagh 'taking a trip into the great world in a very unexpected manner'. But though always averse to the extremely sophisticated social life of her times, she nevertheless loved to hear about the London scene with all its gossip, from the letters of her friends whose lives were mainly set within that scene.

Hester Grenville was intelligent, well-educated but not an intellectual woman. The correspondence reveals nothing of her childhood or early girlhood; the earliest letters to her are from her favourite brother Thomas in 1742, when she was already of age. It is from the letters of two girl friends, Jane Hamilton, who became Lady Cathcart in 1753, and Elizabeth Wyndham, later Hester's sister-in-law, that throw most light on her enviable life as the adored only sister of five vigorous brothers, passed mainly in the beautiful and wealthy setting of Stowe and Wotton. She also moved about and like most members of her circle paid lengthy and frequent visits to spas. Bath and particularly Tunbridge Wells (though not Cheltenham) were well like by her. While it may seem strange today when spa visiting, if carried out at all, would essentially be confined to the elderly with rheumatic and similar complaints, the spas in Hester's day were not only frequented by young people of both sexes but were regarded by their parents as places where suitable matrimonial prospects would be sought and found. It is at Tunbridge Wells that we first hear, not only of Hester's love of riding, but also of her excursions on horseback accompanied by possible suitors. Jane Hamilton's letters from the Hot Wells of Bristol also speak of riding and her indignation when a young man asked her if she ever 'rode double'.

And so passed the first thirty-three years of Hester Grenville's life, trouble-free, calm and placid. Excluding the first ten years of childhood her long life falls approximately into three sections of about twenty-five years, girlhood, marriage and widowhood. To meet the difficulties and sorrows of the two latter periods, she was sustained by the physical and mental strength built into her by her carefree youth, and by her own innate courage.

1   Basil Williams, *The Whig Supremacy 1714-1760*, 2nd (revised) edition, OUP 1965
2   *History of Parliament. The House of Commons 1715-1754*, HMSO 1970

Chapter 2

1754-1778

PITT AND HESTER: A LOVE STORY

When Lady Hester Grenville married William Pitt on 16th November 1754 both had had a birthday that month: Hester's thirty-fourth and Pitt's forty-seventh. There is no mention of this coincidence in any exchange of letters, neither in those between themselves nor in comment from friends and relations. The only birthday publicly celebrated was that of the reigning king; private birthdays, even those of children, were a private matter which together with age were not apparently, in their circles, a subject to write about. This first marriage for both, in an era when the average expectation of life was in the early forties, was late by the standards of that day and indeed by those of any day.

Neither Pitt nor Hester had had any serious affairs of the heart before their marriage. In Hester's case this was understandable, given the mores of the time and her congenial and happy family life. There is speculation by some of Pitt's biographers that she had always cherished a special affection and admiration for him since childhood, when he was a frequent visitor to Stowe and Wotton. But the evidence is slender and unconvincing. For Pitt his restless nature, his hypochondria, political ambition and lack of means all contrived to keep him single. He was also exceptionally fond of his third sister Ann, who never married; she filled an emotional though strictly honourable element in his rather bleak personal life. When therefore his sudden courtship of Hester in September, on a visit to Wotton and their engagement to marry became known, there was both pleasure and surprise among their friends and members of Hester's family.

Pitt spent most of the six weeks before the event separated from his fiancée at Bath, a pattern in their lives which was to continue until a year or two before his death, when he was too ill to make the journey to his beloved spa. Pitt's obsession with Bath, though hard to equate in modern terms with a happy marriage has, thankfully, left to posterity a periodic, at times a daily record of love letters which passed between them at this time, and later when his work and Hester's dislike of London again contrived to keep them apart. From the outset of their marriage of twenty-four years, few wives can have suffered so much separation from a much loved husband, much of it voluntary on his part, as did Hester. But her devotion to him never faltered.

Pitt's letters in the engagement month of October speak of little else but his great love for Hester, of 'gratitude, passion and adoration without end'. There is reference to a misunderstanding but which is now 'over, forever erased, out of memory', and in this letter of 27th October he fears that her esteem for him may not last forever. Two days earlier he had asked Hester to write to his 'poor sister Ann' who was not well enough to come to England from France, and on her agreement to do so he writes back with 'tears of gratitude', describing his sister as 'an almost expiring poor woman' (she died in 1781, twenty-seven years later).

Hester was at her home, Wotton, and at Stowe during this month. For the first but not the last time in their lives together she is concerned about the terrible weather for Pitt's journey to Bath on 9th October. On the 13th she writes, prophetically '. . . the evil of absence [which] is a necessary one and must be submitted to'. Her thoughts range wider than Pitt's; her brother Henry Grenville - 'the Governor' - is going to Bath and wants one of Pitt's servants to engage rooms for him; these should have a bedchamber, a separate room for wardrobe and baggage, a parlour for seeing company and two garrets for his servants. All the brothers agree that the engagement should no longer remain a secret and 'the Dowager approves without her usual *But* '. She accepts that Pitt wants to make some sort of permanent second home at Bath, and suggests that meantime the wallpaper of his present rooms should be matched to the chair covers and curtains to avoid a mixture of colours. Both Pitt and his fiancée, especially Hester, are shaken by the news of the sudden death of the Queensberry son and both refer to it in a similar phrase 'an event to make the happy tremble'.

The correspondence now moves to the latter part of December. Once again Pitt is alone at Bath, his wife in their official residence at the Pay Office in London. They spend the first Christmas of their marriage apart. Pitt writes to her on the 25th but makes no mention of the day; Hester does so. On the 26th she writes that 'I eat my Christmas Pye with the little Cathcart in her little parlour where everything is on her own scale'. There is no other mention of any festivity. Pitt is busy building a house in Bath and wants her opinion on its embellishment but Hester is cool about the project; he must follow his own judgement in 'the grand affair' proposed by him. At the end of the month she is returning to Wickham in Kent, the home of her relations the Gilbert Wests, where they spent their honeymoon; there she will love her solitude, being 'given up to reflections like those that sweet place will inspire'. But on this visit she finds herself left on her own to care for the West's dying son Richard, and his death early in January brings from Pitt once again the phrase 'an event to make the happy tremble'.

Pitt returned to London early in January 1755 but is back again in Bath in September, when the correspondence resumes. Hester, remaining at the Pay Office, is eight months pregnant with her first child and her 'situation' is now one subject of the letters. She is under the care of Dr John Hunter who is satisfied with her condition. Pitt in his letter of September 29th assures her that 'either sex will be equally welcome' but goes on to deplore the lack of progress in his housebuilding in Bath. Three days later he enquires tenderly about her 'state'. 'Tell me what you do. Do you take the air? Can you bear a chaise? Do you eat, can you sleep?'. On the 25th she replies to his anxious enquiries: she 'airs every day in the chaise' and 'eats enough for two'. She sleeps better in her 'sweet blue bed' because of the cooler weather. They exchange news of family and friends. Hester pays social visits and Pitt comments on Governor Lyttelton's adventures in France as a short term captive. He, Pitt, is living a country life but missing his 'most amiable partner'. She finds writing difficult because of her increasing size. She is dismayed at his delayed return; he assures her this is on doctor's orders. 'My heart is too passionately yours and my nature too sensible of all that comes from you, not to feel . . . the smallest intimation of supposed inattention to you'. On 3rd October she 'forbids [herself] from feeling a disappointment . . . if [the delay] is really necessary'.

Two months later Hester has had her baby and Pitt is back again in Bath. He had arrived on December 24th dirty and uncomfortable and unable to get the lodging he had hoped for. Hester tells him that she must 'adhere to my old maxim and suffer my regret upon a necessary evil' but she misses him even more than on his last visit to Bath and wishes him a merry Christmas. She is house-hunting and he has news of a possible house to rent in Upper Brook Street. Pitt's youngest sister Mary is staying with her and on 25th December they 'ate their Christmas Pye in Brook Street' (a Grenville home) and spent the day there. Meantime Pitt has dined with Ralph Allen and 'roamed his hills on Poppet'. She is worried by Henry Grenville's report on the delays and bad workmanship of the Bath house, which will upset Pitt's plan for settling in in the spring. Pitt is touched at her concern: 'the sweet peace of soul' her letters bring. From 23rd December to 5th January Hester writes every day, Pitt almost as often. Her news of the baby who refused to smile when the Dowager visited; Pitt's assurance that 'poor little Dame Hester is not less dear to me than a son and heir to our no-estate cou'd have been'. The Upper Brook Street house and the owner Mrs Nesbitt's terms for leasing: £100 per annum 'without stabling or offices without [out of] doors'. She regrets the inside kitchen 'but we must learn to live without roast beef on Sundays'. In this letter of 3rd January 1756 she expresses, albeit guardedly, an uneasiness about the Bath house, not lost on Pitt who replies on 5th January that the house is too far advanced to recede: he could 'never imagine that any plan cou'd be long practical for me, without a house at Bath . . . for the evening of my days'. Hester's letters describe a full social life mainly with and around the Grenville family but there is occasional depression: 'the day [January 2nd] is heavy and dull and I sympathise with it'. However, three days later she is joyous at the prospect of Pitt's return.

In November 1755 Pitt was dismissed from his office of paymaster-general. A year later on 4th December he became secretary of state for the southern department, leader of the House of Commons and actual premier. There is of course no mention of these momentous happenings in the correspondence between husband and wife; they were together at the relevant dates. During this time they acquired the house at Hayes which they were to own, with a short gap in 1766-67, until Pitt's death. His letters to Hester during the years of his greatest fame, 1757-61, are for the most part short and undated, hardly more than notes. His work kept him much in London though he was also able to spend at least some nights in each week at Hayes. But every hour spent apart from one another was a torment and loss to the devoted couple: 'just a moment to write between conversations'. Hester herself, most of whose letters during these years are from Hayes, was also occasionally away staying with the Temples at Stowe or at Wotton with her second brother George Grenville and his wife and, rarely, in London. In her absence Pitt spent more time at Hayes to keep an eye on the children, Hester, John, Harriot, William and James. The two elder sons were born at Hayes, the daughters and James in London. As is often the case where a husband deeply loves his wife, Pitt was a most devoted father to 'her sweet little race'. There is some political comment, and war news, but the children's welfare is the paramount subject: 'Hester ails a little, and her imagination still more'. In a rare dated letter of 30th June 1761 he sends news from 'our Hovel of Hayes . . . new Hayes rises apace to take place of something I must ever love'. Hester's letters are longer and her admiration for Pitt abounds. She sees him everywhere. Writing from Stowe in June 1578 she tells him that alterations there do not please her: 'I cannot now follow your dear private happiness and for the public glory'. She was not starry-eyed about all his family; in this same letter she has 'asked sister Mary to tell Mrs Nedham that I am upon my couch . . . which I hope will prevent a visit'. On 1st January 1760 they were apart and she sends him New Year wishes. She believes that the people of Hayes were so fond of the old year that they did not want to part with it 'for no notice has been taken of the new by bells or any other sort of celebration'.

The correspondence of these five years paints in words an idyllic picture of the brilliantly successful father, the five lively and happy children growing up under the care of their devoted parents (and a hoard of servants) in a setting, Hayes Place, beautiful and loved. All of this is faithful and true; but shadows lurk. There is the occasional complaint from Pitt about his health: 'an increase of uneasiness and weakness' in his left hand 'threatening real gout'. They are increasingly hard up. In an undated letter of 1759 Hester writes that though she hates to bother Pitt about money she urgently needs £30 'for the nurses'. They borrowed from relations, friends, colleagues and even senior servants and by the early 1770s were deeply in debt. Those difficult years were however some way ahead and Hester's letters from 1757 to 1761 were, if anything, even more effusive in their expressions of love than in the earlier correspondence. On 6th July 1759, from Wotton she writes:

> My most Loved Love,
>   . . . the tender expressions of that love which makes all my happiness, my Angel will easier imagine than I can tell him. The overflowing of a Heart, filled with such variety of sentiments of affection and admiration as mine is for the adored object of all my thoughts.
> > Your truly loving wife
> > H Pitt

In the confidence of her full maturity she feels able to write to him in a style unhampered by the hesitations, the taboos of the day. There is now a hint of the erotic in some letters: '[Hetty] sends a kiss to dear Papa, and Mama will have a thousand ready [on] Saturday to pay [for] those dear Ideal ones of last night' she writes in an undated letter of 1760. Her 'pride and pleasure . . . in her loved bowery bedchamber with [his] dear letters upon her pillow'. 'I accept your dear Kisses my most loved and send you ten thousand in return'. She recognises the need at this time for Pitt's 'later hours and oppressive business' but she hopes her 'dearest love will be at liberty to pass his usual time at Hayes with his passionately loving wife'. 'I contrived to compose myself to a quiet sleep after you went, my angel, which lasted till past ten, by which means I had a late second breakfast'. Pitt, the head of a country at war and yet a devoted family man will have craved the myriad of domestic details of daily life at Hayes so amply provided by his wife. The detail is in fact surprising when set against the background of Pitt's frequent visits. There is a part explanation: 'I write to you because I must give expression to the thoughts with which my mind is filled'. She describes the house and its furnishings: 'Mr Fielder has produced a border for the paper, which suits the bed something better than the hangings'. And the gardens 'bear the marks of my Love's hands . . . the Master is plain in all the composition'. 'The hay at the farm is carted and Peter can be spared to take this letter'. The horses are of course important: 'July [coachman] thinks the bays and blacks should be matched together; they go better together'. She hopes that Pitt's ride back to London on Poppet was agreeable. Above all the children. Few indeed are the letters which fail to report some detail of their daily doings, their ailments, their amusing talk, their games. The Pitts were model parents and Hester was a model wife. In an undated letter, probably of 1758 she writes that she knows that 'these times claim all your care for poor England and that she is a rival I must submit to'.

On 5th October 1761 Pitt failed to persuade the cabinet to act against Spain and resigned. He refused any honour for himself but asked that a peerage might be bestowed on his wife. On December 4th Lady Hester Pitt became baroness Chatham.

There is no identifiable correspondence between Pitt and his wife for the next four years. In 1765 Sir William Pynsent, an elderly baronet previously unknown to them, bequeathed to Pitt his estate of Burton Pynsent at Curry Rivel in Somersetshire. At last they had become owners of a substantial landed property. Pitt enjoyed Burton and at once began expansive - and extravagant - building plans and alterations. The separations, as also the correspondence, resumed in 1766. Pitt's illnesses, real gout in the extremities, misdiagnosed gout elsewhere had taken hold, as had the periodic onset of mental instability. He is back in Bath in May and Lady Chatham is left on her own to negotiate the sale of Hayes. What with this undertaking and the arrival of two unexpected families to stay 'I don't know which way to turn' she tells Pitt on 9th May. The next day she expresses her sorrow at leaving Hayes 'so loved a place' but she is 'somewhat fatigued by such continual business and such continual company'. All her labours will however be forgotten the moment she sees her 'beloved husband'. If Pitt was writing to her at this time, which he assuredly was, his letters have not survived. His wife's letters are now mainly from Burton Pynsent, into the management of which she has thrown herself with enthusiasm. On 11th July she writes to Pitt, now in London, that she is missing him but finds 'business with Mr Pear and Madam Keetch'[1] good remedies against loneliness. She is worried about his health: 'my mind seems to have no part in anything I do' and by the 18th she has decided to send the children ahead on the planned visit to Weymouth in the care of Nurse Sparry and the tutor, Edward Wilson, and herself proceed to London to be with Pitt in his illness.

In July 'finding the waters of Lethe at Burton Pynsent no more healing than the waters of Bath'[2] Pitt accepted the King's 'desperate bid'[3] to form a ministry. He allotted himself the light post of lord privy seal and was created a peer. On 4th August he became Viscount Pitt of Burton Pynsent and Earl of Chatham. In 1767 Hayes was repurchased, on a whim of Chatham's and without regard to their precarious finances. There is no hint of criticism in Hester's letters. In this year he became for a time mentally incapacitated and in October 1768 he resigned from the government. From 1770 he was sufficiently recovered to attend the House of Lords from time to time, there to attack the government's American policy and to take part in the Wilkes affair. His last appearance in the House, when he collapsed while making a speech, was on 7th April 1778 and he died five weeks later on 11th May at Hayes.

From the year 1768 there are no surviving letters from Chatham but fortunately his wife's letters are there to continue this story of love and esteem. No matter how capricious Chatham's behaviour, how genuine (or neurotic) his prolonged illnesses, her letters when they were apart (and he was ever restless when not actually confined to his room) are full of affection and encouragement and of the domestic news so dear to his heart. 'All is well with the children' she writes in an undated letter, probably of 1770; 'this day given to a general Rhubarbing, to which everyone readily consented'. In July of this year there is news of Hayes: 'the passages will be stuccoed immediately'. She wishes the 'breath of our sweet briar could reach [his] smoky bedchamber'. On 7th August she takes the two youngest children on an excursion to Blackheath: 'everything favoured our pleasure'. Four days later she writes of a great storm and of dinner guest Richard Berenger's fuss and agitation to get away: '[his] continued attention to [the storm's] progress . . . as he was waited for by a friend whose carriage he had borrowed'. Later that month Chatham is at Burton Pynsent with William and James and from Hayes she rejoices in his 'sweet description of the moonlight on Troy Hill lighting the pillar'. In this letter she jokes about the 'great Heat' and her 'degree of perspiration [by which she] might distill with a water nymph'. The household at Hayes receives provisions from Somerset: 'the contents of the Burton basket provided an excellent dinner'. Just now and then there is a passing comment on national affairs; though in her letter of 11th April 1772 she expresses her true feelings: 'the politicks of the times have made no part of our conversation' and continues with details of Dr Addington's prescriptions for William and James. She has heard from brother Temple and is somewhat disparaging about his employment of yet another architect on the work at Stowe: 'If many Heads can compose perfection, his alterations must inherit it'. In this month, with Chatham still at Burton, she tells him on the 14th that she has no fresh news but that 'foreign aids are not necessary to convey . . . the sentiments of the heart'. Both John Pitt and his sisters are in Mitan's hands; on the 21st they are having dancing lessons with Gallini and 'Pitt' has been invited to the grand masquerade at the

Pantheon; she has given her consent. At the end of the month Chatham is still at Burton Pynsent and she is coping with unexpected visitors despite 'so small a complement of servants'.

The following year, 1773, Hester is at Burton and Chatham in June has gone to Lyme Regis with the two sons, Pitt and William, where she plans to pay them a short visit with the girls and James. To save expense she asks him to send his coach and horses to meet her en route at Chard. Once back, on 1st July, she will not again visit Lyme before Chatham's return 'because of oeconomicals'. Through autumn and over Christmas he is still at Lyme; his absence is 'in the present circumstances of displeasing necessity'. His companions have changed (William had gone to Cambridge in October); Chatham now has Hester and James and she hopes that in spite of his pains he has been able to enjoy the 'Merry Christmas with your merry companions'. In this letter of 26th December she describes their own Christmas at Burton and ends with an urgent request for money. On 30th December she writes: 'How am I to thank you, my Loved Life, for your sweet goodness in employing your own [gouty] hand to relieve my fears' and welcomes the opportunity for Hester and James to 'profit by conversations [with him] which are superior to any they can ever meet with'. These letters to Lyme are filled with lively descriptions of her life at Burton, relations with tenants and servants and management of the estate. The enduring affection for Chatham runs through them but regret at his absence is tempered with her obvious delight in her Somerset home.

Because of Chatham's long sojourn at Lyme, 1773 yields the last continuous run of the correspondence. There are scattered letters in the two following years. On 28th August 1774 Hester is a member of a large houseparty at Stowe: 'last night we danced till twelve' including herself. Temple is out of sorts: 'building plans inspire him sometimes, but our topics rest there'. In January the following year Hester is in London with Harriot 'her Damsel girl' and is writing 'under Mitan's hands'. She describes her audience of the king and queen: 'the deficiency of graciousness' lay in their failure to ask about Chatham, but enquiry was made about son Pitt with the army in North America. This was to be her last carefree sophisticated time of enjoyment in London.

The dated correspondence ends with a letter of 21st February 1775 from Hayes to Chatham in London; it contains a rare commentary on politics, detailed and thoughtful, on the subject so dear to him of the administration and America: 'Lord North wou'd have saved himself by retiring to ground. The doubts he has betrayed as to the line of conduct he pursues . . . will induce him being removed, or removing himself'. She ends this letter, written at ½ past 8 am, 'Good Morning my Dearest Loved Love. The day is so fine I cou'd find in my Heart to wish you were here but *the State, the State* forbids. Your ever loving wife, Hester Chatham'. For much of the three succeeding years until his death Chatham was ill at Hayes, suffering from a multiplicity of mental and physical complaints, real or at times, imagined. To appreciate the care with which he was nursed by Hester it is necessary to consult the correspondence of others; in particular that of Dr Anthony Addington [q.v.] the Chathams' physician. The good doctor's letters to Lady Chatham tell a story of her heroic devotion to a deeply depressed, and depressing, patient. We will never know how Chatham felt about his wife's sacrifice in these last years, her total absorption in the task. We must assume that his love for her transcended the introspection inherent in the nature of his illness. Of her love for him, to the end, we have the evidence.

1   Burton estate employees
2   Stanley Ayling, *The Elder Pitt*, Collins, London 1976
3   Ibid

Chapter 3

THE BROTHERHOOD

Unattractive the men of this family were, rapacious, dull and self-satisfied;
yet with all their faults they were public-spirited and had a genuine love of liberty

Basil Williams, *The Life of William Pitt, Earl of Chatham,* London 1913, vol 1

i. LETTERS FROM RICHARD, LORD TEMPLE 1749-1779

Richard Grenville, first Earl Temple, succeeded to his mother's (contrived) earldom, and to the magnificent estate of Stowe in Buckinghamshire on her death in 1752. Married to a local member of parliament and squire, Richard Grenville of Wotton in the same county, she was the favourite sister and chosen heiress of Sir Richard Temple, field marshal Viscount Cobham. At his death in 1749 the estate became hers, and a few weeks later a string or two was pulled and she became Countess Temple.

Her son Richard was therefore the eldest of Hester Chatham's five brothers and in common with the other four, he was devoted to his only sister and, initially, to William Pitt who, with the three elder Grenvilles and their cousin George Lyttelton, formed the band of young radical politicians under the leadership of their uncle Lord Cobham known as the Patriots or Cobham's Cubs. So it was with the greatest pleasure that he received the news of Pitt's engagement to Hester.

Hester Chatham, though largely resident in girlhood at Wotton made Stowe her principal home after her mother's inheritance until her marriage in 1754. After marriage relations between the couple and Temple, her eldest, richest brother and with the most forceful character, though cordial, even ecstactically so during Pitt's leadership in the Seven Years War, may not have been as easy as that with the surviving brothers. For one thing, he was a major creditor, partly supporting the feckless and impecunious Pitt for many years. He was also a difficult man and contemporary opinions about him are, with few exceptions, disparaging, sometimes vitriolic. He was deeply unpopular with the political establishment. King George II disliked him: 'he was so disagreeable a fellow, there was no bearing him'.[1] Macaulay thought that 'it was his nature to grub underground like a mole'.[2] William Lecky, quoted from The Complete Peerage describes him as 'delighted in forming intrigues, inciting mobs and inspiring libels'. Modern historians are no kinder: 'The political influence of Pitt's brother-in-law, Temple was unwholesome'.[3] 'First prize for trouble making ought probably to be awarded to Temple. . . this prestige-hungry chief of the Grenville clan'.[4]

 Against the background of this catalogue of vituperation, what kind of man emerges from the three hundred and fifty letters he wrote to the Chathams, ninety to Pitt, the remainder to Hester? It must be said, a very different man. We find him here outspoken, certainly, but often charitable; cynical sometimes but very often sentimental; reflective and philosophical. In the letters two themes stand out: tenderness towards his sister, her children and the orphaned children of his brother George Grenville, and a passion for his house, Stowe. A third theme is his dislike of London, and essentially, of political life in general, partly but not wholly because both removed him temporarily from his beloved Stowe. From 1755 to 1774 he was engaged in the reconstruction and rebuilding work which can be seen in the mansion today and in the correspondence it is possible to follow in some detail the progress of the work. His twenty year labours on the house were impelled, despite setbacks, by an almost immoderate devotion: 'I am extravagantly in love - with Stowe' he admits to his sister in a letter of June 1761. Not only the house but also the surrounding park and gardens receives his delighted attention.

The letters to his sister Hester, covering a period from 1749, when he was thirty-eight and she twenty-nine and unmarried, to a month before his death in September 1779 are all gentle, compassionate, concerned and loving, and show a side of this complex man evidently missing from his relations with his fellow politicians and with most of the prominenti of the day. Even during his bitter quarrel with Chatham, lasting about two years from 1766, the letters to Hester, though fewer in number, are still maintained in admiration and affection. His substantial generosity to the hard pressed Pitts is mentioned only with modesty though he must, as a prudent man, have disapproved of Pitt's reckless expenditure.

Though Temple wrote half as many letters again to Hester as to William Pitt, it has been advisable, to round off the picture of the man, to include some letters addressed to Pitt. In accordance with the theme of these studies, largely social and domestic, the subjects of Temple's letters to both the Chathams, where these are mainly political, have been omitted, or only touched upon, in the quoted correspondence.

Temple, like his brother-in-law though to a much lesser extent, was subject to fits of depression (Pitt's depression became clincial) and, like all his generation, though obsessed by illness, he was nonetheless a strong man (he died as a result of a carriage accident while on a tour of inspection of his gardens at Stowe). With his brother James he lacked faith in medical advice, a characteristic noted by his cousin Molly Hood in a letter to Hester Chatham in which she complains of Temple's 'lack of gratitude to his doctors.' In 1764 he was receiving treatment by a doctor and two apothecaries 'who', he tells his sister, 'have been learned enough to say little and do less.'

Lady Temple, who married Richard Grenville as he then was in 1737 is a somewhat shadowy figure; the correspondence throws little light on her character though she is frequently mentioned in her husband's letters. She was Anna Chambers, an heiress of Hanworth, Middlesex - 'a fortune of £50,000'[5] and the wedding was at the Countess of Suffolk's house, Marble Hill, at Twickenham, where the bride was a member of that set. They had one child, a girl who died young. Anna Temple had at some time written poetry; her Select Poems were printed at the Strawberry Hill press in 1764. However, in an undated letter to Hester Chatham she modestly denies poetic talent. What does transpire from her husband's letters is firstly, that she went everywhere with him despite her chronic poor health, and secondly that at no time was there overt attraction elsewhere, much less scandal, in his private life.

In conclusion it must be said that if the surviving correspondence in the papers was the only source of information about Lord Temple, a very different man would be left to the knowledge of those who came after him. Yet not all the contemporary politicians or indeed the historians of his period can be wrong. We must recognise that Temple, as with most human beings, was many sided. In the context of his emotional and highly charged nature and in the times in which he lived, the many sides were perhaps more firmly marked than in most of us.

Richard Grenville's first surviving letter to his sister, even allowing for the circumstances pertaining at that time - the death on September 13th of his uncle Lord Cobham, and his and Hester's mother's inheritance of Stowe - is indicative of the man: his essential conventionality and his meticulous knowledge of etiquette. Although his mother was named as Cobham's heir, Temple already sees himself in the role:

> Stowe
> Sep. 17 1749
>
> Dear Sister
> I am glad to hear that the concern my Mother feels for the loss of Lord Cobham is not likely to affect her health. You say likewise that she approves of the mourning proposed, but as to what you mention of her design to keep on the mourning a year, as succeeding to the title, I am sure when she reflects she will see the impropriety of it. There are but two mournings, the long and the short; the long mourning requires servants and coaches etc. to be put into mourning and lasts a year for a father, which is the strictest of all mourning except that of a widow. Now we are all to mourn for Lord Cobham as a father, that is the strictest mourning of the kind we go into, which is the short one and last six months only. This is a precedent set to us upon several occasions by himself, and pursued by me upon all occasions with respect to my own family, his or my wifes. An heir never can be supposed to take a deeper mourning that a son and if I did, or my mother, we must both go into the long mourning with servants and coaches, which is what you say my mother does not think right to do, as she approves the other. This weighty matter of form being thus explained, I have only to add that we continue well and pretty much in the same state as you left us.
> I am ever yours most affectionately
> R. Grenville Temple
>
> [PS] Lady Cobham who mourns as a widow goes in only for a twelvemonth. We think of burying Lord Cobham this evening or to morrow. I shall not direct to your Ladyship with any addition, as I have since heard more instances of the kind I mentioned; so that great event remains at least doubtful for the younger children.

An outbreak of cattle disease (taken seriously then as now) in a tenant's farm, also referred to in letters of George Grenville's wife Elizabeth, receives mention in Temple's next letter to his sister, as do the pleasures of the theatre. He is now Lord Cobham following the (engineered) conferment of an earldom on his mother, three weeks after she succeeded to Stowe:

As I was a writer of evil tidyings about the Pollicott Cows, so in justice I ought to send favourable ones when I can, and we have now the greatest reason to flatter ourselves that we shall hear no more of this Plague at Lucas's, it being almost three weeks since the first fell, without any following her. I am sorry to hear my mother has been out of order. The flourishing state of the playhouse is no small temptation with me to a London life and I hear there is a Polly that will recall to my mind Ideas of about twenty five years standing; how soon I shall hear of her is not quite certain tho' I believe some time next month. When I see King's [his land agent] receit of the Pollicott rents, if I find any more due to you, as you doubtless hope there is, I will order it to be placed to you.

Temple's letter to his sister at the time of her engagement to William Pitt shows the degree of tenderness of which he was capable:

Stowe
Sunday night
[October 1754]

Dear Lady Hester

I am extremely happy that any part, which the fullness of my heart suggested to me, upon an occasion in which I felt so much for the future happiness of two persons so intimately connected to me, by all the tyes that can most nearly affect every sensation of my mind, should be capable of adding to that satisfaction and delight which you must feel in the important proof you have, so much to your own honour, received of esteem and affection from a person of Mr Pitt's infinite worth and discernment. The whole course of my own Life has been such an uniform testimony of my high opinion of him, in which I cannot allow even you to exceed me, that I do not entertain the least degree of surprise that his great and amiable qualities should have made the deepest impression upon your heart and that it should be warm to every expression of his praise. You will hear therefore with double pleasure that nothing can equal the kind, obliging, affectionate manner in which he has been so good as to mention this matter to me. . . I feel happy and proud in being able to hold out to the world an acquisition that does so much honour to every part of the family and to you so particularly. Every attention of mine to the interests of both of you, like every wish, is full of nothing but real kindness. . . I have had several times a mind to have step'd into the coach to morrow morning to have seen you both [at Wotton] in your present condition, but upon the whole Mr Pitt being to set out so soon for the Bath, I thought I ought not in conscience to break in more upon you than by the perusal of this answer to one of the kindest and prettiest letters I ever received, and so I put a period to my own Love letter, for I think it is a little less, and I mean that it should be to both every thing that can be wished from
Dear Lady Hester's most affectionate brother
Temple

A year later, in a charming note, Temple makes an offer to the newly weds:

My dear Lady Hester
    I cannot defer till to morrow morning making a request to you, upon the success of which I have so entirely set my heart, that I flatter myself you will not refuse it me. I must entreat you to make use of all your interest with Mr Pitt to give his brother Temple leave to become his debtor for a thousand pounds a year, till better times. Mr P. will never have it in his power to confer so great an obligation upon Dear Lady Hester, his and your most affecte
                    Temple

Indeed, Temple need have had no fears that the offer would be refused: William Pitt had no scruples ever about accepting gifts of money or 'loans', no matter from whom they came, always provided that they were from wholly private sources, divorced entirely from his official work. Earlier that year Temple is grateful for Pitt's advice and skill in the all-important question of the projected improvements to Stowe:

Aug 5 1755

My dear Pitt
    I have two reasons for writing no political news, the first that I know none, the other that I make it a rule never to trust any that I do know to Messieurs Shelbooke [Shelburne] etc. This much I learnt from that great and good man Sir G. Lyttelton. Now to the more important object of Stowe; all our wise country masons Ideas concerning Signor Borra's plan for the house stand exploded to the highest degree, and to your immortal honour be it said that the afore mentioned Signor Borra not only approves but I think has now adopted every part and particle of the alterations in the plan you originally prepared from the beginning to end. Where the Devil you picked up all this architectural skill, what Palladio you have studied I know not, but you are an Architect born and I am edifyed and delighted. So is Jemmy, that Goth, that Visigoth, that antipodes of taste. He enters now fully into all the glorys of our future front. If you do but build sons and daughters upon as excellent a model, you have a lovely race in Stowe. Now let me finish my Dull Epistle, and tho' I am the very reverse of the man I was, I am ever most Kindly and affectionately Yours
                    Temple.

From 1756 and for the next six or seven years, the years of William Pitt's greatest fame, Temple's letters are addressed mainly to him; in one year alone, 1758, there are six letters to Pitt and one only to Hester. Temple was an emotional man, and his letters to his brother-in-law at this time are largely congratulatory and full of excited comment on the triumphs of the battlefield, particularly in North America, thus:

Stowe
June 29 1758

    A thousand congratulations to you upon this great and happy event and I hope the consequences will prove the victory to have been compleat. Louisbourg is the consummation devotedly to be wished for and I think sanguinely to be hoped; when that news arrives we may embrace indeed. Undoubtedly we have never sworn by Styx or Toryism or Patriotism, never, in no case whatever, to send a man to the Continent, and the Emden regiment is a proof of it; but that of sending three squadrons to reinforce the Hanoverian army at this time must wholly depend upon circumstances and objects of which you are the judge and of which success will be the best vindication.

Sunday morn.
9 o'clock [July 1758]

  Joy Delight Rapture Fame Triumph Glory and such like stale and hackneyed words are so worn out of late that unless I have a new language adapted to such events I can neither express what I feel nor what such unexampled miracles deserve. Could we have known the good fortune of the preceeding day, when we met at Wotton, what a Heaven it would have been!. . . I long eagerly to embrace you and Lady Hester with something like a Louisbourg joy and so we do it all, all. Adieu ever most affectionately, my Dear Louisbourg brother
T.

  The letters to Pitt continue in regular sequence until the political quarrel between the two men of 1766, but the contents, though of interest, do not belong here and we return now mainly to the correspondence with Hester. In 1760 he tells her, not for the last time, of his dislike of London:

1 o'clock
Jan 3 1760

  It would be an inadequate piece of ingratitude in a gentle swain of the right side of 50, if, unable to express his gratitude in person as he intended for your last kind epistle, he did not make you the best return, Poor Man! he can, by setting pen to paper with a view to inform you of the very interesting news of his Safe arrival at Stowe, the better for his journey. By way of answer, send me word that you and all yours are perfectly well, in which case I think I may trust I shall have the pleasure of seeing you in St James's square, when I next plunge myself into that abyss of Fog, Sulphur, Fever, cold and all the excretions on this side of Styx.
Love to your Loving and loved husband concludes this piece of galantry from, Dr Lady Hester, your truly affectionate etc brother
T.

  Temple was a robust man but, as with his contemporaries, ever alarmed by illness, however minor:

Stowe
June 9th 1761 9 o'clock

  In joyful return my Dear Lady Hester for all your kind enquiries and those of Mr Pitt, during my illness, I think I can do no less than trouble you with an account of my Life and conversation since I took leave of my beloved ass at Knightsbridge in my way out of town, her last Cordial Cup! I got here yesterday, bore my journey surprisingly, walked a little, rid out on horse back, dined, went to bed, and then out in my little Chair round the garden, the whole evening. Delightful weather, Stowe superlatively charming. As soon as I get down my tea,

my horse, my horse and I intend my tottering fabrick shall be so repaired, washed over and beautifull that in three days there shall not be the least appearance of any havock. Enough of myself, except that I am not only the Hero of this epistle but you truly loving friend and brother.
[PS] Cows milk agrees with me perfectly.

Three days later, he has recovered and is elated at Hester's possible intention to come to Stowe for his fiftieth birthday party:

Stowe
June 14th 1761

I am much obliged to my dear Lady Hester for her kind intention, meditation at least, of flying on the friendly wings of sisterly affection to see the recovered Bloom of fifty, shining and glittering by candlelight like the tinsel of my dear Opera. I am extravagantly in Love - with Stowe... never, never was any thing half so fine and charming!

Still on the subject of his age, he writes on 25th October:

I never am in danger of any complaint you know, at Stowe: perfect health and as perfect happiness as long winter nights will allow a man of 50, I enjoy, and so does Lady Temple.

Lord Temple was a self-centred man but he possessed a redeeming insight to his character. In the course of a letter regretting the loss of a valued servant, he reveals that:

Stowe
July 22 1762

I rise every morning a little after five and stick to business very handsomely. I dread the thought of confusion and so bestir myself accordingly.

And to Pitt some months later:

Stowe
Jan 6 1763

Be a Philosopher as much as you please in mind, the times as well as your time of day require it, but a Hercules in body. If year following year has stol'n something from us, at least it has stolen us from something and that reflection brings along with it some consolation to my mind and Pride also. . .
I relish my Rusticity most exceedingly tho' I am ashamed to call myself a Country Gentleman; from that disgraceful title Good Lord deliver me!. . . Stowe is a Beauty who in her old age grows warmer and warmer, especially in my new manner of enjoying her below stairs. I wish my own warmth encreased with my years too, but upon that chapter I am silent.

In 1765 William Pitt's inheritance of the Somerset estate of Burton Pynsent was of great interest to his brother-in-law, whose active and practical mind turns at once to the design of the proposed memorial pillar to Sir William Pynsent, the bequeather. To Hester he writes:

Stowe

Aug 4 1765

I am particularly happy in the description you give of Burton-Pynsent, as I think it will rise into high favour and afford much rural Delectation. Sir William has already elected a monument for himself to his eternal honour in the successor he has chosen, but if in these times gratitude rises 114f 4i high, it will equal Lord Cobham's Pillar, statue and all. Of this the statue is 10f 4i, as near as I can guess by what I have heard and I cannot get other information. The whole cost about 830£ but much depends on the facility arising from neighbouring Stone Pits, Lime, scaffolding etc. The Diameter of the Pillar is 10f 6i, the channels in it are not admired and I believe were not authorised by Gibbs. I have a sketch from him for a Dorick column upon a Pedestal, the diameter intended to be only 4f but that may be encreas'd to any dimension. If you wish a Plan of either I will order it and send it as soon as I learn your wishes.

And to Pitt (with a hint also of proper financial management):

Stowe

Novr 5 1765

I am thank God most perfectly well, more and more delighted with my Palladian Arch, having freed it from the incumbrance of the two neighbouring abeles; it looks very majestick indeed. The dreadful time of settling the years accounts is likewise now arrived, so that I am not idle, in order to be quite at ease the rest of the year. I shall with the greatest pleasure facilitate, as far as in me lyes, the favourite object of enlarging round Burton Pynsent, at the expense of Hayes, and I wish your estates in Somersetshire may not only rival the great Peter, but extend as wide as the sight from the top of the monumental Column on the bleak Promontory which, through determined purpose, not blind chance, I shall most certainly be next summer, as well as the rising towers and I hope flourishing plantations which your active mind has plan'd and expeditious right hand already executed.

This is the last surviving letter from Temple to Pitt for over two years. The quarrel, arising from Temple's manoevres to gain a superior post for himself in Pitt's forthcoming ministry, began in 1765 and came to a head in July the following year. The dispute was deeply felt by both men, not least by Temple as shown by two rather chilly letters to Hester Chatham, who was trying without success to mend the rupture:

Pall Mall

Jan 20 1766

11 at night

My dear Lady Chatham
    I am much obliged to you for the kind expressions contained in your letter and shall certainly call upon you as soon as I know you are in town. I did wish to be sure to hear an account both of your own health and Mr Pitt's from the Bath,

but you deprived me of that pleasure. Many unfortunate events have fallen out both for the public and affecting the comfort of my private life. Misapprehensions are oftener, I believe, than Realities the cause of much unhappiness and I refer myself only to your recollection of what has passed betwixt you and me in many unreserved conversations, manifesting towards you such real esteem and affection in one who is above dissimulation and very much your affectionate brother
Temple

Pall Mall
Jan 24 1766

It is no small satisfaction to me to find by your letter of yesterday that the long discontinuance of our correspondence on your part did not proceed from any resolution of putting an end to it, but from various occurences which prevented me from hearing from you at all during a very considerable and interesting Period. I do not mean to enter into observations upon all or any part of what has passed since the day of my Dissent from Mr Pitt. I have my recollections and events have verifyed my opinions. I can appeal to my own Heart and I know the Purity of my own Intention, sufficient to vindicate me to myself and enable me in some degree to bear up against new scenes of Family Disunion. I share in every Grief you feel and I am sure Happiness of every sort was at hand.

However, family affection prevails, and through the spring and summer of this year the correspondence between brother and sister continues, with news from Stowe, and a description of a round of visits to the estates of the Wyndham brothers, earls respectively of Thomond and Egremont, brothers-in-law of George Grenville. Temple observes the properties with a connoisseur's eye:

Stowe
June 15 1766

We returned last night from our Shortwood [Shortgrove, co. Essex] and Petworth parties; the former consists of a very pleasing hill, a serpentine river of very clear water and a Bridge from which the place opens to you and affords a very pleasing scene. From thence we took a ride to the famous Audley End. I neither like what remains of the House nor the situation; Sir John Griffin has already disposed of ten thousand pounds there but never can make it a delightful habitation. Petworth stands high indeed in my estimation; Lawn, Timber unrival'd, Concave, Converse, vast extent, pleasing prospects and very good taste as far as it is done, plead most strongly in its favour. The day we arrived was distinguished by the finishing a little Rotundo, something larger however than that at Hagley, and which fairly beats upon the whole in point of situation all the Rotundos I have seen and adorns a most perfect natural piece of Gardening. The wood in which, or rather at the side of which it stands, connects with the house and is very beautiful in all its parts. In short it will vie as a greatly pleasing seat with any I have yet seen; I think far superior to Woburn, in the Woburn style. The Park and Woods at Stowe suffer with their neighbours by the comparison, and the very bleak and cold evening of yesterday, with this morning the same, bear hard upon Stowe even in my estimation. So much for my travels.

The fine weather is returned and with it my Love of Stowe tho Candour still necessitates me not to see, even with a fathers eye, my twigs in competition with the stately timber of Petworth. I have been exceedingly flattered however by the Prince de Cröy and the Duke de Havre; the first is the only foreigner of real taste as to our English style of gardening which I ever met with. He draws himself and is a brother gardiner, in raptures at every change of landscape. He really prevented my being tired of walking with him.

There are no more letters until December 1768 when, unrecorded, the quarrel between the two men is at an end, but signalled by three affectionate notes from Temple to his sister, and a longer letter at the beginning of the year that follows:

Stowe
Jan 5 1769

I waited my dear Sister with much impatience to hear from you the state of Lord Chatham's gout, as my own unmerciful Heart began to relent, and I am for the present fully satisfied. I wish with you that he may now have respite sufficient to enable him fully to recruit and meet the next attack with fortitude. We have passed our time here in the most perfect solitude and I can say in the most perfect Content, all the Day with wheelbarrows, all the Evening with Accounts..
We do not think of seeing the smoke, and smelling it too, of that stinking Metropolis till the 16th soonest.

It is not, however, until June that Temple addresses a letter directly to Chatham. As might be expected, some residual embarrassment is concealed under a jocular tone. After expressing pleasure at 'this proof of a recovered hand' in a letter from Chatham, he writes back:

Sunday near 4
[June 1769]

The political Barometer is at full stand. The D. of Grafton exhibited last night almost as much love and tenderness to his future Bride in the exalted Box of the Dutchess of Bedford as he manifested last year in the humble Pitt to that Divinity Nancy Parsons, by men called Horton. This marriage connects him I think very closely with the Bedfords whom he is to govern or who are to govern him. In that light, as unconnection was his only strength at St James's, connection may prove his weakness. The Butes may be alarmed. Tomorrow for Stowe! I think I shall behold the smoky face of London again about the close of next month in way to or from Lord Thomond's. I shall most assuredly treat myself with a view of Hayes and its kind inhabitants on that occasion. Hoping for the high Delight of seeing you and yours at Stowe as soon as warm weather has compleated the ardently wish'd recovery of hands and feet I remain my dear Lord most affection-ately, and unalterably your Lordship's and Lady Chatham's together with the young fry
Your most loving Brother
Temple.

With relations established again on a base of affection and esteem, Temple's letters for the next few years both to Chatham and to Hester are numerous, and newsy. That is, until 1775 when the letters to the former cease, probably because of Chatham's now chronic state of illness; but those to Hester continue without break until his death in 1779. Two deaths which occurred soon after the friendship was renewed, and which probably contributed to the renewal, brought a dramatic change into Temple's life. In December 1769 Elizabeth Grenville died, followed a year later by her husband George. Temple was guardian to the seven orphaned children, none older than twenty, and, after the father went, the three boys and four girls were taken from Wotton to make their future home at Stowe. These sad events, neither sudden, both certainly expected, are described by Temple in letters to his sister. Elizabeth Grenville was Hester's closest friend from girlhood:

Wotton
Decr 5 1769

The dreadful Blow was struck this morning a little after 5 o'clock; at one time last night we were not without some small Ray of Hope that it might <u>possibly</u> have been warded off for the present, but without any promising expectations for the future. She dyed at last easy after having suffered most excrutiating Torments for many days. No words can surpass in expression the true account of her magnamity, sense and dignity. The fine words of Horace concerning Regulus's Departure, which Lord Chatham will translate for you most ably, were verifyed to a tittle.

Ten months later he meets his brother on George Grenville's last hopeless visit to London accompanied by a relay of doctors:

Sunday evening
Oct 21 1770

I am just returned from meeting my Brother G. Grenville in the neighbourhood of Towcester on his road to Town. He looks shockingly, and I should be indeed alarmed did I not place great confidence in that of the Doctor who attends him to Dunstable this night, where they hope to meet [Sir William] Duncan.

George Grenville died on November 13th in his London house in Bolton Street.

The great quarrel of two years past was at an end but sensitivities linger. Hester is in London on a rare social visit:

[Pall Mall]
Monday night
March 4 1771

I am much concerned my dear Sister that any word of mine, mistaken or misunderstood, for one or the other I think it necessarily must have been, should have given you so much heartfelt anxiety and wounded so deeply. I am still, at this moment entirely at a Loss how to guess it, which is the best Proof of my total Innocence as to Intention. It is not I believe you know, my Custom to deal in bitter Hints or double meanings and you must have surely been sensible how impossible it was that any thing unkind or offensive could drop from me, in my own house, and at a time when you had so kindly seated yourself by me. I took it for granted from your Letter that it had passed in the Box, and in that case I thought it most wonderful and unaccountable, that you could Serve me with the Letter, in the way you did and without giving me the means of any possible explanation. . . When I know the unfortunate <u>Word</u>, I may recollect the turn of the conversation and if you are sure I used it, explain a meaning very different from what your imagination suggested. In all events I am most assuredly certain that I could use none which in my understanding and construction could carry the most distant allusion to any thing that tended to lessen or depreciate you or yours. Let us banish entirely every Recollection but that of kindness and goodwill.

[PS] I dont know whether we are not now to wish that Ld C. may have a fair but kindly fit of the Gout. I still grieve to think how unhappy you have accidently at least been made. I shall always be happy in seeing you, but put yourself to no inconvenience. Mahomet is ready to go to the Mountain, and you know you are growing into it very fast. I am just released from a grand Festival Dinner here.

There is no further allusion in the correspondence to the misunderstanding, if that is what it was. Instead there is the excitement in October of Charlotte Grenville's engagement to Sir Watkin Williams Wynn:

> Stowe
> Oct 20 1771
>
> My Dear Sister
> Sir Richard de Grenvile in days of yore was one of the 12 Knights who conquer'd the County of Glamorgan in South Wales. Charlotte de Grenvile has at her first appearance entirely subdued the whole County of Denbigh in North Wales and returned triumphant, her Brows with Laurel and with Mistle bound! Watkin the Great is now actually doing homage within these Walls. A Treaty of Alliance was yesterday agreed upon and Cupid and Hymen are called in to be Witnesses. Every circumstance that accompanies this most happy event is of the most pleasing kind. . .

After noting that Sir Watkin's fortune is 'for the present 28000', but that it is expected to amount in a year or two to 34000, the happy uncle continues

> Sir Watkins Mother is much pleased with the Match, as indeed the whole Country; if He had not proposed He would have been Dethroned. In short I shall never have done if I allow myself to go on to the whole extent of my feelings.

The wedding took place at Stowe on December 21st. It receives no mention in Temple's letters but others report it in detail. Mrs Molly Hood in particular at second-hand disapproved of Lord Temple's wedding speech, which she found vulgar and unacceptable.But there is nothing amiss in the wording of his letter to Hester announcing the birth of a son to the newly-weds, and his proposed departure to stay with them in North Wales:

The Birth of a son and Heir apparent to a Prince of Wales has ever been a matter of great satisfaction and Joy, and as it was the only object wanting to compleat the Happiness of last years event, Taffy has by his safe arrival given sincere delight to us all. We shall set out on Monday to join that happy Society and for other good purposes of Business and Pleasure. My rising Walls no longer detain me; I have with great difficulty compleated almost half of what I intended; it rewards me however by turning out much better than I even expected. I am sorry to hear that you have been as you style it unwell, which I suspected not or I should have enquired. But volunteer Letters suit not with one who has been tormented with so many and various Businesses almost every Post. Deluges of rain are a common complaint and contribute to make me leave Stowe with little Regret.

Some at least of the 'Businesses', by implication irritating to him, of which Temple complains are the negotiations in that summer and early autumn through the Chatham family lawyer, Nuthall, over Chatham's wish to break into his wife's Trust money:

Stowe
Sep 8 1772

My dear Lord Tho' I never can be tired of any Business in which I am engaged in your Service and that I execute it with Zeal, yet as these are of different sorts, some may to a kind wellwisher of you and yours be allowed in their nature to be more agreeable than others. At my return to this place on Sunday last I found your Lordship's letter, together with one of the 4th Sep. from that facetious Man of Business in so many departments, Mr T. Nuthall, whose fellow if not easily to be met with, witness your marriage settlement not witnessed, his peremptory and repeated assertions that your Trustee had no Power to advance the Trust money on Mortgage. . .

And so on. With relief he turns to news of Stowe and mention of Hagley, home of the Lytteltons, cousins to both families:

After many disappointments I am now going on prosperously here; the North side is charming and the South will be very magnificent, attended of course with much expense, but what is worse with infinite trouble. I hope however the worst is over. For Hagley news I have none to add to what you must have heard from the once juvenile and lovely Lips of Madame Hood. . . Tomorrow I enter upon the Delights of a Race at Newportpagnel, of which Proh Puder! I am a Steward.

Though Temple appears to have been somewhat accident prone, the mishap he suffered early in 1773 does not seem to have been in anyway due to fool-hardiness:

Pall Mall
Jan 28 1773

With my well right Hand I return, my dear Sister, the best thanks of my poor left arm for the kind enquiries of Burton Pynsent. I am now getting out of

Pain of which I have indeed had a reasonable share... I was coming very soberly from the Play, the night after I came to Town, viz, Wednesday 20th; unluckily my chairmen turned down the Strand where, meeting with another chair, the tops struck and with the violence of the Concussion threw down my chairmen who, falling on the Poles overturned the chair with the more force into the Street off the paved way; broke the windows all to shatter and gave me so violent a Blow, that I thought my arm was broken betwixt the Elbow and shoulder. However, upon feeling it repeatedly I soon grew convinced to the Contrary; the chair was set up and in it I came home to make my melancholy case known. Had I stirr'd at all I suppose I should have been cut to pieces, but I resigned myself most quietly to my Fate.

His recovery was slow and hampered by an attack of gout precipitated by the accident:

> Pall Mall
> Feb 25 1773

All my Golden Dreams of Speedy Recovery have vanished, as soon as formed; I must content myself with the mending more slowly that the pace of the dullest ox in the heaviest yoke in Somersetre. Gout is gone but has left me such a swelling quite up to the top of my Thigh, as does not seen even disposed to abate. My arm too mends in the same proportion.

By mid March he is better. After the customary comment on the state of Chatham's health, he writes

> Pall Mall
> March 18 1773

For my own unworthy self I can only say I air at the rate of a hundred and fifty miles a week. I can walk almost without a stick, but have still a swell'd Leg, the remains of gout; a swelld hand and lame arm which keep me confined. As it was in the beginning is now and ever shall be for aught I see to the contrary, world without end; to which however I say not Amen. Ever most truly your affectionate Brother

Temple

In June he is back at Stowe. The opening sentence in his letter to Hester expresses as well as anything he has hitherto written, the depth of almost spiritual love of the place and the mission on which he is engaged to add to its beauty:

> Stowe
> June 29 1773

The first solitary moments at Stowe were taken up with comtemplating the the Progress which had been made in the great works, to the completion of which I at last stand engaged.

Another excursion to North Wales is planned, and as always there is Chatham's state of health to deplore and the rebuilding of Stowe to extol:

Stowe
Aug 1 1773

I was much mortifyed my dear Sister to hear from the last accounts of your sovereign Lord and Master, that he was still upon Crutches, but I will hope that in spite of the late cold weather and Rain, he has contrived to throw them away. For my own Part I have taken to the Cold Bath and think I have found much Benefit from it already. . . Our Welsh journey takes place later than we intended; Aylesbury Races claim me on the 5th and Conway Races Sir Watkin on the 16th... If I must speak with Truth, I must say with as much Modesty as I can, that my Building does turn out far better than even I expected from the Plan. . . A great undertaking it is indeed! Whilst Royal Villas as yet speak only by their foundations, my North Front is entirely finished and the South is so far advanced that we shall even get up to the Base stor[e]y of the Center this year.

The Welsh trip was somewhat marred at its outset by the death of the much liked and justifiably admired cousin, Lord Lyttelton:

Stowe
Sep 11 1773

I am much obliged to you my dear Lady Chatham for the very kind interest you take in the great misfortune which has befallen me. . . Poor Ld L. was to have been of our Welsh party and would have greatly added to the Delight of it, instead of which that fatal event threw a gloom upon the whole.

Nevertheless, Temple's active and enquiring mind was aroused by all he saw and found in Wales

My eyes however were feasted with the lovely aspect of that Delightful Country and the inhabitants of our little Colony of Relations are extremely amiable as well as the rest of the neighbourhood. I was pleased above measure with the view of Conway as you descend to it; a most picturesque ruin of a Castle standing on a rocky eminence over the River Conway bedeck'd with mountains, a most beautiful wood on the side, lovely hills and a long reach of the River to your left, the Sea on your Right, numberless enclosures constitute I think a more pleasing scene than any at Mount Edgecombe. The ruined Castle of Caernarvon is likewise very fine and the approach to it. From thence we went to a Lake called Clanberris on the side of Snowdon, six miles they said long, encompassed with Mountainous Rocks.

The party seemingly were greeted with a feu de joie from the local inhabitants:

We were welcomed by many discharges of Powder from the clefts in the Mountains which echoed like a ratling Peal of Thunder.

Thirteen year old William Grenville was of the party and had written verses in praise of his uncle:

The great William Grenville attended me. . . We had much Poetry in those parts, Prologue, Epilogue, chrinonhotontologos, many complimentary verses but

this great Man, almost 14 has in his first attempt at an ode beat them all. . .
The whole country is full of Romance so that Poets cannot fail of Inspiration.

Late in the month, on their return from Wales, an alarming building accident occurred at Stowe, resulting in the death of a workman. Hester Chatham had already received an agitated letter from Catherine Stapleton, who was present when it happened, describing the accident which undoubtedly had put the lives of several members of the household in danger. Lord Temple's account by contrast is restrained to vanishing point and puts the fault on the unfortunate workman who died:

> Stowe
> Sep 29 1774

> I will not dwell a moment on the folly of the poor man who it turns out pulled a new cornice on his own Head and with it endangered so many other Lives, not to mention the damage done and Delay occasioned

He continues without pause to express his pleasure in the news of the engagement of Hester Pitt to Lord Mahon:

> but I will hasten to the warmest congratulations on the happy event which you have communicated to us, so promising and so superlatively pleasing in every circumstance that can contribute to the increase of every Domestic felicity...
> On both sides each can prove their sixteen quarters of them, is something of the Phoenix kind, not to be met with, scarce in hope from any other quarter.

Temple was genuinely delighted about the engagement, and to compound his pleasure makes a generous offer to the young woman, through her father Chatham, as custom decreed, and expressed in the most graceful terms:

> Pall Mall
> Nov 16 1774

> My dear Lord
> While you was stating to me the Plan of the intended settlements on the approaching happy Nuptials, this method of epistolary application occurred to me as the properest, to ask the favour of your Lordship's interest to prevail with my amiable niece kindly to accept from Uncle Temple a thousand pds to equip for immediate Service the good ship Hester to be commanded by that gallant officer the Mahon; may the good Captn aforesaid arrive safe in Port is the earnest wish of, my dear Lord, your most affectionate Brother
> Temple

> [PS] As a quondam first Lord of the admiralty, I have a right to insist upon it that this is in my Department and it will save me all trouble as Trustee.

The last surviving dated letter to Chatham written a month later is on the same subject:

Pall Mall
Dec 19 1774

> Before you can receive this poor Lady Hester Pitt will be no more. I am however Barbarian enough to congratulate your Lordship and all the inhabitants of Hayes on the loss sustained, as she passed immediately into Elysium, where that she may continue as much loved and honoured as she hath hitherto been is my most ardent wish, as well as that of Lady Temple, who joins with me in every warm expression of kindness. As I take it for granted that this letter will arrive before the Bride and Bridegroom can be up and on their way to Chevening, I would beg to add all that even your Eloquence can express by way of sincere felicitation there, on an event so pleasing to all Parties, and most particularly to my dear Lord's most truly affectionate
>
> Temple

On this happy note the correspondence addressed directly to Chatham ends. Comrades from early manhood, brothers-in-law, Temple was a true admirer of Chatham's marvellous achievements in the war. But what were his real feelings about his sister's husband, so different a man? One can only guess. It may however be significant that Temple was at Chatham's side when, on 7th April, four years later, the statesman collapsed in the House of Lords a few weeks before his death. The picture entitled 'Collapse of the Earl of Chatham in the House of Lords' by John Singleton Copley shows Temple close beside him.

Meantime, and until the crucial year of 1778, there is the steady correspondence with Hester to examine. Always worried about his health, he writes on the following 26th April from Pall Mall:

> For myself I am agreeably better but still a weak vessel. My opera scheme ended in smoke, for towards evening I feel very shabby.

In July he is suffering from a bout of depression. Comparing himself to Chatham in the matter of illness, Temple writes:

Stowe
13 July 1775

> If I had not heretofore known how to compassionate Ld C's sufferings, my late experience would have amply taught me, not from the Pain, but from the inexpressible dejection which frequently made me sigh after a sound sleep in the Grave in preference to this mortal existence. His case and mine have been in many instances wonderfully similar, pray God his may end as happily and speedily.

In August he is bothered with constipation and Hester is desperate for money. After the usual concern about the bad news of Chatham's state, he writes with less than grace:

Stowe
Aug 6 1775

As to my own Health I continue to go on prosperously, except being occasionally plagued from a costive Habit with Purgatives, which always make me sick... The great distress you describe in the present moment is too grievous for me not, in this instance, to be my own Pope and give myself absolution. I have therefore sent an order to Mr Coutts to sell out stock to the amount of the credit you ask, being part of what was destined to my own engagements, now grown pretty extensive.

Three weeks later he is in better heart - and presumably shape. In a postscript to a letter of 22nd August he tells Hester that

NB. I can eat 2 platefuls of mutton and 4 of Roast Beef besides other Trifles at one Meal! A good English stomach of 64!

The exclamation marks may indicate that this quantity of food at a sitting was unusual.Family affairs are the main subject of his letters for the next two years. Two births raise comment, the first that of a girl to the Mahons, Hester Chatham's first grandchild.

Pall Mall
March 15 1776

Having troubled Lord Pitt at the Opera to express to you my Kindest compliments and wishes on the then approaching event, I did not set pen to paper for the mere formality of telling you, what you must be assured of, that I was most happy in the safe Delivery of one whom I so much esteem and love. The joy would have been doubled had it been of the masculine gender and in that case I do not know whether I could have resisted troubling you. Lady Temple desires me to add her very affectionate congratulations.

And a boy to his nephew and heir presumptive, George Grenville:

Pall Mall
March 21 1776

Mrs Grenville was this morning about ten brought to bed of a little animal of the right sort, as like to grandpapa Clare as possible, according to universal testimony of young and old which you may believe, if you please.

Understandably, for dynastic reasons, Temple must deplore the gender of the Mahon's first child and extol that of the Grenville's. Nevertheless, history has a different story. The famous, though eccentric, traveller Lady Hester Stanhope has found a place in memoirs and biographies to the present day; the second duke of Buckingham has faded into obscurity.

Lady Temple died suddenly the following year. A week later Temple writes, with great restraint; he was devoted to her:

Pall Mall
Apr 15 1777

My dear Sister

I am perfectly well and exceedingly miserable, much obliged for your kindness and that of Lord Chatham. My nephew is at Wotton. I hasten to assure you and yours that I am ever your and their most affectionate

Temple

Two months later he is still feeling her loss. On 20th June from Stowe:

For myself I am and have been as well in Body, as sick in mind, which is saying not a little. In the last I do not mind, but grow more and more miserable, though I have met and meet with kind friends, who leave nothing undone in their Power to perform on the article of affectionate consolation.

Temple and Chatham had long held different views on America, but the former now admits to a closing of opinion between the two. Chatham had made a small recovery, though short lived:

Stowe
Novr 25 1777

I rejoice indeed very sincerely my dear Lady Chatham to hear so good an account of the recovered statesman and that in many material Parts his sentiments and mine agree; in short that we remain pretty much the same as when we last talked matters over. . . I am grown a perfect Tory; so blind as not to see the true English Whiggism of not keeping America subject to the Crown of England (that is the King in his Parlt) in all cases whatsoever. But that is a Point of long canvassed Debate and is alas! now I fear quite out of the Question. The greatest temptation to me to cast a Glance into public Life would be to agree with him, whenever the Fortune of Events will put it in my Power.

Temple has been responsible for the rebuilding of Buckingham church damaged by a major collapse three months earlier. The letter continues:

In the meantime Be it known to you that this day is an important one indeed; a Festival on whether the Bayleff is to lay the corner stone of the new church. I am and have been all day along in the highest odour with the Corporation; but I have had infinite trouble and am going to receive the reward of all my labours, in a manner, perhaps as signal, as Ld Chatham did through the streets of London some years ago. An ox roasted on Castle Hill, with a Hogshead of Strong Beer from Stowe, and a brace of Does at the Cobham arms, are but a Part and Prelude to the great events which are at every moment ripening into Birth.

William Pitt, Earl of Chatham died on the eleventh of May 1778. Two letters from Temple to the widow mark the event:

Pall Mall
May 12 1778

On receiving the expected news I instantly went to Lord Mahon's to consult with him him whether he thought it probable that a visit to you from me would at present afford you any consolation and whether it might be possible for me to prevail so far with you to bring you to Pall Mall.

But Mahon was not in favour of this plan and Temple submitted to his view, ending the letter

Every service in my power you are always sure of. What can be wished for more, since in a good old age we must all submit to Fate, than to quit this anxious and humiliating scene, covered with public Regret and glory.

The following day he was able to give Hester the good news of Parliament's decision to award her a generous annual pension and to pay the debts; and to name the friends who were foremost in bringing this about:

Judge only of my Joy, if I may use that word at present, by your own. Joy it is to see such gratitude and such welcome Proofs of it. The settlement expected will probably be 5 or 3000 p. an, to attend the Title. . . Mr T. Townshend, Ld Shelburne, Dunning, Barre, Ld Nugent and the Rockinghams in the person of Ld John Cavendish, have stood amongst the foremost. I had almost forgot Mr Pulteney, who expressed a wish that if there were any Debts, they too should be paid. I hope all these circumstances will add comfort and alleviate your heavy Distress.

[PS] The debts are to be paid.

In the eighteen months of life left to him Temple's letters to his sister continued on much the same lines as before and at intervals of about one or two a month. His subjects however now include observations on the unacceptable delays by the Treasury in payments of her grant (delays which continued for several years), and a keen interest in William Pitt: Temple's perspicacity had already recognised in the very young man all the signs of future eminence. There is a further visit to Wales to describe, and of course life at Stowe. Wales is now familiar ground for a visit, but even in January, most enjoyable:

Stowe
Jan 19 1779

You are very kind my dear Sister in interesting yourself so much in the event of our Peregrinations. The old has been carried in the middle of Winter some hundred miles to be sure in gratification of the wishes of youth, and so far from having cause to repine at the consequences, too much cannot be said in Laud and Praise of it. Good health, good roads, good weather, a week of plays [at Wynnstay] and much amusement, all concurred in making the Party very agreeable, without the smallest Rub or Disappointment.

Stowe
Feb 2 1779

     The delicious season which we enjoy renders Stowe delightful and we make the most of it; amongst other celebrated Performances that of Fox hunting in Phaeton and Garden chaise has not been the least delectable; in three days we have killed three foxes, in at the death of all, the last after a chase of one hour and fifty minutes hard running. Coach women Hester and Catherine. Yesterday we had no success but great are the hopes for tomorrow... I wish I could have heard that your Treasury matters had been settled as they ought, both for your interest and Quiet.

In July he has no particular news:

Stowe
July 18 1779

     Breakfast dinner and supper at Stowe are so much things of course, that they furnish no Novelty worth dwelling upon especially too as Fox hunting is not yet quite come in.

But

     By the last post however I received a very kind letter from the great William of Cambridge, signifying to me a thought of declaring himself a candidate for that University [seat]. I cannot possibly form any opinion of the solidity on which his Hopes may be grounded, nor is it clear, intending to follow the Law, that so early an Introduction into Parlt is desirable. At the same time it is very flattering to be sure to think at that at his age He is already an object, sufficient to call the attention of so learned a Body.

Uncle and mother are in happy accord on the subject of William's political ambitions. After praising her 'perspicacity and sagacity', he writes on 29th July, with modesty, that

     I am entirely a stranger so that it is impossible to give an opinion. The warmest good wishes go along with young Cantab in every Pursuit, but not without anxiety in this. The Report here is that many Horses are to start for the Plate, amongst the rest Ld Euston, who is said to have declared.

And so, in this year and in those to come, which promised to Lord Temple a serene and trouble free old age, in his lovely and loved home, and with all the interests to engage him in the maturing of his Grenville wards - and the young Pitts - his destiny said No. On September 11th he suffered a skull fracture after a fall from a phaeton in a wooded road of his domain and died some hours later.

ii. LETTERS OF GEORGE GRENVILLE 1746-1770

George Grenville was two men: firstly the politician and public man, ambitious, tactless, obstinate and ungenerous. So says his biographer[6] in the Dictionary of National Biography, while conceding that he was able (though narrow-minded) with 'considerable financial ability, unflagging industry and inflexible integrity.' Reading these and observations in similar vein from other historians, it is hard to believe that he had another, different side to his nature. It is in the letters to his sister and those of his wife that we find his other persona.

Grenville's career is well documented. He was the second son of Richard Grenville and Hester, Countess Temple; he lived for the greater part of his life at the family home of Wotton in Buckinghamshire. He entered parliament as member for Buckingham in 1741, a seat he held until his death. He rose quickly to ministerial rank in 1763. But 'the king had long been tired of his minister's tedious manners and overbearing temper[7]' and he was dismissed on 10th July 1765. His last political action, an important one, was to bring in a bill, a few months before his death in 1770, to reform the means for deciding the outcome of disputed elections.

George Grenville's role in Hester Chatham's life was a particular one: Wotton was the house in which she grew up, and she continued to make it her main home, with Stowe, until she married William Pitt in 1754. The papers contain some twenty letters from Grenville to his sister but only nine to Pitt. These latter are, however, warm in tone, mainly congratulatory on the war victories, and with news from, and descriptions of, Wotton, the home he so greatly loved, and to which he hurried back to from London at every opportunity his political duties allowed. Neither he nor his wife were given to much visiting (except to Stowe, twelve miles away from Wotton) and the correspondence yields only a few letters from elsewhere. George loved his wife and children; in his letters there is found no trace of the character defects of arrogance, insensitivity and other flaws noted by contemporary and later historians.

There is however a significant gap in the correspondence between 1761 and 1769, during which there are only two surviving letters from Grenville and three from his wife, though there is evidence from Hester's letters to her husband that she visited Wotton during these years. In short, George Grenville and Pitt were, if not openly quarrelling, at least in severe disagreement after 1761, and it is not until 1770, his final year, lonely from the death of his wife the year before, that all antagonism is dispelled, and the papers contain ten long and affectionate letters to his sister, with family news and affairs; his own and Chatham's health; Lord Temple's improvements at Stowe: '. . .busy about his colonnades for the North Front.' He writes often of his loved home: 'your poor old favourite Wotton [is] in its greatest beauty' and of his growing children, the four girls now under the care of the invaluable family friend, Mrs Stapleton. His last letter is dated September 11th; he died two months later. The seven children left Wotton to live at Stowe under the guardianship of their uncle, Lord Temple.

George Grenville's early letters to his sister, written when he was thirty-four and Hester eight years younger, are fraternal, affectionate, occasionally admonitory in an elder brotherly way, a little pompous and long winded, but always indicative of an easy uncomplicated relationship between the two.

Stoke
July the 31st 1746

The tables are turn'd between us, my dear Hetty, and I who but a fortnight ago was writing a letter full of reproaches to you for your idleness and neglect of me, am forced to throw two long sides of paper (for so much I do assure you I had written before I received your first letter) into the fire, and am now oblig'd instead of talking big, to submitt and humble myself before you... Consider too, that you was within six hours of being in the wrong, for if I had not receiv'd your letter the very morning that I did, mine had gone in the afternoon and therefore you ought in reason and in conscience to place it to your account, as you was the occasion of its miscarrying... I dont dare quarrel with you, my dear Hetty, but it is not fair [that] in the very letter you bid me give an account of myself and of Bristol waters, to take not the least notice of the effect of Tunbridge waters. In this I will set you a good example by informing you of my life and conversations at the wells... I rise a quarter before Six and as there is five long miles to the wells, am obligd to ride softly not to heat myself. I get there between 8 and 9, and stay there till between 10 and 11 and return an hour or two before dinner. After dinner which is seldom over till four or five, a little walking or if that is impossible by the weather, which has been often the case of late, Back Gammon for want of Chefs is the word, and then sweet conversation and a walk up and down an old hall till supper, and so to bed.

You see this scheme is full of health, but not of Edification, for I have almost forgot to read or write, except once or twice an Admiralty letter, which gave me the headach, and made me remember it... The exercise or the waters, or both together, have certainly done me a great deal of good, and so desirous am I to deserve the performance of the promise made me, that I am trying to get excluded from the Admiralty by staying here longer than even Ld Barrington's dispensation, for I shall not set out from Hence till the 8th of August, which will bring me to Town on the 10th, where I expect to hear a good account of you... All the important news of Bristol wells you have seen in the newspapers, how a Gentleman gave a public breakfast where there were present 140 people, how Lord Jersey is gone to London to try the Scotch Lords, how the Dutchess of Norfolk has been very ill, and how the Duke came from London, how he found her better and went back again...

You tell me that you shoud have been sure of a letter if you had staid in London; to be sure I shoud have had more to have said to you there as you see more people. I shoud have desired you to tell those that enquire after me that if the waters do me as much and as lasting good as their enquiries give me pleasure and happiness, I shall never have occasion to drink them again. Adieu. God bless you.

Admty Office
Augst the 28th 1746

Considering how well I love you, My dear Hetty, I cannot conceive the reason why I am sometimes so long without writing to you, and to do justice on both sides, as long without hearing from you. I won't mortify myself with believing one moment that it is the least mark of yours to me, I rather think from what I have always felt that the pleasure in hearing from those we love more than in writing to them, for the same reason that I had rather hear them speak than speak myself, and consequently when the vanity of letter writing is out of the case, it is only to entitle one to an answer, and is no more than paying a debt, or working for a salary which tho it is very honest employment, is not so pleasant as receiving the income and spending the money we borrow. But as we have both try'd each other and find that no evasion will do, let us act de bonne foi for the future and only expect as much as we give.

Deploring the shortness of her letters 'consisting of a half sheet of small gilt paper doubled together with large margins on the top and sides,' he goes on to say:

> Write me good sizeable letters and don't begin dating them like the watchman's cry 'past twelve o'clock and a cloudy morning', not that I shall always insist on long letters for as Hotspur says 'I woud give ten times as much to a deserving friend, but in the way of bargaining, mark you me, I'll cavil on the tenth part of a line. . .'

Hester is at Tunbridge Wells and has complained of being unwell:

> I do assure you I have been very uneasy for you, or rather for myself, not only because it hinderd me hearing from you, but for a reason more interesting to me than that, which you scarce deserve if you want to be told it. I own I heard some expressions thrown upon your conduct at Tunbridge. I was told that you rode out at improper hours, that you breakfasted before you drank the waters and drank the waters too late, and many other articles of complaint.

George Grenville's long drawn out courtship of Elizabeth Wyndham probably begins at this time, and in this same letter she receives her first mention, though not by name. His information about Hester

> came from good hands, from a <u>charming spirited honest young Lady</u>, who was at least as good a witness for me, and I am sure a less suspicious one than your <u>charming spirited</u> honest Capt Geary. . . What I expect is a thorough abjuration of all your errors, all your favours, agues, inflammations, heats and colds. . .
> I am told wonders of your horsewomanship but seriously ten miles an hour is rather too much fatigue for an invalid. Pray remember that is an error; and confine your praises to your genteelness on horseback and not your Spirits.

Two weeks later, Hester is still at Tunbridge and George has received news of her from the third brother James - Jemmy - who has joined her at the spa:

> Admty Office
> Septr the 13 1746

> . . . Jemmy indeed gives a very good account of you, and insists that a bottle of wine does you more good than a bottle of water, and hints that you have got a red face but except that says you are in perfect Beauty.

He has news of the fourth brother, Henry Grenville's career:

The good news I am going to tell you [is that] Harry's affair is at last determind and you may now wish him joy I think of being Governor of Barbados. The D. of Newcastle sent to me yesterday to tell me that he had mentiond it to the King who receivd the Proposition very graciously, and made no objection. I go with Henry to the D. of Newcastle's on Tuesday to fix the day for his kissing hands. Rejoice with us my dear Hetty at this good news and make it compleat by coming up to town in health and spirits. The Gates of Shene will be open for you, and I fancy it will be found that you are not so absolutely recoverd that you still want the country air and a little riding in Richmond Park, at best this will be the case if the inhabitants of Shene are allowd to have any skill in Physick.

There is mention in this letter of Henry Grenville's future wife, the beautiful Margaret - Peggy - Banks:

There is a copy of verses writ by young Horace Walpole calld the beauties, in which half the women about town are changd into goddesses. Amongst others, Mrs Lyttelton and Fanny Macartney have their share... but what is wonderfull the Author has forgot Peggy Banks. See the effects of being a hundred miles out of Town.

One further letter of 1746 survives before George Grenville's marriage in 1749, after which for some years it is Elizabeth his wife who takes over as chief correspondent. Hester's own marriage to William Pitt on November 16th of 1754 brings a letter to Pitt at the end of October. George Grenville is the brother in charge of the financial settlements of the union, and it is on him fall the negotiations with Pitt's solicitor Thomas Nuthall.

Wotton
Octr the 31st 1754

My dear Pitt I was just sitting down to answer your very kind and affectionate letter when I receivd one by an express from Ailesbury from Mr Nuthall containing many difficulties and Queries which I am sure you will forgive me answering before your letter, and notwithstanding that letters from Attornies upon law business are not allways the most agreeable, yet everything that can hasten and dispatch the preliminaries of that day which will if possible unite us still nearer, must be my wishes and inclinations almost as strongly as it can be yours, take place of every other object and consideration. I wish you had settled it for an earlier day with Lady Hester but when we parted she told me it was absolutely impossible to take effect till the 15th... Mr Nuthall has not yet sent me the drafts but says he thinks I may depend upon them by Saturday's post... My stay here should not delay you an hour, so reasonable do I think the impatience you express, or rather so impatient am I myself for every thing you desire.

After the wedding and for the next five or more years, George Grenville's few letters are addressed to William Pitt. It is doubtful that the two men, so very different in temperament, could ever have lived in great sympathy one with the other. Grenville probably felt the dichotomy, common to others, between his admiration of Pitt's astonishing success as a war leader and his doubts on the great man's mental and physical stability. The principal subjects of Grenville's letters of this time belong to history and have no real place in this study. By 1760 their friendship, if it ever existed was at an end. There is one letter only of 1761 and one of 1766, this last icy letter coldly formal written in the third person, and with a grievance:

Bolton Street
Saturday morning
Febry 8th 1766

Mr Grenville presents his compliments to Mr Pitt, and is sorry that he was not in a Condition to remain in the Committee last night after he had spoken, as Mr Grenville found Himself under the necessity of giving an Answer to many passages contain'd in Mr Pitt's speech, which He apprehended Himself to be personally calld upon, and to which He earnestly wishd Mr Pitt could have heard his Answer. Mr Grenville is obligd to Mr Pitt for his assurances that nothing was further from his thoughts than to mark the least want of Personal Regard towards Him. Mr and Mrs Grenville join in returning their Thanks for his Enquiry after Mrs Grenville's Health, which They hope is better than it has been, and shall be glad to receive the like favourable Account of Mr Pitt and Lady Chatham.

The break between the two statesmen is now total and not to be revived for over three years:

Eton
July 5th 1769
Wednesday morning

Dear Sister
On our arrival here last Night we found your kind letter... Mrs Grenville and I feel very sensibly the affectionate concern which Lord Chatham and you have shown towards us upon the Occasion of the very alarming Accident which has happend to our youngest son. We had the Comfort of finding Him quite free from every Complaint except a little Weakness which must necessarily follow what He has gone thro'... We flatter ourselves with the Blessing of God that we shall soon see Him perfectly re-establishd in every Respect. Mrs Grenville has been ill with a Return of her former bilious Complaint, but is now getting better, to which the good account of our poor Boy has not a little contributed. We sincerely hope that Lord Chatham and you are in good Health and that you have no such painful anxiety with Regard to Any of your young Family as that which we have lately felt.
I am Dear Sister, Your affectionate Brother
George Grenville

But Elizabeth's end was close, though the fluctuating nature of her illness keeps this sad knowledge from her husband. They even still entertain:

Wotton
Octr 12: 1769

We feel most sensibly My Dear Sister the Concern which Lord Chatham and you so kindly express for Mrs Grenville's illness and your solicitude receives better account of Her Health which, thank God, I hope I am now able to give to you. Since her last Severe Attack, She has had no Return of violent Pain, and her Complaints are in some Respects considerably abated... We flatter ourselves that the Disorder is gradually lessening by the approach of the cold weathers and by the Use of the Parreira Brava, from which she found such surprising Benefit three or four years ago, and which she now takes mixd up in Pills with Almond Soup.

After comment on the doings of members of both families, George continues:

We expect a House full of Company next Week at the fishing of our Lake, tho I daresay that our Expectations in this, as in most other Fisheries, will be greatly disappointed.

Elizabeth Grenville died on 5th December. It fell to the already seriously ill George Grenville to attempt to keep together a home for his seven children, the eldest of whom, Charlotte, was not yet twenty. In this he had the support of Catherine Stapleton, already in post during the latter stages of the mother's illness and now prepared to place her remarkable and generous mind and her practical skills to the support and comfort of the family. The widower is aware of her value to them, and the children, especially the four girls, love her as deeply as she does them.

Bolton Street
Tuesday April 24 1770

I feel myself My Dear Sister very much obligd to you and Lord Chatham for your very kind Enquiries after us. We all arrived here safe and well last night and are extremely glad to hear by your Letter that Lord Chatham is so much recoverd from his last attack of the gout. The hopes which you give to us of calling upon us in Town make us flatter ourselves that you are yourself free from any Complaint as well as our young Friends. I shall endeavour to come and see you at Hayes as soon as I have little settled my Busyness in Town. In the meanwhile I shall be happy to see Lord Chatham and you whenever you make an excursion from the Pleasures of Hayes to the Hurry both of Busyness and of Jolleness in which the Inhabitants of this Place are constantly engaged. Our kindst Compts attend you all, and Jem, my Dear Sister, Your most affectionate Brother

George Grenville

Back at Wotton, and after lengthy comment and sympathy on Chatham's gout 'that cruel companion' George writes:

Wotton
June 10th 1770

I have so few thoughts which can afford me Pleasure that I beg to indulge in all those which do. Tho we have had some cold Weather, yet the Country has Green'd and is most delightfull. I have enjoyd it by being as much abroad as possible. Our Leaves and Flowers, I mean by that our Lilacs and Liburnums are in their highest Glory. You are so partial to Wotton as to believe this upon Report, but I cannot help longing every Day to show it to Lord Chatham and to you and to our Young Friends, whom I hope you will make us happy in bringing with you. Our Great Work which is, as you know, nothing more that a Wooden Bridge, goes on apace and I am promised will be finished in a little more than a month. I have not yet been at Stowe but George has passd four or five days there and brings me an account that Lord and Lady Temple are perfectly well, that he is extremely busy about his Colonnades for the North Front, and making out the Foundations for altering the South Front.

He hopes that the Chathams and their family will join him and his when he goes to stay at Eastbury, the home of the Henry Grenvilles, in July:

This would double the Pleasure to us and we would make any alterations of our Scheme in our Power to obtain it. We must however be back again here before the end of July for the breaking up of our Eton Boys. Some private busyness calls me to London for a few Hours and I shall set out from Hence to morrow to return again on Wednesday. Mrs Stapleton takes this opportunity of performing a promise she made of a visit to Lady Blandford and goes with me thither tomorrow.

But there was to be disappointment, the Chathams did not join him at Eastbury. Illness as ever the reason:

Eastbury
July the 2d 1770

Your letter, my Dear Sister of the 28th of last month came to me at Wotton the Evening before we set out from thence for this Place where we arrivd yesterday. This prevented me from telling you till now how much mortify'd and concernd we all are at the account contain in your letter. We flatterd ourselves with the Hopes that Lord Chatham and you and our young Friends would be of our Party here, instead of which we have heard with much Concern how much you have been alarmed by the Illness of two of them attended with the same violent Cough which gave you so much anxiety in the spring.

Commenting on the wet weather and its evil effect, even in midsummer, on old and young, he continues:

I do not wonder that Lord Chatham has felt it as very few Persons who have any chronical Complaints have been quite free from the effects of it. . . Charlotte whom you so kindly enquire after is much better than she was, but I think not yet quite recoverd from her Illness. She and George are both here but the latter is just setting out for Weymouth to bathe and drink the Sea Water, where he will continue for a month and then return to us at Wotton.

The plan is to move on to stay with the Suffolks (particular friends of Elizabeth Grenville - 'the Marble Hill family' -) at Charlton House in Wiltshire. While there they receive alarming news, the shock too much for the ailing man. On return home he describes the event:

Wotton
July the 24th 1770

The very next morning after our arrival there [at Charlton] we were greatly alarm'd by an Express from Eton informing me that one of the Boys in the House where my two sons boarded, was seiz'd the Day before with a very bad Scarlet Fever (of which he is since dead), that many of the Boys and almost all those in the same House were sent Home for fear of the Infection and desiring my Directions what to do. I immediately resolvd to send for them Home and Miss Stapleton insisted that she and Charlotte would go back to Wotton the same morning to keep the two Boys separate from the Girls, for fear that they would be infected, and promised to send for me directly if there should appear the least symptom of their being ill. They set out accordingly, and the next day I felt myself so much out of Order that I was forcd to keep my Room, and for the greatest part of two Days, my Bed; but two Doses of James's Powder set me up again, and I have had the Comfort at my Return Home to find all my young Folk perfectly well and free from any Complaint whatever. . .

Whilst I was absent Miss Stapleton carried over the whole Family (except George who is at Weymouth) to Stowe and their Report is that my Brother is extremely deep in Lime and Mortar and that He and Lady Temple are both very well.

At last the Chathams have been to stay at Wotton, but George Grenville's health is now declining fast:

Wotton
Sept the 11th 1770

You would not have waited till I had heard from you, My Dear Sister, to have returnd my sincerest and warmest Thanks to Lord Chatham and to you for the very kind visit which you made to us at Wotton, but I have been so very much out of Order since you left us that indeed I have scarcely been able to do any Thing. Fortunately for me Sir Wm Duncan, whom you met upon this Road hither, was here and has put me into a method which he hopes will soon give me some Relief. He seems convinced that the severe Pains which I have lately felt proceed not so much from any Cold as from my Nerves being universally relaxed and unbraced. He has therefore directed me to take Dr Huxham's Decoction of the Bark twice a Day and to be in the Air especially on Horseback as much as I can, and I am considerably better than I was and I think that the Bark agrees with me and does me Good tho I have yet had but little Trial of it.

Two days later and the Temples are evidently worried about him and with good reason:

[Stowe]
Sept the 13th 1770

Lord and Lady Temple came in without the least notion of their kind intention in their Way from Eastbury to Stowe, to which place they carried off me and George the next morning. Charlotte stayd behind to wait for Mrs Stapleton who had made an Excursion to carry my two Etonians to Eton that morning. . . On Fryday (tomorrow) she and Charlotte come hither to us, and on Sunday we intend to set out for Packington if we hear nothing from Lord and Lady Aylesford to the contrary. . . Lord Temple is returnd in perfect [health] and extremely pleased with the Colonnade in the North Front which is now almost finishd on one side except the stuccoing. It is indeed very pleasing and very magnificent. Lady Temple too is very well and free from the Gout tho she is still lame in two or three Fingers which continue to be arranged in Flannel. The success of the North Front has given fresh Life and Encouragement to the Plans for the Garden Front, which at present engross most of our Time and Conversation.

There was to be little further fresh Life and Encouragement for George Grenville, who died on 13th November. His agonising last journey to London, accompanied with a relay of physicians and by Catherine Stapleton is described in her letters to Hester Chatham.

His death was sad in so far as he did not live to see any of his children fully grown-up and his four daughters married, but there will surely have been satisfaction for him in the full restoration of friendship with his sister Hester - and with her husband - though his love for her had, without doubt, never lapsed.

iii. LETTERS FROM JAMES GRENVILLE 1744-1783

James Grenville was Hester Chatham's third and probably her favourite of the four brothers who survived into later age, and who preceded her at yearly or two year intervals from 1711 to her own birth in 1720. It is easy to see why. He was a loveable man, lacking the ruthlessness and political ambition of the two eldest, Richard, Lord Temple and George, who became prime minister in 1763. After Hester married William Pitt, James's great and lasting devotion to her beloved husband will have cemented the love engendered by his charming nature.

There is evidence in plenty of James Grenville's gentleness, of his philosphical acceptance of the twists and turns of existence, of his modesty, in his own letters to his sister, and to Pitt, and in observations about him in the letters of others. He was the only brother who is referred to always by a pet name, Jemmy or Jem. He was also something of an eccentric. In a letter to Hester from her sister-in-law Elizabeth, the wife of George Grenville, there is an engaging portrait of him in 1751 at a family gathering at Stowe: 'We found Mr James Grenville so wedded to Buckingham [election] and Thucidides in the original that he has never appear'd since our arrival except of the first day at dinner in a shirt three days old and a wig over one ear'. He was one of the trio of Grenville brothers who with William Pitt and their cousin George Lyttelton made up the 'young patriots' under the leadership of the Grenville's uncle, Sir Richard Temple, Lord Cobham. He entered parliament as member for Old Sarum in 1742, and later obtained, through Pitt's influence, junior ministerial rank, becoming Pitt's deputy paymaster-general in 1746. His political star waxed and waned with that of Pitt. After attaining a Treasury lordship he resigned from parliament in 1770 and thankfully retired to his

Somerset seat of Butleigh Wootton, only a few miles distant from the Chathams at Burton Pynsent. It was thus that during the first five years of Hester Chatham's widowhood he was the brother with whom she was most closely in touch, until his death in 1783. James was, like his brother-in-law, a long term sufferer from gout, but his illness was without the mental torment which accompanied Pitt's sufferings. He also, like Pitt and most of their contemporaries, had faith in the curative properties of spa waters; in doctors he had none.

We learn from sources other than the correspondence that James Grenville married a Mary Smyth in 1740, but she is nowhere mentioned in his letters. They had two sons, Richard and James, who were twins, though this fact also is never alluded to. The boys were devoted to their father and he to them; they made their home with him at Butleigh, and James, an MP who became Lord Glastonbury in 1797, remained on in the family house after his father died. Neither son married. Both young men were facile letter writers and the papers contain many letters from them to the Chathams: James junior in particular was especially fond of his aunt. Richard was a career army officer, and both men benefited from the patronage of their cousin William Pitt.

James Grenville and his sons cannot be classed as men of outstanding distinction; it is doubtful that without family influence they would have risen to the moderate public stations they attained. But in their letters to Hester Chatham they leave an illuminating record of Somerset life, as led in a bachelor household of country gentlemen of relatively modest means. James senior, though willingly and happily removed for his last twelve years or so from public activity, was nevertheless no hermit; his letters are full of references to, and shrewd observations upon, political, national and overseas affairs. Above all it is in his philosophy of living that the charm of his letters resides.

The first surviving letter adopts, as would be expected from an older brother, a jocular and facetious tone. There is no mention of his four year marriage or of his twin sons aged two.

[Lisle]
September 24 1744

Dear Meg of Wooton
        Though I have very few minutes to spare from flattering Parsons, table hunting Captains and clamourous insolvent tenants, yet you behaved so very nobly in writing to me, that I could not for shame [three words mutilated] justice to acknowledge it. Pardon me, Madam, for saying into the bargain that I know too well the dangers attending any marks of slight and disrespect to the fair, to be guilty of the least neglect of their favours. Not that I own myself to be so much guided by fear in the present occasion as Inclination. Flattery has too many charms for me to resist even where charms are wanting in the bestowers of it. I leave you to judge what it must be when it comes from your self, and when perhaps more than one hand has been employed in so very charitable a disposition of it. But having made these acknowledgements, I confess it is a great satisfaction to me to find that you understand the nature of your Duty, which certainly is to have, as you modestly express it, a constant attention to every thing that may give my worship pleasure...

All the brothers took a friendly interest in Hester's gentle love life: her suitors are given fictitious names, these doubtless easily placed by Hester:

> I am not a little glad that there is a prospect of getting you off to Simon Truelove. He really deserves to have you, and it is impossible to hope for a more advantageous proposal. My dear Meg, you grow old, and it is time for you to think of a decent retirement from business. Tho' you have serv'd me with a great fidelity and attention yet you will soon become incapable and burthensome... Besides, with regard to my business you will be better able to manage at present by marrying Simon than in any other manner... Therefore let me hear by the very next post that the thing is concluded, otherwise never tell me again of the hardship 'of the times' nor expect me [to] supply your unnecessary demand...
>
> I intend to stay here some time longer, for it is incredible how we strike amusements out of this damned Dull place, like fire out of Flints. Hunting, shooting, dancing and what not... I take my leave jusques au revoir, being with most profound veneration dear Meg,
>
> Your most affect.
> [signed with a squiggle]

Three years later there is a letter to Hester about their mother's health, without an address and containing a cryptically worded passage which may possibly throw light on James Grenville's relations with his wife:

Novr 11th 1747

> I thank my Dr Hetty a thousand times for the good news she sent me in her own fair handwriting. By last post George's Letter had given me the greatest apprehensions of my Mother's state: but your Accounts had made it all easy...
>
> I am dertermin'd to stay here in the Country at this season, and at a distance from all the fine women and pleasures and employments of the Town for that very purpose and no other. Tho' I find you impute my stay to other causes and cant help adopting the Ideas of a Town Lady to people in the Country, whereas who ever heard that People in the Country were kept there thro' sickness. People in the Country, my Dr Hetty are never sick. Town Ladies indeed are never well. But Country Gentlemen are never out of order. The real motive of my stay is perhaps too full of vanity for me to own publicly: nevertheless to you the partner of [my] breast, I must own all. Know then, it is to disappoint a fine woman whom I doat upon and who uses me ill, that I dont shew any impatience of coming to London. She shall know that I can endure being absent from her.

Predictably, James Grenville was of all the brothers the most delighted at the engagement of Hester to William Pitt. In a letter of 13 October 1754, he writes to Pitt, his 'dearest Friend':

> ... I can say with the greatest truth, that from the first moment of my having the happiness to know you, which I thank God was almost as soon as I had what one might call knowledge of any thing in this world, I ardently wished that every event might happen that could possibly give comfort and satisfaction to you, and at the same time tend to establish and cherish that real friendship and warm affection which I ever felt for you, and which I always valued as one of the most pleasing as well as (with respect to myself) the most usefull in circumstances of my whole Life.

Letters from James are scarce for the next eight years; he will of course have been closely in touch with the Pitts. From 1762 the correspondence is directed mainly to Hester, now Baroness Chatham in her own right.

As with most of his comtemporaries, middle age has brought a spate of minor illness to James, accompanied by the prevalent hypochondria due it must be supposed to the helplessness of the physicians at that time - and before, and for a century to come:

Pinner
Saturday 8th Jan. 1762

My dear Sister

I have received your two friendly salutations and many thanks do I return you for them. I could easily ask pardon of any one when I am in the wrong; I can do it to your Ladyship even when I am in the right, so profound is my devotion. The excellent qualities which adorn your Ladyship's Life, both publick and private, make it very difficult for one not to commit a fault in any state of conduct compared with your Ladyship's. . . However I have to say for myself that my errors have flowed from the frailties, not of my mind as you may think, but from those of my body, and these too not in a manner censurable either by the church or the state, but from Colds catched upon Colds, and a Hacks upon my lungs which have been so violent that I cannot describe how much I have undergone, but it is now quite over and I begin again to visit the fresh air. . .

Hester Chatham's growing influence in her husband's public life, (but always subservient to his wishes), is recognised by James Grenville, and others. He continues:

I wish you every prosperity and happiness that the year can bring to reward your wishes, and [that] the many years may derive as much honour and glory to Mr Pitt as the last, but less publick Calamity to this poor Kingdom in the conclusion of it. As the news papers have published a paper purporting a declaration of war against Mr Pitt by his Majesty of Spain, I think it necessary that he should hasten his preparations and get my Lord Temple and the Attorney Genl to Town early or at least as soon as the Holy-days are over. I will meet them. Mr Pitt ought to consider that the match is hardly even between him and the Spanish Monarchy, since including the days that he may be ill and not fit to take the field, he and Lord Temple and the Attorney and your humble servt, even with you to help us, cannot fight above ten thousand in a month, and that Monarchy may supply fifty or sixty thousand upon a pinch, besides the war in Portugal

Pinner
Sunday 8th [?] 1764

My dear Lady Chatham

I proposed passing these last five days exactly with you and Mr Pitt at Hayes. How do you think I have employed them? In getting the better of a fever and a bloody flux upon my bowels. I believe I did right in staying at home tho' not half so cleverly as I intended in being with you. . .

And with a graceful nod towards the Pitt children, including a nice pun:

Pray make my best Compliments to Mr John and Mrs Hester and in short to all the young Ladies and Gentlemen. I want much to let them know what good things I heard of them quite beyond the Severn Seas (they know where) in Wales, and of their improvement in the Sciences and in Languages and in every thing that can make them either amiable or estimable.

In 1765 William Pitt has inherited Burton Pynsent and taken up part time residence on the estate. They are now close neighbours of James Grenville at Butleigh from which comes his first letter from there, addressed to Pitt:

Butleigh
Octr 23 1765

I send you a canister of spruce tops which were brought here last night from Captain Hood. The rest of the cargo has been dispatched to Bath from which place I expect its arrival every day. I have had the Curiosity to make a trial of a tea dish full of it this morning. I cannot much applaud the relish of it - but I take this to be a circumstance of no very great importance, since I find it sets well upon the Stomach. You will observe from the directions that some Molasses will be wanted for brewing up the Essence. I apprehend you may easily procure some from Bristol. . .

I am glad the kind visit you made to my magnificent palace was executed without any bad consequences. You must have been very merry upon your return, for every body heard a vast singing all along the road quite to Burton from Butleigh. Some people say it was William's voice, some say it was James's. It gave great scandal to sober travellers, who impute such loudness to the effects of too much liquor. . .   Jemmy [son James] presents his best respects to you and Lady Chatham. We hope to finish our matters so as to set out for Bath next Saturday, but nothing is absolutely certain under the sky. Some mementos of the gout, which seems to be flying about me, will however quicken my march. If not I will take one more look into Burton Pynsent before I leave Somerset for the winter.

Back in London in December, he writes to Hester on the 21st that he would like to visit them at Bath but that

to do which requires at this time of the year a very bright spark of alacrity to set out in defiance of all the difficulties of short days, long roads, falling rains and winters cold.

and with another cryptic allusion to his private life:

I have now been in this Town seven or eight days, not abounding as you may imagine in many blessings nor in many good works. Yet I protest in some instances of a private kind, and particular to myself, I have Reason to be much comforted and pleased with what has passed.

The three years that follow are those of Pitt's, now Chatham's decline into serious ill health, mental and physical. The devoted James suffers with him all the way, and has his own troublesome ailments to report. Writing from various addresses, in or near London, Clifford Street, Mount Street and Pinner, his letters to Hester are in effect notes of affection, sympathy and concern. Thus:

Pinner
May 15th 1767
late at night

My dear Sister

  The languor in which Lord Chatham was this morning after his ride makes me extremely desirous to know how he found himself in the course of the day, and of the ensuing night. I wish from the bottom of my heart it was possible for me to suggest any method of alleviating his sufferings but after turning it over as much in my mind as I am capable of doing, I am now forced to believe that patience and mild weather are the only true and safe remedies to his present uneasiness. Let me implore you my dear Sister to support both yourself and him with that confidence which I am persuaded will not deceive you. I know how much you undergo, and am sensibly affected with every circumstance of your uneasiness. I am so in the greatest degree with the pains which I see still continue to oppress him. Be so good as to favour me with a line from you by my servant, and if possible let me have the satisfaction of hearing that Lord Chatham was easier in the evening. I am my dear sister

Ever your affectionate brother
J Grenville

In July but not precisely dated James has news of his own state. He is recovering from an attack of sciatica:

  . . . As for me, I am much the same as yesterday, rather better. The operation of cupping was most plentifully bestowed last night and has I believe prevented increase of my Complaint. I kept [to the] house this bad day.

After his long absence from parliament, Chatham resumed the sinecure office (of his own choosing) of Lord Privy Seal on 21st March 1768. But not for long; that autumn he resigned. The faithful James is dismayed, even devastated:

Bath
Octr 22 1768

  I learn from report that Lord Chatham has resigned the Privy Seal. The vast irreparable loss which the public suffers by being deprived of his Authority and abilities in the King's service, is infinitely to be lamented by every thinking man in the Kingdom. I feel the importance of it with a true and sensible concern. I shall only add at present that I ardently wish that you and he may shortly enjoy that comfort and satisfaction from the recovery of his health which you have so much deserved and so long wanted.

Two days later he writes of the effect the resignation will have on his own career:

Bath
Oct 24 1768

  The part which in regard to my own little personal interests was open for me to take in the present distressed and unhappy conjuncture was very easy and obvious. But I have trod one path only from the first beginnings of my Life in any

Political concerns; and my perseverence in it through all the distractions and disturbances of those times which we have experienced, has been my support and happiness. I have always looked up to the intergrity and wisdom of Lord Chatham for the direction of my own sentiments and conduct towards the publick. Therefore any resolution that I might have fixed for myself in the present shattered state of things would have been imperfect towards the repose and quiet of my own mind, if it wanted the authority of his Sanction.

Nevertheless, he intends to carry on and to

steer my insignificant course as nearly towards those views as I can, till (what I pray to God may soon happen) some fortunate event by the re-establishment of Lord Chatham's health shall restore to the disordered state of this country the only hand strong enough to save it.

But James Grenville's 'political enthusiasm seems at this time to have waned'[8] and in January 1770, after resigning his offices he left parliament. Part of the year he spent clearing up some House of Commons business of Chatham's, before retiring thankfully to Butleigh:

Pinner
Friday night 14th Decr 1770

I was much concerned at being obliged to leave Bolton Street this morning before you came there. I wanted to take leave of you, to assure you of my warmest wishes that you and yours may enjoy all possible health and happiness. I entreat the favour of you to convey my most affectionate respects to Lord Chatham, and be pleased at the same time to let him know that on enquiring into the state of his private cash, as Paymaster General, Mr Lambe informed me that there was about £100 balance due to him, which could not be liquidated sooner. Mr Sawyer has his cash book and will discharge the balance to Lord Chatham's order whenever he pleases to honour him with it. ..

[PS.] There are a thousand volumes of Ledgers and memorial books belonging to Lord Chatham at the office. What would he please to have done with them? They will almost fill a room, as I am told.
I go the day after tomorrow to Somersetshire.

James Grenville had another thirteen years to live. He was not unhappy and certainly not bored in his retirement. He had the companionship of his two sons, James and Richard, subject to their career duties in parliament and the army respectively. Although neighbours, Chatham's restlessness, and the long periods he and his family spent away from Burton, mainly at Hayes, a custom continued for a time by Hester after her husband's death, ensured that there was still need for a continuance of the correspondence between brother and sister, albeit at fairly long intervals:

Butleigh
April 17th 1771

    Although I am an idle man, and have little concerns with any of the strange affairs which daily arise to astonish this astonishing world, yet I feel with as much sensibility as any man living such circumstances as affect the welfare and happiness of those I love. It was therefore with much uneasiness that I received the information which my son lately sent me of Lord Chatham's being ill and very much indisposed with severe pains in his head. . . I now write to you, my dear Sister, not merely to assure you of my warmest wishes for Ld Chatham's ease and your comfort, because I should think such assurances from me would be superfluous, but to desire the favour of a line from you if you have any satisfactory account to give me; and at the same time I take this opportunity to express for myself every mark of that sincere attention and affectionate regard by which I am, as well by every tie of mutual friendship, attached both to Lord Chatham and to you.

James could become quite lyrical when writing of his ailments:

[Butleigh]
March 15 1773
Monday

    As I am now my dear Sister restored to a good state of health as well as to a right state of understanding, I take this first opportunity to acquaint you with my situation, and to express my thanks to you for your kind sollicitude about me, during the course of my late indisposition. The Legion that possessed me, body and limb, is gone from me; and instead of continued fever, great pain, want of all appetite, entire loss of all sleep, inexpressible weakness etc I am now free from all those evils and in the enjoyment of most of the opposite blessings. In short, I have made my passage, and have ferryd my boat over to the other shore. . .

Despite recovery, he proposes to go to Bath:

    thinking that drinking the waters for a few days, and perhaps bathing once or twice may be of service to carry off any lurking remains of my Rheumatic fever.

On 29 March he writes from the spa, with qualified pleasure at news of Chatham's improvement:

    I was in hopes of hearing that his advances towards an entire recovery had been more considerable... I feel by experience that the returns at an advanced time of Life, from severe illness to perfect health are very slow in their progress. .

He knows that before ending his letter, Hester will want news of himself, something he says is

    the most perplexing thing to me in the world, [to] give an account of myself. I made my journey to Bath with great ease. I am stronger and better than I was; the waters agree with me, only I am forced to forbear taking them for a day or two on account of a cold which I have catched, attended with a slight soreness in my throat. However, I am not for aught that I know one pin the worse for it.

A month later, on 29 April, and perhaps a little depressed, he writes:

> As for myself, I am what I shall ever be, a patched up old man [he was 58] much mended from the effects of the waters or something else, but without one bit of new plank or cordage belonging to my sides or rigging.

James Grenville, the politician, is aware, though now with a degree of detachment, of the state of affairs in the American colonies.

Butleigh
Sunday morning
[March 20 1774]

> I find the Parlmt or rather the Ministry, are deep in American affairs. To all which I only say with Spenser that
> > those who once have missed the right way
> > The farther they do go the farther do they stray.

As the situation in America grows menacing, James's detachment gives way to concern. He tells his sister:

Butleigh
Monday February 7th
1775

> I hate oppression where ever I see it and from whatever quarter it proceeds. I abhor it in Bengal and of course feel a particular aversion to the making of another Bengal of America. If since you was last at Court, you have any interest with the Ministers, employ it now, and exhort them to let the means that have been proposed, for procuring a reconciliation with the Colonies, take place; to the end that we who agree with them in being lovers of Peace may all join in avoiding a Civil war with our fellow subjects, upon the grounds of asserting a right to do what, in my apprehension, is little short of a Robbery in the first instance, most probably to be accompanied with a murder afterwards. I will trouble you no further on these topics, but thank you for your kind regard about my health. It is much better than it has been for a long, a very long time past. The rains of heaven have been pouring down deluges upon me, storms of wind have been raving round me, but I, like poor Hammond's lover in an elegy, am a fixed Rock in the vast Atlantic of our Moors, unshaken and alone.

On a long visit to Bath that autumn, or possibly two or more shorter stays, James was part of the time with the Temples - 'they are a never failing friend to me' and he is involved in the Bath election arising from the death of one sitting member. Two unsuccessful contenders for the seat were Lord Mahon, the Chatham son-in-law and their son John Pitt. James is fed up with the result:

Bath
November 21 1775

> Your two young men deserve in everything they undertake, success. They will not find it to my great regret, at Bath; and it is a greed amongst us to drop all

futher pursuit of ends that grow less attainable the nearer we approach them. In short, I have broken the Ice, as well as I could, and am fallen in... and here I takes a long farewell of electioneering transactions, which I thought never to have meddled with again, nor should [I] if a spark of zeal, not common to me these later days of my life, had not prompted me to step aside into a path where I was utterly unacquainted.

At the end of the year, on December 28th, in a letter from the spa for which he asks Hester's 'pardon for the blots': 'I write in Company of people chattering around me' he explains one of its attractions for him:

You see I am a truant to Butleigh for Bath. I came here, not on account of health, but to meet some friends, for society.

James's pen was busy in 1776, and to a lesser extent, the following year. His letters to Hester treat always of Chatham's health and occasionally of his own; of his worry about his son Dick on active service in America 'that dreadful theatre of civil war'; of Stowe 'this place of real magnificence'. But his depression, engendered by the American war is paramount and cannot be concealed. After applauding Chatham's political stand against the war, he writes:

[Butleigh]
Friday Dec. 15 1776

I am not given to speculations on Politics farther than my fireside or my next door neighbour, having withdrawn myself from everything but that of being a human creature in society. Therefore I shall trouble you at present with none of the wanderings of my own mind. But tho' I am, like all the country round me, dull and ignorant, I am not quite so indifferent. I see Towns laid waste, civil wars raging, foreign ones threatening and all but actually commenced, Docks fired, Stores burnt, Treasury wasted, fruitless expeditions, campaigns however honourable to officers and troops, yet neither decisive in regard to the future, nor cheerfull in the midst of present success. Peace if intended or wished yet slow, tardy, remote and not quite approaching even to the outlines of reconciliation. It is not possible to be quite blind nor insensible in such a state, but once more farewell to such topics.

Regrettably, a number of James Grenville's later letters are undated. Some of the dateless letters are, however, worth recording, expressing as they do, in his neat turn of phrase, the essence of the man himself and of his views on the world around him. All are to Lady Chatham. The first four were probably written at some time in the two decades before Chatham's death in 1778, the remainder during her widowhood.

Butleigh
Sunday morn.

I am in great hopes, my dear Sister, to receive a good account of you this morning. The East wind blows chill and frore. I have a good opinion of the gales which came from that quarter; I know they labour under a bad reputation with some people, but with you and me they produce valuable effects: they strengthen the heartstrings and bend the mortal sinew to a proper tone of firmness and elasticity. Therefore let them blow, and pour out the treasury of the East upon your poor sore throat; as for me, they have done me good and I am now mended.

[Butleigh]
Saturday evening

I have known the day when a Lady's invitation in the absence of her husband would have been more welcome that his presence. I cannot forget those times so much as to decline any opportunity of seeing a fine woman who condescends to wish to see me tho' alone. But if I should do it, my protest to present any intention of coming to see Ld Chatham will still accompany my design. . .

PS. You will forgive my mistake about the piece of paper that I write upon. I have this moment finished half a bottle of Port and am at Table with one or two friends. This, that is all this, made me inattentive to what paper I was using and prevents me repeating by a transcript what I have already assured you of - my love and best wishes. Excuse my keeping your servant so long. I was abroad when he came, and my dinner was more than ready before I came back.

[?London]

Matters mend with me tho' slowly. My fever is I think quite over, some pains in my head and Temples still remain to keep me both low and humble. It really concerns me that Lord Chatham should continue so extremely lame in his arm, but it is in vain to pray or preach to the Gout or Rhumatism. I have tryed all things to appease their rocky hearts; nothing does. . . I thank you for the offer of broths etc but I find in the King's Arms, just near me, full supplies of all sorts of materials. I have taken some Physick this morning which really agrees with me and affords relief to my head.

[?Butleigh]

The first line of your letter gave me infinite pleasure - the latter lines restored me to a certain degree of compromise, after a long exhortation to a thing that the very thoughts of is an oppression of me. By the Lord that made me I will neither hear nor see nor welcome any Physician. I pray for a truce from intrusions that are disagreeable and vexatious. I am somehow lead on to write more about so worthless a subject than the thing is worth and I can ill afford the trouble - or the time. I beseech my dear sister, beseech you to let me take my own ways without enquiries. I will make no answers and mere civilities are nothing.

[Butleigh]
Monday 6th March

I was anxious about you till I received your note - it cleared up my doubts. Though I wish to see you, yet I do not wish to gather the fruit till it is in good order. Discretion is a great virtue, it leads to safety, and is proper for me to recommend even to you, contrary to my inclinations.

Ever yours
JG

Tuesday
[?1780]

I wish you could put your heart at ease and not anticipate misfortunes, which I hope in God and assure myself are as remote as any of those evils to which in every instant, and in every instance, the condition of human life is exposed. There is not, there has been no danger. Reduced strength is not soon repaired. You must have patience.

[Butleigh]
Tuesday eve

I come a begging to your trees, whose renown for bearing excellent fruit is spread far and wide, desiring the favour of them to bestow a few budds upon me for the purpose of rearing sons and daughters to inherit their virtues at Butleigh. In short I want to amend the breed in my garden; and where can I apply so properly as to yours? Your Gardiner will be so good as to direct my operator to the best sorts. . .

I hope to hear by the bearer, that is by a line, a single one, under your own hand, that you are free from any complaints in point of health, and if possible from every other circumstance that flutters about us mortals even in the sunshine of our lives, to sting and plague us in spite of our philosophy. The mildness of weather and my two Greys call me forth.

During his last full year of life, 1777, Chatham's ailments were to some degree in abeyance, but not so those of his brother-in-law James Grenville, who nonetheless treats them with his usual humour:

Febry 3d 1777

I write at last with confidence and pleasure to congratulate you upon the chearfull accounts you send me of the happy amendment, which you describe in the state of Ld Chatham's health. I trust to it with an implicit faith and am strongly impressed with a belief that the storm is not only abated, but past. A very long and dark one it has been, full of danger to him and of consequential suffering to you.

Monday May 19th
1777

The dearly beloved Gout, Scurvey, Fever and Rhumatism have been holding fete Champetre in my body; after lighting up every chamber in it they took their anniversary dance. The Company thank God is almost all gone and I am rubbing, scrubbing etc. clearing away the smoak, dirt and nastiness they have left behind.

Butleigh
June 30th 1777

I am to acquaint you that the wind is in the North and I am not so well as my brethren of ancient days, Hercules and Achilles. It will change in an hours time, and I expect to be as stout and as much a Hero as both of them together.

Chatham's death on 11th May 1778, the supreme watershed in so many lives brings, as would be expected, a letter of charm and simple affection from James to the widow, a letter almost alone among the countless number she will have received which has somehow been permitted to survive:

Thursday May 25 1778

Knowing what your mind has to sustain under the impressions of such a loss as yours, I venture to write these few lines to you. They are meant to put you in mind that you have been taught in the school of many trying vicissitudes to bear the misfortunes of Life with firmness and dignity. Now try, for your own sake and upon every acccount of tenderness to those you love, by all possible means, to bear even this last, this great shock, as great as Life itself to you, with resolution. Lord Chatham's memory lives in the heart and voice of every individual. His name is covered with Glory and renown. Such a departure is hardly an end of Life. Let this give comfort encouragement and consolation.

The nearness of Butleigh and Burton Pynsent, about twelve miles apart, where Hester spent most of her widowhood - all that time after Hayes was finally sold in 1784 - was without doubt a pleasure and comfort to brother and sister. They enjoyed a mellow friendship enlaced with affection, not only for each other, but also for the other's children, Richard and James Grenville and the five Pitts. The death of Hester Mahon in 1780 and of James Pitt half a year later in the West Indies, brought sorrow to overshadow what was in effect a trouble free time for both James Grenville and Hester Chatham. His health was not good but the spirit and humour remained to enhance his letters.

Butleigh
July 25th 1778

Your summers confinement in London is, I hope, now finished. It was in every respect oppressive and hurtfull to the state of your health. Let me entreat you to withdraw from the effects of such relaxing heats, and make me happy in granting me a request which I make to you in very earnest terms. If you must go to Hayes when you leave London, stay there for as short a space of time as possible. It is the land of recollection, and cannot fail to present to your view objects that recall to your mind images of things better not thought of than dwelt upon at present. Execute your intended plan for visiting Burton Pynsent, but not at once, nor immediately; let it be done gradually and for that purpose accept an invitation to an humble friendly quiet corner of the world accommodated, if I mistake not, in every respect to the dispositions of your mind. I mean the sober sympathysing solitude of this very place where I am now writing. I flatter myself that I consult your ease, and I need not make many solemn vows to assure you that I consult my own happiness in pressing this request upon you. No company will obtrude upon you, the few that are, or that will make a part of our society are known to you, and will join with me in the satisfaction of seeing you and in paying every attention that their love and duty can suggest. Our first interview, though not in good nor auspicious days, shall not be what you describe; at least my efforts shall not be wanting to make it otherwise.

The invitation is extended to include Harriot and William:

[Butleigh]
Augt 3d 1778

When I last wrote I did not know that Mr Pitt and Lady Harriot meant to accompany you to Burton Pynsent. Nothing can coincide more with my wishes than to have the pleasure of seeing them at Butleigh at the same time with you; and I am happy to find that it is in my power to include them, by easy arrangements, in my invitation. It does not suit my dispositions to sacrifice great pleasure to small inconveniences; in the present case there are not inconveniences at all.

Miss Readings [retired housekeeper] anniversary visit to me would have taken place in a short time but the postponement of it is a matter of perfect indifference to her. As for my own engagements abroad, I have but one, proposed for the latter end of the month but left, as it must necessarily be, to the determination of future contingencies and easy to be dispensed with.

The great lawyer and politician, Lord Camden, who held the post of lord chancellor in Chatham's last administration, was also the dead statesman's executor and thus in close touch with the widow. Hester has asked James whether he has heard from Camden; his reply, in this same letter, is characteristic of his literary style:

Lord Camden's motions are almost always a secret to me. His correspondence and mine is interrupted by very long intervals. It is a fire fed by a certain innate warmth of its own; and by no means resembles a constant blaze. Upon your own account and my own, I am impatient for his return.

Did Hester Chatham, with Harriot and William stay with James en route to Burton? Probably yes, for how could she refuse such an invitation? The few remaining years go on. For a time James writes less of his health; his interest in national affairs, despite his total absence from any part in them, is still keen and his observations pertinent. There is rumour of invasion and he is sceptical:

Augt 19th [1779]

I cannot say that I give faith to certain parts of the narrative. For instance I question the whole action and several other particulars. In short, I doubt all except the next approach of something like that cursed thing, a superior naval force equipped with a view to make a landing if possible, which may perhaps have passed Sr Charles and his whole fleet, by which he is to the westward of them, and they of course in command of our Coast instead of being so ourselves. . . [But] whether the invasion or not, at all events I beg that neither fright nor flight nor anything else may prevent our seeing each other. I can take a morning call upon you with much ease. The Greys are fat and in good order.

[Butleigh]
Feb [1780]

Very far am I, my dear Lady Farmeress, from thanking you for the books you sent me by Saturday's post. If I dared, I could from my heart be angry. After doing so right a thing as giving mine to Lord Chatham, who wanted them, how could you do so wrong a thing as sending a bookseller's present to me who did not want it at all. You degrade me from the rank of wholesale farmer to the condition of a wretched retailer - butter, sugar and candles - pounds, shill. and pence. I have a good mind not to tell you that I hear the transports which sailed from Plymouth are driven back by a storm into Cork. The transport in which Lord Chatham is passenger amongst the number... Sir George Rodney has had good luck indeed but the sea and the winds have not left him in possession of many marks of victory - if victory and superiority of 21 ships against 8 are the same thing.

The letters of the last three years of James Grenville's life, years of increasing illness, predictably are concerned mainly with family and local matters, his own and Hester's. He has given her a ram:

[Butleigh]
Saturday [1780]

I cannot hesitate about affording some charitable relief to your farmerly distress, though not so well, nor so much to my glory as I could wish. You must send a man and a cart to convey the illustrious traveller to his seraglio. Such Gentlemen never travel on foot. In the meantime my shepheard shall have orders to make the best choice he can for you.

[Butleigh]
April 2d 1781

Many thanks to you my dear Sister for your very kind affectionate letters. .. You seem to think I exaggerate in the praises of my young friends. I assure you that I do not. What I feel with warmth, perhaps I speak so, but I know that the grounds I go upon are good. They are not pictures but reality and in short, be they what they may, I indulge them with pleasure. What can I have in this late hour and dark shade of Life more pleasing, than to look forward to rising merit.

James has delayed answering a letter from William Pitt who, in company with all who know him, he already greatly admires:

[Butleigh]
17 May 1781

I have, if indolence be a sin, many sins of that sort to answer for, and among the rest, a most abominable atheistical Sacriligious delinquency of omission to another part of your family, Mr William Pitt, who was so good to write a very obliging letter to me about the postponing the visit he kindly intended to make last spring to Butleigh. I intreat you to intercede with him for me, and to procure me a pardon. You must take care to say nothing to him about indolence, for he wont understand your meaning. I know he is quite ignorant, and knows nothing of the matter. Yet perhaps you may cautiously venture to explain it to him, by telling him it is a quality belonging to the old and the weak, and deserves compassion some times, though never the esteem of the young and active.

James's philosophical turn of mind and his appealing metaphors grow rather than diminish as his life shortens:

See the perverseness of the human mind! You give me, in my need, to my heart's desire, an excellent mare, commit her to my care as a faithfull deposit, consecrate to my use what you might apply to your own, and trouble yourself with enquiries about her giving or not giving me the satisfaction you wish me to receive from her. I too am on my part desirous to applaud, thank and employ the gift, for the sake of the giver. Yet have I been but once abroad with her since the day of her arrival here, and as you command I shall now resign all my interests in her except those of very sincere acknowledgements to you for your kind intentions. See the perverseness, I say again, of the human mind! Though she has no fault, yet I dislike her going, and like the queen of Garbe, prefer the services of my ugly, pitifull, mean Dwarf Poney to the dignified figure and just proportions of your mare. I cannot account for so strange a preference, except there should be a pleasure in being vexed which none but the vexed know.

Augt 19th 82

As to your enquiries about myseslf, or my appurtenances, I return you the tribute of my thanks for the kindness of them, and have to acquaint you that I travel on smooth and fair, neither dancing nor quite crawling. Mr James is preparing to leave me in the space of a very few days, and then I am again a noun substantive, all alone without any adjective whatever. Perseverence and habitude are mighty reconcilers to solitude, but if the clouds and storms permit an excursion, the distance of Burton from Butley, and the transition from singleness to singleness is not quite so great as one of best fish made yesterday, out of water into the air. I blame it much for leaving its element, the sally cost it dear, and the pleasure could never have made amends for the pain. But hermit to hermit and cave to cave is not uncongenial, nor unnatural, and this makes me desire you to give my affectionate compliments and respects to your fair company, whose invincible love of retreat, and of rural delights would, if the seas were safe, drive them abroad, to any solitude to avoid the persecution of Town amusements and Country irregularity. I wish they could bear the thoughts of them with less antipathy; a small relish for them is absolutely necessary to those who are born to social enjoyments, and to please and be pleased in Life.

Not long before his final illness, which may have been a stroke, James's political views, which he had consigned to silence, reassert themselves with passion spurred by the negotiations of the peace treaty of 1783.

Febry 24 1783

Sure they must be very much in jest with us, and hold the understanding of their poor neighbour in great scorn, those I mean who for 19 hours together after setting up whole nights waking, watching, cursing, execrating, blasting, damning, censuring, abusing, railing, reprobating, and everything but rejecting, the Peace, in its beginning and in its ending, in every clause and in every line of it, would yet persuade us to believe that they are not only not against it but that they are the most determined friends to the support of it, and the most scrupulous conscientious and devoted professors of the sacredness of its current obligations, of any men in the Kingdom. It may be so - but to my frail judgement the doctrine seems rather mysterious and almost contradictious. . .

Now my dear Sister, this is all that I think about the matter; except that (knowing nothing) I suspect there may be something of the passions concerned in this operation, and shifting of the scenes. For example, some people may perhaps love the peace less than they hate Ld Sh[elbur]ne. But Philosophy says that true virtue loves the good even more than it hates the bad. Therefore I cannot give a clear solution to the dilemmas that you seem to suggest to me in your letter; besides which I am so old and so cold and so dull that I am not good at expounding of mysteries.

James Grenville died on 14th September; he was sixty-eight. It is from the pen of his son James junior that we have a description of his last days. In a letter to Mrs Stapleton three days before the death he writes:

[Butleigh]
Thursday morning

Tho' I haved endeavoured to prepare myself for the blow, it affects me as it approaches more than I can express. I have no comfort to impart to you (except what is a very real one) that the last moments are without the least pain, and we have the fullest confidence, and are now certain, that the advances being so gradual the sad scene will close without a struggle.

And to Hester Chatham:

Butleigh
Sunday 10 o'clock a.m.

My dr Aunt
The last crisis has taken place; my poor Father expired about seven o'clock this morning. Tho' I have so long expected the shock, it still affects me more than I can express, but I cd not reconcile it to my mind, painful as the task is, that any other pen shd communicate to you this afflicting intelligence. I propose staying here till the middle of the week, that I may have the satisfaction of knowing with certainty that every necessary direction has been given and that nothing has been omitted which relates to the last duty. The gratification which I shall afterwards feel will amply compensate for any aggravation (if any such there shd be) to my personal suffering.
God bless you, my dear Aunt, let me have the satisfaction to hear that you preserve yr health which will always be an essential comfort to
Yr most affectionate and dutiful nephew
J. Grenville

The younger James Grenville, of all Hester Chatham's nephews - and nieces - was indeed the most affectionate and the most dutiful towards her. He wrote to her regularly and frequently for the next fifteen years, keeping her posted with national and family events. His undistinguished political career was rewarded by William Pitt with a peerage in 1797 when he became Lord Glastonbury.

This long correspondence, covering fifty-three years from father and son to sister of one and aunt to the other, may perhaps stand as a sort of memorial to two kind men.

iv. A LETTER FROM AND CORRESPONDENCE ABOUT HENRY GRENVILLE 1754-1766

Hester Chatham's fourth brother Henry Grenville, born in 1717 and the last to die, outliving James in 1784 by only six months. Essentially he was closer to William Pitt than to Hester: the ten years he spent as governor of Barbados from 1746, and the three from 1761 as ambassador at Constantinople, meant that he had little contact with his sister during these, the most significant years of her life. His wife Margaret Banks, known always as Peggy, whom he married in 1757, was a noted beauty and socialite, younger than Hester and, if near silence in the correspondence is the criterion certainly not a friend. The two women would have had little in common.

Henry Grenville was a member of parliament for fifteen years from 1759, for three constituencies, the last predictably that of Buckingham, but his talents, if any, lay not in politics, but rather in his long spell as a colonial governor which left him for a time amongst his family with the sobriquet of The Governor. The papers contain but a single letter from him to his sister; even this has the second part to Pitt. It is a letter of great rejoicing on hearing news of their engagement; the warmth probably due as much to his affection and admiration for Pitt as to his love of Hester.

London
Tuesday morn.
[1754 ?October]

Be this letter, my dear Hetty, devoted to congratulation and joy on the most welcome news you could possibly send me. I can use no Expressions that will do justice to the Sentiments I feel on this occasion and therefore must refer you to your own heart as the nearest pattern of mine, to suggest to you. I am so charm'd with the manner in which the important Declaration was receiv'd that I shall love Stowe the better for it as long as I live; indeed the Rank, the Character, the great personal Merits, and virtues of the Party concern'd made it impossible that his proposition cou'd be receiv'd in any other Light or that every Grenville in the World shoud not breathe the same sentiments, and All feel Equally proud, Equally flatter'd and pleas'd with an Alliance which reflects so much Honour on us All, and which serves to strengthen our Tyes and Connections with a Man, of all others, the most lov'd, the most esteem'd and respected by us.

My brother Jemmy is return'd from Butleigh and came in upon me just after receiving your very unexpected letter. In the fullness of my Heart I cou'd not forbear making him a Partaker in my joy, and accordingly acquainted him with the Event. I thought myself at liberty to do this, as all ceremonys are now over at Stowe, and I told him I was sure He wou'd have receiv'd a letter of notification by this same post if his arrival in Town had been known or even guess'd at. He receiv'd it with the highest Demonstrations of satisfaction, and express'd himself in the kindest Terms imaginable. We drank together a bottle extraordinary on the Occasion. . .

Adieu, I now drop my Pen to you and resume it to make my Complimts to my dear Mr Pitt.

I find it as difficult to thank you, My Dear Sir, in Terms equal to the sentiments I feel for the favourable Impression you have taken of me; as it is impossible for me to express the sense I have of the great Honour you do our family in your Preference and Approbation of my Sister. You must not wonder if you see me hereafter one of the proudest men living, since I know nothing that can so much contribute the making me so, as the Honour of a closer Alliance and more immediate Connection with you. The Happiness I feel on this Occasion is more than you can imagine or I express; it is not only that of a Brother whose Heart is most eagerly sensible of every Increase of happiness or Honour that can attend his Sister, but it is likewise that of a man who, in his own particular feels the advantage which his situation will give him, of a title to your future friendship, and of strengthening his acquaintance, and Cultivating an Intimacy with one of the best, first and most distinguish'd of men.

There are no further letters from Henry Grenville but there are occasional glimpses of him in those from Hester to Pitt. Immediately after the engagement, Pitt took himself off to Bath closely followed by Henry. In her letter to Pitt, Hester writes:

Wotton
Octr 13th [1754]

The Governor accompanied him [brother James] but left a commission with me for you, which he would not have troubled you with, but that he flatters himself you will be tempted to forgive him in favour of the hand it passes thro', may one trust to yr goodness? Lodgings is the subject of his business, and he would beg the favour of you to give orders to one of your servants to take for him the following number of rooms where he can find them in the quarters nearest to you, which is the quality most essential to them. A Bedchamber, with a Closet or second room for the reception of the Wardrobe and baggage. A Parlour for seeing his Company and two Garrets for his servants, which concludes my charge from Him, except presenting his best Compliments and saying that he proposes being at Bath Saturday next at farthest and making you his Excuses himself.

Four days later she writes from Stowe:

Yesterday I came over here according to my Intention and had a meeting with the Governor in the midst of the noble town of Buckm, which past in the most agreeable manner in the World. I think by his calculation my Letter and Him are likely to arrive much about the same time.

And the following year, the underlined word says much:

[Pay Office]
Dec. 31st Wednesday
[1755]

I am better my Dearest Love and intend performing my dining engagement at Col. Elliots. I have already made a visit to Lady Temple, and since my return have had here both Mr Henry and Miss Banks, One _after_ the Other.

No glimpses for ten years and then from Hester to Pitt:

Pall Mall
Tuesday May 5th 1766
7 o'clock

The Instant I got out of the Coach, Mr Johnson inform'd me my Brother Henry and his family arriv'd yesterday. I writ immediately He came to me, and I afterwards made a visit to Her, and carried the young Folks. My Brother, I think, looks better than when he left England, Mrs Henry much the same, and little Louisa not the better for her Foreign Travel. Many Lamentations that you had left this part of the World before their arrival. He wou'd have writ to you, but as they are full of a Thousand Things, I undertook to tell you what they wou'd have said. They come Thursday to Hayes.

Thus brother Henry passes out of the correspondence but not so his daughter and only child, Louisa. Within a year of the death of Hester Mahon, the widower Charles, in five years to become the third earl Stanhope, married Louisa Grenville. What we learn from the friends of Lady Chatham, though doubtless biased, does not speak well of her, and other sources confirm their opinions: 'Louisa Stanhope, who seems to have all the frigid pride of the Grenvilles without any of the charm of her mother, the gay and merry Peggy Banks of long ago'.[9] She was cold towards, and overstrict with, the three motherless girls, her step-daughters and, perhaps more significantly, her eldest son Philip Henry, at nineteen left home and put himself under the protection for a time of his formidable half-sister, Hester Stanhope. Wheels indeed turned full circle.

v. LETTERS FROM THOMAS GRENVILLE 1742-1747

The death of Thomas Grenville, a naval officer less than a year older than his sister, was the first of Hester Chatham's many sorrows. He loved her dearly; his letters speak from the heart. He died of wounds at sea, serving under Anson in the action off Cape Finisterre on 3rd May 1747. He was twenty-eight years old. Thomas wrote regularly to Hester from 1742, mostly from sea. He has just received news of his promotion to captain:

Romney off Toulon
Ju: 13th 1742

My dear Hetty

You may imagine it was with extreme pleasure I receiv'd your letter of the 12th Feb. when I had not had one from any soul in England for six months before and I was very glad to find it was not owing to your Idleness but to my ill Luck that I had not heard oftener from you. You must have heard of my good Fortune, so I will not tire you with a Repetition of it, and I think it will be needless to say any thing of my gratitude to the author of it, because if you have any opinion of me at all, you must conclude I am penetrated with the deepest sense of what I owe to him. . .   We have a great many ships here at present, but I do not believe more will be done now than in Mr Haddocks time, with a much smaller number, and that for a very plain reason, for I do not see any thing more can be done. The Spaniards and French are at Toulon and likely to be there, for I cannot think they will stir this summer.

After comment on family events he ends

Adieu, and believe me dear Girl most affectionately your
TG

Thomas was not immune from the incessant striving after naval prizes, so much a feature of his time. He writes from Villefranche:

Villa Franca
Aug. 29th 1742

You are either a little idle Bitch or I am a sad unlucky Dog, for I have not seen a line from you this four months; I desire you will tell me in your next what it is that takes your time up so, if it is your Lovers, I excuse you but upon no other Account. . .
You may have heard I have been a little lucky in meeting with prizes lately, but I have had a little ill-luck to balance it for I very narrowly mist a Spanish courier with 8000 pistoles, off Genoa about a fortnight since, having sent my Boats after him, which took the Felucca he was in, but he had unluckily just time to put ashore and get to Genoa with the money, notwithstanding my people landed and were within five minutes at furthest of taking him. This was a disappointment to me, for of the 8000, 2000 would have been my own proper share.

He is in port, rather bored with inaction.

Spithead
Jn: 28th 1744

Dear Hester
It is too true that we are still here, and what is worse, God knows when we shall be any where else. The other day we were in the greatest hurry imaginable to sail, now wise folk say we shall not budge; for you must know that the long expected much desired Dutch Squadron, instead of coming to Spithead as the Sincere Creatures promised, had fairly given us the Slip and is come round Scotland, in order to meet their own homeward bound India Men. In the meantime Secret Whisperings are buzzed abroad that another invasion is coming over as soon as ever the French have Ostend. . .   My Duty and compliments to all with you and tell them how much I wish to be with them; for it is certainly much pleasanter doing nothing at Stow[e] than doing nothing at Spithead.

But he is soon on the move again and in this letter he mentions the gift he intends making Hester from the proceeds of his prize money:

Falkland
Spithead
Sept: 23 [1744]

An Express arrived two hours ago with orders to our Admiral to sail immediately, an Account being arrived of French men of war in the Channel to the No. of 16 some say twenty. We go out twelve sail, and I believe cleaner ships than the French, so we apprehend nothing from them. . . I wrote my Mother word that I intended to appropriate the two or three hundred pounds I got upon my last Cruize, towards making you spend your winter agreeably in Town; and I wish'd you might feel the good effects of it by the summer; I mean that you should not lye along another cold winter. So make the best of use of it you can.

There is the frustration of a further delay:

Falkland
Spithead
Nov. 11th 1744

I have been here since my last to you in daily, nay almost hourly expectation of sailing, which has been the reason of my not writing to let you know it. . . I have been disappointed so often that I scarce believe we shall ever sail. Now, every hour produces alterations in our orders. . . Never was an Admiralty so irresolute as this at present, which we at a Distance suppose to arise from the miserable distracted situation in all our affairs both by Sea and Land.

Five months later and some prizes under the belt, though still not to the amount he had hoped:

Falkland
off Kinsale
Ap: 13th 1745

Fortune that Bitch (a very civil beginning of a letter to a young lady speaking to one of her own Sex) has used me like a Dog, for I am return'd from my hopeful Cruize without the poor Comfort of a single prize; but still I am not so poor as when I went out, no thanks to her tho', for Hamilton, who I share with, has sent a very rich prize hither which I reckon will put between two and three thousand pound in my pocket, and if I had had tolerable luck I certainly must have doubled that sum.

He ends, after news of another possible sailing followed by shore leave and in hopes of a letter from Hester:

I desire too your letter may give an account of Life and conversation of that strange good, odd pretty whimsical sweet creature Hetty Lyttelton, and of the wild witty and wanton Harriet [Speed], for as I look upon them both as my mistresses since the Love Letters they wrote me, I cannot help being solicitous about what trade they drive in my absence.

Letters to Hester continue from naval stations through 1745 and the ensuing year, broken by their meetings in London and at Stowe:

Spithead
Septr 10th 1745

In all my hurry I can not help writing to you to let you know of my arrival at Spithead, having lost Sr Jno Balchen in bad weather. How long I shall stay here is yet uncertain til I hear from the Admiralty: but if they take my ship into Dock to clean, it is not impossible that I may just steal to Stow[e] for a day from London, where I shall ask leave to go to settle my affairs, tho' this project admits of great Difficulties, I can tell you. No news of Sr Jno Balchen, it being upwards of three weeks since I lost him, but they say here that he is gone in search of the French Fleet, which is believed to be cruizing off Lisbon or Cadiz. If that is the case, I am sorry I parted company with him. . . I have no good news to tell you of my success, for I have taken nothing but still I shall be three or four hundred pounds in pocket by this Expedition, being in company with the fleet when four French men were taken, of which I have my share; next Cruize I shall take something myself.

Downes
Jany 11th 1745-6

A mock French Invasion causes so much terror and alarm ashore, and so much hurry and fatigue at sea, that I do not much wonder at the little interruption of our Correspondence lately, for I account for your silence by the former and you will be good enough to excuse mine for the latter reason. At last I am a little free and I am now getting under sail in order to change the troublesome busy scene in the Downes for the calm and retreat of Spithead. I was once, and that very lately, full of sanguine hopes of seeing you before the End of this Month, but a small Cruize which I am to sail upon from Spithead intervenes, and will probably put off that much wish'd for pleasure a month longer. . . I wish Mrs Grenville and you and (I dare not say M. Banks, tho' I wish it confoundedly too) had spirit enough to form a frolicksome scheme of coming to see the sights of Spithead within this week; if this finds you at your merriment in London and not at your Lazy Wotton employments, it is not impossible nor impracticable, but I fear the French and the Rebels and the Pretender have so sunk your spirits that they will not rise to any Noble uncommon frolic.

Hester has written to him about a disagreeable event or problem which is troubling her:

Augusta
Plymouth
Apr: 5th 1746

I am just returned, my Dearest Hetty, from a cruize, which as usual of late I have nothing to brag of in, and which your mysterious letter, that I got upon it, has served to make very unpleasant. The thousand reflections that has given birth to me in my mind, and the impossibility of resting upon any, have caused me much disquietude, the result of all which can at present be only this assurance, which you may depend upon being sincere that, whatever subject of discontent you may have, and with whomsoever, I will take such a part with you as shall become the professions I have always made you of the most inviolable, invariable

Friendship and affection, and which you may remain assured, I never will depart from the least little. I am at present full of hopes of coming to London very soon, and your letter makes me desire it with much more eagerness, especially as you seem so cautious of trusting any of the breathings of your heart upon paper.

Thomas's generosity towards his sister, born of his love for her, ever increases. Hester has been suffering from inflamed eyes while at Tunbridge Wells:

> *Defyance*
> Lisbon
> Octr 27th 1746

These three lines will inform you of my arrival here, occasion'd by a small accident very common to people that go to sea, of carrying away a mast. I shall remain here about three weeks and in about six you may expect to hear of me in England...

I hope you have not been deterred from staying [at the spa] as long as you ought from the expense attending those places. You are well enough acquainted with my Ideas about that, and I shall really be vexed and angry at my heart, if you have not made all the use of the love and affection I have for you, that was proper and necessary for you, for fear what I left with you should not be sufficient... I desire my Brother Grenville will by virtue of this letter supply you with as much as you want of the money of mine in his hands. And I beg most earnestly of you that you will make no womanish scruples about taking it, for you must consider I am now at Lisbon, where I must get four or five hundred Moydores before I come home; and I know no way of laying it out with so much pleasure to my self as by procuring health and happiness to you.

> *Defiance*
> St Helen's Road
> Janry 20th 1746-7

I have but time to write these three lines to let you know I have just anchor'd here after a long and tedious passage from Lisbon of five weeks. The Ship must dock here and it is not impossible but I may contrive some way of seeing [you] before I go to sea again. I hope you got some of the letters I wrote from Lisbon, and made use of them that I meant you should, and shall be very angry if you have not...

Adieu my dear Hetty. The many things I have to say to you I hope to tell you a pleasanter way than this. In the meantime be assured I am, what I ever will be
> Your most truly affectionate Brother
> Thos Grenville

Almost as an anticlimax, there occurs in Thomas's last three months of life, his election, arranged through his brothers, as a parliamentary member for Bridport. A letter of 22 January to his brother George after receiving the news, ends:

Thanks to you, thanks to Dick [Richard Grenville later Lord Temple], thanks to Jemmy [James Grenville] and adieu till Saturday afternoon.

His last letter to Hester reveals his feelings on his new status:

[*Defiance*]
6th April 1747

My dear Hester

      Here I am, safe arrived from Bridport, after much besmearing of lips, noise and drunkenness. You cannot think how glad I am that it is over, not only because the thing in itself could not be agreeable, but because I think I have done infinite service to my interest there by this journey, insomuch that I believe I may defy the Devil or Dr Ay...h to shake me there. . .   We sail on Tuesday, of course I am in some hurry. Compls to all my fair ones in town, whose absence costs me here some pangs. Tell Harriet, one of the Kisses I gave her at parting was for Jenny [Hamilton] and I beg she will be honest.

                Adieu, ever yours
                    TG

i. 1   James, 2nd Earl Waldegrave, *Memoirs* (1821) p 95
     2   Thomas Babbington Macaulay, *Essays* (1843) p 762
     3   Peter Brown, *The Chathamites* (1967) p 25
     4   Stanley Ayling, *The Elder Pitt* (1976) p 244
     5   *The Complete Peerage*, Ed. G E Cokayne, London 1887
ii. 6   G F R Barker
     7   Ibid
iii. 8   *History of Parliament. The House of Commons 1754-1790*, Namier and Brooke, HMSO 1964
iv. 9   Tresham Lever, *The House of Pitt*, John Murray 1947

Chapter 4

LIFELONG FRIENDS

Among the various traits of this human and sociable century
was an unwearied addiction to the arts of friendship

Peter Quennell, *Four Portraits*, Cresset Library 1987 (1st pub. 1945)

i. LETTERS OF HESTER LYTTELTON, MRS JOHN FITZMAURICE 1763-1790

The Lytteltons of Hagley Hall in Worcestershire were first cousins of the Grenvilles of Wotton. Both families were descended from Sir Richard Temple of Stowe through his daughters, Christian who married Sir Thomas Lyttelton and Hester, wife of Richard Grenville of Wotton. In each family a daughter of the next generation married a Pitt: Christian the eldest daughter of Sir Thomas was the wife of Thomas Pitt, Chatham's 'unsatisfactory' elder brother, and Hester Grenville married William Pitt, first Earl of Chatham. Hester Lyttelton and Hester Grenville were therefore doubly related. Both were younger sisters of five brothers, they were close in age, and for Hester Grenville, an only daughter, the relationship with her first cousin was probably the nearest she enjoyed to that of a sister.

The correspondence is patchy; the letters only become frequent after 1780 when they were both widows. Even so, the greatest number of letters in any one year - in 1780 - was only eight; the remaining sixty or so, of which fifteen are undated, cover the years 1763 to 1790, with a long gap between 1767 and 1779.

Hester Lyttelton's husband, John Fitzmaurice, holder of minor political office in Dublin, was a nephew of the first earl of Kerry and a considerable landowner of an estate called Springfield in county Limerick. He had been married before and his grand-daughter Anne, whose marriage to Sir Robert Tilson-Deane, first baron Muskerry, gave rise to a long lawsuit prosecuted by Mrs Fitzmaurice after her husband's death, which not often fails to be mentioned in her letters and is also followed with interest by members of the Pitt and Grenville families and of course her own, the Lytteltons.

Hester Fitzmaurice had the gift of the pen; her letters are witty and descriptive of her social life and surroundings. The first ten letters, from 1763 from Ireland are the most intrinsically interesting of the collection. On 9th May she writes from Blackrock where they had rented a house on arrival; the sea journey was rough and they had had to lay-to for several hours, an ordeal borne with fortitude by Mrs Fitzmaurice. Later that year they moved to Merrion Street in Dublin and in her letter of 3rd December she describes the furnishings of the house; they took part in the social events of the Castle and the clothes worn by the participants at a ball are described in detail and with humour. In

April the following year they leave for Springfield with a stop at the Curragh for the races en route. In the west they live in quite a whirl of amusements, visits, race meetings, centered on Mallow 'the Tunbridge of Ireland'. For the next three years they move between Dublin and Springfield but have begun to think again of a return to England.

After the long gap in the correspondence noted above, Hester Fitzmaurice, now a widow, writes to her cousin on 27th January 1779; in this letter there is the first mention of the complicated lawsuit, mainly centered on ownership of the Springfield rents. For the next four years she lives with her Lyttelton relations at their country homes, Hagley in Worcestershire and Arley just over the border in Staffordshire. She loves the English countryside and her 'woodbine bower'. Rural sports at Arley are encouraged by her hosts, Lord and Lady Valentia. Hagley reminds her of the happy days when she and Hester played as children together.

In 1783 she decides to set up on her own; for the next two years her letters are from Warwick, the quiet provincial town of her choice where she already has friends. The letters from there have a special flavour and charm: the low-key but quite active social life. She enjoyed visits to Burton Pynsent, and to Hagley in October of 1784 for the coming of age of her nephew George Lyttelton, son of her favourite brother William Henry, Lord Westcote, but confessed she was thinking of her 'snug, neat apartments in Sheep Street' to which she was shortly to return. But Hester Fitzmaurice was getting old and by September of the following year she is back at Hagley for good under the permanent care of the Westcotes, moving with them to London (which she dislikes) for the annual visits. In her last letter, a short note from the capital, she writes of illness, from which she probably did not recover, but which we can be sure was borne by Hester Fitzmaurice with courage and good humour.

Blackrock
May 9th [1763]

I hope my Dear Lady Chatham receiv'd an account of my being well after my journey to Park Gate and I am sure it will give her no single satisfaction to hear of my arrival at Blackrock, after an expedious and as favourable a Voyage as possible. We made it in about 16 hours, but for want of the Tides serving, we were obliged to lay to all night, which made me suffer a little, but I believe no more than what was beneficial to a Bilious Constitution. A second 12 hours of the same severe discipline wou'd have been a little too ruff for me I believe. Thank God I am now perfectly well and much pleased with the place I am to call my home till we can purchase one to our mind, and as far as I can judge of the inhabitants I cou'd not any where meet with more agreeable Domestick Companions. Mr Henry and his Lady are cheerfull and sensible and we have a young girl who is an enlivener of the Society. Lady Arabella Penny lives next door and I find we have many genteel neighbours besides, and are only 3 mile from Dublin. On one side of the room I am now sitting in I have an extensive view of the Sea, bounded by Mountains, and beneath them the Town and various ships coming in and out perpetually, there is now 25 in full sail. The opposite Windows afford me fields and beautiful shaped Hills, Woods and fine white Houses, one of which is Lord Fitzwilliams, and he gives me great encouragement to enjoy his Woods and Parks as much as I please. I enter into all these particulars as I am confident my Dear

Lady Chatham is sincerely interested in my happiness, and I beg her to believe few things constitute more to it than that confidence as she ever will have in me a more faithful cordial friend and Devoted humble servant.

H Fitzmaurice

Mr FItzmaurice charges me never to forget his best regards to your Ladyship and Mr Pitt, mine always attend him. My love to Miss Mary and all your little family. Madame Passerene is my next door neighbour, she made last night great enquiries after good Miss Pitt. She, her husband and his nephews make us a Concert when ever we please.

Merrion Street
[Dublin]
Dec<u>br</u> the 3rd [1763]

I know it will give my Dear Lady Chatham pleasure to hear I have quitted my rural scenes, and Country Squires, for the pleasures of the Town and polite society of the Castle etc. My long journey has added to my health and spirits and enabled me to go thro' the fatigue of furnishing our House in Merrion Street, allmost as Elegantly as Sr Richard's except (what is not worth mentioning) a few Original pictures, marble statues, or such kind of baubles, that I conclude he has pickt up in his travels, if he has fine representations I have realitys. The Sea on one side, and Lord Kildare's magnificent beautifull marble House, with a fine Lawn before it on the other side, which are objects very uncommon in a Town. I was at the Castle on the Princesses Birthday and found the Ballroom a noble one and well fill'd. Lord and Lady Northumberland appear'd, one in Irish Velvit and the other in stuff, with silver nett of flounces. There was not many follow'd their example, but I did not fail to show my patriotism, as well as her Ladyship, by going in a Scarlet poplin, for which I had many blessings from the Mob. I shan't think my self so well drest on the Queen's Birthday, tho' by Lady Shelburne's generosity I shall then shine in Pompadour and silver, indeed rich cloaths are greatly worn here, which I am sorry for.

Merrion Street
April the 7th 1764

Dear Lady Chatham
I won't tell your Ladyship a word how I have past my previous hours since I wrote to Miss Mary, but to preserve it, I will assure you in a fortnight I quit without regret Dublin for Springfield, but for fear the change of scene shou'd be too sudden Mr Fitzmaurice proposes to give me the deversion of the Curra horse race in our way thither, which is a great meeting, and lasts a week. Lord and Lady Northumberland honour it with their presence. I believe it is the finest Course in Europe . . .
PS. Entre nous if I was not forty I shou'd think I was breeding. I find a change tho' I am not sick.

Arrived at their estate in the west, Mrs Fitzmaurice writes with pleasure and lively interest of the social life in which they are participating and the prospect of a camping excursion, accompanied by 'allmost all my servants.'

Springfield [Castle]
[Co. Limerick]
July the 9th 1764

I am just return'd from an agreeable [visit] I made to the Races of (?) Rathclare and the amusements of Mallow Wells, the Tunbridge of Ireland [but] a spot much more beautifull as it affords a charming river and Noble Ruin and fine shady walks, which are embellish'd by the Speaker and Doctor Delany. I was pleased to find so pretty a place of the kind, within 12 miles of me, in my way home I saw a fine Garden and Park of Lord Donera[i]le's. Next week we propose quiting our Chateau of Springfield for a Cabin on the Seashore, from thence we shall ramble to every romantick Lake and view (worth the observation of us lovers of Nature) thro'out the famed County of Kerry. I take a very sensible amicable young Lady with me, a second cousin of Mr Fitzmaurice and all most all my servants, so that I think I have all possible amends made me for not seeing England this year. I live in hopes the next will compleat my happiness in a joyous meeting with all that are near and Dear to me there and consequently present to my thoughts where ever I am.

February of 1765 finds the Fitzmaurices back in Dublin, for six weeks. She had expected to pass the winter in the country but

Mr Fitzmaurice changed his mind . . . it is a long journey for so short a time but travelling I believe is good for us both, so I am contented.

More travelling and May finds them back at Springfield:

Springfield
May the 21st 1765

I hope this will find my Dear Lady Chatham and Mr Pitt at Burton, as much delighted with their blooming Orchards and rural scenes as I am with mine, to which I am just return'd from Dublin where I spent 4 months instead of 6 weeks, as we first intended. We vary our schemes so much, that I think our English expedition uncertain but at present we have thoughts of passing the winter at Bath and perhaps the next summer in France as Mrs Henry [stepdaughter] presses her Father much to pay her a Visit at Cambrey and he seems to think a tour thro' that Kingdom will be conducive both to our health and pleasure.

The following year, 1766, in January, Hester Fitzmaurice writes from Springfield that she has heard news of the Chathams from her sister Mrs Ayscough so

you see my Dear I gain a little intelligence of you but none will content me that does not come from a hand that has afforded me one of my greatest gratifications successively for these (shall I say how long) 30 years past, save a correspondence of that duration can never end but with our lives. If it does, I shall have nothing to upbraid myself with.

Still considering future plans (the Fitzmaurices were as restless as most of their contemporaries) Hester writes in March from Springfield that

Mr Fitzmaurice and my self both liking Bath and it being a place not too expensive for us Irish Gentry, I believe it will not be many months before we pay a Visit . . .

and so evidently they did that year or the following before again returning to Ireland:

Dublin
Octbr the 22nd 1767

It was a great mortification for me to leave England without bidding my Dear Lady Chatham farewell, tho' it is long since we mett or even corresponded, I have so much confidence in her friendship to make no doubt but her Ladyship will be glad to hear of my having cross'd the seas with as much ease and safety as I had reason to hope at this time of year. While I was at Hagley I heard Lord Chatham was perfectly recover'd, a continuation of that good news under your Ladyship's own hand wou'd greatly rejoice both Mr Fitzmaurice and me as no friend you have more sincerely wishes your happiness or has felt more for you, tho' I forbore to trouble you with an assurance of it. Our house being lett, we are at present at Lady Shelburne's in Stephens Green; when we shall leave it for Springfield I am ignorant and allmost indifferent. If writing shou'd be disagreeable to your Ladyship I hope you will employ some pen or other to let me know how you and yours do, our united good wishes and compliments attend them all. Adieu Dear Lady Chatham, Your ever faithfull etc.

H Fitzmaurice

It was indeed Adieu so far as the correspondence went. Nearly ten years later Hester Fitzmaurice, now a widow, and Hester Chatham just over two years away from that state, were once again in touch. In an undated letter, annotated in Lady Chatham's hand 'Decr 8th 1776 Gerrard Street' Mrs Fitzmaurice writes:

As neither a tedious absence, or a lamented loss of Dear Lady Chatham's correspondence, had power to lessen my well founded esteem and affection for her the mark I have this minute receiv'd that I still have a share in her friendship, gives me the highest pleasure. I thank your Ladyship for her kind enquiries after my health, thank God few are bless'd with better. I am griev'd to hear such constant bad accounts of that of my worthy friend Lord Chatham and feel much for your sufferings in consequence of it, heaven support you under them.

Three years later she has received an invitation from Hester Chatham to stay at Burton Pynsent. Such invitations were rare and this one only a year after Chatham's death indicates the degree of affection Hester had for her cousin. In this letter there is the first mention of Mrs Fitzmaurice's lawsuit against Lord Muskerry and his wife Anne, her late husband's granddaughter, over the Springfield rents. The case dragged on in the Irish courts for years, undoubtedly undermining her health; in few letters does she fail to refer to it.

Berkeley Square
Janry the 27th 1779

I am infinitely obliged to Dear Lady Chatham for the Interest she takes in what concerns me, the proof her Ladyship gives, that our long separation has not lessen'd the share I possessed in her esteem and affection so may happy years of my earliest days, is the best consolation I can receive in my present unfortunate situation. At this juncture, I not only lament the loss of my good friend Lady Litchfield [Lichfield] but the impossibility of my making my self the best amends for that loss, by the enjoyment of my Dear Lady Chatham's company in the quiet retreat you have the goodness to offer me. While my lawsuit is undecided I must not absent myself far from the Lawyers and Attorneys engaged in it. I have taken a Lodging in Berkeley Square till the 4th of next June by which time I hope I shall be more at liberty to wait upon your Ladyship in what ever part of the World you may be settled in, probably by that time you will prefer Hay[e]s to Burton Pynsent.

My deceased friend has left me 1000 pd. Lord and Lady Westcote desire their compliments.

The visit, to Burton Pynsent, takes place three months later. She will travel down with Lady Chatham but other arrangements are needed for luggage:

Berkeley Square
May the 14th [1779]

Dear Lady Chatham
I hope nothing will prevent my having the happiness of being with you at Hay[e]s on Tuesday by dinner. I have enquired and find the Taunton Waggon sets out on Monday 10 oclock, by which I will send my Trunk directed to Burton Pynsent and must [hope] it will arrive safe, or your poor Friend will be doubly ruin'd. With a grateful heart for all favours I conclude my self My Dear Lady Chatham's Most affectionately devoted
H Fitzmaurice

For nearly three years, 1780-83, Hester Fitzmaurice divided her time between the Lyttelton properties of Hagley, near Stourbridge in Worcestershire and Arley, or Areley in Staffordshire, home of her niece, Lady Valentia, daughter of the eldest brother George, first baron Lyttelton of Frankley. She wrote often to Hester Chatham at this time, partly spurred no doubt by childhood memories, and also to pour out to a sympathetic listener her troubles with her protracted lawsuit.

Arley Hall
May the 15th 1780

Dear Lady Chatham
I am sure it will be a satisfaction to you to hear I am well and happy with my kind friends at this quiet rural retreat after having finished my business that called me from one which must ever have strong attractions, no need to say Burton Pynsent . . . I left the books with Mrs Willbear [Wulbier] and the Telliscope with Mr Ramsay. Lady Harriot will speak to Lord Mahon to fix on a proper charge, I told him you wou'd not lay out more than three guineas.
Ever your Ladyship's most affectionate obliged
H Fitzmaurice

The following month, still on the 'Telliscope' and with news of her 'cause'

I am much obliged to you for wishing your new Telliscope cou'd give you a sight of your friend enjoying these rural scenes in a Woodbine bower, indeed I often sett in one with honeysuckle, roses and sweet brier under a Tassel'd Canopy form'd by a beautifull Labernian [laburnum] and converse with my dear Lady Chatham there in imagination, and I regret it can't be in reality. Arley, Hagley and Burton Pynsent are all equally delightfull in their different stiles . . . You ask what is the opinion of my friends and Lawyers, concerning my cause, they think it may last by artfull Management of Sr Robert's agents some years longer, but in the meantime they hope a Receiver will be appointed . . . A blackbird is whistling under my window Nancy Dawson most merryly but I think the wild ones in the woods make better musick.

And rural life at Arley

Arley
July the 5th 1780

We have lately had fine Haymaking weather Here which I hope has been the case in your part of the World. Viewing the Haymakers is a pleasing amusement every where and Here all Rural sports are much encouraged by Lord and Lady Valentia. Yesterday it being the time of a Wake (not an Irish Wake) they gave a shift to be run for by Girls and a hatt to be won by throwing a weight the hardest and ribbon cockades and breast knots to be given for the best Village dancers, after which sports abroad a short dance in the House and cheerfull supper made the second[ary] Gentry happy. Mary had a smart young Gentleman Farmer for her partner . . .

Soon she

propose[s] enjoying the old oakes in Hagley park and my old favourite companion my Brother [William Henry Lyttelton, Lord Westcote]. Arley has afforded me much satisfaction in every particular these last three months.

Hagley
Sepbr the 21st 1780

Dear Lady Chatham
Lord and Lady Westcote being gone to pay a Visit to Lord Plimouths [Plymouth] I propose making myself amends for the loss of their company by a black and white conversation with you which I assure your Ladyship I prefer to a Tete á Tete <u>walk</u> with the Gallant Sr Richard Reynells. I suppose you will smile at my mentioning a walk but I am improved in strength since I was oblig'd to call for Mr Croft's assistance to get me back from Blackbird Haunt [on her visit to Burton Pynsent]. . . Miss Lyttelton is of the party to Lord Plimouths or I am sure she wou'd send many compliments to Lady Harriot, she often wishes for her in her Rides and walks which afford scenes much improved since the happy days when Hetty Grenville and Hetty Lyttelton bounded over the Lawns together with the same tender friendship I then felt and a great encrease of esteem.
I am ever My Dear Lady Chatham's most devoted
H Fitzmaurice

Two weeks later, still from Hagley, Mrs Fitzmaurice has an interesting comment on the faith, then so widely held, of the efficacy of blooding in reducing tension:

> I think it was fortunate you was blooded, the day before you knew yr son [Chatham] was well under your own Roof, as extreme of joy has sometimes proved as fatal as excess of grief. Few people, I believe, have experienced the sensations of both in a higher degree than my Dear Lady Chatham.

In a letter of 20th December Hester Fitzmaurice makes the only reference in the correspondence to her childlessness. After describing at length the anxieties about the health of the Lyttelton children, she says 'I am pleased to have escaped a Mother's anxiety tho' I have lost her joy.'

Mrs Fitzmaurice spent the next two years staying either at Arley or Hagley. The two estates, though in different counties, were less than ten miles apart. As always her keen sense of the beauties of nature was much in evidence in the letters. In a partly dated letter of 1781 from Arley she writes:

> I enjoy good health and many tranquil pleasures at Lord Valentia's most Hospitable rural retreat, which is now in high beauty, my senses of seeing, hearing and smelling are constantly regaled with a profusion of flowers, an abundance of barges sailing up and down the Severn, beautifull woods, which afford the most delightful melody of birds, even nightingales to [?] both day and night.

In another letter of 16th January she writes of Christmas at Arley:

> I arrived at Arley last Wednesday and found my friends well and keeping Xmas in the old stile, a Welch harper playing to a cheerful circle round the fireside, and the pretty honeysuckle dancing.

But change for Hester Fitzmaurice was on the way. In 1783 her niece Lady Valentia died from, so she told Lady Chatham on 23rd May 'a universal decay of nature' for which the Bristol hot wells could do nothing; she was forty-one. Arley would cease to be a second home for her. Hagley remained and there she passed the summer of 1783, but the Westcotes were often away and on 23rd September she writes to Harriot Pitt and asks rhetorically

> and where do you think I shall take up my winter quarters, not at Worcester or Bath but in a decent Lodging in the heart of Warwick where I shall have the society of an old friend and her family, who are sensible and worthy females, and one daughter has a musical Clergyman her husband.

And so Mrs Fitzmaurice becomes, for a time, a contented provincial lady but not before, in a final letter from Hagley of 18th October, she writes to express her disapproval of Lord Valentia's action following the recent death of his wife:

> Lord Valentia is gone to Ireland, it's strongly reported he is soon to be married to Sr Harry Cavendish's daughter, a Girl of 18 who has a fortune in her own power of 13 thousand Guineas. I hope he will make a wiser choice, and the

Lady also. He owns he has Matrimony in his head, which is rather too soon to prove the goodness of his heart but he [swears] his wife on her deathbed requested him not to live long single.

Hester Fitzmaurice was incapable of writing a dull letter even from the new abode of lodgings in a quiet provincial town:

> Novbr the 17th [1783]
> [Warwick]
>
> Your most friendly letter my Dear Lady Chatham is the first that honor'd my Lodgings and none will ever be more welcome to me where ever I am. You tell me you wish to learn all things relative to my present situation, which I have the pleasure to assure your Ladyship is not uncomfortable. My apartments are a parlour, bedchamber, drawing room, and a closet nearby and neatly furnished, my room below stairs is larger than your Ladyship's bird room [Lady Chatham kept an aviary at Burton of exotic birds], so that I can have four card tables in it, when I am disposed to return the invitations I meet with. Last night I play'd at Quadrill[e] at a Mrs Goodwin's who is 94 and rivals Mr Dean in the preservation of her powers both mental and bodily, she told me she wou'd be happy to make one at a card party when ever I wou'd send to her. I mention this to confirm Mrs Stapleton in her opinion. An exceeding pretty well bred Lady has just paid me a Visit from the Priory (a very pleasant place near the Castle) her name is Wise. I believe her husband's family is known to you, he has a very good fortune and lives handsomely. I think I shall pass my time here as agreeably as any where except with those I have long loved. My friend Mrs Warner offers me the free use of a good library, which is no small benefit, as I am still fond of reading. I can not yet judge whether I have any chance of the amusement and improvement your Ladyship is so good to wish I may receive from an acquaintance of some learn'd natural philosopher; this Town is particularly calculated for study there being no business carry'd on.

and more thoughts on the Valentia remarriage:

> Just before I left Hagley Lord Valentia inform'd his Attorney [that] his match with Miss Cavendish was settled to the satisfaction of all parties, that she had a pretty good fortune independent of her Father and had expectations of money from him and that she now presented him with 2000 to pay debts. He hoped before a month to present her to Mr Roberts at Arley, his Cara Esposa. I agree with your Ladyship in being at a loss to account why the young Lady shou'd make him her choice or her father consent to their union. I suppose the Vicsse was the temptation to both, unless the father was afraid of her doing worse, as two of his daughters set her a bad example. His Lordp has been kind to me therefore I shall be glad if this match continues to make him happy . . . I am pleased to find your Ladyship goes on improving your farm and shall be delighted if I am an eye witness at it next summer.

In a postscript, she refers obliquely to the non-rural aspect of Warwick: 'I think a Daisie now a great curiosity.'

The following year, 1784, Mrs Fitzmaurice moves from lodgings to a rented house; after political and family comment she writes on 9th April:

I find the manner of living and the air in this place agrees so well with me, that I have taken a little House about the length of this street out of Town, which will afford me all the advantages of being in it with the quiet of the Country and a little [. . .] and flower garden of my own, with the pleasure of shade and birds from my near Neighbours who are Persons capable of preserving my body, and Soul.

In the autumn she is visiting both Burton Pynsent and Hagley. At the latter she writes of her nephew George, aged twenty-one, about to set out on his grand tour of Europe which will last 'three or four years'. She hopes he will distinguish himself and 'deserve the name of George Lyttelton.' Harriot Pitt has evidently been indisposed and Lady Chatham has thanked Mrs Fitzmaurice for her good advice:

> Warwick
> Novr the 26th 1784

Dear Lady Chatham

I had not the pleasure of yours till yesterday and I am too much oblig'd by all the kind things it abounds with . . . I am proud of my skill in disease and happy that my good guessing Evans was the person to care [for] Lady Harriot, has been of service to her. An old Woman often knows more than a Physician. I hope by this time her Ladyship and the Chancellor [William Pitt] are with you and for a week at least. The weather again mild which I am pleas'd with for your sake and my own, as I have been able to pay a Visit on foot three streets length today and I can assure your Ladyship I have sweet rosebuds, and sweet briar now in my garden and I have sett the Maiden barberrys and made my Neighbour West happy with the shutes from your Carnation Tree, and have promised her some eggs from my Chathamites so that I owe you the power of obliging my friends. You cant think what a long leged fellow the crowing Gentleman is grown, his Wifes are pretty but neither he or they are such compleat beauties as their producers. I congratulate your Ladyship and Mrs Stapleton on the escape of your dogs [?from quarantine] and am very glad they are out of confinement, as I am sure you must have mist them exceedingly. I will now drop the subject of birds and beasts, and touch upon that superior animal Man, from whom you wish me to receive a higher entertainment that the conversation of the Ladys can afford me. I expect some from an acquaintance I have just made with General Powell who is just arrived from America and appears a sensible well bred man and he is settled Here. To night the Balls begin, but as I cant dance with the General I dont design to grace it with my presence this evening. Yesterday I had here a smart party, and some folks who found entertainment for themselves, being young men and maidens fair. They all praised the Counsellor's Lady's taste in fitting up her withdrawing room, now mine. . . I have lost my best companion Mrs Warner for some time who is gone to Waterstock to comfort her old Mother who has buried her daughter lately but I have still the advantage of her Library and have read the Bishop of Chester's Sermons with so much approbation that I wish your Ladyship may not have read them and then I think you have a pleasure in store. I have now been even with you in filling my sheet[1] and you will not pay for it the ruinous sum of 10 pence which yours cost me.

Adieu dear Lady Chatham, yours ever

> H Fitzmaurice

The correspondence yields three further letters of 1785 from Warwick, but these lack the freshness and delight in the writer's surroundings of the earlier letters; her mind is now increasingly obsessed with the endless lawsuit and a sourness has crept into even the most trivial situations. On 17th May she writes:

> I wish you could see how much your kind favour ornaments the chimney piece in my parlour which is hung with a plain blew paper, and that I think calls for prints or pictures and I cou'd fully adorn it if I had those Lord Muskerry's Deed gives me.

At some time later in the year or in 1786 she has left Warwick for good and has come to rest in the bosom of her family living under their care for the rest of her life.

> Septr the 18th [1786]
> Hagley

> Dear Lady Chatham
> A thousand thanks for your most friendly letter, which my heart has often paid, tho' Ill health and low spirits has prevented your sooner receiving them under my hand. At present I am better but far from being at ease, as I have no hopes of any favourable turn in my affairs.

In this letter she refers to the death [on 12th September] of their cousin Molly Hood, wife of Admiral Alexander Hood, later Lord Bridport:

> I condole with you my dear Lady Chatham on the loss of our old friend and relation, it's some consolation to think she died without a sigh or a groan, and escaped the infirmities and other ill effects of living beyond 80 which I think she was.

The lady's husband was much younger than his wife and this fact is delicately reflected in Mrs Fitzmaurice's further comment on her death:

> The Admiral inform'd Lord Westcote of his loss the day after it and sais he is much afflicted, indeed I believe his friendship for her was very great and she deserved it.

A year later she has no regrets at leaving Warwick and is thankful to be in her old home:

> [Hagley]
> June 1787

> I sett out a great deal this warm weather and some times exert all my strength and mount the park Hill, thank God my health has been uncommonly uninterrupted ever since I breath'd my native air instead of that of the Town of Warwick . . .

In the winter she does not leave the house but

> when the sun shines I creep out but not far, as it is too cold [November 16th] to sett, and I keep in good health by only taking the exercise range this House

affords me and ... I have some pleasure in looking at the Park and its peaceful inhabitants thro' the Gallery Windows.

Hester Fitzmaurice is never now long apart (if at all) from the Westcotes, and moves with them when they go to London

Germyn Street
Janry 16 (1789)

I am sure it will give my good friends at Burton Pynsent pleasure to hear I am happily settled with my Brother's Family in Germyn Street, their resolution of spending many months in Town tempted me to break my promise to my self of never leaving the Country, which I much prefer. I had a very cold journey but I did not suffer from it, as I only travelled in the morning, and while the frost continues I shall not quit the fireside.

Predictably she does not enjoy living in London and her health suffers, as she tells Lady Chatham in an undated letter written later that year. Apologising for her 'long silence' she says

[1789]

I was not quite unable to sett pen to paper, but I had no heart to do it only to make complaints to your Ladship and cou'd tell you nothing in regard to my health or affairs that was pleasing. Ever since I have been Here I have suffer'd from a most violent defluction, cough (and lately) feverish disorder, the former is not so bad as it has been but I fear I shall not get rid of it till May. We have now a second winter which will keep me in the chimney corner ... I content myself with seeing a few of my old acquaintance who are so good to come to me and excuse me Visiting them. I have not been in any House but this, and have only gone to Church twice and thrice taken an airing to fetch my little favourite boy William from School at Parsons Green. Last night I went early into a few streets to see the Illuminations, and had a specimen of the beauty and grandeur of them. I had not courage to go at the time they were compleated, tho' Lady Westcote ventured herself son and daughter, they were kept in the streets by the thronge of coaches till 12 so I applauded my self for not being of her party. The King's perfect recovery is a joyful event indeed.

Still later in the same year she writes thankfully from Hagley:

[1789]

I am very well and happy at being once again settled for some months at delightful Hagley whose sweet air and high Verdure are peculiarly relish'd after having been three quarters of a year smelling the smoke of London and beholding nothing but its dirty brick houses, from the windows in Jermyn Street, which I very seldom quited indeed. My brother has now got a pretty house in a better wholesome situation being in Mortimore Street near to Cavendish Square, they are so good to offer me an apartment in it which I cant refuse tho' a Winter journey is rather a formidable undertaking for an old woman [she was 69 or 70].

In December Hester Fitzmaurice, after a trying journey, is happily settled in the Mortimer Street house. She

> travell'd in my Brother's Chaize and arrived the fourth day just as dinner was sett on the Table, which you will think was not overhurrying my old <u>flesh</u> and bones, indeed I found they were shook sufficiently.

In this, her last but one surviving letter, Mrs Fitzmaurice ends, perhaps appropriately, with a bitter complaint about her lawsuit:

> I have not heard from Ireland since I last wrote to your Ladyship, nor received a penny of money, sure never was [a] poor Widow worse used by Lawyers and their exployts, but enjoying the society of my dear Brother and His Family makes amends for all my misfortunes.

One last note dated on the outside in Lord Westcote's hand 'London April 21st 1790' brings to a close the correspondence between the cousins: in this she states she is 'very much an Invalid' and her complaints 'present from Bile and general relaxation.' She has been prescribed bark vitriol but she is a 'bad preserver in taking Medicines' and that the doctor 'sais it must be a work of time to restore [my] appetite and strength.'

But she had no time.

ii LETTERS OF JANE HAMILTON, LADY CATHCART 1747-1767

The correspondence begins in 1747 when Jane Hamilton was twenty-one and Hester Grenville five years older. They would probably have met earlier (they moved in the same social circles and had many common friends) but Jane evidently considered their friendship dated from that year: in a letter of twenty years later she refers to 'our antient friendship from the year '47.' Jane, sometimes known as Jean and called Jenny by her mother was the youngest child of Admiral Lord Archibald Hamilton, governor of Greenwich Hospital and his wife Jane, daughter of James, sixth Earl of Abercorn; her second brother, to whom she was close, was Sir William Hamilton, diplomat and archeologist, later husband of Emma.

Jane grew up under the shadow of an unhappy marriage. She disliked her grumpy father and adored her mother, at one time the reputed mistress of Frederick Prince of Wales, father of George III. The family home was the enclosed surroundings of the Hospital, with drives - 'airings' - and walks in Greenwich Park, the only outdoors activities, but with spells in London and at Chiswick, where her mother had a house, undoubtedly a royal favour, and where she often stayed, alone or accompanied only by Jane. After Lady Archibald's death in 1752, the prince's widow appears from a letter of Jane's (to whom the house had been bequeathed by her mother) to have laid a claim to the property which had been put up for renting.

In 1750 Jane is with her parents at the Bristol spa, Hot Well, and two years later there is the great adventure of the prolonged visit to France, with her parents, brother William, which however ends in tragedy, the death of her mother. However, the following year Jane met and married, as his second wife, Charles, ninth baron Cathcart and lived in happiness with him and their seven children, in Scotland and in the south, until her early death - she was only forty-five - in St Petersburg, where Cathcart was ambassador, in 1771.

Jane's life was an eventful one, both before and after marriage; this combined with a lively nature, power of observation and ability to convey all three through the written word, gives a special flavour to her letters.

In the first surviving letter Jane is somewhat breathlessly thanking Hester for a present, the nature of which we shall never know:

> Greenwich
> 26 Sept 1747
>
> I have been in the utmost impatience since last night to write to Dear Miss Grenville to return her my most sincere thanks for the <u>Great Favour</u> I have received from Her. I find I can no more express in words how much I am obliged to you than I can say how great a Value I place upon what you have sent me.
> I can truly say of Both that Imagination can't exceed the Reality. It makes part of a Subject that words could never express but Insufficiently. But you have already shown me that you do me Justice by that and the other kind and obliging things you writ in the Note that contain'd what it its self was more than I ever could equal but in Gratitude and Inclination, made my Obligation to you infinitely greater. I cannot be sorry to be thus endebted to you tho' I am ashamed of the trouble I have given you as it was unintentionly. . . That your Fancy has been employed in it, will give me pleasure as often as I see it. I would say that it entirely answer'd my Idea but that it exceeds it. You have made fine what I intended to be nothing more than pretty. It is now both and has an Air of Distinction very suitable to my <u>Veneration for the Contents</u>.
> I will not detain you any longer upon a Subject that I hope Actions will speak for me in and give me the Joy of proving in facts how much I am and with what sincere Esteem Dr Miss Grenville
> Yr most Obliged and Faithful servt
> Jane Hamilton

Two undated letters of 1748, both from London and written to Hester at Bath, give a lively, sometimes surprisingly critical description of Jane's life in town, but in these letters she is undoubtedly reflecting her mother's views on people and events; they went everywhere together. At this time she had hopes of a romance with Hester's second brother, George Grenville, hopes which were to be dashed the following year when he married Elizabeth Wyndham.

> [Easter 1748]
>
> My dear Miss Grenville
> I could not help sending to enquire at your House if any tidings of you was come from Bath, tho' I must own I was not surprized to be Answer'd in the Negative and could readily place it to the ac[coun]t of those premature things one does thro' impatience. . . I rejoyced that the weather was pretty tolerable while

you was upon the road, it has been and is now bitter bad, Snowing and Raining most unseasonably. But I begin to recollect that when one is out of town one fancys that there's a great deal of news in it and to show you there is not at this time any considerable, begin with the inconsiderable. Peg with Lady--- as usual was hist at the last Oratorio. The Company in that Box was so unreasonably noisy that it got the better of the Patience of the Audience and tho' the Beauty and Wit are powerful advocates, Handel's friends prevail'd and preffer'd his music, unaccountably to be sure when two senses were to be charmed by not attending to his Oratorio. It was the fashion to be Musical that week. Mons. Haslang gave an Entertainment of Music in his Chapel after wch there was a very fine Collation. This was good friday. Mama and I had tickets given to us by a R[oman] Catholic and went in the places wch was left for them wch at other times are for the Servts wch has affronted those that are constant frequenters of the Chappel. But it was Politesse of Mons. Haslang who gave up the best places to the English Quality, accordingly the first that presented to fill them was Miss Banks and Miss M Rich. We sat very inconveniently behind, it was very Hot. The Music not at all Solemn as we expected, the Words Italian and in short it was just like an Opera only Casavini was the Virgin Mary and Reginelli was John the Baptist. We were very soon tired of seeing them personally [and] we went away at the End of the first Part. Ld. Ashburnham was most happily seated at the foot of a Divine Bank from whence the finest hiss proceeded but as they were not Zephirs, which was what we shd have been the better for, we Chose to retire into another Climate. . . Mama joins with me in impatience to hear the act we wish of yr Journey and the success of the Bath Waters with you and Mr Grenville. I beg my compts to him. Mama desires hers to both you and him. I can only add that I am yr Most affecte

JH

Monday Evening [1748]

I have industriously contrived to spend this Evening at home and to secure my entertainment for that part of it wch I shall pass in my own little room, am set down to Converse with my Dr Miss Grenville. Your letter wch I recd [on] Saturday lyes before me and Claims what I am not a little happy to pay, my best acknowledgments. . . I am greatly satisfied with the effect of the Bath Waters. I expect in another letter to find Mr Grenville can bragg of as great an improvement as you have already found. Two or three days of fine weather and two of heavy warm rain has greatly advanced the spring. I hope it will settle at last to good, which will make your time pass away more to your own mind and the good of your health, for except Mrs Edwin I dont find that the Company you meet is very desirable. But I am vastly glad that her Society is agreeable to you. To be sure her Zeal is very edifying and her Hymns almost Divine. I really think she has some reason to have hopes of you, for you commended her and her Religion exclusive of her Voice wch I must own is an article of Importance to me whenever I have the pleasure of being in her Company. . . Now for a London Article and where can I begin it better than from Blandford House. I was there for a little while last night (the only time since you saw me there.) I went to make Mama's excuses, who was ill of the Headach. . . The topic of Conversation of the Assemblée seemed to turn altogether upon the Masquerade that is to be next Thursday. I go after bragging till very lately that I shd not. One comfort is that a Domino is soon put on so that my Dress gives me no trouble. Lady D Hobart and Miss W[yndha]m and several others go in Dominos too but the Gentlemen are very angry at it but those that don't care for that will go their own way. . . I've had a letter by this Mail from my Br William. They are at present encampt within five Leagues of Maastricht, wch held out till the 28th. I find by his manner of writing they all think the Campaign will soon be at an end. He says it can't possibly be otherwise wch agrees with a repport that came from St James's today that the Peace with France is actually concluded and others say the Conferences at Aix La Chappelle are broke up, so one is uncertain what to believe tho' not at all uncertain to wish it were true. A summons from Papa's room will relieve you from this tedious epistle.

Back in Greenwich for the summer months, Jane writes of a quiet, uneventful somewhat lonely life with her parents, her mother never quite well and her father often out of humour: 'Papa's excessive low spirits which makes Mama have no heart to undertake a party of pleasure.' A visit from Hester in May therefore, was a high moment of joy:

Greenwich
29th May [1748]

I hope I need not tell you that the agreeable surprise of seeing you gave me inexpressible pleasure. As it really did, I trust it was apparent in my looks wch I have wisht more than once to be expressive when I could not content myself with words that might sound like Compliments tho' I shd only Speak that I long of all things for such another day. Having walkd with you in the Park has added to the pleasure of every Walk since, by recollecting all the places we turned our steps to, Beech's Prospect etc I wish of all things you could persuade —— [George Grenville]. I mean impossibility so I wont proceed. Papa and Mama having been taking an Airing this Evening in the Post Chaise I've made use of that time in Walking and have taken a vast round [of] Black Heath and the Park, not without wishing for my two Friends at every step, for it was vastly pleasant. I've left Mama at Chess; I am obliged to seize Moments for one way or another I am always employed and in consequence of being in a Hurry I send you this intolerable Scrawl but I could not defer writing to you longer... Greenwich is in Great Beauty, vastly come on since you was here. You have given me the greatest of pleasures next to seeing you in saying the Day you past here was agreeable to you. Such another can't come too soon but such is the fate of human things will be too soon Over. Mrs Edwin would draw some very good Conclusion from this traite de morale. I shall, the Hour of Sup[p]er been arrived, end well since it is with sincere Assurance of being my Dr Miss Grenville's most faithful and affecte friend and obliged humble servt

J Hamilton

A year later Jane is with her mother in the Chiswick house, where it is evident that life was much more stimulating and amusing that at Greenwich.

Chiswick
24th June 1749

But its time I shd write a little seasonably and as one ought to do when one is near the smoke of London to those that are far from it. I hear the gaities begin to dwindle and that it is grown very empty. The Peg is safe return'd from her naval expedition but has had the pleasure and variety of being out in a very great storm. Col. Walgrove was of the party. If I may be allowed to say so Ldy Frances Seymour is not the beauty you have heard, well enough for anybody, very well for so great a fortune. Sr John Peachey sent in his proposals wch were return'd unopen'd but he says that's no answer and that he shall never think himself refus'd till Ldy Frances tells him as much herself. He was at Court the day she was presented and the act of her behaviour puts me in mind of a haughty Lady, Honoria was her name, that you have read a story of among Dryden's Fables. The Duke continues his flirtation with the Grecian beauty, who goes constantly to all public places but at the same [time] desires gentlemen that are sans consequence to walk with her avowedly saying it is to keep that Great Admirer off. Mr Garrick was made happy Thursday last. They were married in town return'd to Chisw: before dinner and remain here still. We are very well with our Neighbours tho we dont meet very often. Ldy Burlington particularly has gain'd me very much by great civilitys last time we were there. Mama was set down to cards and I had the pleasure of walking for an hour and a half at least tete a tete with my Lady herself, wch was at first great constraint but quite wore off in a little time by her great good humour. I suppose you have heard Prince George is to have the sixth vacant Blue Ribband, I mention it so because Mr Doddington, who was here Wednesday, told Mama he had been at Council the day before and that the other five were given away and that one refused. It seems His Majesty was resolved to do it as of his own good pleasure and lock'd that secret up in a more private recess than even the Cabinet. By the way Ld Chesterfield has been very ill but is recover'd. I hear too that he is violently in Love with Mrs Pitt and has said he wd give half his Estate to Kiss her little child. To be sure, if so he wd give to kiss herself more that he is worth in the stile of that good Patriot or Courtier that proposed giving the King twenty shs in the pound or more also. Mama said that and pray tell Miss Speed her wit upon Mr Ly[ttel]ton was sterling and diverted us vastly. Having very freely troubled you with one message, I will likewise add to it my Compliments wherever you think they will be acceptable.

Greenwich
24th Augst 1749

I was rather sorry than otherwise to leave Chiswick. I'm afraid Mama wont be so well here because she will use less exercise, wch sounds odd but it is always the case here. We have objections, that is Mama has, to both walking in the Park, where we once met with a fright and Airings, as Papa was once Robbd. I wd gladly for my part forget both these adventures. The weather has been very fine but only Papa has made the proper use of it and he goes out in his Chariot round the Heath as usual and Suns himself every morning in our Kitchen Garden wch is now made as neat and pretty as such a Design and such a Space will admit of. As my early hours have been both a subject of envy and admiration to you, I must tell you there is now an embargo laid upon them. Mama thinks me thinner for the little sleep I allow myself and has orderd me Asses milk the day I came here and to sleep after it wch I do because she desires it but not without much reluctance.

In the summer of 1750 the rather uneasy trio of Jane and her parents sets out for the spa known as Hot Well at Bristol.

Hot Well, Bristol
Sunday 27 May 1750

My dear Lady Hester
We are just arrived at our Lodging in wch I can't sleep comfortably till I've given my Dr friend a proof of how much she is in my thoughts, indeed you wd have had more than one letter from me since the last I recd from you but that I felt so angry upon a Certain Subject that I kept myself from writing because I think I can't as yet rail with [the] safety I wish. I might say with justice Tomorrow is the Monday I've waited impatiently for as I shall consequently for a letter from yr Dear self wch I hope will bring me some news of importance. As there is no altering persons, I don't know what is to be wish'd but that their conduct will

explain. So no more till I hear from you... I must observe the Silence I've prescribed myself, so now you shall hear of our Journey. It has been very prosperous. Pray tell Mr Berenger with my Complits that his books have been a great amusemt to us on the road. Notwithstanding, I must own it has been a most tedious journey, Papa being so low and Weak and I may add to that, impatient. To make amends Mama has had no headach tho' she has not had one tolerable nights sleep. I am now come to Monday morning, for I had not opportunity equal to my inclination yesterday. We have been at the Well, there is hardly any body here, the only names I can tell you are Lady Londonderry and Sr Charles Howard. Poor Papa is full of grievance and Mama has got a Violent Creek in her neck, or rather I believe something Rhumatic and is otherwise not over well but I hope it is only owing to cold and want of sleep and that she will soon recover here. She likes the situation of our Lodging mightily. We have a charming rural prospect and are not far from the Well. I am not settled enough to enlarge more and unless I cd say very different things from the contents of this, am sensible it is full long enough. Will you be so good to mention particularly how Ldy Charlotte Edwin does, we have constant actts but Mama will be glad to hear from you as you see her Physician.

Believe me most affectionately yrs etc

JH

On 4th June Jane has 'persuaded Mama to ride upon a pillion and that I accompany her Single Horse, and that we are to ride this way three times a Week.' She believes it will do them great good. On the 18th she comments at length, if a little obscurely, on what Hester has seemingly told her about an unsuccessful love affair. She writes:

I think all uncertainty is now at an end and that is so material a change for the better that I look upon it like a fever become intermitting in wch case the progress of it is to be stopt by a never failing remedy in those Cases. I wont say that your Head will have the conquest of your Heart for I have always seen that in you they both concur to make your actions right.

She is touched that Hester should have confided in her:

My Dr Lady Hester gives me the strongest proof of her friendship and the highest pleasure, for these are synonimous terms, in putting it in my power by my opinions to chear your Spirits when they tend in need of the revival of a friend. How I regret we are not together.

And takes the opportunity to express her views on men, women and love:

If friendship did not come into the aid of Love how soon must one write Bankrupt under that Selfish passion and yet we are all drawn in by specious pretences to suppose something noble and worthy, as the virtuous are ever the most unsuspecting. Well, let the Men boast of the Superiority of their understanding and take the privileges of being stronger than Weak Women, as we are called. I am for my part content it shd be so, for we have truth and virtues on our side wch they readily give up to us as not worth contending for.

Nothing remarkable has happen'd here since my last except the bad actt Mama has received of Jacco the 2nd, who is departed (the phrase of the gardener who gave the actt.) and that very suddenly having only been ill a few hours. Mama is so bent upon replacing the loss of the first, wch was the great favourite, that we are taking all imaginable pains to get a Brazil marmouset but it seems they are extreamely scarce. Will you be so good to mention this to His Excellancy at Barbadoes [Henry Grenville] when you write next... You will be so good as to mention that one of the material characters of the right sort of Monkeys is that they are strongly perfumed and likewise have a sort of Whistling notes like a Bird. Mama is so greatly entertain'd by this specie of Animals and we have so much time that requires some domestic amusement to pass tolerably... I only Dance Minuets at the Balls, the weather having been prodigiously hot and another good reason, no proper partners. We hardly ever go in the long room.

But nine days later she has found a partner (albeit one aged fifteen) as

I had Lord Villiers for my partner the first part of the Evening. He is indeed the handsomest and genteelest Boy I ever saw and dances in the greatest perfection. I was in great spirits at that Ball notwithstanding that it was immensely hot.

Hot Well
8 Augst 1750

The Tuesday before yesterday The Brother arrived and stayed till the Monday following. I was extremely struck at first sight and felt at my heart as having seen no pleasing apparition. I recover'd immediately and can answer for it that my looks told no tales then or any other time. He seem'd at first to view me with curiosity and was so very clear sighted as to be, as far as I cd discover, perfectly easy as to my ignorance, very good humoured to me and I to him, only think 'ont, except once that he askd me if I rode double upon wch I shot forth a look of great disdain, wch he took notice of as being the first time he had seen me angry. I felt great relief in the sincerity of that one moment.

Hot Well
15 Augt. 1750

The 20th Inst. we are to set out upon our return, so this is the last time I shall write to you from hence... My time has been lately very much taken up with Galloping and I shall go on the same way for the three or four remaining days. Upon the whole I've past my time well here.

On the return to Greenwich, domestic life for Jane resumes. Letters to Hester over the next two years are scanty: the two young women may have met more often, or perhaps because there was nothing much new to write about. On 2nd September, two weeks after the return, Jane writes that she 'lives all day in Mama's room' and 'dedicate[s] the time before breakfast to Music, having an Organ and organist at my disposal.' Her mother has 'suffered terribly from headachs, Worse than ever but is taking new Medicines and began Bathing in warm water wch has been prescribed.'

Hester's cousin, Richard Berenger, the King's Master of the Horse, paid them a visit on 'his Proud Steed' but would not stay to dinner. Jane hopes that on his return journey 'he may have escaped the Collectors, as they are called, who infest the environs of London worse than ever.' But change was on the way. In June 1752 four Hamiltons set off for Paris, Jane, her parents and her brother William, a visit which was to bring death to Lady Archibald six months later but which did not end for Jane until the following May. In her letters to Hester from France Jane is constantly worried and at times deeply anxious about her mother's ill health, but the letters also reflect the interest and freshness of view of an intelligent young woman on her first trip abroad and are of singular interest.

Paris
20 June 1752

My dear Lady Hester
    I quite long to converse with you this only way that is in my power, I have thought of it a thousand times, have hardly had one inst of leisure since I set out from Greenwich. We arrived here Sunday Evening abt nine without any accidt and had a passage of three hours and a qr just before the storm that we were afraid wd alarm our friends in England. Mama was several times so ill upon the road that she was quite low spirited so you may judge if I was not too, but no headach the whole way... From Calais to Chantilly the dining place of the last day, the country is extreamly wild, no villages interspers'd and but few woods or tolerable prospects, none fine. The Port towns at the distance of six miles and often nine which is a post and a half, [are] very ill served with horses. But indeed we found that more than most people, as we were three Post chaizes wch takes up [to] nine and six saddle horses, wch is more generally travel in Company I suppose, so that even with sending on a Post before, we often waited till horses came in from the field. And then such Poverty among the people that I never saw before. Every thing changed from Chantilly, a most delightful place belonging to the Pce of Condé wch we saw only from passing on the road, for our Dinr was ready the inst we arrived and we set out immediately after with a Postilian as well dress'd as Ld Bristol wd have been if he had taken a fancy to try his skill in such an undertaking. Powder'd, curld, long Cue, Gold laced Hat, flourish'd Ruffles, white waistcoat, in short the prettiest of figures for he was very much a Hervey. We went thro' the forest of Chantilly, the whole road we pass'd is made at a vast expence paved in the middle and room for two Chaises to pass at a time of each hand of it and many fine avenues of (young) planted trees (for it has been done by this King's order) for many miles together. From St Denis, the last post before you arrive at Paris, objects crowd every inst upon you as you may imagine. The whole length of it is one fine avenue of a great breadth and planted on each hand with a double row of trees. Enterd into the gate of Paris where we were stopp'd, but civilly, and a slight examination made of our trunks etc. We travers'd the whole town to get to our Hotel de Provence, Rue Condé, F[aubourg] St Germain. We were surprised with the narrowness of the Streets, Darkened too with the hight of the houses and frighten'd too with the concourse of people we seem'd to be driving over but they are most alert in getting out of the way. Our Lodgings are very good and furnish'd in a very Elegant mannr in the french taste, but to tell you every thing there are numberless inconveniencys to rub thro' from English servts, and french ones not understanding one another The Confusion of Babel is a great stop in our way, and then at the first settling one feels all one[s] wants and that they are many. Cela est mortifiant but the longer I live the more I see that the greatest ingredient for human

happiness is a good easy temper. Je vous en fait mon complimt for I think I never saw it more conspiculously than in your Ladysp. Je fais de mon mieux pour vous resembler mais cela coute quelquefois. Don't ansr to this. We were recommended to an Abbé whom we have found of great use. He went with Mama, Br Wm and I, in our fine Berlines (wch is a Carosse de Remise) to shew us the Thuilleries yesterday. I never was so struck with any thing in my life, the Louvre is by much the most magnificent Palace they tell us that is in Europe. It is built round a Court, you see one front from the Key [quay] of the River Seine, Pass a very fine Bridge from wch you see several fine Public Buildings, enter the Garden where you are surprised with a view of the delightfullest Grove you can imagine, Cut into arcades and gothic arches, the work of art but yet has the appearance of la belle nature. The trees are limes and horse chestnuts and are now in their highest beauty. We walk'd thro' a great Place to get to these walks but were turning back every moment to look at the long range of building, another front of the Louvre we were leaving behind us. Groups of marble figures placed properly before the green trees have the finest effect in the world. We set in one of the grande allées for an hour and a half and saw all the fine people pass in review before us. The Ladies walk vastly well and dress the same except those of the highest rank, that wear such a quantity of rouge that it's down right shocking. They wear the blue corn flowers in a bouquet, stuck not on one side but just before. They dress their hair in twenty different ways, all pretty and not like their imitators in England, much more becoming. But their way of holding themselves and walking is wt sets them off the most. . . The men don't make half so good a figure as the Ladies and even they don't please my Br but I imagine cela sera toute autre chose when he converses wth them. . . I have not mentioned Papa, he bore the journey surprisingly and is well but complains as usual. My Br is very alert and clever. Compts from Mama. Remember me to enquiring friends. Adieu my Dr Lady Hester, I love to hear from you.

Paris
14 July 1752

Mama has hired a house ready furnish'd belonging to the Marqs de Crillon at Marly. It is a charming situation, stands high, good air, fine prospect, looks into the King's garden near the prettiest airings that can be and but two miles from the forest of St Germain, an hour from Versailles and two from Paris. The house just holds us and Mama is pleased with the thought of going there. Papa is secretly so and in short we are glad that this situation is determin'd upon and that we shall be there some mths. Mama is to drink asses milk; as for goat's whey, Fontainebleau where it's to be had is reckon'd bad air and a miserable place to be in and besides this the doctr does not aprehend the necessity of it as he thinks it certain her lungs are not affected. . . Mama and I are vastly taken wth the Tablier de menagère wch is the fashion here to wear at home. It is a copius Short apron with a broad Bavette of Lutstring of any Colour you please, green or black the most worn. I have affranchis myself from the Slavery of Curling or rebours the french way. Fanny [her maid] can do my Hair very well en touppe and that becomes me better. The other c'ettoit un Visage d'une Aune. You see I am in spirits today. . . I feel every day the advantages of our Fortunate Island and thank my stars that I was born where there is Liberty, property and no Popery. I dare not say wt I wd of the contrary here for fear my letter shd not reach you. Mama has this moment told me that she finds wt the Docr has given her answers beyond expectation.

[Mama] is vastly pleased with our Situation here, indeed it is a charming one and the finest Air that can be from wch I expect great amendment in some time. The house is hired ready furnished of the Marqs. de Crillon, the price 12 Hund livres for Six months wch is reckon'd a great deal both in that article and some others that were objected to as too disadvantageous. He wd not recede in the least, that it was not his business to let Houses, that this was to be sold but he wd let it first pour faire plaisir and that if had had the honr to be acquaint'd with My Lord or Madame he wd have offerd them his house for nothing and that shd still be the case or his terms entirely complied with. It ended there as you may imagine. I only mention this to shew you the <u>nature</u> of a french compliment, for no Jew cd have extorted a better bargain. But no matter, for that it serves our purpose to admiration, is neat and agreeable, just holds us all. Below stairs we have a good enough dinning room, a Sale de Compagnie off of it, very pretty and well furnishd petit cabinet with a Lit de repos where Papa sits all day very quietly, leaning upon great cushions of green damask and all conveniencys abt him quite to his mind. Above we have all good bedchambers, mine joins to Mama's I have a closet besides and a Balcony before Mama's windows and mine. . . I have my little table and books before me and when ever I look up see over our little garden, a delightful prospect. . . The village is between us and the garden but still that is but one little range of low Houses wch we over top from the Rooms below. This you'll say is very fine but I have a great deal more to tell you yet. The airings just at our Door are the finest you can imagine. The Coaches are allowed to drive in the Park and Forest of Marli wch joins to the garden and shews great part of it. It is like Richmond Garden and you can go for miles together thro' the finest avenues, groves, thickets, lawns, cornfields, out of wch you Spring game at Every step and when you are tired of this, as it's the vice of our natures to be of every thing we are too much familiarized with, we have nothing to do but to turn our Steps as we did yesterday and through the finest and most (ormanentl'd) road found ourselves in an Hour and that in a heavy coach and only a pair of Horses, at Versailles. We only drove round it to view the outside. We were astonish'd to find it more immense and magnificent than any imagination we had form'd of it. The Chapel is all Gilt on the outside, the Windows looking glass and some painted glass intermix'd, the whole the richest scene I ever saw. As for the Louvre, I grew so familiar with that that my admiration vanish'd in a great degree especially after the fault of the Roof wch is vastly heavy, being pointed out to me and finding that a great part of it is only a shell, the other side dirty old Buildings or poor appartmts wch are inhabited by artificiers the King lends them to. But to return to our Marly, we like it infinitely better than Versailles; all there is the work of art, here Nature has been kind. The House is not fine but its in a singular taste wch I'm sure you would like. The Pavillions wch are placed at little distances of each side of the Corps de Logis, form some thing more than a semi circle, they are all joind by coverd walks with trilliage en forme de berceau, the trees bent over in the most regular and artificial manner, the space within is Parterre terraces, vast flights of Steps, large Basons of water with fine Marble emblematical figures which all play every Sunday in all parts of the garden wch is full of fine Statues in various stiles, all agreeable and the prettiest vases and urns that I ever saw. . . My Br is vastly pleasd here too. Papa is not so much changed as to be contented but he is well and tho he dont express it in words, we often see that he is much diverted.

We are more and more Delighted with the part of France we now inhabit, which is very like England and no bad complimt to it neither. Ldy Caroline Petersham, her Ld and Sr John Bland and a Monsr de Laner that I suppose you are acquainted with and that will be in England again next Winter and that appears to me to be a very pretty man, were all here a week ago to see the Waters Play and Mama. Her Ladyship detests Paris and the ways thereof, longs to return to England. Madme Hay gave them a great supper of seven coarses, all wch Ld Petersham payd with interest by losing four hundred Pound to the Husband. Gaming goes on at a great rate. Ly Car[oline] was quite at a loss at first how to put on Rouge [and] ask'd if it was to be worn upon the nose or chin, after wch Sr John Bland said before several people and herself 'Ldy Caroline dresses just as she did in England only she wears a little more Rouge.' Ld and Ldy Coventry made us a visit yesterday, she is excessively admired at Paris, notwithstanding the Beauty first mention'd had told us the contrary. . . It is scarce to be credited if one did not see it again and again, what absurdities vanity and envy will produce in a Handsome Woman that values herself upon being thought such and turns the whole bent of her mind upon gaining admirers. I am sure that is not Ly Coventry's case, all her Beauty is dedicated to please her Husband, she has eyes for him only. And such is the charm of novelty, that she pleases the more at Paris from that circumstance. At least they talk to her and of her upon that ton. She ansrs by an interpreter for she does not aim at a Word of french wch she hardly understands the least of. I am not sure wether that too is not a favourable circumstance. She wears no Rouge or White either. I am persuaded [that] whoever has thought her painted saw her thro' the optic of envy for she speaks with so much innocence upon the subject and look'd so fair yesterday in broad day light that I can never disbelieve what she says. . . The Paris friseurs have done their utmost to spoil her hair. . . to make it look like wool, more frizzled than ever was the head of a Negro. Notwithstanding all this and looking thin and somewhat out of shape she had more beauty yesterday de reste than I have seen in France. The run of the people are really ugly wch is partly owing to their wearing no Hats and being all day long exposed to a much hotter sun than ours. . . In one of the intervals of Mama's best health we went, us two, in her Caleshe one morning last week to Versailles and with the help of an Excellent french footman, who put us in the method, saw the great apartment and gallery which is all very fine but not so much so as we expected from the outside. A Suisse [guard] seeing us strangers invited us to see the King's bedchamber which is furnish'd finely, the bed Yellow and Silver with a little Red, great Plumes of White Feathers upon the Top. But Louis le Grand's bedchamber wch remains just as it was when he died, is much finer, the Bed is the Richest Gold stuff that ever was made and finer than any they make now and this was embroider'd besides. Magnificent glasses and a lustre de Cristal de Roche. Pictures etc. all in the highest taste. The Windows look upon the great Avenue and he used to divert himself from his Bed with seeing the people of the Court pass and repass from this. We saunter'd about just by ourselves and in our negligé till the hour of the Queens going to Mass. She was carried thro' the rooms in a Sedan Chair [of] Wicker gilt. Three of the Mesdames [daughters] follow'd, they all pass'd close to us, we follow'd them in to the Chapel and plac'd ourselves so well that we saw them as well as it was possible. The Chapel is very fine and the whole service, wch is music pleasd us extreamely, in the stile of an Opera for it did not come up to the seriousness of an Oratorio. We were vastly edified with the unaffected Piety we observed in the Queen, who appeard to us to be an agreeable well looking Woman, bearing up with resignation and patience the neglected forlorn situation the King leaves her in now, whom she loves with great tenderness and was once as much in his favour as any favourite he has had since, not excepting the present [one]. The Mesdames were cover'd with Rouge, they have black Eyes and strong features and great resemblance to the King, at least we judge so from his Pictures. The Original we have yet to see for he was not at Home. They look very lively, the gentle and the modest are not the characteristics they seem to be distinguishd by, except the youngest, who for that reason and not yet arrived to be upon a footing with her Sisters, minded her Prayers and had no airs at all. . . We return'd home in good time and in the shade highly satisfied with our morning expedition. The Dauphin to the great joy of France is quite recover'd. The Dauphiness has gain'd great reputation by her care of him in his illness. She looks like a pretty woman and genteel, we saw her from a window of the apartment at Versailles talking from the garden to Madme Adelaide, who was at her window. She was without hoop and as Pepin our french servt told us ingiving us notice we might see her, that she was walking and 'pas mieux habilé que vous Madselle.' All the ladies of the Court that we saw look'd very trumppery indeed, they wear black lace Lappets. As for the head, it is so little and cover'd with ribbonds etc that no black can appear. The Mesdames wear mantelets of the same Lutstring or taffety, rather that their Robes are of wch is that clouded confusion that you have a gown of, wch is the most fashionable kind of thing wore here. They are of all colours, generally the ground of a dirty white, they never chuse a clear white, they say it's unbecoming to the complexion.

Marly
1 Septr. 1752

I have been another expedition since I wrote last. I was delighted with [it] and Mama so much so that she was the better for it instead of being fatigued. We went for one Day and Night to Paris, saw the whole Court of France assembled in greatest pomp and brilliancy in the Church of Notre Dame to hear [the] Te Deum for the Dauphin's recovery. We were placed so as to see every thing. . . It was by much the finest sight I ever saw, we were very lucky to have the opportunity wch might not happen again for years. The illumination of the town at night was like enchantment.

Marly
15th Septr. 1752

I am in great spirits wch makes me seize a single quarter of an hour to give my Dr Lady Hester an act of the cause. It is now that you are to congratulate me upon Mama's recovery but the road she has arrived to it has been very rough. . . We have the pleasure now of nursing her up with broths and jellys but I really thought the Docts wd have starved her. My Br in the midst of our fright gallop'd away to Versailles and Brought one of the King's Physicians, we found him a very sensible man and it was a satisfaction to find him concur with the other. . . Mama has been out to take the Air today, she is in a coarse of Mineral Waters and the plainest diet, no milk or garden things. The Scheme of the South of France is totally at an end, neither Papa or herself are equal to such an undertaking and as her lungs are out of the question, it is not thought necessary. Paris air is very good and we shall winter there.

The early winter of 1752 brought the deaths of both mothers of Hester and Jane. Countess Temple died at Bath on 6th October and Lady Archibald Hamilton in Paris on 3rd December. Hester, though a dutiful daughter, had not been close to her mother and was surrounded with many relations to comfort her; but Jane, alone in Paris with a father she never really liked and with her brother William still a young man, was shattered by the loss of a mother she adored.

Paris
4th Novr 1752

My Dear Lady Hester
     Your letter from Stowe found me in the utmost pain and anxiety for you. I cannot express how much I feel myself obliged by your manr of writing, which shews me the justice you do my sentiments for you. I shall never forget your goodness in allowing me a share in your thoughts in the circumstances in which you wrote. . . I am vastly pleased with the offers you have had from all your brothers and with your answer to them all. Mama was guessing you would live with yr Br and Sister Grenville, I told her I believe you would chuse to have a habitation of your own, she thinks it wisely determined but we both hope there will be an alteration in the scheme and that you will not live single. . . We are just arrived at Paris the day before yesterday, the Weather is vastly cold, it is quite ridiculous to see the variety of immense Muffs that are wore universally even by the lowest of the people. . . Mama has got a great cold and is very weak but notwithstanding recovers upon the whole as one could wish. I am contented and happy upon her subject, so you may imagine it goes well. . . Adieu. God bless my Dear Friend. Yrs with the highest esteem and unalterable affection
     J Hamilton

Paris
15th Novr 1752

     Now that I wd talk to you of Paris wch by the way I have not improvd my acquaintance with very greatly as Mama has kept house with a cold. . . There is talk that Madme Pompadour is thought to be in a Consumption which is thought to be catching, so that they will do all they can to wean the King's affection from her. She is so apprehensive of it herself that she is jealous upon the slightest occasions and gave an instance very lately in desiring a Lady of the Court and who is agreeable and has a great deal of wit and is often of the Private partys, to retire seeing her better drest than usual, her Diamonds new set and as she apprehended, an air of design. She told her plainly she shd not sup with them and that they wd make her excuse and tell the King she had the migraine. This was executed but the King insisted she shd be sent for, she came in all her finery and being asked why she had intended disappointing them of her company for so slight a reason, she said she was very well but had obey'd La Marquise, upon wch the King looked at her very drily and she remaind much mortified. She is so much hated at Paris that these sort of reports may very likely have no other foundation.

Paris
8 Decr 1752

My Dear Lady Hester
     Little did I think when I was grieving for you that it would be so soon your turn to offer consolations to me. . . It is no uncommon thing to lose a mother but few Daughters could boast of such a one as mine. I thank God that I had the honour to belong to her. . . the business of my life will be to imitate the worthy example I have seen in her. I am still stunn'd with the stroke and can scarce believe that it is not a dream. . . My friend, my companion, my adviser is gone, who will now tell me of a thousand useful admonitions that will escape unheeded and grow into habits. We took Sweet Council together and walk'd as friends. . . Sunday the 3rd,

at two o'clock, the Doctrs having tried all their skill, bleeding in the foot, blisters upon the legs and all the most powerful medicines and cordials wch they thought prolonged her life for some hours, shewed me their despair by allowing me to give Dr James's powder... At five on Sunday Evening without one convulsion but with a gentle sigh that good and great soul took its flight to Heaven... My Br's conduct throughout this melancholy scene has pleasd me vastly and [he] has been most affecte, senceable and friendly to me. Papa has not been able to be made more unhappy than he was before so you may judge what his mind is wore to, he is good humour'd to me, trusts me now in every thing relating to the family in Mama's stead and I have assur'd him I will never leave him as long as he lives and do every thing as much as it depends upon me to lessen the weight of this calamity. He has been so good to confirm to me the gift my Dear Mama has made to me by a letter of request to him, at most every thing that belong'd to her and that she had purchased... What it will amount to I dont guess... All her riches consist in her Jewels, some furniture and another little article you shall hear of when I can explain more at large. [The house at] Chiswick mortgaged for the value and instead of money there is debt but that can be cleared out of the fund above mentioned. [All] this after being ten year a favourite and in the principal employmet in the royal service. Pray tell me what people say. I doubt you will have heard the bad news before this but it was not in my power to write sooner. I was determined against removing the sacred remains for reasons that will immediately occur to you. She is deposited in the best manr this country will allow among Protestants in a burial ground destined to them, and after much terror upon the subject am now satisfied that she is safe from molestation as in any other spot whatever... We are to stay here all winter, Papa says it would kill him to remove, we shall live very privately and quietly. We have met with great civilitys from many Dr Mama had gained the hearts of. Mine beats and bounces abt but yet I am well.

After her mother's death Jane stayed on in Paris with her father until early in May 1753. As was to be expected in a young woman of lively temperament, her spirits gradually revived. Many prominent women in Parisian society were good to her, notably the French duchesses of Mirepoix and St James and the English duchess of Queensberry, whose brother Lord Hyde met an untimely death in April from a fall from his horse, the subject of Jane's last letter from Paris.

Paris
23rd Janry 1753

My Dear Lady Hester
    I have this day a second letter from you and true it is that I was before in yr debt. I cannot enough thank you for both. That letter wherein you gave me advice that I think the senceablest in the world and what I mean exactly to steer my conduct by... I hope... that you will examine me attentively and use the utmost freedom in advising and admonishing me. You will always be in the right and always gentle and you will make me happy. My Br and I are upon very good terms but with him and the other Br also, it will require managemt. and temper to preserve peace and Harmony... I am perfectly well and my mind in a state of tranquility when I dont trespass upon it too far by recalling some sad ideas that take me from myself and make me unreasonable; that I am not so generally my looks wd shew you, for they are much recover'd. The Dear Dhs of Queensberry deserves and has a large proportion of Love and gratitude from me... Ldy Browne is my sheet anchor, she treats [me] like a favourite child... Madme de

Mirepoix I am half in Love with and admire her every time I see her still more and more. I am seldom left in an Evening to be alone but when I am, I think it no misfortune. . . As for our affairs, a great deal of business has been done since my last wch has caused me much writing and trouble. I have desired my sister to act for us and for me particularly. I have not had her ansr and before you get this you will know more than I do abt Ld. Walgrove taking or not taking the [Chiswick] House, wch I was told he had a mind [to do] and that I wish him to take. I hear the Psse has sent Br. Frederick word that she is going to build up a wall before the wind side of the great room. . . it will be a great disadvantage and perhaps hinder any body from taking the house. Her RHs may do as she pleases, I shall be the principal sufferer but nothing shall oblige me to become an humble Petitioner to her said RHns This entre nous.

Paris
28 April [1753]

My Dear Lady Hester
    I could not let the post go out without a line, tho' you will certainly have heard by the express that yesterday poor Ld Hyde's fate was decided. This is the usual phrase but according to my notion it is the living and not the dead that are to be pittied. I am very anxious to hear how the poor Dhs of Queensberry does, its well she did not determine upon coming here. Every thing that was possible has been done in every sence. The family have the greatest reason to be pleased with Ld Albemarle and Ld Stormont. The people of the highest distinction upon the french have interested themselves in this case by enquiries and regrets, the world has reason to be sorry for it has lost a most benevolent and amiable inhabitant but much is to be said to comfort his friends for he had not comfortable health and spirits and from this act his life might have given him the greatest pain. I am too much taken up with this to mention any other subject. I believe I mentioned in last abt the time our journey is fix'd. I hope we will set out the eleventh sooner it could not be. Poor Fanny suffers more and more but all in a way of recovery. I hope we shall not be obliged to leave her behind. The rest of us are well. I, yours as usual etc.

[Letter not signed]

Jane married Colonel Charles Schaw Cathcart, ninth baron, as his second wife on 24th July 1753 in London. It was a very happy marriage. They had seven children, four sons and three daughters. Her friendship with Hester Grenville continued without a break, and lasted through Hester's marriage to William Pitt in November 1754, until Jane's death, at the early age of forty-five in St Petersburg, where her husband was ambassador, in 1771. The letters written after her marriage, though always lively and with interesting descriptions of Scottish country life - and long journeys to and from Scotland - are necessarily concerned mainly with the growing families of Cathcarts and Pitts. The two women often met, especially in the first year of Hester's marriage, when she was living at the Pay Office residence and Pitt was often away at Bath. Though five years apart in age, a quite substantial gap in a period of mainly short lives, the twenty year (or longer) friendship of Jane Cathcart and Hester Pitt pursued its tranquil course untroubled by dissension or misunderstanding.

My dear Lady Hester has been particularly kind and good in her enquiries so without waiting for an ansr from you to issue from this place I set down to whip off a letter in a minute to tell my Dr Friend that I am quite well [after the birth of her baby] and very happy, so you are sure my Lord is so, and the child thriving, indeed she is so to a surprising degree. I have the additional pleasure of recommending myself extremely to the people here by the task I have undertaken and by shewing her, and no body has thought from my looks that it seem'd too much for me. My Lord is so careful and attentive for me that I am sure I am safe from harm. The Dear Creature fait les honrs de son Paÿs, on ne peut pas mieux, et me rend le chez moi ici tres agreable. Les Gens que nous voyons sont de trés bonnes gens, il[s] ny en a que peu en nombre ici mais nous irons dans peu dans un autre de ses terres ou le voisinage est trés grand et de plus considerable du païs. Je vous dit cela seulemt pour vous mettre au fait et point par preference. I believe I told you in my first letter I thought this place very pretty, I think so more now than at first. There is a vast deal of profitable business going on wch employs a vast number of Hands and feet, not to say horses, wch looks lively and the business we have to do both within and without Doors is only polishing, wch we cd not have done to our minds by ourselves. I was in hopes I had got a Mare that wd have carried me safely as I don't chuse to walk a great deal, I was out upon her once, but yesterday My Lord rode her and wd have been thrown if he had not saved himself by very good Horsemanship. So you may believe I shall not be trusted. She is quiet but this was a fright she took only upon [the] taking off a Hat that was floppd and that the wind blew near her Eyes. My Ld catchd it but was obligd to drop it as she continued out of her wits all the time he held it. This you know will not do for a Woman's horse, it's a sad thing it shd be so difficult to find a proper one. I've very little time to read and find none for L'Ennuy [ennui] vous sentez bien le fort de ce panegerique. I doubt you wont come as far as this to make us a Visit but when I have settled myself in order I shall take an opportunity to claim yr promise or rather put you in mind of it for I receive none but volunteers, it's too far to complimt any body without one is sure of as much as will prevent repentance.

I received the pleasure of Dr Lady Hester's ansr to the last but one of the letters, so I flatter myself I shall have another soon and write this in the mean while. Pray what do you mean by the rival parties? Consider I live out <u>of the world</u>. I have fishd out who Ld W is said to be thinking of marrying but pray let yr news my Dr friend be imparted as to an uninformd person. You ask what part of Scotland are our Head quarters, this at prest till our house in Air[Ayr]shire is built but that is the favourite situation. I shall write to you from thence next. We are to turn the minister out and lodge ourselves in his House. Our Scheme of Visiting the Dhs of Q[ueensberry] is frustrated by the badness of the roads and our fear by the act that it may be too hazardous to venture our little chaize. There has been a great deal of rain but of late fine and hot weather, a great appearance of a plentiful year. My Ld has a field of thirty acres of Oats much higher than the tallest man and all our second crop of clover has been mistaken at a little distance for Pease. I am not romancing. I have rode out several times upon a little Horse calld the Devil, a very peaceable beast and quite safe but so hard a trotter and so slow a Walker that I apprehend I shall be forced to change it for one of more expedition and smoothness of carriage if that can be found with as much safety. I am perfectly well and the Child the most thriving that ever was seen. Pray tell Mrs [George] Grenville she has two creases in her wrist like her secd son, she will understand the merit of that and of her being at the same time as hard as marble. I spare you all other particulars. . . We are making improvmets and visiting Estates and settling acts of Farms, arrears etc all which are so rational [and] pleasing employmts that they afford the greatest satisfaction. I leave [all] this the day after tomorrow, stay at Ed[inbu]r[gh] two days and so proceed by Glasgow to our shire of Air where we shall arrive before the month is out. You see I have wrote a Rhapsody of things without method or order, that is an indulgence that I always use most fully when I write to you who are only anxious to hear I am well and happy. My Ld desires me to offer you his most particular compts, mine wait upon the friends you are with and best wishes attend you all from her who is ever much yrs

JC

St Quevox near Air
[St Quivox near Ayr]
12 Sept 1754

Yours of the 1st Inst: My Dr Lady Hester is the last recd, one of mine was not come to hand when it was wrote. I mention'd in that the success of my Lord's law suit. We are now in a Minister's Manse - House - wch just holds us, it is for the convenience of being just near the [?site] where the house is to be built. That fine plan we were so fond of in winter is laid aside for one that will do infinitely better and that my Lord has contrived entirely himself, this is a bridge of 112 foot in length over the river that runs at the foot of the garden [where] are the works projecting for immediate execution and as you may imagine furnish us with much occupation and entertainment. This is one of the finest places I ever saw, from the great variety and extent of natural beauties well understood and improved in the highest taste by my Lord's Father thirty yrs ago so that the plantations are grown up and besides we have the greatest quantity of natural Wood of Oak, beech, Ash etc. I ever saw growing along the Side and banking up for an immense height the Sides of a most beautiful river. The grounds are shaped in the happiest manr and we shall have in the front of the House a Plain border'd with Hills top'd with Groves and on the one Side the River and its Woody Banks. I shant indulge my inclination in extending wt I cd say of so beautiful a part of Scotland wch we are so happy to be at home in (or at least shall be) as it will keep cold for conversation but by what I have said I hope you will think it deserves the warmth you will see I feel for it. The Weather has been charmingly fine for the fortnight we have past here. We are out the whole day and every day, have a great deal of Company about dinr time and very good senseable agreeable hearty people they are for the most part but the morngs and evengs are on our own. The child is everything we can wish and desire. We propose staying here this mth out. So much for the subject of yr friend, I know you wd be uneasy not to know as much and for Details I refer to verbal discourses.

In this same letter Jane, feeling cut off from the social life she had been a part of, begs Hester to send her news and gossip of friends and acquaintances:

I think this is the month Mrs Grenville lies in, I shall be earnest to hear the act I wish of her and that the painful hour is happily over. I am glad you have had so agreeable a party tho' I know Wotton must ever be so to you at all times. Poor Ld Halifax was indeed to be pittied but I think he was also invited by the happiness he saw to renew the state, you will laugh and I intend you shd for in good earnest wt I have said is good for nothing else. I hope yr guess about Mr Spencer will be confirm'd. I fancy, at least hope that Ld and Ldy Brooke will be in town by the time you get this, they were to set out the 9th. Pray how does Mr Grenville and His Exce etc etc? These are the sort of things I wish to hear, whatever interests you most and not an ansr to the things I write, but there is no improvement to be wishd in yr letters, I only regret the long time they are travelling. Ld March I heard was at Edr some days ago, I expect we shall see him here but perhaps not of some days as the Leith races are the 17th. We did not go to [?Dumfries] from the difficulties of the road. I had the pleasure to see Hamilton [Palace], it is a very noble fine place altogether and form'd much in the taste of some of the Palaces I have seen in France. The Dhs's Daughter is vastly like her, they were not at home. Adieu My Dear Friend, believe me most truly and affectly yrs etc

J Cathcart

Jane was delighted with the news of Hester's engagement to William Pitt:

Sauchie Lodge
4th Nov [1754]

My Dear Lady Hester
            One of the happiness's in my friendship with you is the absolute and mutual confidence that each of us have in the affection of the other, wch has made me quiet tho' I have neither wrote to you or heard from you as much as I could wish. I have payed it off as well as I could with thinking and am indeed truly delighted with my thoughts upon your Subject. As Mr Grenville was so good as to say of My Lord and Me so say I of you and Mr Pitt. I will burn my books if you are not happy together but as you well remember my wishes have long ago given you to him. . . We leave this place at the end of the week and propose to set out from Edr in eight days from this. . . Compts to yr Brs Sister and Friend

The correspondence continues after Hester's marriage on 16th November but with much longer gaps. The Cathcarts were established in their new built house, Shaw Park early in 1757 and two more children had arrived.

Shaw Park
[Alloa]
22 June 1757

My Dear Lady Hester
            I congratulate with you upon the Recovery of your Dear Babes [Hester and John] from the Hooping Cough and I am sure you will no less glad to return the Compts to us upon our Children's recovery who we took the measure of inoculating (all the three) since my last, and thank God the two Eldest who took the illness have had it most favourably, the youngest did not take it but has had an Eruption for four or five days and fever before it came out, to which the Docr gives no name and does not allow to be oweing to inoculation but imagines to proceed from the approach of Teeth. It is certain that it was quite unlike the Small Pox but I am easier since she was infected that she has had this little fever to clean her blood, she was heavy before it but is now as well and lively as Ever. The others released from their three weeks Confinemt are rung about the garden in perfect health and are like Birds let out of a Cage. . .

Not all Jane's concerns were domestic. She continues:

> I beg you wd put yr self to the Expence of Purchasing a small work lately come out, calld the Temple of Virtue, it is the work of the Minister of the next town to us, he is a most ingenious and worthy man and as fine a Preacher as ever I heard, a great deal of fire and imagination and so much real Piety that it's impossible not to be from such a combination both an attentive and instructed hearer.

In a letter written from Shaw Park on 8th May 1758, Jane pays tribute to Hester's serene temperament and inner strength, characteristics noted by nearly all her women correspondents:

> I rejoice to find you are so much stronger that I cd have thought, 'tis really surprising to have been able to recover so well [when] suffering so much anxiety at the same time, but of that I am convinced there are different species, I know you are totally free of that kind, that is attended with a peevish impatience wch adds its own peculiar restlessness and uneasiness to the original grievance from whence it springs.

About this time Cathcart was evidently becoming restive and anxious to re-enter public life:

> Shaw Park
> 18 Augt. 1758
>
> You are vastly good My Dear Lady Hester in shewing me by repeated proofs that you willingly give me a share in your time and thoughts at those favourite Seasons devoted to the true pleasures of life, which you enjoy at Hayes. . . We propose to set out for London at the head of our whole infantry, a circumstance which will make it necessary to anticipate Short days in cold weather. This is a bold measure but as the necessity of returning hither next Summer is not absolute, as it has hitherto been, and as my Lord would embrace with pleasure an opportunity of being employed in any way where, consistently with the good of his family, he might be useful to the Public, if anything of that sort should arise [and] having left any of the children behind would be a great embarrassmt as we should be uneasy were they to take so long a journey under any convoy but our own. You will say this is a change of measures in us country folk, the truth is many things were necessary to be done here before we could be at liberty to make a long Absence. The heaviest of these are now accomplish'd and tho' we both agree there is nothing like retirement, the country and one's own home for happiness, yet that consideration with my Lord will never stand in the way of what may produce any Service or advantage to his Country or family.

The infantry continued to receive additions. Following the birth of another son in 1760 Jane writes:

> S[haw P[ark]
> 21 Jan 1760
>
> My Dear Lady Hester
> I am not a little happy to find myself recover'd and able with my own Pen to thank you and Mr Pitt, wch I do in the warmest manr for the kind congratula-

tions address'd to my Lord wch gave us both the most sensible pleasure, as it's certainly the most flattering thing in the world and when applyed to our happiness what greatly encreases them, to have them shared by those who are in possession of our Esteem and friendship. My recovery has been an exceeding good one and I am engaged in my usual business of nursing with a most promising appearance, for a more healthy or quieter child never was seen. Our Old children are vastly fond of this new plaything, Jane asked with great _empressement_ when she was told she had got another Br, if Mama knew it.

During the next few years the Cathcarts spent more time in England, both in London and in the country, with spells at the inevitable spa (for them Tunbridge Wells), than in Scotland. These were not good years for Hester. Pitt's (now Chatham's) failing health and in 1766-67 his total mental breakdown were known to Jane:

[Dover Street]
Monday 11 May 1767

Dear Lady Chatham
As you are so much out of town and necessarily have such a load of Care and anxiety upon your mind without any relief from any out of Doors friend, as I think must hurt your own health to a degree of not being able to hold out unless you fall upon some expedient that will lighten your own part, I can not from this consideration with hold my Pen from telling Dear Lady Chatham that if she can find out any sort of way or manner in which I can be of the smallest use to her, she will make me happy now or at any time by telling it and that there is nothing so small or nothing so material that the antient friendship from the year '47 won't perform with the utmost faithfulness, being with the greatest regard Dear Lady Chatham you most affectionate etc.
J Cathcart
If you don't think of seeing me don't write, for that is only adding to yr trouble, unless you are so good as to have some Commands for me.

But there were also some jolly times arranged by Jane for the two young families despite Hester Chatham's great worries:

Dover Street
Wednesday 17th June 1767

My Dear Lady Chatham
I had your kind favour yesterday and as it happen'd the pleasure of having your three Eldest Children at the same time with all our Children. They brought a strong invitation from the two (whom we were very sorry could not come out) that they might meet to day in Bond St. wch being told is permitted _every where_, I mean Lond[on] and N[orth] End, is accepted and our Boys kept a day longer from Eton that they may all be happy this Eveng together. We had the finest Cricket Match in our Court you can imagine. You never saw anything more like a School Boy than Ld Pitt, wch I think says a great deal for his Education. The Young Ladies danced: Ldy Harriet in particular I think a genius in that talent, her little feet and all her little fair figure is delightful. Ldy Hester's Stile and Air is different and that is all, for I shd be very sorry to give a preference against her to any of the family. There is an openness, a Solidity and goodness in her that makes one quite her friend. She was as Womanly and Careful that her Br and Sisr shd not over _Eat_ or over _heat_ themselves as Dame Sparry herself could have been, wch at her age [11]

is delightful, as she has as much of good humr and liveliness as any of them. Now I am distressd that I have not said enough of the other two but I really dont chuse to say more, it looks like what it is not and tho' you shd be so good as to thank me for being what you call partial, I wont allow that I am so in the least, I shall only say that I think I know them and judge of them as you do: at least, as the <u>prevailing outline</u> in each. Nature in them bids very fair and the nurture is what it shd be. I did not intend to have wrote many lines because I wont touch upon things I am <u>heartily sorry for</u>, among the rest that you have not succeeded in a view that am sure you have strong reason for wishing to succeed in or wd not have so much as given the least hint of desiring. I think it will stalk about like a Ghost with the present possessor and that he will at last relent and give it back again. The Weather too is still inhumane but must change soon because it has lasted so long. Adieu then My Dear Lady Chatham, you and your Lord and Children have mine and my Lord's best wishes and highest Esteem. I shall drop you a line when we are at the Eve of departure. Our Servts go the end of the Week and all our baggage, so we must soon follow. I shall hope for acts from you directed to Shaw Park, by Alloa, N. Britain, that will give me the pleasure you have not yet been able to convey to my wish, and that the children say 'Mama looks better than she did at Bath.'

A reminder of Jane's death in 1771 (if indeed Hester needed one) came three years later in a letter from the widower:

Shaw Park
Nov 6 1774

Madam
    The Friendship which so long and uninterruptedly subsisted betwixt your Ladyship and her who was so dear to me, makes every Mark of Respect and Distinction which it is in Power to show your Ladyship appear to me as a Tribute due to her memory, which indeed from every consideration I must willingly pay. I therefore address your Ladyship at this time, believing you will rejoice in whatever promises to conduce to the Happiness of her Children, to inform you that as soon as I get to London I shall have occasion at the Desire of the Marquis of Tullibardine [later 4th duke of Atholl] and his family to ask the Queen's Consent for my eldest Daughter to accept the Prospect of marriage his Lordship has done her the Honour to make to her, and am further to acquaint your Ladyship that my second Daughter [Mary] will be married at the same time to Mr Graham [later Lord Lynedoch] a Gentleman of exceeding good Family, fortune, character and accomplishments. The adven[ti]tious circumstances in both offers are as agreeable as possible, but the real and essential ones [are] the Characters of the young Gentlemen, their Plans of Life, their Connections, their being neighbours to me and to one another, and the mutual Inclination of Parties, unsuggested tho' highly applauded by Friends are what give a Parent the truest satisfaction. Your Ladyship will I hope forgive me for having indulged myself in the Pleasure of communicating these Events to you before the Report of them will be likely to reach you. In the same View I should be glad your Ladyship would mention them with my best Respects to Lord Chatham and to Lady Hester Pitt, to whom I offer my best Compliments. Altho' the Circumstance of the Ceremonial is a Restraint upon my talking of them till we all get to London, which will be before the end of the month, soon after which I imagine all will be concluded. I have the Honour to be with the greatest Truth and Respect Madam, Your Ladyship's most obedient and most humble servt.
    Cathcart

iii. LETTERS FROM MOLLY WEST, MRS ALEXANDER HOOD 1765-1785

Mrs Mary Hood, always known as Molly, was the first wife of Rear Admiral Sir Alexander Hood, later, after her death, Admiral Lord Bridport. Her father was Dr Richard West, prebendary of Winchester; through her mother, also Mary or Maria, she was a granddaughter of Sir Richard Temple of Stowe and so a first cousin of Hester Grenville. Molly West was contemporary with William Pitt and, it was thought at one time, a possible bride for the statesman. She 'admired Pitt to a degree perhaps more that strictly platonic.'[2] But it was not to be and instead he married her much younger cousin.

The Hood brothers, Samuel, first Viscount Hood, and Alexander, distinguished naval officers, had no money; they were the sons of a country clergyman, the Revd Samuel Hood, vicar of Butleigh in Somerset. Alexander's marriage in 1761 to the wealthy Miss West, some twenty years his senior, not only forwarded his career but also brought him close to, sometimes uncomfortably so, to the Pitts. Molly Hood was something of a snob, and perhaps because of this and also because of her early infatuation with William Pitt, the Hoods virtually devoted a large part of their lives, the unstinting use, empty or occupied, of their London house in Harley Street [then No 7] and, above all, of their money as loans to the extravagant and improvident William and Hester Pitt, Lord and Lady Chatham.

Molly Hood was a prolific letter writer, nearly three hundred of her letters to Hester Chatham survive, covering the relatively short period from 1765 to her death some twenty years later at the age of eighty. It is difficult to judge from the correspondence alone exactly why the Hoods should have chosen to take the Pitts so completely under their wing; Pitt was in decline politically and would not have been able to any great extent to further Hood's career. And why did the Pitts allow themselves to be so obligated to the Hoods? Ayling in his biography of Pitt describes Hood as 'this most loyal of friends (and long suffering of creditors)' and adds that 'the Chathams seemed more than willing to treat him as a milch cow'.[3] Whatever the reason, the letters both of Hood to Chatham and of his wife to Lady Chatham stand as testimony to a friendship based on the rather improbable and uneven relationship of givers and receivers, with one lapse, for many years.

Unlike her brother, Gilbert West, poet, author and distinguished civil servant, Molly Hood was not intellectually gifted. She was however sociable, knew and dined with many men and women of distinction, and entertained generously. She was consequently well informed about court and society affairs in general, and quite ready to pass on news and gossip of this world to Hester Chatham who, though never anxious to participate herself, nevertheless enjoyed hearing about London life.

Though essentially Mrs Hood was an amiable, well intentioned woman, not to all, but towards those she admired and liked, it is possible that Hester Chatham was not really fond of her; the letters, unlike those of another cousin to both women, Hester

Lyttelton, Mrs Fitzmaurice, give no clues to her feelings. Even for Lady Chatham, long inured from the deplorable example of her husband to living in chronic indebtedness, the relationship to a creditor of her own standing and status must surely have weighed heavily at times on her sensitive nature. Molly Hood's death in 1786 may well have brought to her a kind of relief.

Tunbridge Wells
July the 10th 1765

Dear Madam

My best acknowledgements please to accept for your very obliging letter. With Concern Mr Hood and I received the account you gave of the Inflamation in your eyes which we hope is now quite over, and that your Ladyship will have no return of that troublesome complaint. It is a pity that Virtues cannot shield the Great and Good from feelings evil. Mr Pitt, too, we find had not quitted his crutches which we flattered our Selves he had done some time ago, but Alas, that and every other Good have only been in Ideas of late and such Cruel disappointments would sit more heavily upon us, if we did not rest our minds upon the kind assurances you gave us of the continuence of yours and Mr Pitt's friendly regards towards us in all Situations, an Honour and pleasure which must ever be Invaluable to us. The Weather has proved of late pretty favourable to the Water Drinkers, and we hope to the Haymaking at Hayes. We wish Miss Pitt joy of her Blackbird's Nest and of the Cape gooses production. We imagine it will not be long before you set out for Burton. We meditate paying our respects to you there before you leave that place if we possibly can. Miss Pitt will give the greatest pleasure by favouring me with an account after your arrival of the State of all the travellers, as we shall be full of anxiety for them, particularly Mr Pitt who has not had the trial of a long journey a great while. Mr Hood, and I, are much indebted for the kind wishes from Hayes for our Healths, which we think will be improved by the Methods we pursue at this place. We are tempted to make a little purchase of a Farm on Mount Ephraim as our Healths may require these Waters in other seasons, and if we can do without them, and our Income will not admit of a Summer residence, we can easily let it. Mr Hood joins with me in wishing Health and prosperity to all at Hayes.
With the most perfect regard, Dear Madam
I am your Ladyship's Most obliged Humble servant
M Hood

Later, still on their round of spas, the Hoods have seen Pitt in Bath. Her letter from Harley Street of November 8th contains a hint of criticism of Hester Chatham for not being with him:

I know your tender feelings and how much you must suffer by his absence but yet I cannot wonder at the part you have taken. Such parental tyes as your Ladyship and Mr Pitt feel the force of being sufficient to conquer the present Inclination of your being together but we trust it will not be long before you with your sweet little family join him to proceed altogether [to] this Metropolis where one hears a general Voice of his coming etc. etc.

The following year the Pitts (now Earl and Countess of Chatham) having made use of the Harley Street house while waiting to move into their own in Bond Street, Mrs

Hood writes from Sunning Hill on August 17th to her Dearest Madam regretting that they had quitted

> our Humble Dwelling in Harley Street before the pavement in Bond Street is finished, as the Noise from your rooms exposed to it must be intolerable. Let me therefore beg My Dear Countess that you will still make use of both Houses occasionally, and believe the value Mr Hood and I shall set upon our House, must rise in proportion to the use you made of it.

In an undated letter of September 1767 Molly Hood, writing for some reason in the third person, throws a sidelight on the death in Monaco, aged 29, of Edward Augustus, second son of Frederick, Prince of Wales. In this short formal note she refers (once) to her husband for the only time as 'Capt Hood'; throughout the rest of the correspondence, as hitherto, regardless of his rank he is designated by her 'Mr Hood.'

> Thursday, Earns Hill
>
> Mrs Hood presents her compliments to the Countess of Chatham with a thousand thanks for her most kind and obliging letter.
> Capt Hood set out for London with the greatest expedition yesterday having by an Express received orders to attend the Landing at Greenwich, the remains of the late Duke of York
> Mrs Hood proposes to stay only till Saturday at Earns Hill [Somerset, where they were on a visit to the Richard Combes] and then to return to Thorncombe and to London if Mr Hood does not give her hopes of coming back to her very soon.
> Mr and Mrs Hood were much relieved to hear so pleasing an account of the sweet little people at Burton Pynsent. What woud they not give to free Lord and Lady Chatham from their complaints.

In search of a country home for themselves in Somerset, Molly Hood gratefully accepts Hester Chatham's invitation to base themselves at Burton Pynsent for a few days. She assures Hester that they will bring 'whatever may be wanting for our accommodation' and will take every care 'not to be troublesome to any of your servants.'

There is a short delay to the plan:

> [Harley Street]
> May the 13th 1768
>
> Dearest Madam
> Mr Hood and I have for some days past intended to pay our regards and thanks in person for the kindness and goodness Lord Chatham and your Ladyship has shown to us in regard to our going to Burton Pynsent which we thought to have availed our selves of the latter end of this month, but the strange circumstances of the times makes every thing uncertain to Us. Mr Hood is ordered to his Yacht to secure his Men from being seduced etc. etc.

Finally in July they arrive at Burton; three letters of ecstatic (and sycophantic) description follow, of which this is the first:

My dearest Madam

Mr Hood and I arrived last night at Burton Pynsent and extremely Happy we feel our selves in this delightful place, which is doubly pleasing by its belonging to the Earl of Chatham and your Ladyship who always entrance every obligation by the delicacy and kindness with which you confer your favours. We are in possession of that part of the House your Ladyship thought the most pleasurable for us and we both break out with frequent approbation of your choice. Your obliging attention in all respects, we are very sensible to. Mr Hood has been to the pillar but I have contented my self with looking up to it from the Portico, where I have set almost the whole day from not being able to quit the dignified and sweet Scenes which present themselves from it. We have procured a little Horse of Mr Combe for the Chaise, so I shall fully enjoy every Beauty of this Lovely Spot at my ease. A great deal of your Hay was carried yesterday and much will be brought in before the evening closes, for though we have not been quite without Rain, it has not occasion'd any interruption. Some has been spoiled and the Corn is in danger unless the weather shoud be more favourable than of late, and there seems now to be a prospect of it. The loss among the sheep has been very great where the lands are low in every country. So many sheep adorned Troy Hill to day and surrounded the Portico, that the Landskips were not a little improved by them. Mr Hood is just walkd to wait upon Mr [George] Speke, in consequence of a polite message from him to say he would come any morning when convenient to Mr Hood. All the Animal tribe are well, one of the Beautiful Cats made us a visit and we gave the best entertainment in our power. The joy she exprest was as if her old friends were returnd; was that so and in perfect Health, Mr Hood and I coud feel no greater joy. However we trust that Heaven has the Blessing of Health to bestow, on which so many others depend. It is true it has been witherd for a time, but the Benign Hand of Providence very frequently suffers these evils to prevail for a time from whence arises the greatest Mercies. May your Ladyship and the Earl of Chatham fully experience this, is the most earnest wish of Mr Hood and, My Dearest Madam, your most faithful Humble Servant

M Hood

We are to all the sweet little people everything they can desire.

Chatham's resignation from the office of Lord Privy Seal and virtual head of the Cabinet will have been a blow to Molly Hood, ever conscious of rank and importance, and to her husband for the loss of a powerful patron. But she writes generously:

Harley Street
Oct 22nd 1768

We are so sensible to the Earl of Chatham's warm and delicate feeling towards the King, and the good of the publick, that his Noble Nature must have sufferd extremely from the weight he had upon him, the being discharged of which will we make no doubt bring about his recovery. . . And the time may come when he may break forth again to renew his good deeds. He is with held for a time perhaps, only to exalt him the more hereafter. . . Pardon me for saying so much but where the Heart is touched, it is Natural to go to great lengths.

1769 finds the Hoods visiting Stowe and Wotton. The Stowe visit begins a sort of plain-speaking friendship between two forthright people, Hester's eldest brother Lord Temple and Molly Hood:

Sunning Hill
Sept the 3rd 1769

It is impossible to say how much the absence of your Chearful Society was lamented at Stowe... But the Beauties of the place so far from sympathising with our gloomy aspects were adornd in all their brilliancy which made Lord Temple often cry out that day when he obligingly drove me round the gardens: 'they have not seen Stowe, how unlucky they did not give us a day more.' We past a week there, being very kindly pressd to do so, which made us not a little happy, as we cou'd not fail of having very pleasing reflections upon the restoration of Domestic Harmony and happiness in a family always united in worth, though seperated for a time [a reference to the protracted quarrel between Temple and Chatham]

On moving direct from Stowe to Wotton, twelve miles away the Hoods should

have passed our time very agreeably by the obliging reception we found, had not Mrs Grenville been much out of order with her old complaints [she died three months later.] Your Ladyship's letter to her came in time to give us the Satisfaction of hearing that you arrived and lay at Hayes the second night from Stow[e] but our pleasure was allayed by your account of your dear Lord having been too free with the fruit, which occasion'd a little disorder in his Bowels.

They are now

again become quite the Cottagers [at Sunninghill] to pursue regularly the plan for Health in early hours and exercise. The medicinal spring we find very salutary, and the rides, drives and Air are really fine.

Later that year and throughout most of the two following, the Hoods in their kindly way, concerned with the depressing effect of Chatham's chronic illness on the life of the family, are engaged with entertaining the three elder children, John, Lord Pitt, Hester and Harriot, and sometimes all five.

Harley Street
Friday Dec 15th 1769

Mr Hood and I were happy to find by your obliging letter that your cold was going off. The Gout has of late been so friendly to my Lord, that it be a sort of Ingratitude to Suspect the Visit [of the gout] he was now made will be unkindly long or that a happy interval of ease, will not take place at the proper time. Tuesday is the day fixd for the Jubilee. Our Young Friends I hope will be perfectly well to receive the entertainment; if they come on Monday we shall feel our selves the more obliged by lengthening out the pleasure of their being with us. I send this by Mr Gallini [dancing master] that your Ladyship may settle with him the hour of his coming to our House on Wednesday morning.

Harley Street
Sunday Mar the 18th 1770

Your Ladyship's kind Note brought by Lord Pitt demands my best thanks... The gallant resolution you have taken of going to the Mansion House on Thursday is indeed no small Undertaking especially as all the implements for the present mode of dressing are so much in disarray, however a Noble Spirit conquers all things [in the end they did not go]. Your Ladyship will find that Lord Pitt lay at the Lodgings in Pall Mall, which I think you will approve, as we are so circumstanced as to have a very complaining Family and one of the Maids confined to her Bed.

Molly Hood was a close friend of the much admired Elizabeth Montagu and appears to have acted as a sort of intermediary between this famous lady and the Chathams.

> Harley Street
> May the 8th 1770

> Mrs Montagu has fixed on Saturday next to dine at Hayes in hope of its being a convenient one to be received, but shoud it not be so, be so good to let me know, to have it deferd to another day next week.

She enlists Mrs Montagu's help in the arrangements for the Pitt children to see Garrick at the play. In an undated note from Mrs Montagu, addressed 'To Mrs Hood', this lady writes:

> I have this moment left Mr Garrick - he is ill, and acts no acts on Monday. Tuesday I have fixed for our young friends, you must send your servant to keep nine places in the Center front Box, the place of all places to be seen and to see in. If the young people pant to see Mr Garrick perform you may assure them from me, that for them, and them only, I will engage him to appear at their summons. Adieu my dear Madam.

In the event Mrs Montagu herself accompanied the young Pitts to the theatre. Molly Hood in an undated letter, probably of 1770 or early in 1771 writes:

> Mr Hood had the Honour of your Ladyship's Note, and will immediately communicate the contents of it. We are happy to hear the young people returnd well and had received so much pleasure from the Spectacle in the Haymarket, and the polite attentions of Mrs Montagu, who I had fears for, as her fatigue was great and she exposed herself to the cold by setting behind her company just where the door of the room opened to the street; however she will not own she sufferd as your Ladyship has seen by her letter to me inclosed last night to Lord Chatham. I hope when you mean to go to her, you will let me know, and command me or my coach if of any use to your Ladyship. Shoud Lord Pitt gain permission to appear at the House of Lords on Tuesday, Mr Hood will attend him there and bring him to Harley Street, where a well aird Bed will be at his service.

She is called upon (or perhaps offered) to shop for the girls:

> [Harley Street]
> Jany the 10th 1771

> I am afraid I am brought into disgrace at Hayes for the choice I made and for not apprehending that Blue without any mixture was the prevailing wish of the Young Ladys. I went this morning to fall on if I possibly coud with the last idea given, but unfortunately without the success hoped for, and now being confined to that Shop, the change must be deferd till the middle of next week, if the Blue

water'd flowered Tabby [a kind of taffeta] has the preference to any other of the silks Mr Pane has sent, who is so desirous to oblige, that he begd he might send those of the favour colour I looked at by the Bromley coach this afternoon. The trimming I cannot get without bespeaking, as it ought to match exactly. The delay I flatter my self will not be any great mortification as the weather will not allow of any amusement, the streets being in some parts of the Town dangerous, and the best company will be in the country till the meeting of the two Houses.

The annual round of spas takes in Cheltenham not previously visited by the Hoods and therefore inspected with a fresh and lively eye; they were well pleased with what they found:

Cheltenham
July 5th 1771

We are flatterd with the prospect of receiving benefit from this salutary spring, as it agrees perfectly. Mr Hood now can eat with an appetite and bears a great deal of exercise without his usual langour. He explores the country and finds out for me variety for my drives, though I am not unentertaind when I am confined to those of a little distance, as there is a great deal to please the eye. The meadows are parklike ground and many fine trees scatterd about of oak, elm etc. The cornfields very spacious and Heaven's Blessing is upon them, to employ the hands and gladden the Hearts of Many, I never saw such luxuriant crops. The boundarys are Hills prettily diversified in shape and cultivation, and so intermixd with objects that a life and gaity is given the whole... [There is] so much rural felicity in this place that we shall be sorry to leave it on the 22nd, though thank God in every Situation we possess content, which is more than a Duke of Grafton or a Lord Suffolk can say.

From Bath in September, after the usual anxious comment on Chatham's state of health, and praise for Doctor Addington's 'salutary advice and cordial comfort', she continues with a reference to public calumny directed to Chatham:

Wednesday Sept 18th 1771
[Bath]

This moment your second letter is brought me, for which a thousand thanks are due. We are rejoic'd that my Lord goes on mending which is a proof that the gout has taken his leave. We honour the People of Exeter for their distinguishing so properly [Freedom of the City] and hope their example will be followed in other Cities, and my Lord only wants to have justice done to his publick and private character. How monstruous absurd is the turn given to his visit into the West etc. etc. They begin to tear him and to take every method to impose upon the uninformed. Tho', in general, all they say is to be despised, yet there is an article in one of the papers we wish to have cleared up relating to the War Office accounts.

and Elizabeth Montagu's visit to Hagley

The tenth Muse Mrs Montagu and Muse's Friend Mr Garrick went from Hagley before the Foreigners came there... You must forgive a Water Drinker's scrawl.

For the last three months of the year the Hoods were at Greenwich, where Captain Hood was Treasurer, or in their Harley Street house. They were however as restless as others of their same status and wealth and, ignoring the difficult travelling, paid frequent visits to stay with friends, or by the day:

Royal Hospital
Oct 30th 1771

The weather being fine we enjoy it as much as we can, and make little excursions frequently, which renders our situation at Greenwich not unpleasant. We spend all our mornings abroad, and are shut up in the evenings which suits our Health, and our Taste. I have got my old Friend Mrs Ives with us who is an agreeable companion. Mr Hood entertains us with reading two hours, as soon as Tea is over, so we go on with comfort, and think retirement no bad thing.

Family news predominate in the letters for the next few years, interspersed with court, society and political gossip. The engagement of Hester Chatham's niece, Charlotte Grenville and subsequent marriage to Sir Watkin Williams Wynn calls forth excited comment from Molly Hood, beginning in this same letter of October 30th:

I take it for granted that timely information has been given at Burton of the Great, the important event that is very soon to take place in your family. I have had it only from common fame, which says a Ball was given by Sr Watkin Williams [where], Miss Grenville had a fall in dancing, received some little hurt, which drew the attentions of the company and he in particular distinguished himself by giving his [attention] in a peculiar manner. All powerful Love seized him, the consequence of which was a journey to Stow[e], where he proposed himself, and Cart Blanch, and was of course joyfully received. Lord Temple is in great spirits. The young Lady, and Miss Stapleton, I hear are in town, very busyily employed in preparing wedding cloaths.

Greenwich
Dec 3rd 1771

No wedding yet takes place. The Lover lays upon a couch, the young Lady constantly there - the Mother employing her to make Tea. Many tears have been shed, but are now pretty well dryed away, and a countenance resumed of chearfulness. Five thousand pounds worth of jewels are added to those given by the Mother, and every other article of expense bear the same proportion, to the amount in all, twenty thousand pounds. It is well the Estate is entaild else Vanity woud soon see an end to it.

Back in London for the winter, she writes on Christmas Day, but without mention of the festival; the letter contains a hint of criticism of John Pitt's way of life:

Harley Street
Dcr the 25th 1771

We are sorry that Lord Pitt has been indisposed, a little moderation in his pleasurable exercises is necessary to be observed, and then the Brushing Hounds[4] will be the best specific. . . Since we left Greenwich a little shock of an earthquake was felt. In this great Metropolis we seem to want an alarm from Heaven, till then, the care to secure our selves from Thieves and Housebreakers who are becoming such Artists, that Bolts and Bars do not avail; our doors and shutters are filld with Nails to prevent pieces from being cut out for an entrance, which was done at a House in our Street very lately.

Charlotte Grenville's wedding is to take place at Stowe.

Harley Street
Decr 26th 1771

I wrote so lately to your Ladyship that I have little more to say than to beg our sincere and warm congratulation may be received at Fair Burton upon the happy marriage which is celebrating at Stowe, with every mark no doubt of that joy the friends assembled can shew upon the occasion. The Bride woud rather dispense with her Uncle's jokes I believe, if they are of the sort I heard when I met him at Lord Lyttelton's.

Three weeks later she has been to see the wedding presents and to hear about the ceremony.

Jan 18th 1772

Upon the late wedding, formal visits have been paid, on all sides, and Lady Williams Wynn has allowed me since to make her a morning visit. Sr Watkin only was with her, so I was at liberty to see her jewels, the Bridal suit[e], and a guilt dressing plate, that last a present from his mother to Lady Henrietta Williams Wynn, very fine and a full Table of it. Her jewels consist of a necklace, earing[s], stomacher, Bouquet sleeve knots, ornaments for the Hair, all very beautifully set and of great value. She was presented in a white sutten with a little silver flower, covered almost with a silver triming that was light and pretty and perhaps genteeler than if it had been richer. To day she is to be in a gold striped stuff, mixd with colours, and a triming assorted to it. Her behaviour I was pleased with, modesty and ease with a proper degree of politeness. There was a great check to the jollity intended at Stowe, by Lord Temple's gone and the Bride being far from well for some days, owing I suppose to the agitation of her spirits and hurrying down to Stowe on the wedding day without a female friend or any refreshment but a cold chine packed into the chaise. A strange diet for a Bride; one shoud have thought she had been going to a Fox Chase instead of a marriage Feast. The conduct of the whole and his Lordship's pleasantry upon the occasion has been food for the Tea Tables. I believe you will wish him at a distance when your daughters marry.

The affairs of Molly Hood's Lyttelton family are understandably much in her mind and in her letters; in particular the unpredictable behaviour of the heir Thomas, and the sorrow and anxiety he brings to his father. But Mrs Hood tries to see good in him:

Sunday Feb 23rd 1772

Mr Lyttelton [Thomas] was here yesterday. He spoke of the Honour Lord Chatham had done him, with a sensibility that bespoke Virtue. I really think that upon many occasions he has Noble Sentiments and that a time may come when they may spread forth in his actions. A young man, or rather youth, thrown out into the great World, with the reins about his Neck and unlimited credit, to indulge very strong passions, and then being at once curbed, it can not be a matter of wonder that he fell into great Vices and distressed situations. . . He certainly has judgement to distinguish the good or bad in characters, therefore it is to be hoped he will embrace the one and cast the other in his own. Poor Lady Valentia [Lord Lyttelton's daughter] is in a deplorable way, debts surrounding her. My Lord [Valentia] in Ireland, attacked in his property from three quarters, and his cause still suspended and he liable in his own person to fall back into the way of life he was happily drawn from. Lord Lyttelton is born to Domestick Evils beyond belief.

She has more news of the Wynns, now back from their northern travels

March the 12th 1772

Lady W-Wynne is returnd vastly well. Sr Watkin not so, but bleeding and other disciplin will set him to rights. He prudently drank Lemonade instead of wine in Shropshire, else he might have suffered greatly, as drinking prevaild so much, that all the gentlemen at his Ball, were not fit to mix in it, tho they did, which was distressful to Lady Williams.

Of all Lady Chatham's correspondents, only Molly Hood, possibly from the jealousy of which she accuses her, appears to dislike Catherine Stapleton, friend and kinswoman of the Grenvilles, and eventually resident companion at Burton until Hester Chatham's death.

Harley Street
March 18th 1772

Jealousy begins to appear already and a foundation for enmity seems to be laying in the minds of all those Mrs Stapleton has influence over against Mr Lyttelton; your Ladyship will judge of it by the inclosed copy of a letter I had occasion to write to her, that I might not be subject to be rudely treated any more. A quarrel I am sure, I woud wish to avoid, and the least seperation. She has not however taken the least notice since, and I have not met her any where and this is the first time I have mentiond what I have related. The conversation arose between us by my asking her if she had seen Lord Lyttelton, as he had a charming letter and delightful verses lately sent him. She replied No, neither do I desire it, I wish he was gone, I wish he was gone, I really thought her Head was turnd, but I found by her not having heard of them, she had taken an Idea that they were young Lyttelton's, instead of Lord Chatham's, so that part may [be] cleard up as soon as her burst of passion woud give me time for it.

Still fuming, she writes a week later on the same subject:

I am happy that your Ladyship approves of my conduct, if I know myself, I rather err in passing over too much than in resenting, and if the conversation had been a private one, silence upon it afterwards would have been my option, but it being resumd by her again, I always was in danger of the same sort of Treatment which it became necessary to put a stop to. I writ I thought in so guarded a way that she might have thought fit to answer it, and returns of civility might have taken place again as usual, but as it is near a month since any intercourse has been it appears that the part taken is to drop it, on her side, which to be sure is absurd to the last degree.

From about this time the Hoods actively engage themselves in attempts to sell Hayes Place, and so relieve the ever increasing financial pressures on the Chathams. Many of Molly Hood's letters over the next few years treat of their, unsuccessful, efforts to find a purchaser or a tenant. In pursuing this aim, and perhaps to get an overall view of the property, they go to stay for a few days in the empty house.

> Hayes
> Monday July 13 1772

> The short time we have before we expect to be summond to Hagley, made us impatient to embrace the friendly invitation of taking up our residence here, which we have done since Thursday, and for three days lived eight hours in the day abroad. Mr Hood early finishing his rides, and drinking at the salutary Well at Bromley, devoted himself to sauntering with me, and a real joy we both felt in treading that ground so distinguished by the lustre of those characters to whom it owes its various beauties... Mr Hood carrys this to Bromley, he is a good postman for all the neighbourhood.

They visit Burton and the return journey is described, including a stopover at Mrs Montagu's:

> Royal Hospital
> Saturday Octr the 10th 1772

> We chose the road that was new to us and therefore slept at Frome, instead of Bath. The next day we proceeded as far as Hungerford in order to breakfast with Mrs Montagu on Wednesday, which we accomplished very exactly to her time, and passed six hours most agreeably... Your Ladyship may easily imagine what the chief Topicks of conversation were, as we had been at Hagley and came from Fair Burton; lively and witty as the subjects gave occasion.

and as ever anxious for Mrs Montagu to meet Hester Chatham:

> Nothing she [Mrs Montagu] said woud give her more pleasure that to pass a week under your roof, as she loved to see Dignity in private Life. Had she ever received an invitation, you woud have been sure of her obeying with alacrity.

From about this time onwards the Chathams fell ever more deeply under obligation to the Hoods, not only for help in trying to find a buyer for Hayes, but also as a source of loans. Mrs Hood, seemingly ever dazzled by Chatham's past fame, and perhaps also from a degree of nobler sentiment, writes with a tact and charm not normally associated with creditors. The services required came from Hood, but all the money was from his wife's family, the wealthy Wests.

Most flatteringly kind your Ladyship has been in every expression of your friendship to Mr Hood and me, which we prize more than I can pretend to say. Our obligations to you and your worthy Lord command every tribute due [which] hearts and understandings can give were they enriched with those powers which belong to your own; but such as we possess, like the widow's mite, we present very cordially. . . Mr Hood begs pardon, if your Ladyship did commission him, when at Burton, to transmit ten pounds to the poor woman at Portsmouth, as he did not understand or it slipd his memory. Upon your letter he immediately sent a bank bill by post to his Brother, which has been paid to her and her receipt for it he has. She has lost her old Habitation from being turned out of the gun wharf for drunkeness.

And on the so far unsuccessful search for a buyer for Hayes:

It is certainly a bad time of year to strike any Bargain, and possibly if a different one is suggested, it may be prejudicial to the whole. Another spring may bring forth the completion of our wishes, when things are more settled in regard to money, which at present is hardly to be got from any Quarter. . . This alone may possibly be the reason that Hayes is not inquired after.

But all is not business; a stream of family and social news and gossip, and sometimes a measure of political comment, continues to flow to Burton Pynsent, apparently at Hester Chatham's request, as we learn from a significant sentence with which a letter of October 1772 begins:

As your Ladyship may not think I am unmindful of any of your commands, I will relate a few of the little anecdotes very lately come to my knowledge.

Jan 21st [1773]

All the family from Stowe arrived yesterday in perfect Health, but a little accident has now confind your Brother, but hope no other consequence will happen from it. He went out in a Hackney chair last night, and in his return another chair of the same sort in passing by that he was in, with violence threw down his men, and the chair was carried by the force into the middle of the Street and broke to pieces. My Lord received no other Hurt but upon his arm - which is a little swelld up and he contents him self with only the application of arquebusade. It may properly be in the papers worse represented, therefore I wishd you to know the true state, lest you might take an alarm.

Molly had a great eye for dress:

Harley Street
January 23rd 1773

Mr and Mrs [Thomas] Pitt, Mr Wilkinson [father in law of Thomas], Mrs Montagu and Miss [Elizabeth] Carter honoured us with their company at dinner a few days ago, all in great spirits, which produced chearful conversation. Wit and humour made scandal go glibly down, and a proper ridicule upon folly and vanity; some of your relations had a share of the latter, which I will represent.

Lady G at court, in a garment of Feathers, the idea just coming out of the Nest. The fine gentleman her son, had a Silver Tissue, compleat suit, embroidered all over with gold squares and spangles in the middle. On New Years Day, he had on a suit with a Border of Pearls; what fair Lady strung them was not represented. In another suit I heard of among many more, all full of pretty fancies, were Buttons with Cupids, enamelld, and other charming devices to adorn etc.

Feb 23rd 1773

I think there is nothing stirring worth your knowledge, at least we mix so little with the World, that we are ignorant if there is. The Masquerade, I will just name for the entertainment of my young friends, as their cousin Lady Williams was distinguished by her dress, which was very advantageous to her person. It was a vandike, very finely adornd throughout, her hair in ringlets upon her forehead became her much. A vast number of jewels, well disposed among which was one that Sr Watkin purchased lately that belongd to the late princess dowager, bought by a Jew for four hundred and fifty pounds at the late auction of all her jewels etc. etc. and repurchased for six hundred the next day. This was a single drop of pearl which was presented by Sr Watkin to Lady Williams, and was worn hanging from her neck. Her finery only appeard at the Pantheon, for at Lady Darlington's where were two hundred masques, she and Sr Watkin were coverd over with callimapea, which gave offence to come with a covering of their splendid dresses, which woud have been better understood to have shown there than any where else.

Sunday Mar 21st 1773

I wrote on Saturday by the post to your Ladyship, I now therefore shall continue my self to a few anecdotes which may not be unacceptable. To begin with that which is interesting, there is a faint hope of a purchaser for Hayes. Mr Hood dined lately with Lord Shelburne who told him he had recommended it to Mr Tollemache and that they meant to go there together to make their observations on that sweet place. . .

Now I proceed to little occurrences and court intrigues. The two Duchesses receive company twice a week, and a party is forming for the Dukes. A discovery was made yesterday, by Mr Hood and Colonel Maitland in their ride. The Duchess of Gloster passd them alone in her coach, but in return from Hamstead Heath, the Duchess of Argyle had been taken into the Duchess of Gloster's coach, and the post chaise of the Duchess of Argyle followed at a little distance. It is said the Duke of Argyle is much dissatisfied. . .

Poor Lord Lyttelton is much to be pittied, more Domestick evils come to his share than could be imagined, but when he takes his part, he has a happy method of calming his mind, and becomes the same man again. The rapid match, and rapid separation [of son Thomas] have been fatally bad to all parties. The young man took a disgust to his wife as soon almost as she became his.

She can now find nothing good to say about Thomas Lyttelton:

Tuesday evening 23rd [March 1773]

Domestick concerns in Hill Street which are now come to their crisis, Mrs Lyttelton and Lord Lyttelton being determined upon a separation. The plan to be proposed to Mr Lyttelton is to give him his choice of an amicable or legal one, she to have five hundred a year at present and a thousand if he survives his father. . . He has lived for those last two months with only laying at Home, now and then at the gaming Table at the Savoir Vivre, and with women. . . A dreadfull fate he has brought upon him self, by his giving way to tumultuous and unwarrantable passions, lost to his family and the World.

A rare reference to naval affairs and a war scare:

April 21st 1773

It is very certain that a great equipment is ordered, and three pounds advance to every Seaman. This intelligence came forth but yesterday and it is supposd was from the deliberations at the Council the preceding evening. The Stocks fell amazingly upon it. Evils surround us and I am afraid will multiply. As an individual, a war is very tremendous to my mind in various ways. The two brothers [Hood] will not be idle if there shoud be Action to call them forth.

Nevertheless

The gaity of the Metropolis exceeds all discription, three Masquerades in one week produced the utmost astonishment in the foreign Ambassadors, who said it was beyond anything abroad, at the time of their festivities. . . I am just told that the Fleet will consist of sixteen ships of the Line, six frigates, three sloops, two Fire ships, one Hospital ship.

In May the panic is over 'and the ships are orderd to return to their different ports as Guard ships'.

The Hoods now seriously consider acquiring a permanent home in the desired county of Somerset. The announcement of this intention contains an oblique observation intended no doubt as a hint to the improvident Chathams:

Tuesday July 20th 1773

Mr Hood has had it much at Heart to make such a purchase as might put a country residence in our power but that he has been disappointed. His indulgence woud do everything for me but we must square our expenses to our income, which will not allow of two Houses. He is gone to Town today, and will call at Mrs Wulbier's from whom you will soon learn a further account of us.

Both the Chathams and the Hoods have turned down invitations to meet for a combined visit to Hagley. Mrs Hood gives their own reasons in this same letter:

The Hagley party will be much too lively for our quiet spirits, which rather seek the decent chearfull Society of valuable friends, who direct their talents to the benefit as well as entertainment of those who converse with them; so I believe we shall steer but one course this year, and if I hold out to another I must give up all thoughts of going from Home as age and infirmities are making quick advances, almost to make me afraid of a present undertaking, but my ardour to see friends I love and respect, and Mr Hood's objecting to go without me prevail, and will carry me once again into Somersetshire if no evil arises in the meantime.

The purchase of the estate of Cricket St Thomas is now completed; a warm and excited invitation follows:

The Lady of the Manor of Cricket St Thomas presents her respects to the Lady Farmeress of Fair Burton, and shall be joyfull to see with her their worthy Lord, their Lovely Daughters and their Hero, the little Seaman, and the Sea Bathers [John and William at Lyme] will be summoned to the meeting repast at the new farm of two hundred year[s] old, where the Lords and Ladys, esqrs etc. shall be seated at an immovable Table, which shall be spread with homely but wholesome cheer. The guests of course will find a Hearty Welcome. Fair weather - or else nothing can take place.

Chaises will be ready to accommodate those who wish to explore and a certain mare will be brought of course. The effusions will not take place till the looked for Day, when the Hall shall have on the floor a winnow sheet.

It is not known whether any of the socially shy family accepted this invitation. Perhaps there was not a fine enough day for it.

Correspondence resumes on the Hoods return to London after a visit to Burton. Lord Lyttelton has died and the behaviour of his son Thomas on his succession to the peerage and to Hagley is watched with interest and reported at length. Always concerned wherever possible to find some good in the young man, Molly Hood's blame for his shortcomings now switches to the wife. The letter begins with a graceful thanks for the visit:

Harley Street
Oct 23rd 1773

Nothing sure can be more pleasing to the mind than the mutual intercourse of kindness between friends, and my dear Lady Chatham keeps that up in the highest degree. What shall I say for your last welcome proof of it, received last night; where you so lively draw us to the sweet and amiable circle in the dressing room, indeed we were so happy when we enlarged it, that you may always think us present in thoughts and wishes. Our journey was rendered extremely pleasant by the fine weather and very delightful roads, which gave a spirit to our preceedings, and with ease we came to eat our mutton at Home the fourth day. In consequence Mr Hood, having wrote to Lord Chatham from the Devizes, I deferred till now the acknowledging our feelings upon the time we passd at fair Burton, where all tend to inspire respect, Love and gratitude. We coud not want therefore in conversation in travelling, when such Topics were so recent to engage our hearts to dwell upon

and continues with Lyttelton affairs and description of a classic matrimonial dispute:

We met Mr [W.H.] Lyttelton about Hammersmith who promised to dine with us today... [His nephew Thomas] deplores extremely not seeing his Father and woud give the world he had been present at the last melancholy scene. His Heart is certainly penetrated and his resolutions at present correspond with it, except in regard to his wife, who has cut up every possibility of a reconciliation by her deviding the Father from the Son. Every thing else might have been removed on his side had she not taken this step, but I suppose when she did it she was aware of it, and as the separation was entirely her seeking, she meant it shoud continue and therefore considered what woud render her situation the most desirable, which was to have the countenance and protection of the late Lord

Lyttelton and all his friends, and to receive all the honours and advantages that his house in Town and at Hagley coud give, where she was to be mistress of both. My Lord left her his House in Hill Street for six months. The furniture being the present Lord's makes it very awkward for her to go into and there is a strange report, but I think and hope it cannot be true, that people are ordered by her to guard it, all entrance denied; a thousand idle reports will be spread, which to prevent she woud do wisely to get another and relinquish that immediately.

In this long letter she notes that

the Irish Estates are in danger of being taxed with two shillings in the pound if those who are possessed of them are absent. A bitter pill to many should it take place

and ends with a further reference to the new Lord Lyttelton:

Mr Lyttelton has just left us, our discourse has been entirely upon the subject of Hagley and what passed there since Lord Lyttelton's death. He said his nephew had conducted himself with the greatest propriety and the plans he had resolved upon were very sensible. He called at Stowe and represented there matters of fact which all tended to the honour of Lord Lyttelton, who he thinks must do well if he will but follow the judgement of not being led away by his passions.

Two months later with some rather predictable news on the Absentee Landlord's bill

[Dec 1st 1773]

Lord Shelburne has just been with me, he so good to call from the Cold Bath which he frequents. He came to Town last night and was happy to find that the idea was at an end of taxing the Irish absentees.

Twenty-two letters of 1774 survive. News and comment on family, Lytteltons, Wests and Pitts, and friends predominate. On the death of Chatham's rich Dorset patron from whom he was expected to inherit a fortune but did not owing to Thomas Hollis's sudden demise, she writes

Harley Street
Jan 6th 1774

It is very true my dear Lady Chatham that we do feel deeply the important events which touch our worthy good friends at Fair Burton. The loss of that most excellent man Mr Hollis is a cutting one indeed.

In the same letter, William Henry Lyttelton's second marriage:

Mr Lyttelton has aquainted Lord Chatham with the approaching change of his condition. Moderation and a rational expectation of happiness are very characteristick of the Lyttelton family. The Lady has no fortune at present.

Attempts by the Hoods to sell Hayes continue but there is a rumour that the Chathams intend to return there to live. This does not meet with Molly Hood's approval and backed by a conversation with Lord Temple she does not mince words:

Harley Street
Feb 13th 1774

A report has been spread that upon you having let your farms at Burton, that of fixing again at Hayes were Lord Chatham's intentions, but I think we have pretty well checked those ideas out. Lord Temple who I was alone with had heard and gave credit to what has been said of the kind intentions of Mr Hollis and lamented very much that they were not executed. This led me very naturally to join with him and to wish that Hayes, which still remained a dead weight, was parted with, as there would be a great difference in receiving the interest of the money it ought to sell for and getting very little for it, that your family were now coming out into the world and called for a large supply even upon an economical plan.

However a few weeeks later, she accepts the inevitable, given Chatham's whims and fancies, with a good grace:

Harley Street
Mar 3rd 1774

We begin to count the days for the removing all the dear and most invaluable family from Fair Burton to sweet Hayes, where we hope for a joyfull meeting, by seeing health and happiness throughout...

We have been full of dining parties from the weddings of Mr Lyttelton and Mr Balchen West and shall be glad when they are over.

Captain Hood's post as treasurer of Greenwich Hospital since 1766, has come under official scrutiny, resulting in a demand upon him ex. officio to deposit £5000 as security. Molly takes the opportunity obliquely to compare Hood's attitude to money affairs with that of the Chathams:

Sunday evening March 13th 1774

The Town is full of gaity but not of the sort for us to partake of; content and repose is what we chiefly aim at, but even that has been broke in upon by a malignant spirit that has arose among the Direstors of Greenwich Hospital and affected the office of Treasurer in a very unprecedented manner and I may add oppressive one. For by a Minute of the Board, five thousand pounds was ordered to be laid out in the funds... and some of them said they did not understand that the Treasurer should have any money in his hands... Mr Hood immediately transferred stock of the amount of five thousand pounds by which he loses twenty per cent to his office this year [which] I suppose will not be anything to him; but this really is not the worst of it, as he has the fortitude and resolution to form his mind, and way of living , to his circumstances... This unexpected call for five thousand pounds and the remaining sum for his purchase with the promise of a thousand pounds to Lord Chatham, has given him many anxious thoughts... Nothing he has so much at Heart as to answer any wishes of his Lordship and in this he hopes to succeed with his Banker if not some other way.

In July they go to Dorset, mainly it would seem to clear up the problems left behind in the house rented by Chatham and occupied by him for a long period in the previous year, the lease still in force:

Lyme
July 16th 1774

We got to Lyme the fourth day and by leading our two young Horses they performed very well. Our three female servants got in before in a post chaise, to get things in order, so in a few days we shall be settled, and reap the advantage of Lord and Lady Chathams goodness which is always operating to our pleasure wherever we are. The young woman who had charge of the House has aquitted her self so ill that we chose to have nothing to say to her after we took an inventory of what is delivered to us. It is reported of her that many Beds have been found sheeted and lain in at a time and seamen have been seen coming out of the House and riots have been heard... She pretends there are accounts to settle and therefore we cannot do anything in it but only said we had no occasion for her services. Fleas and dirt she has left, but the comfort is we have cleanly servants to get rid of both soon.

Still on the fleas and with practical suggestions for the care of the house:

Lyme
July 18th 1774

I have wrote so lately to your Ladyship, would not have troubled you so soon again, but from a view of your geting clear of two people that are very unfit to be intrusted with the care of anything; we have now more at large heard of their goings on. The female let out the bedrooms for threepence a week each and they were well filled; no wonder then that we found what such company must naturally leave behind, and it was well we had no other impediments to the pleasure of being here, than offensive smell, dirt and fleas in great abundance, all which we shall however get rid of by degrees with care and a good look out...
For the future Lord Chatham may put the care of the House and Garden upon a much more secure and less expensive footing if he thinks proper, as Mr and Mrs Padecombe have offered their good offices to find a staid and steady person to lock up the house when uninhabited, and open and air it properly for a trifle, and likewise a man now and then to clear the garden of weeds; this is all that it calls for, as every sort of thing it produces will be had upon easier terms from the market.

In a final letter from Lyme, Mrs Hood looks into the question of repair liabilities:

Lyme Regis
Oct 22nd 1774

The collector has been to collect the Taxes for Mrs Code's house; we not being certain what Lord Chatham was to pay, desired Mr Smith to show us the Lease, in which is specified one hundred and five pounds a year rent, taking rise last Michaelmas, to which is added the Window Tax and to the charity and poor. These belong to the agreement on Lord Chatham's side, with the repairs of Windows only. All other repairs belong to Mrs Code, and it is well they do, as the house and out-houses are in a most shattered, ruinous condition.

The big event for the Chatham family in 1774 took place at the year's end with the marriage of the eldest daughter, Lady Hester Pitt to Charles, Viscount Mahon, later the third Earl Stanhope.

Harley Street
Dec 20th 1774

My dear Madam

The happy knot being tyed, it is impossible to withold my pen from breaking in a moment to join in the joy that naturally surrounds Hayes and Chevening on a union that must bring lasting happiness to the two illustrious Houses. Mr Hood, and I, shall take the first morning to pay our warm and sincere congratulations to all parties when we think we shall be the least troublesome.

I am my dearest Madam your Ladyship's most faithful humble servant
M Hood

In the following two years, 1775 and 1776, three domestic topics predominate in the letters: Harriot's London debut and subsequent social life, carried on from the Hood's Harley Street house under the joint chaperonage of Mrs Hood and the newly married Hester Mahon; the Hood life at South Cricket; James Pitt's naval education. In the wider sphere the American war understandably draws frequent comment and few letters fail to mention Chatham's health; the Hoods' financial help to him does not pass unnoticed.

Harley Street
Mar 14th 1775

Your young people my dear Lady Chatham are all so amiable and behave with such a propriety that they command love and admiration. What other impressions of a little deeper sort the fair maiden has made, time must discover. A certain marquis was at Lady Middleton's last night and afterwards at the Festino, where the lovely maid appeared in all elegance and beauty. He did not approach her at either of these places but I shoud imagine however that his eyes did her justice at least. Mr Hood and I do not allow of your objection given, we shall expect and hope to see Mr James Pitt to morrow. In case he comes then Mr Hood will attend him to Deptford, but if not he will defer going there till the Thursday following with him. As your Ladyship will hear from Lady Mahon I will say nothing of the motions of the sweet sisters.

We wish my Lord coud make more hasty advances, but as they are sure ones to his perfect recovery, we must be contented to wait for that happy event.

Adieu my dear Madam, most truly yours
M Hood

There are problems at Cricket from labour shortages:

South Cricket
July 10th 1775

We have just begun to mow which must make a late harvest, tho' a very fine one I think it will be. Not a labourer can we get to smooth a hoe and make things neat about us; and as to inside work to give tolerable conveniences, the trials we have made by our village jobbers have put us to double the expense of knowing workmen, and to our disappointment have been forced to undo what they did.

They are embarked on rebuilding, despite the uncertain political situation:

Cricket St Thomas
August the 3rd 1775

If it was not for the calamities which are thickening and fears for those who are dear to us, Mr Hood and I shoud feel our selves happy in our sweet retreat. We live as cottagers, in all rural simplicity, and are surrounded by those only who came by their labour, their daily bread. The gentry of the country take not any notice of us, I suppose from understanding that we are not in a proper situation to receive them. A lucky circumstance, as we can fill up our time without having it broke in upon. A great deal of business is going on, Haymaking now over and many avocations arise. Old Houses too are pulling down to make way for the farm House we are beginning upon for our humble dwelling next year.

In the spring of 1776 Harriot is in London staying with the Hoods, to take part in the balls and other entertainments of the season. But there are problems on this visit: her sister, Hester Mahon has had her first baby, Hester Stanhope, on 12th March and is not around therefore to assist Mrs Hood in the duties of chaperone, and undoubtedly this lady is feeling the strain as is evident in a number of letters written to Hester Chatham, three of them undated. The letters are of particular interest: from them we gain an insight into what it was like for women who sought, or were obliged to seek, to dress in the high fashion of the day.

[Harley Street]
[March 1776]

Delicate as it is, I cannot acquit myself without expressing to you my dearest Madam that Mr Hood and I did begin to be alarmd least that dignity should be wanting in Lady Harriot Pitt that markd Lady Mahon to the World as your well educated daughter, so sweet a creature as Lady Harriot is,in her disposition. Her understanding too so very superior, it is a pitty that she should receive the least infection from characters or persons that are much below her imitation; but from the mode of the Bon Ton, she is certainly in danger if not timely prevented. The dress of her Head which makes her sit double in a coach and her stays little at Bottom and broad at Top are certainly to be remarked with some other Ladys who like to be distinguished, and who may run some hazard to their healths by such enormous fashions. An old woman who sees so little of the great Ladys as I do can have very little weight on these occasions, and indeed tho' I know a line shoud be drawn, I am unequal to the task of saying how far it shoud go; a monitor too of some authority is necessary to keep the proper bounds. Your sweet daughter can only fail in these kind of things, that one so young must be naturally led into. Therefore the check that she will receive from your maternal goodness, and the advantage of returning to her prudent sister, her conduct I am sure will be adjusted to your Ladyship's wishes. I go with Lady Harriot to Mrs Tho. Pitt's ball this evening and will stay to bring her home. To Mrs J Pitt's I am not invited and was under a difficulty about a person proper to go with Lady Harriot Pitt. I am sorry to have her deprived of this expected pleasure but upon the whole it may be right to avoid it as Mrs Pitt has rather been deficient as well as her husband to your Ladyship and family in many points.

Lady Chatham, now aware that Harriot's visit has not been a total success has called her home in a hurry:

[Harley Street]
[March 1776]

The amiableness of sweet Lady Harriot Pitt's disposition was strongly markd by a chearfull readiness to comply with Your Ladyship's commands for her return, tho a Ball was in view, and almost secured to her by consent, if not approbation. I felt upon some circumstances in regard to Mrs J Pitt's conduct last night a regret for having so easily giving up my charming guest before Thursday and in consequence of it, I begd Lord Pitt, who said he shoud go easily to Hayes, to represent to your Ladyship my wishes for Lady Harriot staying with me to partake of the diversion of dancing, but the chaise is come before your Ladyship could receive them thro Lord Pitt. I must now return a million of thanks for the trust reposed in me which perhaps gave too strong a rise to my fears least any thing should be done that was not exactly conformable to your Ladyship's wishes, knowing how very exact and delicate you carry all your ideas for the conduct of your lovely offspring. I can with great truth assure your Ladyship that Lady Harriot is in all respects regarding the interior most perfect, and her conduct is sensible and modesty is the pleasing covering from which Lord Shelburne can discover many excellencies which she really possesses. It is only little things that your Ladyship has therefore to attend to regarding the dress of the times, to keep it a little down, and some little tricks which when unobserved she may fall into such as throwing out her chin more than usual, and bending forwards, which I took the liberty to put her in mind of, and which she obligingly tried to correct.

Explanations are still due for the not very happy events of Harriot's visit in March, resulting in her abrupt recall to Hayes:

Harley Street
April 15th 1776

I am afraid your Ladyship from your maternal care and tenderness received impressions I did not mean to convey. Indeed I shoud be very unjust to sweet Lady Harriot was I to say any thing she did was essentially wrong. I only apprehended the fashions of the times might draw her further than I judgd your Ladyship would like her to go, and therefore thought the apprising you of them woud be right, that the line might be drawn for her Ladyship to observe, it being quite out of my power to advise on many occasions when she was so good as to ask it. I own I felt a distress, well knowing the rectitude and propriety to be observed for a young Lady of her consideration at setting out in Life, and forming connections suitable to her rank. It has much grieved me that I should throw out my fears to your Ladyship before Mrs Pitt's ball, and I really was concerned at Lady Harriot's being abridged of that diversion, which I had no idea of, or when I wrote, of being deprived of her company till the day after it... I cannot wonder that Lady Harriot shoud be struck at the precipitate and unexpected summons to Hayes, and suggest other reasons that her good Mama's wanting her at home. The whole now being over, the subject had better not be resumed.

Towards the end of the year the American war, and the open support of France and Spain including the use of their ports to American ships, directed the thoughts and actions of the British government towards naval increase. Captain Hood's anxiety to return to active service, successful after the inevitable wheeling and dealing in high places, now finds an important place in his wife's letters.

[Harley Street]
Novr 29th 1776

Mr Hood, and I too, have early enterd into those ways of the World that are unavoidable. Business, and proper attentions to the high and mighty he has given throughout, and I have joind him only in family connections and friendly ones. On Wednesday he was at the King's Levee, who was gracious; so was her Majesty when he paid his duty at the drawing room the next day... A visit he made immediately after his arrival to Admiral Keppel, who received from Sir Hugh Palliser Lord Sandwich's desire of knowing whether it woud be agreeable to him (Keppel) to take command of the King's Fleet... Mr Hood has asked for the Alfred, tho' he coud not get a positive promise for her. He fixed upon a new ship that he need not be to change through the course of the war, should the natural enemies of this country bring on one.

In this same letter Mrs Hood reports on one of several conversations she has had with Lord Temple. These two understood each other:

Your Brother my dear Madam was here. He talked in that style, and when asked how he accounted for the warlike preparations and the assistance certainly given to the Americans, he only said in regard to the assistance given, it was only similar to what we gave to the Corsicans.

In an undated letter of this year she reports, rather unkindly perhaps, on another conversation with Temple about John Pitt's unexpected return from America and 'resignation' from the army:

[1776]

In the morning Lord Temple came and set with me an hour at least. He talked of publick and private affairs very freely. In regard to the latter they were confined to your family chiefly, as I always lead him that way in hopes to draw him to that sensibility towards them, as might produce essential kindness. He deplored the various and distressd situations occasiond by Lord Chatham's long illness to him, and his; that he was sorry the young man was thrown out of the army; that had not his father determined for him, he ought to have gone, as an officer was to obey orders without enquiring the fairness of them. I said I hopd there might a time come when he might return again to his profession in the military Line as many others had done... He answerd [that] Lord Chatham's son woud always find favour with all parties.

In the final year and a half before the watershed in Pitt family history of Chatham's death in May 1778, Molly Hood's letters continue on much the same lines as before, with perhaps more emphasis on Hood's coming departure to sea, on the loans to Chatham and on the naval career of James Pitt in which Captain Hood is closely involved. One letter of lyrical praise of Burton Pynsent stands apart from the others, devoid of double meanings and covert criticism, in its simple admiration for a beautiful place:

Cricket Lodge
Sept 20 1777

My dearest Madam

Health and pleasure I hope has arose from this joyous weather to Lord Chatham, your Ladyship and the whole House. It had so good an effect upon me, that on Thursday I ordered my chaise and made an excursion to Burton. I met Mr Jermyn who conducted me through the grounds and up the pillar, from whence my eyes were feasted with the gloriously enobled scenes so varied and enrichd, that it appeared as if nature had designed it for the present great owners of it. The Shepherd's Cott, tho humble, I found my self exalted in, and which I could with difficulty quit, so sweetly delightful the views were. The dairy farm was in remarkable beauty, the verdure there being fine. I could not go down to it, but recollected the charming drives I had at times with my dear Lady Chatham, in surveying all the diversified glories of the place... It may be a matter of wonder how I came to be alone; the truth is that Mr Hood was to have accompanied me but unsuspected business detain him at Home and my eagerness to embrace the opportunity fixd upon, least any disappointment should happen, was the reason. The riches of your farmyard now Harvest is in I was much struck with having never seen so many ricks together before. I visited all the rooms in the House and for the credit of the maid servant I must say there was more marks of method, exact care and cleanliness than I ever observed throughout elsewhere. The red bird and others I paid my compliments to. I eat my little dinner and drink in water prosperity to your whole House, and in about an hour after took my leave and returnd to drink tea with Mr Hood, who told me I had performd so well, he should not be afraid to trust me again, whenever I was disposed to make small sallies...

With the most perfect regard I am at all times,
My dear Lady Chatham's faithfull and affectionate Humble Servant,
M Hood

Eight months later Chatham is dead, Hood has hoisted his flag on *Robust*, taking James Pitt with him as acting lieutenant. The widow and the grass widow, are writing to one another; Hester is making use of 7 Harley Street for a London visit:

S. Cricket Lodge
July 11 1778

When I saw your hand I was in expectation that the happy event of Lady Mahon being brought to bed had taken place. I wish your maternal attentions are not too much for your own precious health, as I find even in the country that the heat has been very oppressive... I do not like of your being in our habitation without the sweet Lady Harriot Pitt, even for a day, as I know full well how, and in what way your mind would be filled with passd ideas. But let me entreat you my dear Lady Chatham to turn your thoughts as much as possible to the blessings you are still in possession of, such a young family who else can boast of, who feel your preservation of the utmost to their happiness, as well as advantage.

She is missing her own husband

My kind Mr Hood has so invariably been almost present since our separation,
and a summer cruize does not bring the dreadful ideas of a winter one.

Sadly, the following year an event occurred which was to involve the Hood and the
Pitt families and which caused a breach in the friendship, never properly healed: this
was at the first of the double courts martial of Admirals Keppel and Palliser when Hood
gave evidence, the veracity of which was brought into doubt. His explanation was later
accepted by the court. It must be conceded that the action of Lady Chatham and her
two elder sons in removing the youngest, James, from Hood's ship *Robust* was unkind
and uncalled for and beyond all normally accepted standards of friendship and
gratitude for sustained kindness and generosity.

A clue to the reason for this decision is to be found in Mrs Hood's first letter of 1779,
in which she conveys Hood's decision to withhold leave from James Pitt, which would
not have pleased his mother, and mentions all the officers from *Robust* may be called
to give evidence at the trial, a prospect which would have horrified the publicity-shy
Chatham family.

Harley Street
January 2d 1779

Mr Hood I parted with about one o'clock, which was after your Ladyship's
letter came. In answer therefore to that part of it relating to further leave of
absence, I am sorry to say that he thinks it quite improper in the state things are
that Mr J Pitt should seek so soon again such an indulgence. The first lieutenant
Mr Inglefield had only ten days granted him and Mr Lumley no more, who had
two hundred miles to go...
Mr Hood will be at Portsmouth tomorrow morning, and will have much
business not only in regard to the Robust, but [also] that which the sad and serious
court martial must necessarily occasion. Mr Keppel calls upon all the officers in
the Foudroyant, and possibly all those in the Robust may be summoned to give
evidence, another reason for all the Lieutentants to be forth coming.

Despite this setback to the friendship, the correspondence carries on for the rest
of the year much as before; but suppressed hurt and anger flares in a letter of late in 1780:

Cricket Lodge
Oct 25th 1780

When I answered Lady Harriot Pitt's letter, I had little expectation of giving
your Ladyship the trouble of making any remarks upon the subject of it. But as
your penetration is great, I must own that the air of dissatisfaction which you justly
observed appeard in my letter was what my Heart has felt for many, many months
passd, and how could it be otherwise when reflection furnishes the mind so
frequently with strong marks of the most solid esteem and Friendship which
subsisted between your late noble minded Lord and Mr Hood, which then too was
strengthend by your Ladyship's kind partiality, and the young part of your family
were taught to love the man so flatteringly distinguishd and who I am confident
paid every tribute in his power by devoting himself for a long course of years,

where respect, adoration and love were his only calls, he being very sensible how much he sufferd in his Interest by such an attachment and, I may add, injurious treatment on that score. That these things were so I am sure your Ladyship may well remember, and when I wrote to Lady Harriot they all broke in upon me with their full force, nor feeling the slight omission of congratulations which I should have been ashamed to have noticed, if all had been as it was in happier days. But the reverse Mr Hood has certainly experienced, for no mark of Friendship had he received from your Ladyship or Family, but cold and reserved were all to him in high degree since the fatal breach. And for what reason private connections were to be broke and marked to the World makes it very strange indeed, he being the same man he ever was.

But long habits die hard and for the few years more left to her, Molly Hood continues to write to Hester Chatham, chatty letters of family comment; of their life at Cricket Lodge; of Hood's political and naval career. As with all of Lady Chatham's friends, the remarkable rise to national fame of her second son William does not pass unnoticed by Mrs Hood who, always a good wife and therefore mindful of her husband's career in this age of patronage, has put aside resentment and the correspondence continues. One further outburst occurs in an undated letter of 1785, addressed to Catherine Stapleton, previously so much disliked, now living more or less permanently at Burton Pynsent:

Cricket Lodge
Wednesday [1785]

Dear Miss Stapleton
I rejoice much that dear Lady Chatham has lost her cold and is able to enjoy abroad the fine days we have lately had, which we hope will produce every advantage to her Health and pleasure. She is very good to take an interest in what concerns the inhabitants of Cricket Lodge. What I said in my letter to Lady Harriot Eliot was not to convey an idea of complaint that we had not the honour and pleasure of her company and Mr Eliot's as she intended, neither of not seeing Lady Chatham. For so full of fears was I at the thoughts of a moonshine return that I was upon the point of sending a servant with a letter to beg that Lady Harriot woud not think of coming, was it her Ladyship's intention to take that uncertain light. The Ladys therefore I intirely acquit, but not for the same reasons can I Lord Chatham, who in the long time he was at Burton, might certainly have mounted his horse or got into his equipage any fine day he pleased, had his inclinations kept pace with our wishes to see his Lordship, Mr Pitt too, who had flatterd Mr Hood by repeated promises, quitting the country twice without coming was a serious disappointment especially as he woud have gone very little out of his way in calling here when he was passing on to Mr Bankes. To be debarred of the honour and pleasure of seeing him, you may easily imagine after depending upon it, must be most truely mortifying, and must hurt the more as my poor dear Mr Hood is the most injured man alive; and tho' he has stood the brunt of malice and bore up against the frowns of inveterate party, for many years, yet he wants the Balsom of friendly acts to heal those wounds given to his Fame, and Fortune, which can never be but by a publick ostensible mark of Mr Pitt's favour. These circumstances, and he being a member for Bridgewater contrary to his judgement and inclination, and being distressd by having thirteen hundred pounds paid from his pocket for his seat, has given in the scale an additional expectation to be distinguished. Unless he is very soon, he must feel painfully that his long and

faithful services in his professional line, and his strong attachment of friendly zeal to Mr Pitt's person and administration are of no avail.

Your letter has drawn the above explanations from me, least you should think my mind sent only to such little disappointments that I ought to be ashamed of laying any weight upon. The best of wishes present to Lady Chatham and accept them yourself, from Mr Hood and your faithful obliged servant

M Hood

This late letter appears to be the last surviving of the correspondence. Molly Hood had not much longer to go: she died just twelve days before Harriot Eliot - her 'sweet Lady Harriot' - in 1786. But her husband, the poor injured Mr Hood, survived her for many years, to marry again and to be promoted to Admiral and the peerage.

iv. LETTERS FROM ELIZABETH WYNDHAM, MRS GEORGE GRENVILLE 1744-1769

Of all Hester Grenville's friends from girlhood, it is Elizabeth Wyndham who was the dearest to her. It is easy to see why. Both were women who made no pretence to take part in the growing feminine intellectual life of their time; both loved and appreciated the beauty of country life and loathed London, though forced because of their husbands' political careers to live in the capital for quite long periods; both were devoted mothers, with strongly marked leanings, especially in Elizabeth's character, towards the domestic arts. Amongst the surviving correspondence, Elizabeth's letters are the earliest of all Hester's women friends - in fact the earliest of all the letters except those from the Grenville brothers. Her letters show that she possessed an ironic wit, totally untainted by malice, always an endearing trait in a friend. She also had courage: her health in the last ten years of her not very long life was obviously appalling; whatever disease afflicted her it was evidently very painful. Yet at no time does she bemoan her misfortune; she mentions her ailments but only to dismiss them with wry humour.

Elizabeth Wyndham was born in 1716, the daughter by his first marriage to Lady Catherine Seymour, of Sir William Wyndham, a noted politician and ardent Jacobite. Her two brothers, Charles and Percy later became, through a complicated inheritance, the second earl of Egremont and the ninth and last earl of Thomond respectively. Left early an orphan, Elizabeth appears to have got on well with her stepmother, Maria de Jonge, widow of William Godolphin, marquess of Blandford, whose name and title she retained after her marriage to Wyndham. Elizabeth made her home with Lady Blandford at 'Sheene', now East Sheen near Richmond, before she married and almost all the early letters and many written after marriage, mention her stepmother in affectionate terms. This lady's sister, Isabella de Jonge, wife of the fifth earl of Denbigh, also receives friendly notice.

The correspondence opens when Elizabeth was twenty-eight and Hester four years younger. Both young women were to be married (in their thirties) to prominent politicians, and had hitherto lived most of their adult lives among people of note in the political world; Elizabeth's letters and by implication Hester's also, contain from the outset political comment and observations on national affairs. Living near London, she passes to Hester news and gossip of the great world; of the theatre and the 'crowds at Ranelagh.' More seriously, several letters of 1745 refer to the rebellion, named for that year.

Elizabeth Wyndham married George Grenville, Hester's second brother and a future prime minister, in 1749. Why it took so long to seal the knot is not revealed; she was a frequent visitor to Stowe and a favourite of the Grenvilles' maternal uncle, Sir Richard Temple, Lord Cobham, squire of the great estate of Stowe in Buckinghamshire, a field marshal and much else besides. After her marriage Elizabeth goes to live at Wotton, the original home of the Grenvilles situated about twelve miles from Stowe, which was to become her home for the rest of her life. This house had been allotted to George Grenville when his mother succeeded under Lord Cobham's will to Stowe, and his elder brother Richard Lord Temple became their mother's heir.

Wotton, where Hester had spent most of her childhood, was a house dearly loved by both women. Elizabeth's letters are ecstatic in its praise: the beauty of the grounds with the lake, the shell grotto, the charming walks. She grudged every moment of the time she was obliged to spend away from it. Here she and George Grenville raised their seven surviving children, four girls and three boys, and here she died in 1769 aged fifty-three. Peter Jupp, the biographer of her youngest son William, the future foreign secretary, pays tribute to Elizabeth, and provides a not very flattering glimpse of her appearance: 'much of the credit for creating the family environment in which Grenville grew up rests with his mother Elizabeth... Looking prematurely aged as a result of the scars of smallpox and troubled with a stammer, she devoted herself to bringing up her large family, a task... she clearly enjoyed and which perhaps compensated for her lack of ease in society.'[5]

So be it. But she had many friends, and there is no lack of ease in her frank, open and affectionate letters to her girlhood friend and future sister in law, Hester Pitt, Lady Chatham.

Elizabeth has been on a visit to Stowe and Wotton where the two girls appear to have made a pact to write regularly in future to one another:

Sheene
Sep: the 8 1744

I have forgot Dear Miss Grenville in what manner the preliminaries were settled between us about writing, but being determin'd not to retard my pleasure by my own fault I have begun; the maxim at least you will approve of tho perhaps you may wish I had put it in practice on some other occasion. I must trouble you with my compts to Lady Cobham with many thanks for her figs wch I sent for immediately after my return; they were prodigiously good. Imagination is still occupy'd with Stowe, I often accompany you in our evening walks and as proof that I am thoroughly mindfull of the Garden and all its appurtenances, I have begun my negotiation for painted glass and have at present great prospect of success. I have had the pleasure of seeing Mr George Grenville who I think looks perfectly well; he proposed being with you very soon. I hope you have still the amusement I left with you at Wotton, but after this most uncharitable wish, I must add that more benevolent one of the improvement we had begun to make taking place more and more every day. Lady Bl[andford] and I join in compts to all at Stowe or rather to all those whom you shall think proper. I am, Dear Miss Grenville, your most faithfull

Humble Servt

El: Wyndham

The good resolutions about writing are kept up, on both sides, at a cracking pace:

Sheene

Sep: the 19 1744

I hope you will believe me Dear Miss Grenville when I say that I recd with very great pleasure your two obliging letters and am extremely flatter'd with your kind reproach for the shortness of mine... I thank you for your political news, you are very indulgent to me in communicating it and I hope for both our sakes you will encourage so usefull and agreeable a correspondence. I must tell you in return that it was confidently reported here that the Dutch had sign'd their neutrality and given us notice that our troops should return home in safety, but I suppose it is not yet made publick tho' no body seems to doubt of the truth of that event. In regard to home affairs I hear that Ld Bath is to choose Commodore Anson at Heddon, in the place of Lord Montrath. His Lordsps patriotism is once more awak'd and no body laments more than he the sad situation of his poor country.

It seemed preordained that these two politically aware young women should marry politicians, and though in this early letter both George Grenville and William Pitt are mentioned, the marriages did not take place respectively for another five and ten years. The letter continues:

Mrs [Ann] Pitt has heard from her Brother since he came to Bath; he finds himself the better for his journey and was preparing to drink the waters: I enter into Mr Grenville's distress occasion'd by the bad weather he has had [in which] to entertain his company at Wotton, but if our climates agree, he has had the finest that could be seen for these last three days...

I desire to recommend to you the study of Chaucer with geat assiduity and afterwards to propose myself for your scholar when next we meet.

Elizabeth Wyndham's step-aunt, Lady Denbigh, of whom she was fond, 'Lady Denbigh's gayety makes the finest weather imaginable', figures considerably in the early letters. First a passing taunt at George Grenville:

Sheene
Oct: the 7 1744

There is a paragraph in your last letter Dear Miss Grenville which amazes and concerns us extremely. Need I tell you it is that wch mentions your likelihood of staying in the country till after Christmas; this violent measure of Mr Grenvilles is by no means approv'd of or indeed understood by his friends in this part of the world and we are upon the brink of determining it to be one way of hanging out the white flag... Lady Denbigh who you enquire after is extremely busy in carrying on a work at the end of her terrass which you may perhaps comprehend without my describing it, wch would be difficult as I never saw the place. The account she gives me of herself is that she attends her workmen till tis night and then comes home quite tir'd, flings herself upon a sofa and there falls asleep, so that Sunday is the only day she finds time for writing. This sort of life agrees perfectly well with her and she does not seem to think of coming to London till the very latter end of this month or beginning of next.

But the early resolution on exchange of letters falters and a letter of a week later in which Elizabeth notes that

she is extremely pleased to find that the painted glass will be of service to Lord Cobham

and that she has

got another parcel for him wch he will receive soon

was the last that year and for several months thereafter. She has heard from Hester who has gone to Wotton:

London
May the 7 1745

There is an air of sincerity in your letter Dear Miss Grenville capable of persuading almost any body that Buckinghamshire is at present preferable to Middlesex and your journey thither merely an act of choice void of all complaisance to those you are gone with. But I must beg leave to refuse the bait and to attribute all your commendations of the country to the internal happiness you possess of making every place agreeable to yourself and those that are with you; therefore whether or no the beauties and comfort of Wotton (in my opinion) are in itself I leave you to judge..

Elizabeth is having fun in London and George Grenville is there too; the letter continues:

Tell [Mrs Grenville, Hester's mother] that the loss of my cloak has prevented my going as yet to Vauxhall but when occasion offers I shall send to demand it in such a manner as will admit of no refusal. I am grown insolently well within these few days as to be absolutely above all common prescriptions such as country air, exercise and the like and no longer ago than last night Ld Cobham, yr Brother George and myself (persons reckon'd at present to be all of the age of the first) were seen at the same place between the hours of twelve and one at night... The time for going to Sheene is still uncertain and I believe you do not think I shall press it much. London is as yet very supportable and our assembly last Sunday very flourishing.

Elizabeth is young and in love but also aware of the anxieties caused by the Jacobite rising, the rebellion of that year and of friends who are suffering from it:

> I am almost asham'd of so ludicrous a letter at a time of so general affliction as this one, but I hope you only feel it as I do by suffering for the concern of others and from no particular one of your own. I have seen but little of those who are peculiarly distress'd; the scene is too much for them or their friends as I experienc'd Sunday morning with poor Ldy Sebright, who has as yet heard nothing of or from her son and consequently fears the worst. I believe with too much reason they expect an express to night wch will probably confirm her misery and that of many others who are in her situation.

Elizabeth returns to the subject of the rebellion in September and in December, but first she must let off steam about Lord Cobham's protégée, Harriet Speed, permanent resident of Stowe and greatly disliked by Hester and all her girl friends.

Sheene
Sep the 14 1745

> I submit to yr censure for writing a letter at this time without communicating political news but disavow your appelation of a person of consequence. As such, I shd have been unpardonable but otherwise think myself justifiable, especially since Miss Speed had the day before with a modest triumph insulted me upon her having wrote all Ld Cs intelligence to Lady Denbigh, and when I sent my letter to you she had wrote me at the same time wch I concluded contain'd all and more that I cd have told you... I hear the rebels are joined by some few people of family, but younger brothers and such can add no great weight; their numbers however encrease. The pretender has been proclaim'd at Leith and tho' this was and still is treated but slightly by many, it seems to grow more serious than one cd wish, especially if we shd be invaded by foreign forces, wch is much to be apprehended... I find it the fashion to disclaim fear, I hope there is no occasion to do otherwise but I think one must divest ones self of humanity not to be in some measure affected with this affair even as it now stands, because in whatsoever way it ends it cannot fail of having very shocking consequences towards many individuals, and the longer it subsists the more fatal and extensive they will be.

[London]
Dec the 15 1745

> Nothing cd be stronger than the panick in London for some few hours last Thursday upon an express sent to the D. of Newcastle with certain advice of the french being landed. It was soon contradicted by another wch prov'd the alarm to have risen from a french ship stranded on the coast and some smuggling vessels. The particulars of all this you have probably had from better authority. I was lucky enough to hear nothing of it till late in the evening when all fears were calm'd. The Duke is expected in Town to night or to morrow, having found it impossible to overtake the rebels, so that we must wait patiently for a good while longer before

anything decisive can possibly happen and wch in all likelihood must be perform'd by Mr Wade's army in or on the borders of Scotland whither the rebels are marching with all speed.

Elizabeth's letters contain no further observations on the rebellion, and thirteen (an unusually large number) written in the second half of 1746 are concerned with social affairs, Hester's presumed suitors, news and gossip about friends and visits. In July Hester is at Tunbridge Wells:

Sheene
July the 24 1746

I can expect no account as yet Dear Miss Grenville how the waters agree with you, but I fancy by this time you have been able to judge what benefits you are likely to reap from your evening rides: dissipation is always prescribed with waters, therefore I hope you will take care not to attach yourself to any thing; the next thing worth your attention is what will attach itself to you - but of this you are to judge for yourself; tho neither the advice of yr friends nor even yr own remonstrances are likely to avail upon this occasion... I am deeply engag'd in the fairy Queen and return you thanks for having furnish'd me with so agreeable entertainment. I scarce forgive the Red cross Knight his amour with Duessa tho the rude pennance he underwent for it mollifies me. I am charm'd with the House of pride and in favour of this poem [and] can reconcile myself to the old english...

She is a little bored, finding the high summer months rather long:

The Twickenham Neighbourhood [Marble Hill household] is quite dispers'd, the fairest part presides over the North and the lesser star is to shine in Kent; how I bear this desertion I leave you to judge but I feel that the month of July grows very tedious. What August will be I cannot tell but I am apt to think I shall be in haste for September. Ldy Bl[andford] desires her compts to you, mine with whatever else you will accept is most sincerely yrs
[no signature]

Things change with a visit from George Grenville:

Sheene
Aug 11 1746

I was going to write to you by yesterdays post Dear Miss Grenville but upon hearing that yr Br George was drawing near this part of the world, I thought you would not be displeas'd at my deferring it till I could give you some account of him. He din'd with us yesterday in his way to London, seem'd to be perfectly well and says he is so (but that you know goes for nothing.) I can say nothing of his looks because his face is quite blister'd and parch'd with the sun...

After relating some social gossip brought by George, Elizabeth ends:

I think it is time to conclude. I have been long on horseback this morning wch has made my hand shake but what has made me leave out words, I cannot so easily account for. Adieu

All her life Elizabeth was devoted to horses and was a keen rider until motherhood and declining health put a stop to it. Hester also was a keen horsewoman before she married. Three undated letters of this period contain references to a favourite horse:

> Frisky and I are just return'd from R[ichmon]d Park

and generously

> Frisky will be at your service whenever you signify yr pleasure at the stable in Gr[osvenor] Square and for as long as is agreeable to you. I wish it was possible for me to appear less selfish in this offer or for you to be persuaded that yr pleasure in riding him is a more sensible one to me that the great advantage I shall find from having him rid by one whose skill I never doubted and shall henceforward look upon as superior to every thing.

an invitation which Hester evidently accepted:

> I assure you my Dear Miss Grenville yr riding out does me a great deal of good and as I am not perfectly well at present I hope you will continue it. I have continu'd to get a great cold in my head but with yr care and my own I doubt not to get rid of it soon. I had the satisfaction to hear by yr Br Wednesday that you had determin'd upon riding the morning you was so doubtful. It pleas'd us both extremely and I am glad to hear of yr attendants because I think the enterprise will seem less terrible than to go out alone.
>
> Shortgrove
> Sep the 5 1746

> I propos'd writing to you from London last tuesday Dear Miss Grenville but was prevented by a rage that seiz'd Lady Blandford and myself for seeing Houses, wch took up all our time till four o'clock. Yr friend Stanley's was of the number; we paid due deference to it and if his trusty maid does justice to two unknown Ladies and a gentleman, her master will hear great flatteries upon it. I really think it prettily done but entreat you to make no discoveries to him of this party; that is if you can withhold such a confidence from a person you are so well with...
> Sunday last being a very rainy day we set out with Ldy Suffolk and Mr G Grenville for Chiswick and persever'd to the House thro such a rain as soon demolish'd muslin gowns, notwithstanding handsome brown camblet cloaks with wch we had provided ourselves, and it was by no means for yr Br's reputation to land at Mortlake with such trollops. However our ticket was return'd and I still hope the party may take effect when you can be of it. We have left all the fine weather behind us to the great grievance of Mr O'Brien who wish'd to have done the honours of Shortgrove to us in sunshine. We are oblig'd to have recourse to gaming wch we follow in various shapes.

Hester is having her portrait painted. Elizabeth writes on 7th October

> Pray send me word how Bardel has succeeded and in what manner he has dispos'd of your two hands, wch he seem'd to be as much embarrass'd with as if you had double the number.

And a month later she is

> going this morning to Mr Bardels to see yr picture and sit for my own. I wish I may not be handed down to posterity the less advantageously for my former criticism.

There are no surviving dated letters of the next two years (1747-48) and a few undated which may belong to this time are not specific, merely recording details of Elizabeth's social life, enlivened with her anecdotal gifts, thus:

> Shene
> Tuesday
>
> The party we had here the day after I saw you was in every point compleat and none of the company [were] sufferers either from the cold or too great exercise. We have a retour two days after at Mr Pester's where we play'd at cards till eight and then return'd here with a new pr of lamps fix'd to our post chaise and wch might be of use if they were properly plac'd. It is absolutely necessary for us to come to Town to have them rectify'd but I shall take care to diferr it till after you are come.
> Ld Jersey and Mr Villiers gave general praise to Stowe with most honourable mention made of Wotton but I enter'd into no particular disquisition of either, reserving that till you can be a hearer. Ld Jersey is gone into Suffk but talks of settling in Town before the Birthday and Mr Villiers has many places where he might go but was unresolv'd whether he would go to any. He produc'd a bottle of Russia Tea upon a slight promise he made me of some last winter and I am so very choice of it that few people are thought worthy of it...
> Lady Caroline and I conclude up-a-daisie are establish'd at Petersham where the lady last mentioned is to come for some days and I am persuaded her chief employment will be to court popularity with the Dowagers of Argyle and Rutland by making up their evening party at cards.

It is difficult to determine why there is this gap in the correspondence, and lacking other evidence it has to be assumed that the two young women met constantly. There is thus no record of any formal engagement but it would certainly be known among their relations and friends that George Grenville and Elizabeth Wyndham were to marry. And so they did, in May 1749. Two months later, Elizabeth writes to Hester from Sunninghill, the Berkshire spa which they find hectically social, crowded and noisy; but they have found an escape:

> Sunning Hill
> July the 4 1749
>
> We have been entertain'd here for these last three or four days with Races, Balls, Concerts and assemblies, at none of wch we have voluntarily assisted except at the Races one day, but have been unwilling partakers of the noise and riot from morning till night. Yesterday we fled from it to Mrs Edwins at Cookham; she was not return'd from Bristol but we took possession of her Library where we eat our cold meat and went from thence to Cliveden. We are charm'd with Cookham, it is the prettiest, gayest retirement I ever saw. The House is small and not extremely

convenient, it goes on fast but cannot possibly be inhabited till next year. We have put an interdict upon the execution she had determin'd upon of the only three Trees upon her ground and least our rhetorick deliver'd by her first minister shd not prevail we have left the following pathetick lines for her perusal:

> Here the rude Axe with heaved stroke
> Be never heard - my nuts to crack
> And lay my Tree upon its Back.

NB. They are walnut trees.

You may judge how romantick and beautiful a situation it must be that could inspire us with such elegance of poetry...

We have din'd one day at Mr Southcotes, we found him laid up with the gout and very much pull'd by a terrible fit of the gravel... We learnt there that Miss Howard, the Duke of Norfolk's niece is going to be marry'd to a younger brother of Ld Houstons, wch is one of her Grace's deep laid schemes, the benefit of wch does not strike at first sight. Pray let me hear from you soon for I long to know whether or no I shall find you as well as the sincere affection with wch I am My Dear Sister

Yrs etc.

[This and all subsequent letters are unsigned]

Sunning Hill
July the 11 1749

We drink the waters very regularly and not one of the society arrives later than half an hour past eight at the Well. The Beau monde we find there of our own acquaintance consists of Sir R. Rich and Miss Mary and Mr Bale; the unknown form a body of about twelve or fourteen but the place of gaiety and resort is the House we lodge in (of a Monday morning in humble imitation of Putney Bowling Green). There was yesterday a hundred or two people at the breakfast and Ball, at neither of which I assisted but went out on Horseback with yr Brother, and because I know you must be interested in whatever regards us, I must send you a state of our Cavalry and inform you that the most incomparable Mare is younger and fresher than ever and has almost lost her Cough. I wish I could make the same good report of Spot, he coughs incessantly and seems much dispirited but is going to be try'd with my meat mashes etc. Our evenings are spent in seeing places, of wch there are great variety in this neighbourhood, and the scheme of life seems so wholesome and wears so pleasantly that I expect you shall find a great amendment in yr Br's looks when we meet again.

They are becoming more reconciled to life at the spa:

Sunning Hill
July ye 20 1749

Mr Grenville is gone to London to attend the Treasury. I hope he will have but one journey more there before the Holydays, for I really think the waters seem to agree with him... I must not omit telling you (for the particular entertainment of Miss Harriot [Speed], that the Ball here last Monday was the prettiest thing I ever saw of the sort. They danc'd about ten couple under the Trees in the Garden and the rest of the walks were crowded with spectators and Tea Tables, all wch I beheld with great ease from my window, and saw the likeness's of Hans, Ld Strafford and many more of my friends dansant a faire rire, wch diverted me extremely. Yr Brother for fear of being accus'd of singularity and unpopularity made one at the (no) breakfast, for none cd he get, the crowd was too great.

Two months later on 13th September, the old warrior, Lord Cobham is dead at eighty. He was something of a surrogate father to Elizabeth and she will have felt sorrow at his going. But in the fashion of her day her letter to Hester describing his death speaks not of sadness, but rather of practical matters, the will, mourning.

[Stowe]
[Sept 13th 1749]

Ld Cobham continu'd much as you left him Dear Sister, till about four o'clock. He then grew delirious and talk'd much of his garden but nothing else nor nam'd nobody. He had convulsions for about two Hours and then dy'd away with great ease between eight and nine. There is a servant dispatch'd to Lady Langham and at his return the Will is to be open'd wch you will know the particulars by the express that brings you this. They found it in the Cabinet below stairs. Lady Cobham desires you will tell Mrs Marsh to make but one gown for her till she comes to Town, and that, such a one as she may wear undress'd. Miss Harriot [Speed] desires you will recommend Mrs Marsh to make hers with a french sleeve. All here much as you left them except myself who miss you every Hour and shall be very impatient till I hear how you got to Town, how you found Mrs Grenville, all wch I shall expect by to Morrow's post wch I suppose to have been more expeditious than the return of the Messenger. Thursday. I am just come from hearing the Will read. The real Estate is entail'd upon Mr G.G. and his heirs male, then to Mr Js Grenvilles Children and their Heirs male and so in succession to yr Br Henry and his to the Lyttns, the Wests and to Mr Berenger. The legacys are as follows: two thousand to Lady Cobm wch he had lent her, her dressing plate and furniture in H. Square and the Coach and Horses; five thousand pd to Mr G.G., one thousand to Miss Speed, one thousand to Mrs West, and 3 hundd pd annuity to yr Mother with some legacys to Ferrand, Squib and John. Mr Dayrell and Mr Glover are executors with 2 hundd pound apiece and all charges allow'd. I run away to write this and have heard no comments. Adieu, pray have my letters put into the post.
All the plate furniture etc. are made heirs to and entail'd with Stowe.

The years 1750 and 1751 find Elizabeth settling down as chatelaine of Wotton. Many letters of these early years, and indeed of the rest of the decade, and of the next, are undated but they contain so much that is worthy of record that parts of them must be given, even though the chronology may at times be doubtful.

Elizabeth has had her first baby and George, a delicate man, has been ill; she has domestic problems in plenty, not excluding the stable:

[Wotton]
Monday [1751]

I rec'd yours yesterday Dear Sister, you had judg'd generously and justly upon the reason that hinder'd your getting a letter from me sooner than today. You will have had but little satisfaction in receiving it, this must make amends by bringing you the good news of Mr Grenvilles being got well again tho' a little weaken'd with regimen and discipline. Nurse is rather better but not enough to make me judge more favourably of her case as yet. The Child and I are perfectly well, but to add to the list of my calamitys my Old Mare has got a swelling in her shoulder for which she is oblig'd to be rowell'd, so that I am on foot heartily praying for relais of feet, for the ground is so uneven that I was most heartilly tir'd yesterday, but the great Lakes and every thing thereunto belonging are in greatest beauty and I hope you will have a great and real satisfaction in seeing them. To return once more to that extensive chapter Calamity, the new Cook is so bad that beyond roast and boil'd (wch she does really well) there is nothing to be attempted to the great grievance and future disgrace of the Squire and his Table, the only resource that presents itself is to try to get our old Cook who I believe is still in our House [in London] to come here for a month in order to put her a little au fait of our taste

Hester's help is again sought

and this negotiation we put into your hands; her scheme was to have gone next Saturday by the Waggon into Wales but I think she will in consiquence of my great gratitude to her difer her journey a month and come by the first Buckm Waggon hither. Be so good to speak to her yourself and to explain that it is only teach the present Cook who is so willing to learn and so cleanly that I cannot think of parting with her.

Despite the nurse's illness they take a short break at Stowe, where Viscount Cobham, later Earl Temple, has already begun the improvements which would last until his death nearly thirty years on:

Stowe
July the 16 1751

I left Nurse full as bad, if not worse than ever and losing her strength daily. I hope Dr Duncan will have sent directions to the apothecary tho' I own I have but little faith in medicines for her unless he cd get her (by good fortune) some of the true balm of Gilead. Mr Mackye I know has some but I fear he is gone to Scotland. We have been here since Sunday and propose to stay till Thursday evening. The gentlemen go to day to the Assizes and to morrow likewise. This place is in great beauty and Lord Cobham very eager about it both within doors and without. I like most of the alterations extremely, particularly the Queen's Theatre and the gothick field.

In September there is an exciting story to relate:

Wotton
Sep: the 30th 1751

The only letter of note brought us by the post yesterday was one from Lady Denbigh giving a most deplorable account of their journey to Paris. They embark'd at five o'clock and were till six at night at Sea in a Calm. and the two Ladies so sick that they were oblig'd to get into a little Boat in order to go ashore but the wind chang'd upon them immediately and oblig'd them to Land upon the nearest shore, there to wait till a Cart could be got to carry them on to Calais, wch was obtain'd so late that the gates were shut and they forc'd to pass the night in a miserable Inn in the suburbs. Their march, tho' disastrous, inclin'd me to laugh at the reading it, as it put me in mind of Scarrons theatrical strolling Princesses mounted upon a waggon like our Countesses, Ld Westmorland taking the place of le destin who march'd by on foot. Lady West:d had poor B-ys complaint upon her arrival at Paris and did not stir out but the Earl is vastly delighted with the splendor and magnificence of the Houses and manner of living of la noblesse, wch made Mr G. peevish till the next paragraph inform'd us that the K. of France keeps four thousand Horses more in his own stables than Lewis the 14th ever had, and spends several millions more than him in his Household. The political consequences that may arise from this extravagance comforted your Brother and I think he already sees France another Capua and its King tributary to whoever thinks it worth their while to buy him. The Travellers are to stay but a week longer at Paris and then to go directly to Pezenas.

From Stowe again the following month with news of the Buckingham election, illness among horses at home and shopping for Hester to do for them in London:

Stowe
Oct the 10th 1751

We arrived here, Dear Sister with grandeur and safety and found the famille, your Captn Smith and Mr J[ame]s Gren[ville], but the latter so wedded to Buckingham and Thucidides in the original that he has never appear'd since our arrival except the first day at dinner in a shirt three days old and a wig over one ear... There has come very bad news from Pollycot since our arrival here but all proper care and precautions are strictly order'd, so that we may still hope you may not repent of the Tabby nightgown. There is another calamity wch does not regard you nor your Beauty neither, but for Lady Charlottes sake I must entertain you upon it: the distemper amongst the Horses is broke out in this country and proves very mortal and it is reckon'd a safe and necessary precaution to bleed them in order to prevent it. I beg you will recommend it to Lady Charlotte for her mare whose health she is bound to take care of since she owes her own to it. A Farrier in this neighbourhood greeted this relapse to all those who did not purge their Horses thoroughly last year...
You will do me a signal piece of service in carrying or sending the inclos'd pattern to the Golden Ball in Pall Mall with orders to Mr Butler to get me immediately half a pd of the same colour.

And eight days later

Wotton
Oct the 18th 1751

The distemper at Pollicot has confin'd itself to one single Cow and leaves room to hope it was a false alarm... I must desire you to send the enclosed Card to my shoemaker who is the same as yours, I have forgot his name, and be good to send orders to Mary to keep them till I come.

A year later and news of the death in Paris on 6th December of the mother of their mutual friend Jane Hamilton:

Wotton
Saturday[Dec. 1752]

The Pease arriv'd with your letter on Thursday my Dear Sister, et sauf le respect que je dois a votre grandeur, I am going to eat some of them to day... We are vastly shock'd at poor Lady Archibalds death and the distress'd situation of poor Hammy who I think is most likely to return to England an orphan, for the weak state of her father's health and bodily strength, join'd to the winter season, seems to make it impossible for him to move of some months, wch is a long period in his life. I pity her from the bottom of my heart... I write to her by this post hoping that she feels like me that the remembrance of friends is pleasant in distress.

A comic episode with a French visitor to relate:

Wotton
Saturday [?1752]

I hope M. de Coulanges has not fail'd to give you no description of what is past description, viz the Lake at Stowe and the excessive beauty of Wotton. He was enchanted with the new path and gives due honour to the inventor. I was willing to have as much of his company as I could during the little stay he made and therefore follow'd him, even to the Marble Closet, wch politeness he requited by leaving the door unbolted, but by a strange English awkwardness I was asham'd and flew back to my Room, where when he arriv'd I accosted him with telling him he would have a very hot day for his breakfast. This great adventure he might be too discreet to tell you and therefore I write it.

Hester not only had to shop for the Grenvilles but she is needed to convey official messages from George Grenville to his office and also to make ready their London house to receive them:

Wotton
Sunday [?1752]

Mr G desires you will immediately send to Mr Tunstall to know from him the precise time the ships are orderd and likewise that you will make strict enquiry among your foreign friends and particularly the Hops if the Earl is set out or when he does set out, what stay it is imagin'd he will make...

Be so good to let Mary know that the Glazier is order'd forthwith to clean the windows and when that is done she must come and beg the favour of one of your men to go to Mr Ball in Vine Street to come and put up our Bed and all the Window Curtains... I must also beg you will send to Roubillon (the Chesterfield people can tell you where he lives) to put him in mind that I expect to find the frame and glass for a picture wch Mr G. bespoke, finish'd. Forgive all these commissions, here I will end them and my letter too, least more shd present themselves. Adieu my Dear Sister.

[Wotton]
Sunday [?1753]

Vive les tablettes says Mr Grenville, and I! Nobody is so punctual in business and commissions as Lady Hester, wch we both look upon at least as <u>necessary</u> an accomplishment as a thorough knowledge in painting and Painters lives. And now my dear Sister, having had my joke I must very seriously thank you, both from your Brother and myself for all your attentions to Horse, Picture etc etc...

I dare not tell you in how great beauty every thing is here, least it should disturb the peace of your mind for the little time (I hope) you have to be absent.

I walk so many Hours every day, that I shall soon want feet to my <u>new</u> stockings in the sense of Mme de Sévigné when she is tir'd of using her own sit-down after her Rheumatism.

Then the great news, the watershed in Hester Grenville's life and which touched all her family to a varying extent. Though it was at Wotton that she and William Pitt engaged to marry, this was evidently kept a secret from the rest of the household until the lovers had departed:

Wotton
Wednesday and Thursday
[September 1754]

Your letter my Dearest Sister was almost too much for me; greatly so indeed in your description of me, tho still far below the mark if you think to judge of my affection for you from outward marks or expressions; I have had no essential proof to give of the first and I am very dificient of the last, being all ways most distress'd for words both to utter and to write where I feel most our mutual friendhsip has been pleasure and happiness to us both. And let me add Dear Lady Hester, mine never so great as at this moment from the perfect assurance of a true and lasting felicity to you wch nothing can bar provided Mr Pitt keeps his health; and happiness is so good a recipe that I trust he will enjoy a more perfect state of health now than he has ever yet known. This subject draws me on so greatly to my own sensations that I shall (like our friend the Countess) not know how to quit it, and indeed I find it impossible to go to another till I have told you that yr letter made me quite silly. I could compare it to nothing but that of a beloved daughter, weaning herself from her mother and I having, as you know, much of the maternal sentiment about me, it still found this nearer way to my heart and more and more endear'd the writer to me. Mr G. had a letter last post from Sir G [Lyttelton] wrote in all cordiality, penetrated with yr approaching felicity and that of both parts of the familly in this union; he tells him he has wrote to Ld T[emple], to you and Mr Pitt. I hope the post has done you justice, tho you do not mention it in your letter to me. Mr G has likewise (tho very unlike), had one to night from Mr Pitt; as you are not acquainted with his stile, nor cannot guess at the subject, I should have been glad to have inclos'd it to you, but he has a most unaccountable partiality for it and will keep it to himself; but thus far it is fair to tell you that he is underhand trying to get every body to be of opinion that ye 6th or 7th etc. But to do him justice, tho he attempts this league it ends with all deference to your commands.

With death never in that time far from happiness, Elizabeth continues her letter on a different note. The Queensberry heir, Lord Drumlanrig, has met with a violent death from a shooting accident:

The poor Duke and Dutchess of Q. answer'd both our letters and yrs, the latter I inclose. Mine is much to the same purpose, saying they all keep up each others spirits which is what supports them. I am glad the truth is conceal'd from her and Lady Drumlanrig and I am most heartilly glad that the first report [of suicide] proves so utterly groundless, for nothing seems clearer than your account of this fatal accident and nothing can more effectually destroy the other story. Mr Nuthall [Pitt's solicitor] has not kept his promise, no rough draft [of the marriage settlement] arriv'd yesterday. This gives something like a fair pretence for protracting but nevertheless you will have a great encounter to sustain, as appears plainly by the letter Mr G. rec'd... Adieu my dear Sister, yr Brother would have spoke for himself by this post but is sure you will excuse him as he is writing to yr other self; and besides we think so much alike and feel so much alike upon yr subject, that he depends upon my answering for him, as I do upon assuring yr two selves of both his and my most constant affection.

Hester will have been busy with preparations for her wedding, but Elizabeth, though apologetic, needs more shopping done for her: her style of dress has evidently been criticised by Lady Blandford and the Suffolk household at Twickenham:

[Wotton]
[probably October 1754]

My Dear Sister
        Having great matters to treat upon I begin my letter this friday night least any interruption should oblige me either to forego my business or small talk. The first great point that presents itself is that I acquiesce to the censure of Shene and Marble Hill and desire in the best manner possible to amend my error mais le moyen unless you are so good as to assist me with your taste and choice of a Gown. I feel all the unreasonableness of trespassing upon yr time, but to who can I apply? If you are so charitable as to accept the commission allow me so far to restrain your natural magnificence as to tell you that two guineas pr yard is the very utmost bounds to wch my purse can reach, and I shall be as thankfull as her late Majesty for having the duty of a french silk sav'd to her if you can equip me decently for less. And as to colour, material etc I leave it intirely to you without reserve, but think not my Dear Sister that yr trouble ends here. You must also transact the important article of the Tippet and stomacher with Mrs Lawrence, with strict injunctions to have all brought home on Saturday morning. I forgot to mention that seventeen yds is my quantity for the Gown and petticoat. When it is purchas'd please to send it to trusty Mary who shall receive proper directions about it, and pray be exact as to the seventeen yards because the Mercers are apt to chuse that one should take the whole piece... I am quite asham'd (not politely but literally) of all the trouble I give you but beg you to engage Mitan for me next Saturday at two o'clock and likewise for the Birthday. I have set it upon card to prevent mistake and you will be so good as to send it him.

If the two women were alive today, it is certain that they would agree that the next three of four years were the happiest of their lives. Content in their marriages, delighting in their growing families, they had the added interest and stimulation of their husbands' ever upward success in political life. It was during this time that William Pitt achieved his greatest fame, as head of the government, virtually controller of the nation, in the Seven Years War. The war also underlined the importance of George Grenville's post as Navy Treasurer for four years from 1756.

But success breeds jealousy and in 1758 it is known (though not from Elizabeth's letters) that all was not well between Pitt and Grenville and four years later their friendship failed. Inevitably, the deterioration in their husbands' relations one with another made it difficult for the wives to continue on the same easy affectionate footing as hitherto. They never lost touch but the letters became scarce and dried up altogether for a time.

Meantime, there are the years rich in happiness to record, regrettably in mainly undated letters, with all the minutae of eighteenth century living to delight them - and us.

The Temples and Stowe were of great importance to both families. In this letter we get a glimpse of the somewhat tenuous figure of Lady Temple, ever in the shade of the overwhelming personality of her husband:

[Wotton]
June the 26th [1755]

Lord Temple surpris'd us by so quick a return, my Dear Sister, occasion'd by the putting off the party at Claremont and Oatlands etc. He arriv'd about nine o'clock to dinner; they leave us today. Lady Temple being neither a great walker nor admirer of the beauties abroad, makes the weather we have had to be the less regretted; but in the six days she has pass'd with us, we have been able but once to venture as far as the Chinese House, and were then caught in the rain. The rest of our walks have been confin'd to the South Garden between the showers. We are greatly flatter'd with Lord Temple's approbation, both within doors and without. He tells us you and Mr Pitt talk of visiting Buckinghamshire; I wish it may prove more than words and in that hope I will say nothing upon the subject of the Library except that it is very pretty and much approv'd. Your party to Ranelagh did indeed surprise me, it was taking a trip into the great world in a very unexpected manner.

After detailing exchanges of visits with neighbours, Elizabeth writes:

Wotton
Augst the 10 1755

These are the principal events that have happen'd since we saw you and I must now proceed to business. Mr Grenville has been oblig'd upon the old black Horse's misdemeanour of gnawing the Trees etc to propose the exchange of a grazing beast with a neighbour, and Peter Parrot says he has a mare of Mr Pitt's at grass wch if Mr Pitt and you have no objection he will turn in the Level and take our mischievous beast in his room. Mr Grenville desir'd me to propose this the first time I wrote; the Mare shall have the same care as the rest of our steeds, and will at least have the advantage of never carrying Butter and Eggs, wch you know we have sometimes suspected others have done at a pinch.

They have a busy social life in town but she longs to get home:

[London]
Sept the 16 1755

Dear Sister

The uninterrupted repose of the Country must undoubtedly convey to its inhabitants the true idea of the direct opposite life of a Town Lady, and therefore you could not expect I cou'd write to you in the midst of so busy a scene which you yourself had help'd to clog by the mighty affairs of the worsteds. But having now dispatch'd all matters of importance, I take the time whilst I am waiting for the equipage to take us out of Town to let you know that I am in the Land of the living.

Mr Pitt may possibly have inform'd you that I not only live myself but make others live also: witness the grand entertainment we gave to him and the rest of the Brotherhood by the help of yr excellent haunch of venison and some Essex partridge. Yesterday Mr Grenville feasted upon Turtle at the St Alban's Tavern and I din'd at Col. Howard's...

I rejoice in this fine weather but it suffocates me in the present moment, but I think in what glory it will show Wotton.

Elizabeth has a cold, caught by fishing in their lake. She takes the opportunity to philosophise on that sport:

[Wotton]
May the 18th [?1756]

I have hitherto escap'd colds notwithstanding the inconstancy of the weather and that since our Cousins have been here we have allways gone out morning and evening; but too presumptuous a Fishing yesterday has given me a little cold in my head. The silence of Angling agrees extremely with the Taciturnity and solemnity of some people while there are others who have really so much vivacity, good humour and complaisance that it atones for every thing else but is often productive of that necessary consequence that those that are never heard are many times forgot, and I perpetually catch myself at making the principal person of those where my inclination leads me...

Pray let us know when you know the time fix'd for Lord Temples coming to Stowe, for if it is to be soon our company would willingly pay him a visit. The Dean loiters so much that I believe I saw a smoke where there was no fire.

The birth on 10th October of John Pitt requires, as custom dictates, a letter of congratulations to the father. Elizabeth writes to William Pitt:

Wotton
Octr the 17 [1756]

Dear Sir

I hope our sincere joy and congratulations have reachd you long before this time; Mr Wilkes carry'd them to London in his pocket last week and promis'd to forward them with an expedition equal to the zeal and warmth wch the good news diffus'd over all the company then present. But as the sequel to that good news was most gladly felt by us last post, so we hope the repetition of our joy will not be an unwelcome acknowledgement to our friends at Hayes....

Health and spirits prevail amongst our little flock and Poppy-Boy assures me he is extremely glad Aunt Hester has a little Boy... Lord Temple has once more caught the flame of gardening and says it now burns as bright as ever, at wch I think all his friends must rejoice from the great pleasure it affords him. Mr Grenville desires his Love and most affecte compts to Lady Hester and you notwithstanding the unreasonable and unnatural preference you gave to her when you wrote your last letter.

I am Dear Sir yr affecte Sister and faithfull Humble Servt
El: Grenville

They have been on a round of country house visits:

Wotton
June the 8th [1756 or 1757]

At last my Dear Sister the tranquility of Wotton gives me leisure to thank you for your two kind letters, the first of wch I found at Boughton and the other rec'd here last friday. The life we led whilst we were abroad allow'd no time for writing and it was with great difficulty that I scribbled a few lines to Lady Blandford in the intervals of a pool at Cribbage. You will have a perfect idea at this want of leisure when I tell you that in the five days we were absent from this place we saw Easton, Althorp, Horton, Billing (belonging to Mr O'Brien) and Stowe, the fine seat of the Earl Temple, wch last I must own still pleases me best. The Park at Althorp I admire exceedingly, tho its beauties are de la vielle Cour, ces longues allées rever'd by my friend Mme de Sévigné is the plan on wch it is laid out but there seems to be a great deal of pine wood and Lawn. The House is melancholly and as damp as a Cellar tho a certain old fashion'd moat that surrounds it is very properly converted into a dry gravel walk and a flower garden. The Pictures are charming and (according to the term of art) in fine preservation. Horton surprises the beholder from the immensity of expense, wch shows itself at every step you take almost as visibly as at Claremont, and gives the conviction that something can be made out of nothing. Ld Halifax's text is that every thing can be done for nothing and indeed he goes on as if he had talk'd himself into a thorough belief of it. He is to rebuild the House next year, wch indeed wants it sufficiently, as you will believe when I compare it to the worst part of Hagley. And now to resume the hurries of Boughton, dinner, ninepins, Cribbage and supper dispos'd of the rest of the day. We had delightful weather tho rather too hot for our expeditions as your Brother has found to his cost, for since his return he has been troubled with his Bilious complaint and was blooded yesterday, wch with proper discipline will I hope quite cure him...

We found all the dear Children perfectly well at our return; George [born in 1753, probably now three or four] is in a man's dress and greatly improved by it, both in his activity and his appearance.

and have had guests at home including an eccentric foreigner:

Wotton
Sep: the 1st [?1757]

The morning prov'd after you left us very inauspicious to allow plans. I almost drownded the poor Baron with only conducting him to the menagerie and back again. The rest of the time they stay'd was pass'd in hearing him sing French songs above stairs to the Ladies while the Count was below upon more serious matters with the gentlemen. Lord Temple let his love of green fruit get the better of his discretion and persisted in setting out for Stowe the next morning in the midst of a fit of the Cholick and indigestion. We sent to enquire after him to day and have just heard that an emetick taken as soon as he came home has quite set him right again.

and a self-confident Scottish guest:

> Wotton
> Monday [?1758]

> Lord Selkirk made a most ignoble entry yesterday on foot while we were all at Church, having broke his post chaise at Waddesdon and walk'd from thence. His reception was equal to his appearance; having quench'd his thirst with our breakfast leavings wch he found upon the dresser in the Steward's Room, he has left us this morning being in full and harty march to Scotland but promises a longer bait at his return in October.

Not all Elizabeth's letters during the middle and later years of the decade record only frivolous or domestic matters. They also contain, understandably, much comment on national affairs, particularly on the progress of the war. One sample will suffice:

> Stowe
> July the 27th 1758

> We read... with great discomfort and disappointment the fate of Olmutz, not that in human events we ought to expect a constant and uninterrupted course of success, but the K. of Prussia has taught us to expect so much more from him than from any body else, with all the powerful weight against which he struggles [that] one is scarce prepare'd to hear of his not succeeding in what he undertakes. But my politicks at present most partially bend my wishes to America, tho in the meantime I shall be most gratefull, thankfull for any prosperity attending the Protestant cause in whatever part of the world..

After noting that

> the Assizes at Buckm were but thinly attended...

Elizabeth returns to a domestic theme:

> Lady Temple is very busy trying to preserve flowers in their proper form and colours. I have furnish'd some hints and we shall hope if we meet with success to have our names enroll'd with honour at the Royal Society.

William Pitt's semi-invalid sister Ann has return'd from France where, despite the war she has mainly lived, bringing a present for Hester, aged three:

> Wotton
> Augt the 6th 1758

> I am very glad to hear that Mrs Pitt bore her journey so well and that you find her upon the whole so much better than you expected. I beg you will offer my compts to her and my wishes for her finding more health in England that she has enjoy'd since she left it. I fancy Miss Pitt [Hester] must be in great raptures with the treasure she possesses; the minute admiration of it is beyond her years but the envy arising from so perfect (and at this time of war inestimable) a model of french dress will not be confin'd to those of her age only.

Towards the end of the decade, Elizabeth had begun to suffer from bouts of ill-health, and in 1759 an event brought great sorrow to the Grenville home: the death in July of the eldest son, Richard Percy, a child of nine always referred to in his mother's letters as Poppy-Boy. We learn of this loss in letters from Hester to Pitt; she had gone to Wotton to be with the bereaved parents; consequently there are no letters from Elizabeth about the death, which may well have contributed to her physical decline. The letter below was written before the child's death in July:

> [Wotton]
> Thursday night [?1759]

> Your letter found me in deep solitude My Dear Sister, for your Brother was summon'd to take his place at Council tomorrow, so he set out early this morning... His absence is particularly distressfull to me at this present time, having had for near a week a complaint that makes sitting, standing, walking and even lying down almost equally painfull to me and I never till now had a perfect idea of the situation often mention'd of sitting upon thorns but notwithstanding my joke, you will be surpris'd to see how I am wore with it, tho nothing can be well more wearing than the constant uneasiness and frequent pain I suffer. You will perhaps think I state my case thus to excite compassion, wch indeed it may well do, but nothing is exaggerated and I should be sorry if the reading it should induce you to derange any scheme agreeable to yourself or those you are with, for the days of my four will be near pass'd before you receive this and why should I wish you to partake of my misery... I flatter myself that Lady Temple kindly ask'd why I did not come to her when Mr Grenville left me. The first part of my letter tells the reason: I could not bear the motion of any vehicle and am besides fit for nothing but home in my present state of suffering.

In this letter Elizabeth gives intimation of her eldest son's delicacy:

> The Gov[erno]r [Henry Grenville] was very punctual in delivering Lady Temple's kind message and invitation to Poppy-Boy but alas there are many impossibilities that attend it, the most capital of wch is Nurse Creswel's present unmoveable state wch hinders her travelling, and that I could not venture to trust him in a new place without her, tho I were there myself.

Though Elizabeth could not face driving while in pain from this illness, she had written earlier full of praise for her transport:

> I still date from Brook Street [their London home] tho perhaps I may be so happy towards the close of this day to be moving towards Wotton, wch that it may be so is my fervent Hourly prayer Amen. Our journey to the Holt was prosperous and I really much the better for it, having sufficiently repair'd all loss of sleep in that Heavenly vehicle call'd a four wheel'd chaise, wch literally speaking has something so powerfully soporifick in its motion that it is with the utmost difficulty I can keep my eyes open while I am in it.

The happy days for both women were ending, as was the correspondence. The slow decline in Chatham's health, culminating in his severe mental breakdown of 1766 was of great torment to Hester. For Elizabeth the creeping onset of chronic illness, coupled with the bad relations of the husbands, will have made writing for her less than a pleasure.

Two letters, both, significantly perhaps, signed, written not long before her death on 5th December 1769, survive. They must serve as a memorial to a lively, warm-hearted and above all, a brave woman:

Wotton
Aug 29 1769

Lady Hesters [daughter] correspondent profited by my misfortunes on Sunday my Dear Sister, and told how unable I was to return my thanks to you for your very kind letter; and indeed I cannot boast of much amendment since. But not being now in acutal pain I turn my moments of ease into moments of pleasure whilst I am assuring you both on Mr Grenville's part and my own with how much happiness we recollect the times Ld Chatham, yourself and your sweet Familly past here and how glad we shall be of every renewal of the same satisfaction. We hope Lord Chatham's disorder has not continu'd and that no interruption either in his health or yours will prevent your enjoying the great pleasure you have had in finding Mr William so well recover'd.

George.... has been at Stowe with Tom ever since Saturday and returns to us today. We wish'd much to have accompany'd them thither but my miserable health made it impossible... The Cabriolet has a double supply of cavalry by having had Charlottes fantastic mare broke into it but at present I am quite unable to use it, and Elizabeth and William take the opportunity of riding the two little Horses every day. Miss Stapleton assures me the chaise Horse is fit for business but you are so well acquainted with her accommodating manner that you would not doubt her saying so if she thought he could be of the least use.

In both these last letters tribute is paid to the invaluable Catherine Stapleton, a kinswoman of the Grenvilles, called to this as to other homes when illness and all the problems which stemmed from it, bore down on a family:

Wotton
Nov: 16 1769

The hopes my Dear Sister of giving fuller satisfaction to yours and Ld Chatham's kind solicitude about my health has made me difer from day to day the answering your last obliging letter; some days prevented by pain, and not well enough on others, to make the account worth sending. But upon weighing the whole I still hope that the turn of the scale is in my favour; and what misleads us all in this particular (if we are misled) is that when I have my five or six days of ease, I am so well and in such good spirits that I am able to enjoy the fine weather and even to take more exercise on Foot than could naturally be expected in such an invalid state. Mr Grenville and I feel all the kindness of your earnest admonitions against our staying in the Country but cannot help observing en passant that like many other Preachers your practice contradicts your Sermon and we, like other obstinate offenders, not only continue sinning but pretend to support by argument the course we follow, both with respect to health and pleasure. The first of these we prove by the good health wch your Brother enjoys and by the blooming cheeks wch surround our Table and I think you will not be at a loss to suggest to yourself instances enough in favour of the latter to help support our Cause.... Miss Stapleton was as usual in intention punctual to the very Hour she promis'd to return hither but Lady Aylesford's illness detain'd her at Packington a little beyond her time. She had the satisfaction of finding and leaving all her Friends and Family well and all kindly dispos'd to encourage her to hasten back to me who was the person standing most in need of her friendly and affectionate attention....

Charlotte has I believe been so particular with regard to the Fishery to her charming Correspondent that I have nothing new to say on the subject except that we could never drain the Lake sufficiently to get at the Eels, which would have been a great entertainment to our young Folks.

And a perceptive observation on the character of John, the eldest of the Pitt sons:

We are very thoroughly convinc'd of the Truth of all you say of Ld Pitt's industry and likewise of the fresh ardour he feels upon commendation, a mind so well turn'd as his will ever feel the utmost satisfaction in being approv'd; and the natural emulation which young people feel (whose turn of Education is near upon the same plan) by being together will, I flatter myself, give satisfaction to the Fathers and Mothers of both Houses. All belonging to this, both old and young, desire to offer their affecte Compts to the inhabitants of Hayes, the young ones in the Dutifull manner that becomes them.

I am My Dear Sister most afftly yrs

El: Grenville

1 See Appendix iv
2 Stanley Ayling, *The Elder Pitt*, Collins, London 1976
3 Ibid
4 A good gallop
5 Peter Jupp, *Lord Grenville 1759-1834*, OUP 1985

Chapter 5

LETTERS FROM FRANCES (FANNY) EVELYN-GLANVILLE, HON. MRS EDWARD BOSCAWEN 1748-1800

But there's wisdom in women of more than they have known
And thoughts go blowing through them, are wiser than their own

Rupert Brooke (1887-1915), *There's Wisdom in Women*

Of all Hester Chatham's regular correspondents the letters of one woman stand apart, those of Fanny Boscawen. She was a member, it is thought an originator, of the blue stocking assemblies, a group of intelligent persons who met for conversation in one another's houses; even in her own day she was considered a noted letter writer, being compared by Hannah More, a younger member of the set to Madame de Sévigné.

The recipient, Lady Chatham, was cultured, intelligent, practical, in no sense intellectual, but Fanny, like all good letter writers, tailored her news to suit the interests and outlook of her reader. Thus it is that nowhere in the letters is there any mention of intellectual activities; her subjects are primarily domestic interspersed with political comment, embellished with the gossip of high society in London which Hester Chatham so much enjoyed. The letters are especially rich in descriptions of home and family life.

Frances Evelyn Glanville, a great niece of the diarist John Evelyn, was the daughter of William Evelyn, who briefly added his wife's name of Glanville to his own by special act of parliament, reverting to Evelyn only after her death at St Clere, near Wrotham in Kent. Fanny was born on May 29th 1719, just over a year before Hester Grenville. Her marriage to Edward Boscawen, a younger son of Lord Falmouth, then a promising naval captain took place in December 1742, twelve years before that of William Pitt and Hester and her five children reflect in the correspondence the difference in age with those of the five Pitts. Edward Boscawen, who rose quickly in the service to become one of Pitt's favourite admirals, died in 1761 at the early age of forty-nine. Thus the bulk of the correspondence takes place in Fanny's widowhood.

Extracts and quotations, let alone complete texts, from the 258 surviving letters would fill a book and it has, therefore been necessary to be deeply selective for the purposes of this single chapter. To this end and to match the general theme of this publication, the emphasis has been largely on the letters of domestic detail and on Fanny's lively and amusing pictures of social life, the whole set against a chronicle of the lives of both women. The always intelligent comment on politics and national affairs has had regretfully to be excluded except in so far as it mingles with the family themes.

The correspondence spans the second half of the century ending in 1800; both ladies had long lives, Fanny Boscawen dying at eighty-five in 1805, two years after Hester Chatham, the frailer of the two. Their adult lives were, as Fanny's biographer General Oglander wrote of her, 'deeply scored by the cares and anxieties of almost incessant war' and Fanny, as the wife, widow and mother of sailors was influenced though never depressed for long by this turbulent background; gaiety and love of life permeate her letters.

There is no record of early meetings though it is certain the two young women will have moved in the same circles. The correspondence begins in 1756 but one letter of 1748 survives. Fanny, though still young writes from the sophistication of six years of marriage; this letter has a reference to Hester Grenville's rare participation in London social life:

Audley Street
16th April 1748

I am quite charmed with your Goodness, My Dear Madame and know not how to thank you enough for yr very obliging Epistle; I expect'd as many lines as would tell me you were arriv'd at Bath, and even that I fear'd you would rather mean than perform. . .

You will expect news in yr letters from hence, but not from me as I don't live with People that can tell me any. We talk of nothing but Duels and Masquerades, the former you'll have a dismal Account of in yr newspapers; and for the latter I refer You to Miss Speed or her Contemporaries, the time when a Place where are not yet settled, so I shall take my Ticket out of Town and wait patiently for a Summons to make use of it. Last Week 'twas determin'd to be at Ranelagh, but I hope and believe that is now alter'd, 'tis very unlucky for me that You (who were grown such a Reveller) shou'd be out of the way at this Revell, wch may possibly be far from agreeable to me for want of such a Companion. . .

I rejoice to hear that Bath is likely to be serviceable to you and yr Companion, as to yr Contemporaries, these if I had met with their names by themselves upon a piece of Paper, I shd have concluded it to have been the Dramatis Personal of some new Farce.

Adieu dear Madam, I won't allow my Self to detain you any longer unless I had some hopes of Entertaining you; I leave that Province to Some One who has the Happiness to be nearer to You and shall content my Self with the Title of Yr most faithfull and obliged servt.

F Boscawen

As was customary following the birth of a child, in this case William Pitt's eldest son John, correspondence was usually between the husband and the wife's relations and friends. In her only letter to William Pitt Fanny writes:

Hatchlands Park
the 13th Oct [1756]

Sir

I am extremely sensible to the Honour of your obliging letter, and if it were possible to double the Joy I feel on this Welcome News, it would be by receiving it from your Hand. I heartily congratulate you on the Birth of your Son, and hope he will be another Yourself, if I may use that Expression, for indeed I know not how by any other Words to form a Wish so advantageous to Him.

I am extremely obliged to You for those You are so good to express for Mr Boscawen's Health; I heard Yesterday that it remains perfect tho' he is now in the 25th Week of his Cruize. I cou'd wish he might be repaid for this Fatigue in the way he wou'd chuse, by escorting some french Men of War to England, but as he has seen none yet, it is hardly to be expected now that the Season is so far advanced. I set out to morrow for Portsmouth to visit Mrs Brett, and help her to welcome Friends from the Sea if any shou'd chance to arrive.

My sincerest Congratulations to Lady Hester. . . Believe me Sir with great Respect you most obliged and Obedient Servant

F Boscawen

But the birth three years later of the second son William brings a letter direct to his mother which charmingly (and prophetically) relates the happy event to the splendid war news:

Admiralty
13th June 1759

I cannot be silent any longer My Dear Madam, You must allow me to wish You Joy and more Joy! Your Son, your Recovery and now, Guadaloupe are such Themes of congratulation that blending them together I must present you mine, knowing You cannot receive any that are more sincere and unfeigned.

I know how much you have rejoiced at Hayes for Coll. Clavering's News: May it be only the beginning of Joys, and many more Messengers arrive this Summer with News as welcome! Therefore I will not give You the trouble to answer me now, but when I have presented you with my congratulations for Quebec and the Destruction of every Boat in Havre de Grace, You shall then express acceptance bounteous.

I go into the Country tomorrow en famille (nothing fearing an Invasion) but wherever I am I do not doubt but I shall have more Congratulations to present to your Ladyship. At all times my best Wishes attend you for the Continuance of your Health and that of your charming Family.

The sudden and early death of her husband, not at sea but at home, is an overwhelming sorrow:

Admiralty
Monday night [Jan. 1761]

I intended to have sent my Son to wait on You, to thank you for your great Compassion and Kindness to me, being very unable to do it Myself. . .

Your kind Compassion and pity of my extreme Misery, I am persuaded of, it is so very great that I know not what account to give you of my State, that of my body is indeed surprising, as I feel little or no pain, but Oh, My Dear Madam, may you never be able to guess at the State of my Mind. The deepest Afflication, the bitterest Sorrow, the most heart-felt Grief is Mine and the Cause so just and great that Nothing but the Almighty Hand that inflicted this dreadfull Stroke can ever lessen its Weight.

Yet Madam I am sensible of the Duty I owe to the Memory and Dear

Remains of Him whose Loss I shall ever deplore. This I will endeavour to perform as well as I am able. Your great kindness Dear Madam demanded this much of me. . .

And in an undated letter on the same subject, probably written in April as she also refers in it to the approaching birth of Charles James Pitt (April 24th):

Monday ½ past 2
[April 1761]

My Health is still tolerable, my dejected Mind is still the same, Time cannot yet lay his lenient hand upon it. Wounds so deep must take a long time to heal, if ever. . .
I had a Gentn of the Law with me upon business when yr kind Message came or I had thank'd you for it immediately, he is just gone and I repeat my most sincere Wishes for yr returning Health after short sufferings which your extraordinary fortitude enables you to bear almost better than Any Body; may you ever be ignorant of the still more Severe pangs of the Mind!

A year later she is still suffering from the blow. In a letter of sad charm she thanks Hester Chatham for seasonal wishes:

5th Janry 1762

How much am I oblig'd to you Dear Madam for thinking of me so kindly when I seem so little to deserve, but that is only seeming; I have often thought of Hayes and of offering to It the good wishes of the Season but on that Subject and to such a Friend I durst not trust my self with a Pen, least I interrupt your Chearfulness while I wish it continual. To feel as I do that I can never again see a happy Year, and am quite incapable of enjoying Those Blessings which the Almighty is pleased still to lend Me, these My Dear Madam are sensations so very melancholy that I would avoid Every Occasion of expressing Them to You; beside that in this particular Season my Thoughts (and even my Dreams) are without ceasing fix'd on the Unspeakable and irreparable Calamity that befell me 5 days after this date. . .

Yet time and a brave spirit have prevailed and rather less than two years later, after a short illness, she tells Hester Chatham:

Hatchlands Park
the 24th Sept 1764

Now I thank God I have recover'd Some thing like Health, have had no Return of fever of any consequence this Fortnight and More. I drink Spa Water with tincture of bark in it; I have quite left off the sad custom of laying awake the whole Night, I take ye Air on our fine downs for 2 or 3 hours together, eat a whole Partridge Every day for my Dinner and am in short quite another Person than I was when I last wrote to my dear Friend. . . I have been taught so much Care and Caution (Chatte Echaudée craint l'eau froide) that I have never ventur'd beyond a ten Miles Airing out and home and never set foot in any house but my Own, and what is worse never upon my own green Grass or pleasant Walks.

Her children are growing up and the two daughters are taking part in London life:

My Girls were at the first <u>Almacks</u> Thursday last and very dull they own'd it was.

But no matter: a great event was soon to follow, namely the engagement of the younger girl Elizabeth to Henry, fifth Duke of Beaufort.

Audley Street
11th March 1766

My Dear Madam

Your Goodness to me on all occasion and the constant Marks of Friendship which I have had the Happiness to receive will not permit me to delay a Moment acquainting You that the Duke of Beaufort has just been with Me, with proposals of Marriage for my Daughter Elizabeth; the great Affection He has for Her is the best Security for her Happiness; and that I can once more open my heart to Joy will I know be a sincere One to my Dearest Lady Chatham. You will be pleased to communicate this News to Mr Pitt with my best Respects, I am sure he interests Himself for all the Children of Admiral Boscawen.

I am at all times more than I can express your Lady's Affectionate, faithful and obliged servant

F Boscawen

She apologises for not answering Hester Chatham's letter of congratulation more speedily and explains that it is

Audley Street
18 March [1766]

not Ingratitude but a sort of tourbillon wch passes all description [that] has delay'd my most sincere Acknowledgments. The Hurry His Grace is in, the daily Visits He makes, the visits of his Friends, the Lawyers, the Clothes the lace Women etc. etc. etc. are more than equal to my time, my Health and my Spirits. Tout cela finira heureusement, s'il plait a Dieu, la Semaine de Pacques. Mean time Ld Botetourt is as kind, as pleased, as happy as if He had chose His niece; already He calls Her by no other Name. I can not boast of any such Satisfaction with regard to My Lady Duchess, but it is to be hop'd Time, and my Daughter's Behaviour may reconcile Her also to her Son's Choice which is so determin'd, so fix'd and perfect that I have really gained a 6th Child, and may boast of a fourth very Affectionate Son.

Wedding plans bring happiness but also a little sadness:

Audley Street
the 1st April [1766]

In vain I fancy'd I would have the Honour and pleasure of visiting My Dearest Lady Chatham last Week to thank her in Person for all Her kindness to me.

Not Business only but Elements neigé à gros flocons obliged me to give up a Scheme so desirable to me; I now write in my last Moments. Tomorrow is the Day that I trust in God will make the Chooser and the Chosen happy at St George's church at 9. They are to made One by dr Boscawen, Uncle to the Maiden, whose hand is to be given by her elder Uncle. One is wanting, even without sending Remembrance back to fetch Ideas of Grief unfit for this Blessing.

As was often the case at that time, there are to be surprisingly few guests, and the extremely early time for the ceremony would hardly have been an encouragement. The letter continues:

My Son the moment He heard the News was forming a Scheme to <u>fly</u> to Dieppe and there embark for Brighthelmstone but wisely waited One Post more as Nothing was said in my first Advices about ye Time When. He was soon satisfy'd that It was fix'd by an impatient Lover of 21, by wch a Sage Brother was entirely distanc'd, Else such a Flight ending happily and agreeably surprising Us, had been pretty. Ld Botetourt, my Daughtr Frances, the <u>illustrious</u> William [second son] who also has a new Midshipman's Uniform on the happy Occasion and (You may believe) Myself are also to be present at the Solemnity, and no other besides those before mentioned. We are to breakfast at Ld Botetourt's after Which les nouveaux Mariés se-jetter aux Pieds de Madame la Duchesse a Ceremony rather awfull to my poor Dear Frances and I and William precede them on the Road to Hatchlands where I hope they will also arrive by [.?.] . . . Next Morning they propose to proceed as far as Reading and the following Days to Badminton with their own Horses wch is pleasanter to me than if they went Post as That is, selon moi, a hurry of Spirits which would not be good for my quiet Girl.

The hazards of travelling, especially at night are a cause of anxiety to Fanny, who writes after a visit from Hester:

Hatchlands Park
Sunday 3d Aug [1766]

I have no Words My Dearest Madam that can express my Sense of your extreme Goodness to Me, in that unparall'd kind Visit, but I had certain actions that Evening which express'd very well my great Anxiety and Uneasiness lest you shou'd be in the dark. I wou'd not suffer my windows to be shut but watch'd continually the close of the day wch was accompany'd here by many more Clouds than I cou'd have wish'd; at length there was an universal Glow of Stars, but alas! not till towards 11 and I cou'd not bear to think you were yet abroad under that fair Canopy. . .

I can not hear from You till Tuesday Morning [and] I shall send my swiftest Messenger to the Post and hope he will bring me perfect Satisfaction; but I have been troubled with many Apprehensions, so true it is that our greatest Pleasures must have some Alloy of Pain.

Her daughter Elizabeth's marriage has transformed Fanny Boscawen's life, opening up for her a new world of great riches; one into which she is received with affection.

I must ask You how you do My Dear Madam, how my Lord does, and if the sweet People at Weymouth continue in perfect Health. What wou'd I give to hear that You and They were to meet at Bath next Week, for thither I go next Monday to stay all the Time at the Gloster Races and Musick Meeting, wch is a week. The D of Beaufort, the Dss and her sister repair thither next Monday. . . My Lord wou'd have persuaded me to be of the Party, but my carefull Daughter oppos'd it, 'it will fatigue my Mother to death and give her the Rheumatism.' His Grace then propos'd I shou'd remain here where Nothing shd be wanting etc. but I know that the Want of all Society exposes me, now that my Eyes are very bad, to put them quite Out, to wch the noblest Library I every saw wou'd be no small temptation; so that unless they left me a Chaplain or some One Creature to speak to, I durst not venture on absolute and profound Solitude for a Week, so I prefer a short residence at Bath. . .

I am a little in pain abt this Gloster Expedition but we took the Precaution of une Saignée Yesterday which together with the Prudence of the Lady will I hope prevent all mischief.

This eventful year culminates in a happening of great moment for Fanny Boscawen, the birth of the Beaufort's first child, her first grandchild.

I am sure My Dearest Lady Chatham will be glad to hear from the Grandmother as well as the Newspaper that the Marquis of Worcester is safe arriv'd. His Lordship did not think proper to conform to the Custom of the times (by travelling fast) but that He came night and day; for I do assure you my dear madam His poor Mother was ill from Sunday Morning till Monday Night, and 24 hours of that time in labour. However all ended most happily and both Mother and Child are well as possible, I am sure I may add that the Father is the happiest Man in the World.

The new arrival

now engages me wholly tho' in perfect Subordination to Mrs Beautanton [midwife] in whom is vested the Supreme Power and Dominion over the Mother and Child and Nurse and Every Body, Her's not being a limited Monarchy. Nous nous en trouvons fort bien for I think all hands agree that when Arbitrary Power is well administer'd it is certainly the best. . .

My Sailor, who has never yet been proud of his sister Dss now reveres her because 'She is useful and has behav'd Nobly in a severe Mal' - his own Words.

In 1767 Chatham's long protracted mental illness was causing his wife, and her close friends, much dismay:

All is tending I trust in God to restore You to that degree of domestick Happiness which I have seen You enjoy and which none deserves so Well; no surely, None so much as Those who are entirely devoted to domestick Duties and Feelings est la le Portrait de ma plus Chère et trés respectable Amie.

But all is not well in her own family and she has a widow's anxieties about her eldest son; the letter continues:

> From my eldest son I have just had a Letter from Cornwall where he has been with his Uncle and his Constituents. The idle life he leads (for so I must call every Young Man's who has no particular Employment) makes me very thankfull to you My Dear Madam for saying you wish all my Wishes for every part of my Family. My very earnest Wish for Him I own is to employ Him not only for the Emolument, tho' that is become very necessary to us since the Marriage of my Daur and his <u>Age</u> of Expense, but because with [out] Parts and Qualifications for Business, He may get an habit and taste for Idleness and become a <u>fine</u> <u>Man</u> <u>about</u> <u>Town</u>, wch is a sorrowful thing and much to be deprecated.

Her daughter the duchess is staying with her mother while the duke is at Portsmouth seeing off his uncle Lord Botetourt to take up his post as govenor of Virginia. Elizabeth has been ill but Fanny reports that

> Hatchlands Park
> the 29th Octr 1768

> I have now the Pleasure to reflect that Even a Mother's tenderness and Anxiety were much exceeded by Her Lord's and that She never cou'd be dearer to Him than She is now; this great Happiness seems (according to the course of this chequer'd State) to require some Alloy, and it is One to suffer so much in her Pregnancy and yet to breed so fast, for we have an Assignation with Mrs Beautanton for the middle of next month I believe.

She hopes for a visit from the Pitt children and

> I beg my kindest Complements to them and especially to Dear Lady Hester in whose Memory I beg a Place; tel her that I wou'd send her Ladyp some bits of the Garments, and also of the Hair of the Queen of George's Land (the new discover'd country in the South Seas) wch I had from Captain [Samuel] Wallis the Discoverer, and which I have kept for Her, but they wou'd make this Packet too big, wch will already cost more than 'tis worth.

Just nine years after the death of her husband, tragedy again struck Fanny Boscawen in the death in the West Indies, while serving with the navy, of her favourite son William, aged eighteen:

> Alresford
> 5th Septr 1769

> It is that which is Hopeless - and which I Pray God you may never guess at - that must bring my grey hairs with Sorrow to the Grave. For if ever there was perfection in Youth I was bless'd with it in my incomparable Child, and if ever there was Reason in Afflication Mine must be allow'd for his irreparable Loss. I had at length recover'd [from] One dreadful Stroke and He was the Salve that

heal'd that Wound. Now they all bleed afresh and I have lost Admiral Boscawen once more. . .

I return Lord Chatham many Thanks for his kind attention to Me on this Melancholy Occasion. Be pleased to tell Him I got the Commission I so much desir'd for this lovely Youth, it was dated ye 20th April, and on the 21st the very next Morning he lay a Corpse upon a foreign Land.

Hatchlands is to be sold:

Hatchlands Park
the 28th Sept [1769]

I have been near selling this Place (which I must now submit to do) to a Gentn lately arriv'd from the E. Indies nam'd Sumner but he has bid only £15,500 for It, and as it cost a great deal More (for here is 405 Acres of Land) I am in hopes to get a little more; perhaps too 'I linger e'er I leave the land' but it <u>must</u> be a few Months more shall decide.

The two succeeding years are uneventful; letters are scarce and meetings will have taken place. From Badminton Fanny writes on June 20th 1771:

No one Occurrence that happens here will furnish a single Paragraph for a Letter and indeed I shou'd not have troubled You if my Gratitude for yr very kind Letter wd have been appeas'd short of an Endeavour to express it.

She has been house hunting and continues

After I had the Pleasure to see You at Hayes I went to a Place where I thought of You very much: it was Great Missenden and after I had seen a House to hire, wch did by no means answer its Advertisement and description, I din'd at a very pleasant Inn where I imagin'd You had spent many pleasant Hours in very good Company. Mr Drake's at Amersham is a charming Place. I think upon the whole my Journey was very agreeable tho' the End of it was not answer'd and I have not yet got a <u>Country Seat</u>, tho' I aim at little more than a Cottage.

A year later she is successful in her search:

Enfield
25th July 1772

Allow me my Dearest Lady Chatham to follow you to your noble Seat with my Inquiries since I was depriv'd of the Pleasure of waiting on You at Your Villa [Hayes] which is always such a Holiday to Me and my Daughter that we wou'd not willingly omit it. But just after You were so good to send to Me and I call'd (in hopes to see You) in Bond Street, I heard of this place. . . I went to see it next Morning and took it in the Afternoon, but such was the hurry that ensu'd in transactions with My Landlord, Ld Lisburne, and My Predecessor Mrs Popham then in possession of the Premises, that I did nor said Nothing that did not relate to Enfield 'till at last I arriv'd here the day after Midusmmer day when Mrs Popham quitted it, such was my Impatience to leave London and reside once more amidst roses and honeysuckles that I cou'd <u>call</u> my Own.

On her return to London from Badminton in January, she had resisted thanking Hester for her letter:

Audley Street
12th Jany 1773

During my Residence there I said to myself No, stay till you go to London and then perhaps You will pick up some little anecdotes, some News or <u>Cackle</u> that may make your letter agreeable, at least to the Young Ladies of Burton Pynsent. . .

Divers masquerades wch were projected and laid aside (so much the better I think). One only is to take place at the Pantheon next Week and one at Almacks some time hence. As yet the Town is empty but I suppose it will be otherwise by the End of the Week.

Another great family event awaits her six months later:

Audley Street
2nd June 1773

My Daughter is going to be marri'd entirely to her Content and also to Mine I thank God. Nor does she depart from that <u>Corps</u> wch has been to me the Source of so many Honours and so many Sorrows! She gives her Hand (Heart and all) to a Sea officer distinguish'd among His Comrades, and likely to be very much so in his Profession whenever Occasion shall call Him forth, Capt Leveson Gower, only Son of Lady Dowager Gower. I have not at present much to tell Your Ladyp of the Goods or Fortune but there are certainly well founded Expectations, and indeed real Rights, suspended by the Law's Delay or some other sinister Cause. However, with a little Economy and a great deal of good Liking I hope there will be no difficulties but what may be easily surmounted.

She makes no bones about the relief she feels at the prospect of marriage for her twenty-seven year old daughter:

I have not felt my Heart so light for many Years, wch I do believe You will be glad to hear, for it is a great thing to marry a Daughter to a worthy and honourable Man dans le siècle ou nous sommes.

The wedding followed swiftly:

Bill Hill
the 20th July [1773]

I am charg'd with the Bride and Bridegroom's Respects and acknowledgement. They went the day they were marry'd to Bagshot Park wch Admiral Keppel had been so kind to lend them. I went thither to visit Them last Week and spent several days very agreeably with Them. Sunday Evening they brought me hither to wait on Lady Gower who had been so obliging to insist that I shd be of the Party when ever they came to visit Her. She is so sensible and so easy, that we are most agreeably situated; this Country is charming and the House (wch is good) in a fine high Situation.

The actual ceremony was as usual sparsely attended:

> Her Ladyp did Us the honour to be present at the marriage (in St George's Church) and the Duke and Duchess of Beaufort were so good to come up on purpose from Eastbourn Place in Sussex, wch the Duchess Dowr has lent them for the advantage of Sea bathing...
>
> Lady Gower seems much pleased with her Daugr in law, and expressed entire Satisfaction in her Sons Choice, wch cannot but greatly add to Mine; indeed, I have in this Event nothing but Comfort (after my bitter Sorrows)!

The following year finds Fanny much involved with her elder daughter's first pregnancy, the confinement and its aftermath. The frequent absences of the husband on naval duties throw mother and daughter closely together for this event.

> Audley Street
> 28th April 1774
>
> I am going out of town for a Month and Mrs Leveson with Me, her Situation obliging Us both to be in London in June (and probably part of July), We are desirous to get a little Country Air while we can... My Villa (to wch we are going) is only 8 Miles off at a place call'd Colny Hatch in the parish of Frian Barnet, not far from Enfield Chase wch we see out of our Windows, and looking upon that great Forest of Oaks gives the whole place an Air of deep Retirement and makes it very unlike a common Guingette within an hour's ride of the Capital.

On June 18th, back in London, she is expecting Hester Chatham for dinner and hopes that

> my Daughter will not just choose that day to take possession of her Lit de Misere... Mrs Leveson has often gone with me to my Villa as she did today, yet She has never ventur'd as far as Hayes nor indeed shou'd I be easy to leave her, for now We expect every day, and as it is the first time one cannot be sure how She will acquit her self. Well, I hope, but 'tis a terrible Affair, and the absence of her husband adds I believe to my Anxiety.

At the end of the month:

> Audley Street
> the 29th June [1774]
>
> My Dear Madam
> You are so good to me upon all Occasions that I cannot help informing you Mrs Leveson has got a son and is doing very well both in the capacity of Nurse and Mother; the Child too seems thriving and strong... I find this Office of Nursing is a great Addition of Business; but I trust in God we shall acquit our selves to the mutual Advantage of both Parties.

In July the rather uncommon decision in such circles for the mother to breastfeed is causing Fanny some doubts:

Glan Villa
26th July 1774

I return you many thanks Dearest Madam for your most kind and obliging Enquiry after Us: I have got my Nursery here with Me and hope the Country Air and Quiet will restore her Strength which is not yet just what I cou'd wish. She owns now that she finds it a great affair to produce a child: she did not use to think there was much in it, or at least suspected that the lying in and Confinement was much more tedious than necessary; but now she is convinc'd that at a Month's End she may be very shabby and good for Nothing. Perhaps the additional Office of Nurse is some demand upon her Strength and Spirits, but yet it seems to agree with Her, as it does with her Son most perfectly.

The next six years bring more family events in the lives of the two women, some happy but others of great sadness, especially for Hester Chatham. Fanny Boscawen's family is depleted by the death abroad in 1774 of the 'idle' eldest son, a sorrow to her certainly but not of the depth she suffered when beloved William died. Both the Boscawen daughters continue to breed fast and Fanny is swamped with grandchildren whose yearly arrival she rarely troubles to note. There are some happy occasions to record: Hester Pitt's marriage at the end of 1774 to Charles Lord Mahon and the subsequent birth of their first child, Lady Hester Stanhope of later fame:

Audley Street
March 13 1776

Allow me my Dearest Lady Chatham to express to You my sincere Joy and hearty Congratulations on Lady Mahon's Safety; to be sure I intended Her a Boy, but at the same time I must allow (as I am entirely convinc'd) that she cannot follow a better Example than her Mother, who also began with a Daughter. She will proceed then to present her Lord and His Family with a very fine Son in a twelvemonth more.

My Son [George] is at Buckingham to recruit, from whence He sends me descriptions of Stowe Gardens that make me remember a charming Walk I took with you Ages ago...

Having for my pleasant subject un heureux Accouchement I am turning Gossip and attempting to tell you News. A marriage or two I must needs produce... Mr Cecil (Ld Exeter's presumptive heir) carries off the great Fortune, Miss Vernon, from all the Maccaronies who wanted her to repair their broken fortunes.

In a short note written from Colney Hatch on July 27th 1778, some three months after Chatham's death, Mrs Boscawen hopes that Lady Chatham will allow a visit from her

but let it be your own time - I only take the liberty to express my wish now before I remove further from London... I hope and believe Dear Madam that You consider me as an old and faithful Friend strongly attach'd to You by the sincerest Affection, Esteem and Respect. Yet I know (alas too well) that there are situations of Mind in which one is rather dispos'd to avoid than seek for the Converse of those One was us'd to prefer.

With Hester Chatham now also a widow and any possible criticism from her late husband out of the way, Fanny Boscawen is able with confidence to include in her letters more comment on national affairs, descriptions of naval actions, politics; the 'shocking' suicide early in 1780 of Hans Stanley, prominent diplomat and parliamentarian amazes her, he 'being entirely free from all. . . cares and griefs.' But before long family tragedy has struck the Pitts again: in August Hester Mahon died after a long illness which followed the birth of her third daughter and at the very end of the year the nineteen year old James Pitt died of illness while serving with the navy in the West Indies. This sad event brings back to Fanny's mind the loss ten or so years earlier, in similar circumstances of her sailor son William:

17th Feb 1781

I know not how to presume, my Dearest Madam to write to You; pardon Me if I venture for indeed I think of You daily, and with so much Anxiety and solicitude for Your Health that I cannot forbear entreating you will be pleas'd to dictate one line just to say what effect upon your Body has this deep Allication of your Mind. Alas! You were little strengthened to bear accumulated sorrow. That which you now endure, I endur'd also: You remember Dear Madam the fine Youth I lost at 18, the day after his commission was dated. He in most perfect Health and Strength. Well I remember how often it was the Subject of my poor distracted Thoughts that had he dy'd of Illness, the Visitation of the Almighty, I shou'd have repin'd less than when He was cut off by his own rashness (for he was often admonish'd that he swam too long.) Vain imagination perhaps, the Loss of the beloved Child is the subject of our Pain, and the Infliction of the Almighty Hand ought equally to be seen in the Midst of the Lake as on the sick bed. . . To submit to it, to resign Yourself is now your Endeavour. I doubt not and I trust in God [that] Every day will strengthen You more and more in body and Mind to acquire this religious composure. Time is necessary - and till much more time has heavily pass'd I shall be in care for your Health Dearest Madam and therefore desirous, very desirous to hear of You or from You.

In July Fanny has delayed replying to Hester's letter from Burton Pynsent because, as always, family demands on her time come first:

Colny Hatch
[July 28th 1781]

The delivery of my Daur sooner than I expected engross'd my Time. She was as happy as possible I thank God in this good Work, and went Her full Time as one may be satisfy'd that sees her great fat Boy. She has now 4 as if in submission to her Noble and kind Mother in law who deprecates a 'Fanny Leveson. . .' Every Saturday I have my two fine Grandsons from Westr School, Ld Worcester and Ld Cha: Somerset.

In this letter Fanny, in common with other friends pays many tributes to William Pitt:

Today I had a Lawyer of Lincoln's Inn din'd with Me; we were speaking of the Riots last Year and he told me that when they form'd themselves into Companies for the defence of the Inns of Court they agreed that the tallest Man shou'd be the Captain: thus Mr Pitt commanded their Company and in speaking of Him I cou'd have lik'd Dear Madam to have convey'd to your Ear all that was said. I ask'd my Guest whether he had seen Mr Pitt lately, he answer'd "Yesterday at Serle's Coffee House where he and other Gentlemen of Lincoln's Inn are in the custom of drinking their Coffee, or tea, for an Hour in the Afternoon". . .

It appears to me that the Admirers of Mr Fox betray some Jealousy and Envy of Mr Pitt, from whence I infer that possessing also the great Talents which he, F, has, He possesses also the Virtues and Principles which he has not, and these will give Him the Trust and confidence of his Countrymen at large, while the other can only have their Admiration as a Party.

The following month she writes from Badminton on August 23rd that she

must be back at my own Cottage by the 15th of September else I shall break my Word with my young Friends the Westmr Scholars who depend on their first Sunday Recess on that day.

And from the cottage a letter of 10th October with a choice piece of news:

Lord Rochford has left I hear £300 a Year and no more to his Nephew and Heir, the present Earl. All the rest of his ample Possessions to his Concubine and her son (suppos'd his).

And with her own surviving son, heir to his bachelor uncle Lord Falmouth, in mind, she hopes

this manniere de peindre won't descend to Viscounts. 'Tis Cruel and unjust where ever it is found accompanying a Title of Honour.

A year later, after comment on news of John Chatham's engagement she writes:

Colny Hatch
Middlesex
July 2nd 1782

I wish my Son wou'd marry too but Notre Oncle (having little cause by his Countenance to like Matrimony) has left us so poor that nothing but a good rich Missey will do for Us, and gold (in that Way) is often bought too dear.

A round of visits in August includes one to Mrs Montagu at Newbury:

Badminton
ye 26th August '82

From Lady Gower's I came on to Mrs Montagu's near Newberry where I spent a day very agreeably with Her, who was in her usual good Spirits and has made by the Help of Mr [James] Wyatt and Mr [Lancelot 'Capability'] Brown vast Improvements within doors and Without since I last visit'd her Chateau.

She has heard from fellow visitors, Lady Bathurst and her daughters, confirmation of a broken engagement:

They told Us no News but what we had before heard that Lord Trentham's Marriage with Ly [Caroline] Spencer is entirely broke off, the young Lady having declar'd She does not like Him; He on the contrary being extremely in love and extremely affected and intends to leave England immediately and promener ses Ennuis upon the Continent: It is indeed severe to Him that the young Lady did not find Out her Dislike sooner, as he has been receiv'd as Enfant de la Maison for this half year.

A year later, back at Bill Hill, Fanny has been unwell, but treats her indisposition, not named but delicately indicated, with tolerance and humour:

Bill Hill
the 16th Aug [1783]

I think many People have been indispos'd thro' the heat of the Summer, myself among the rest, which has indeed been one principal reason of not writing to Your Ladyp. I have had the disorder that goes About, wch is in short One and that One cannot go About with, so that I have not yet ventur'd to Church these 3 weeks, but I reckon myself recover'd and perfectly, only that I have some times very slight Returns, wch make me a perfect Philosopher in diet. Change of air I was assur'd by my Physician wou'd do me good and remove that langour wch so naturally follows these disorders. However I was oblig'd to delay my Journey till I had fortified myself with some doses of bark. I have now begun it with great Success and have had the satisfaction to find my Daugr [Frances Leveson Gower] and her 5 children in good Health, as well as my noble Hostess Lady Gower, who prolongs her Evening Walk an Hour after I am hous'd and is in All respects (deafness only excepted) exempt from the Infirmities of 82.

The general election of 1784 in which William Pitt was confirmed as chief minister, brings news also of the Boscawen 'family' seat of Truro, and even more exciting domestic news:

Audley Street
April 12th 1784

The Happiness You enjoy at this Period of perfect and universal Success. I hope it has done You good, improv'd Your Health, rais'd your Spirits. Pray tell me, and return soon (tho' but by a few lines) these my late but very hearty Congratulations, for our Success in Cornwall has been very complete and Truro is at this minute in a fever of Joy.

With a neat play on the word 'Election' she continues:

I must tell you what has occasion'd my all-Time Silence, but it will cost You another Congratulation for amidst my Son's elections He has elected Him a Wife to our great Satisfaction, as it is good that Young Men shou'd marry. His Choice is Miss Crewe of Bolesworth Castle, Cheshire, whose father is now standing for Chester declaring Himself Pittite. Our young Lady is 19, seems very amiable, sensible and well behav'd as well as well form'd and well educated. Well endow'd the World says and rich as Croesus, but her Mother told me that She wou'd have £10,000 down, wch though a handsome portion We reckon nothing extraordinary for our amiable Viscount. He was so genteel as to ask no question abt Fortune before He propos'd, and the Duke of Beaufort is so good as to undertake the conduct of All those necessary Affairs. She is an only Child and therefore will have more in time no doubt, but her Parents are both as Young as They well can be so that Nothing is to be depended upon but what is settled. . . My Time and Thoughts have been much taken up with this Affair. I see ma belle Fille élue almost Every day and like Her indeed very much, not the less for having no connection with her <u>fine</u> Cousine Mrs Crewe; nor wou'd I chuse to have her Manners resemble those of our finest Ladies.

In some unusual passion she is carried away on this subject:

> You wou'd be shock'd My Dear Madam were You to hear the indignities of the Dss of Devonshire [who] exposes herself every day in her Canvass for Mr Fox. Tout le language des Halles, toutes les propositions les plus Scabreuse does she hear with Ears, what she sees with Eyes cannot be told, I am assur'd. What a Shame! She is in this street they tell me almost every day tampering with an inflexible Oilman, and this has been her sole employ from 9 in ye Morning till Night. She gets out of her Carriage, Walks into Alleys and many feathers replace tails in her Hat, Many black guards in her Suite.

Her son George Boscawen who has succeeded 'Notre Oncle' as the third viscount Falmouth in 1782, seconds the Address in the Lords on the opening of the new parliament. While pleased that he was selected to do so Fanny, as always fair in her judgement even in the case of her son, feels that

Aud: Street
May 29th [1784]

> he acquitted himself so well (as indeed I am assur'd He did) cannot with Me be accounted for otherwise than that he spoke con amore, for I think it is not <u>naturally</u> <u>his</u> <u>turn</u>.

She reports that the triumphant William Pitt was at the

> Musick in Westmr Abbey this Morning, an Entertainment for Ears and Eyes far surpassing any this country has produc'd. I can give You no Idea of it, nor expect You will credit that upwards of 500 Musicians perform in Harmony as in a Concert of 20 hands. I have not been at Either of the Performances but I went to the Rehearsal Yesterday wch gave me a very good Idea of it. . .
> I have been interrupted by a Gossip who wou'd come in to tell me how fine the Musick was this Morning. Their Majesties had 5 or 6 children with Them. The Pr of W was not there either Morning. Thursday Night he was as the same Performance in the Pantheon. . . His RHss had a Ball last Night, the Company assembl'd at 10. The Dss of Devonshire did not come till 12 and He wait'd for Her to begin, 'tho the Dss of Marlboro's Daughters as well as Ly Charlotte Bertie were there, but he danc'd only with the Dss of Devonshire.

George has now married his not so 'rich Missey' and in thanking Hester Chatham for her congratulations, his mother describes her, it must be admitted, in a style more appropriate to that of a newly acquired puppy or young horse:

It is I think very desirable that young Gentlemen, especially when they are so sober and of so domestick a turn as My Son is, shou'd marry rather early in Life, and as He is my only remaining One, I wish'd to see it before I dy'd. I have therefore great satisfaction in this Event, as His Choice is very promising. The young Lady is neither very handsome nor very rich (for of the 100,000£ the Newspapers have generously endow'd Her with, she has exactly the Tythe) but She is young, healthy, very pleasing, of an Ancient Family, has been very carefully bred, chiefly in the Country and of a most sweet Temper and disposition as Every body says that knows Her and My Son wou'd by this time swear to, for I see he is very happy.

Fanny lent them her 'little Retreat' and went herself to stay with Lady Gower before returning home again:

Today I expect them here to take their leave of Me and on Monday they go to Lady Gower's at her particular desire in their Way to Badminton; from thence They proceed to the old ragged Mansion in Cornwall where I hope they will continue to be very happy, tho' the young Lady's Seat in Cheshire is I have hear'd by much the most beautifull Place in that County.

With the last of her surviving children married and the annual quota of resulting births no longer making great news, Fanny Boscawen's letters to her friend Hester tend more to look back and to compare modern social life with that of their youth. Even the weather is different:

Audley Street
Mar 1st [1785]

Methinks our Winters are become much more severe than they us'd to be in Our Time: and they last so long too, such redoublement of the cold fits, that indeed they try the Constitution of those that are old (a peu prés). Those that are young try it [for] themselves and want no Aid; they dance 5 or 6 Nights successively and go to bed by 7 in the Morning.

In common no doubt with all except those of his own inner circle, she disapproves of the Prince of Wales. The letter continues:

Among the fine World last Night I hear'd of a Schism. Lady Eliz: Yorke, having invit'd all the said fine World to a Great Ball on Friday Night, yet not aspiring to the Honor of the Prince's Company - His RH also gives a Ball and Supper on that same Evening and as His Invitations have the force of Commands, All the principal Performers who were engag'd to Ly Eliz. Yorke have rec'd his RH's Commands for Carlton House, so that Ly Eliz's Supper for 100 will be deserted and compose another Elegy on an empty Assembly Room. But when I begin to talk of the fine World, the sooner my Discourse is ended the better.

Audley Street
May 4th '85

Prince Edward, His Majesty's 4th Son is to set out next Week for Luneburgh. One cannot help suspecting that His Majesty's First Son is the Motive for exporting the rest (and a very just One is too universally acknowledg'd.) His RH's present favourites are Lady Bamfylde and Mrs Sawbridge: the latter exhibited a Striking Likeness to Mrs Harrel (in Miss Burney's charming Novel of Cecilia wch I hope You have read) for a general Execution being taken in Mr Sawbridge's House One Day, his fine Lady went next day in great Parade to the Epsom Races with the Prince etc. You will say My Dear Madam that yr old Friend is in a very gossiping Humour to tell You these Stories, but I will proceed with a little tract of Nos Moeurs wch I am sure must be quite new to Your Ladyp. The day of the Ascent of Blanchard's baloon, the Duchess of Bolton gave an elegant breakfast to All the fine World in order to see it ascend, the Windows at Bolton House commanding the Scene of Action; but as Expectation is tiresome there was much Play and chiefly Comerce, for Chintz Gowns etc. One poole was for a Watch of Lady Euston's, the Players stak'd 5 Guineas and as there were 7 of them her Ladysp got 35 Guineas for her Watch, after which the Prince who won it sent it Her as a present from Him.

Harriot Pitt has married Edward Eliot, scion of a Cornish family and for this among other attributes, much approved of by Fanny:

Badminton
Sept the 18th [1785]

I flatter myself it will not be long before the Bride and Bridegroom pay their Respects at Burton Pynsent, and that already Your Health is full equal to the Reception of this happy Pair. I always reckon that Joy is very wholesome and does One a great deal of good; it is a remedy that I wish You My Dear Madam to experience. Another I wou'd prescribe (were you to appoint Me your Physician) and that is to leave Burton Pynsent during the Winter Months (to change the Air) and pass Them in London. You need not apprehend too much Company, I do assure you my Dear Madam; for what you wou'd call Evening wch is the Hour of Society, wou'd be dinner time for All the World, and you wou'd find very few beside myself ready (or able indeed) to wait on you from 7-9.

The birth of Harriot Eliot's child in September a year later, and the young mother's death within a few days, was a tragedy which would have caused Fanny Boscawen much pain and a desire to comfort the stricken mother. But custom decreed that she must wait for Hester Chatham's letter before she could record her own sympathy and lead her friend gently away from her sorrow:

Jan 5th '87

How little cou'd I expect or cou'd I hope for the great satisfaction I have receiv'd! My Dearest Madam I return you a Thousand Thanks for this great Favour and most welcome distinction. The sight only of Your belov'd hand affected me much, how much more the Contents of your kind Letter, the noble Sentiments, the pious Resignation, cou'd not be read with dry Eyes, by One who so truly sympathizes in your Sorrow. That Sorrow cannot be forgotten! No, certainly not but neither do you forget the Blessings that remain: and they still are such as no other Mother (now living I verily believe) can boast of. Mrs Leveson told me She saw Mr Pitt at Court yesterday; She thought He look'd in very good Health. God keep Him so many Years, and You my Dear Friend to see it.

Two years pass without identifiable correspondence; Fanny Boscawen, now in her seventieth year is on the move again, this time because of burglaries, as she writes. First however she returns to a favoured topic, comparison of modern social life with that of her's and Hester's younger days:

Audley Street
May 9th '89

When You retire to rest Our Ladies sally forth to their Parties, when You rise they go to Bed, and when You sup, they dine. Last Night the Duchess of Ancaster Dowr had a Masquerade at her own House wch began and ended there. The Balls are innumerable - a Sisterhood of my Acquaintance whom I thought a sober One own'd they had been at Eleven Balls in One Week; how that can be contriv'd in a Week of 6 Days (for we are not yet arriv'd at Sunday Balls) I do not comprehend but so I was assur'd. The Foundation of All this Festivity and Gayety is indeed most Happy [the King's recovery], and His Majesty continues Thank God in perfect Health, as I was assur'd yesterday at Richmond, where now my Country Mansion is seated, compell'd to quit my favourite Cottage near Finchley Common by no less that 3 Visits from Housebreakers; twice they came in and the last time seem'd to have made a considerable Stay, tho' I was in the House with all my Family and a young Lady my relation who was on a Visit to Me. Happily we all slept undisturb'd, nor was my loss at all considerable, for tho' they broke open drawers, bureaus, cupboards and the linnen Press, yet they totally overlook'd the Butler's Pantry where the little Plate I had was lock'd up, but the terror such Visitors inspir'd made me sell the place and I was particularly lucky in meeting with a better House and a charming Garden between Kew and Richmond. .. It is also classic Ground for There [James] Thomson the Poet liv'd and dy'd, and to His Memory I have dedicated a pretty rural Seat. After Him it became the property of Mr Ross the Agent and as an Agent is apt to be as rich as a Poet is poor I have the advantage of large rooms, numerous Offices and other Improvements wch he bestow'd at a large Expence upon his Purchase, but wch fell to Me (by Auction) at a very moderate One.

In this long letter, for which she apologises 'I have made a long Story of Tout mon Moi' she finds space to describe the riots in Paris which heralded the revolution. It is evident that her sympathies lay firmly with law and order:

I have just seen a letter from Paris wch says the Riot there have been exaggerated, but indeed are serious enough, 120 having been kill'd or wounded. The Soldiers were mercifull as long as possible but by pelting them from the Roofs with Stones and logs of Wood, at length they had Orders to fire and the Mob were soon dispers'd: many are taken and they hang 2 a day in two different places for 6 days; 18000 Soldiers are in and round Paris: 2000 occupy the Quarter (Faubourg St Antoine) where the riots were.

Fanny returns, not for the last time, to French affairs in her first letter from Richmond. After noting the exceptionally wet weather and its effect on the harvest, she observes on the controversial decision of the government to withhold the sale of grain to France (thought by some to be the precipitating cause of the revolution) that

Rosedale
Richmond, Surry
July 17th '89

We are much oblig'd to Mr Pitt for not letting His Charity to the french to come in competition with his Care of Us! I was much inclin'd to be generous, but I was suspect there was some Pride at the bottom; and that remembering so many Wars with France I exulted a little in the Thought of their suing to Us for a Morsel of Bread, and wish'd we cou'd have said with Magniminity 'Give it Them, poor Creatures'! but 'tis too certain (I doubt) that such Generosity wou'd have been ill tim'd.

Fanny Boscawen's last letter of 1789, the year considered to have changed the world, is wholly domestic and social in content. It contains one anecdote which must surely epitomise her wry humour, crisply expressed:

Rosedale
the 15th Novemr [1789]

Miss Fagnini is gone from Hence where she lives with the Duke of Queensberry (whose Daur She is suppos'd to be) and Ld Yarmouth with Her. The rest of the Tale is that She is withdrawn as far as Exeter to deposit a Burden that she did not chuse to exhibit Nearer Home, but as Ld Yarmouth is not une Sage Femme One does not see why He shou'd be of the Party. It is to be hop'd He will not so completely renounce all Pretensions to be un Sage Homme as to marry Her, so little worth as She is of such a Station.

The last ten years of the correspondence (though not of Fanny's life) yield fewer but generally longer letters, her literary style enhanced rather than impaired by age, subject matter much as before.

Wedding fashions are changing:

Audley Street
April 12 1790

We had in our neighbourhood last night a Wedding, Miss Sophia Southwell (a God-daughter of Mine) to Mr Townshend, Lady Chatham's Brother. The Ceremony was perform'd by the Bishop of Peterboro' at Lady Dowr de Clifford's in Stanhope Street and in the Evening (according to the present Fashion) afterwards les nouveaux Mariés went out of Town to Frognall.

And one result of the events in France:

We have a great number of french People of Rank and Opulence (in their own Country) Here, who might put Us in Mind cou'd We forget it a Moment, of the extraordinary Felicity of our own Country.

Despite her robust general health and vitality, Fanny has begun to suffer from some of the infirmities of old age and, unusually for her, her letters now have an ache, a pain or a discomfort to record. She has taken a week to answer Hester's letter but

Audley Street
March 31st [1791]

that Week is however pass'd and now I will not wait any longer for the departure of a swell'd face wch has made it difficult for me to hold down my head to write or to read. Till this unlucky face-ach came to Me last Week, I wou'd have made a very pert Answer to All your kind Enquiries by boasting of perfect Health during the whole Winter, interrupted only by a slight Cold or Two, which taught Me to avoid the Night Air, by using my Chair whenever I went out of an Evening, but the late fine Weather having encourag'd Me to leave off that Precaution, I have now got the only bad Cold as it affects teeth (or rather Stumps) and one side of my Face which however, since it has swell'd is easy, and about to take its leave.

She hopes as always that Hester Chatham will soon return for a spell in London but takes the opportunity of this prospect to go back once again to the topic of the extraordinary hours kept by those of the 'fine World':

tho' as to the Hours and Manners of London, I must confess I know not how to reconcile them to You or to Reason, and I think every year grows worse than the past. Your Hour of Rest and Retirement would arrive before any body had order'd their Coach for the Evening's sortie. The Ladies go to Assemblys soon after Eleven, or if any thing detains them till past 12 they are yet in Time. The Hour of Dinner upon the Card of Invitation is often 6 I am told, but that the Guests are seldom punctual; With this fashionable World yr Ladyp will believe, I have no connection.

Family engagements, marriages and, as would be expected at her age, deaths fill but do not swamp Fanny's letters. In August of 1792 her son-in-law, Admiral Leveson Gower dies, leaving his widow the 'sole Guardian' of their eight children, at present 'a great care' the eldest being only eighteen.

The following year brings an even greater loss, the death of her daughter-in-law; but even in a tragedy of this magnitude the demands of custom and good manners require that comment on a letter from Hester must take precedence over this news:

Rosedale
Richmond
Augt 20 1793

How very kind Dearest Madam to remember Me who seem'd to have forgot Burton Pynsent: but it was not so nor Ever will [be].

I had often promis'd myself I wou'd write to Mrs Stapleton to inquire after Your Health, particularly in the extreme hot Weather; not that I am ever long ignorant, I even knew (before I rec'd your Most kind Letter) of the singular Pleasure you had receiv'd in Ld Stanhope's most interesting Visit - but latterly Dear Madam I need not give any account of my Silence (the former part of it really unaccountable.) Now I am overwhelm'd with a Family Affliction, so unlook'd for, the subject of it so Young, strong, healthfull as was thought, that indeed it has almost subdu'd Me. The best of Sons and of Husbands is in the deepest Affliction. His poor Sister was with Him and has now the sad task to return in kind his Compassion to Her, for this time twelvemonth when Admiral Leveson was snatch'd away at a Stroke, my Son flew from Cornwall to his Sister and came time enough to follow his Noble Friend to the Grave, till business oblig'd him to return to his Family. She is now doing the same kind Office to Him, and it must be a very painfull One to Her as it renews her own Sorrows. But such is the Lot of Humanity. I do not speak Alas! to One who knows It not or had not travell'd the same Road thro' this Vale of Tears! Yes my Dear Madam, the Cup of Affliction has been often presented to You and You have drunk deep. You have many Comforts left Thank God, bright indeed, and illustrious beyond Example I hope I do not forget Mine or fail to remark that tho' death has twice visited the Mansions of my Children within the compass of a Year, yet my Children were not struck.

In the spring of 1794 Fanny is on a rare visit to Bath, mainly it would seem to be with her widower son, afflicted with gout. She find much to interest her in his raising and command of a regiment of Cornish Fencibles. She is meeting part of the cost:

Bath
3d April 1794

Yes, my Dear Madam, our brave Cornish Men have paid a great Compliment indeed to my Son in seeking Him even to his Gouty Chamber (where he has been laid up these 3 Weeks) to command their honorable Corps. . . I think He is much pleas'd with It and he wrote me his Hopes "to catch the fancy of several young Farmers Sons, and Yeomen by the dazzling appearance of the crested Helmet and glittering apparel of a light Horseman."

Her son's letter of 2 April which she has transcribed and encloses contains only

his Thanks to Me for having <u>graciously</u> accepted the Part of this Honour wch he was willing to confer upon Me, that is contributing the Mount this galant Troop, for the Horses must be purchas'd, the little Cornish breed will by no means do, and there is only £250 allotted per Troop for the raising the Men etc. etc.

Her thought are once again with events in France:

Surely if the detestable french could be terrify'd they might be so with our Union, our Zeal and our Resources, but they [only] understand inspiring Terror if not of receiving It. Another Execution, 20 in the day, what butchery! but will these Waves of blood extinguish the Fire of Rage and Animosity? Surely No, but they will smother them I doubt and prevent their breaking Out - but I will not talk of the french, 'tis an Awfull Subject and sinks our Spirits.

Fanny and her Leveson daughter are detained in Bath into the month of May because of the need to be with her son who 'longs to be in Cornwall riding about'. Her time however has not been wasted:

My Dearest Madam
     Your kind, very kind Injunction to write <u>By</u> and <u>By</u> should have been literally obey'd if I had not waited to tell you better News of my Son that I cou'd with truth do the day or 2 after I was honour'd with your most kind Enquiry after Him. He is now so much better that he walks without a Stick. . . and he has already un Pied en l'Air for Cornwall and purposes to stay at Exeter on Tuesday Night. He had the Satisfaction to receive to day a list of the Names of 9 more Recruits. . . but what is better still, He has happily achiev'd the Grand Affair - the Riding Master, and has got the great Mr Dash, him self long establish'd Riding Master at Bath where he breaks in All the Horses, teaches All the Misses and Masters too. . . so You see my Dearest Madam, Our Fencibles have got their grand Diseratum, but You will hardly suspect that I shall take any credit, and me donner les Violons on the Acquisition; but true it is that when I saw my Son so anxious to get a good Riding Master, it occur'd to Me that my Bror Evelyn, a mighty Hunter and Compleat Horseman, now at Bath (with an obstinate lombago). . . that <u>He</u> was the Person to consult, and accordingly I told him our Wants the first time He hobbled to my Cribbage. He said He wou'd consult Dash who was the Man in the World most likely to know some body. This Plan then was immediately follow'd. . . and in 3 days it has been completed beyond our Hopes in the manner I tell your Ladyp.

As she grew older Fanny Boscawen's movements between Audley Street and Richmond have, like the birds, a regularity, predictable, almost inevitable. She no longer enjoys visits that entail long journeys. Even an invitation to Badminton causes her some hesitation:

     Since I receiv'd the Honour (and I'm sure I ought to say <u>Favour</u> of your kind letter) My Dear Madam I have been prevail'd upon to take a long Journey, at least what I call such, and what the Indolence and Infirmities of Age make me unwilling to undertake; but my Son and Mr Daughter being of the Party, and another Daughter requesting, I wou'd not refuse to join them, conquer'd all reluctance and I arriv'd Here with Mrs Leveson and Ld Falmouth last Tuesday. Our very kind reception, the Change of Air and of Place, the beloved Society we enjoy Here has done Us all good I believe, at least I find my Health vastly recover'd.

Reluctant though she is to travel far, age has not diminished Fanny's appreciation and understanding of the times in which she is living. Rarely does a letter omit to give her views on the progress of the war, on the revolution in France and the massacre of so many of her French friends. She reads the newspapers until such time as their contents disgust and alarm her. On 6 November she writes from Rosedale:

     I have been silent lately waiting on some good News to discourse upon, some pleasant Topic to enliven a dull Letter; but alas! Offence and Trouble are sad Themes and to see so many Enemies Within, while those Without are too numerou and successful, is a melancholy Subject of Reflection or Conversation, so that we hate the Sight of a Newspaper.

and in June the following year also from Rosedale:

> My Newspaper is call'd The Times, and The Times are not as yet just what you and I wish Dear Madam.

Much of the family news, marriages and births, is now of the third generation, the grandchildren and great grandchildren, all as ever set against the vagaries of the weather. There is a heat wave and

Audley Street
18 May [1795]

> Now my lilacs are all blown at Rosedale and Nightingales singing. I visit them very often and sometimes take my Dinner There, as my <u>Journey</u> [from London] is only an Hour and 5 minutes. . .
> Domestic Occurrences are good and Lady Worcester is already Out in her Coach to take the Air. (I think We did not use to break Prison so soon.) She left at my door a Request that I would be Godmother to the young Lady, an Honour I shall certainly accept. . .
> My Daugr Leveson is happy in the Arrival of her Lieut Colonel (of ye 63rd) from the Continent looking as Well as if he had been much us'd to go to bed or to fare as sumptuously as We may do whenever We are dispos'd to pay 16sh: for a good Fowl, such was its Price yesterday. But as Scarcity is no good News, I'm sure I will not make <u>That</u> the subject of my Discourse.

Audley Street
27 May [1795]

> I hope this sudden Change from heat to Cold, this <u>freeborn Weather</u> (as Soames Jenyns term'd it) will not retard you in yr Progress: it has however been more free or even licentious than usual; Saturday last we were panting with Heat I was call'd to the Christening of my Great Grandaugr Lady Charlotte Sophia Somerset, We had all the Windows open at 9 at Night and there was not Air enough to affect the Candles - now every body has large Fires.

She has had a visitor with an interesting story to relate:

Rosedale
9th Octr 1795

> I have told yr Ladyshp long stories of my [family] Visitors and now I must tell you of another who came to me strait from Paris wch she left on ye 19 Septr. As a Swiss (Genl Prevost's Widow) she took her Journey all thro' France unmolested, and in 420 Miles never saw a Gentleman's Carriage, only Diligences, Waggons and Carts. At the Inns they oblig'd her to admit to her Dinner the postillions who drove her and sometimes a Dragoon or two that belong'd to the Section. Every Chateau that was not in Ashes, was taken down for the Materials to build Cottages. In miserable Alehouses she often found superb Furniture, fine beds where She had expected to have lain upon a grabbat Pictures wch had been pillag'd from neighbouring Seats. At Anci le franc fine Napkins wch had Made de Louvois' mark upon them. She was twice in the Convention, for sitting in Mr Louvet's Shop wch is a Stationer, He offer'd to conduct Her to the Assembly, wch

He did and He was Presidt that Day. The Next [? day] she went with Him again but He was not again Presidt. The Convn was not so noisy as She expected but consisted of mean looking, dirty Men. She was at the Opera, and at the Play, and walk'd Home from Both (as did most of the Company) at Midnight in perfect Security. No Coaches at Paris with Arms except the ambassrs. They gave her 1160 assignats for her Guinea and told her that 3 Women govern'd France, viz Made Talien, Made de Staal and Made Louvet. The latter I suppose sells pens and sealing Wax between Whiles. Paris was very quiet when She was there, the Poor had their Bread deliver'd out according to the size of their Families and that bread was bad, but at the Traiteurs You might have the whitest and best as well as all sorts of Luxuries if You cou'd pay, and expecially in <u>coin</u> wch was much desir'd but seldom appear'd.

It is evident that of the two elderly ladies, both in their mid-seventies, Hester Chatham though the younger by a year or so, is much the frailer of the two.

We learn from a letter of 3rd May 1796 that Hester can no longer go downstairs unaided:

> I was in Hopes that in Summer You did, as far as a Terras or Garden. but if You cannot get There without being carry'd I do not wonder You renounce It; for to be carry'd down stairs is a fearfull Thing, so I found it a few Years ago when after a Fall I cou'd not walk, my Stairs (at Rosedale) were good, my Servts strong, and very carefull but I cou'd not bear it, and chose rather to remain up Stairs (tho' contrary to my Surgeon's Orders) than endure the Fright of being carry'd down.

Fanny by contrast is barely touched by age except for minor ailments and by her reluctance to travel long distances. Her views on politics and the war remain strong and forthright as they do also on aspects of family life. She had foreseen

Audley Street
7 May [1796]

> that a Mariage then full of difficulties wou'd by the great kindness and Indulgence of the best of Parents be consented to, or rather <u>yielded</u> to. The Duke of Beaufort's Eldest Daur, a very lovely Lady Elizabeth has it seems (long Since) declar'd her determin'd Preference for Mr Talbot, a young Gentleman Grandson to the excellent Ld Chancellor Talbot, and Son of a most worthy Dr Talbot of Guiting in Glostersh: Himself very worthy too I trust and so esteem'd but he is young et qui pis est a younger Son of a Younger Bror of course, far from being so well appointed as our Dear Young Lady might have been (long since) in Mariage. However her decided Preference and at the same time her dutifull Behaviour have at length obtain'd from the Duke a reluctant Acquiescence.

After naming the fiancé's high born relations, from some of whom he has expectations Fanny continues with the information that his aunt

> the Countess Dowr of Shaftesbury endow'd Him also 2 Years ago with the Rectory of Wimborne St Giles in Dorsetshire. . . so that if He displays 'The Beauty of Holiness' (as I heartily wish He may) He may in Time rise in the Church, mean while He has some Fortune in possession some too in Expectance, but All forming a Revenue so unlike the Hospitable <u>State</u> of Badminton that I hope my sweet

young Lady is not mistaken in the Ideas She has adopted of a Cottage and Love, for I guess the best sort of Parsonage House must appear to be a Cottage to a Somerset. However, Here are Two young and amiable People happy - and their good Parents now They have yielded put a very good Face upon it and humour them with a good Grace, the Duke endowing his Daur as liberally as He wou'd have done had She marry'd in her own Line.

Some weeks later Hester's offer to Fanny of a gift from her collection of exotic birds, though refused with grace, yet results in a description of the trees at Rosedale:

> Rosedale
> 25th June 1796
>
> I am thankfull for yr kind offer of the feather'd tribe, but my Domaine is narrow, only Ten Acres (wch is large however for the Parish of Richmond): one Field for a Cow, and a large Garden ornamented with beautifull Trees. Vast Cedars of Lebanon, Catalpas that blow like Horse Chestnuts, a Tulip Tree (Timber), now full of flowers, and a Sassafras Tree suppos'd to be the largest in England a variety of American Oaks and other Exotic Trees and Plants. My predecessor being Agent to many Regimts rec'd presents from All the Officers that visited foreign Countries, and possessing this Place 30 years and loving Plantations, they are arriv'd at an uncommon Size. Previous to this it was Classic Ground, Here liv'd and dy'd the sweet Poet James Thomson - but I must not describe Rosedale for the Post is going - and indeed I am going too, to London to be present at Ly Eliz. Somerset's Mariage and to leave my pleasant Garden for Her Ladyp and happy Spose to inhabit for a few Days before they go Home to Wimborne St Giles, Dorsetshire.

And the wedding, attended only by near relations, here all Somersets except for the two sisters of the bridegroom:

> Audley Street
> 29th June 1796
>
> I told you my Dearest Madam I would have the Honour to wait upon You again soon, for since I answer'd Your kind Letter (wch I had so little deserv'd) I have left my rural Habitation to a Bride and Bridegroom, very happy People, and I hope likely to remain so, as They have enlisted under the Banners of le petit Cupidon. . .
> I came to Town last Sunday Evening, All my Children came to welcome Me and next Day I repair'd to St George's Church carrying the Bridegroom. . . but were soon follow'd by the Duke and Duchess, also the Duchess Dowr, Lady Worcester (her Ld gone to his Regt), Ld and Lady Charles Somerset, Ladies Frances, Harriet and Anne Somerset, and Ld William and Two Misses Talbot, Sisters to the Bridegroom. The Ceremony solemnly perform'd, We return'd to Gr[osvenor] Square, from whence the United set out in their new Post Chaise for Rosedale where Roses innumerable were blooming.

Still somewhat intrigued with this inappropriate marriage (for a Somerset) Fanny has a word to say about the bridegroom:

[He has] I am assur'd an excellent Character. He has also very pretty Manners, his figure pleasing as You may imagine since He has made such a Conquest, tho' nothing striking in my Opinion.

Always sensitive to national affairs, Fanny reacts like a thermometer to the news bad and good. On 25 July she writes:

Publick News is such that I have left off reading my Newspaper. There it lies like a Snake, I don't touch It; only Capt Trollop's Heroism has been read to Me.

But two months later

Rosedale
the 8th Octr 1796

I think I may venture to make a little visit to My Dearest lady Chatham, and even to venture a Word or two of Congratulations, for surely I descern now some blue Sky in our political Hemisphere (to borrow Newspaper Stile). Sure I am it seem'd All clouded over, dark and thick now many Weeks ago, but now is greatly and happily chang'd. Yesterday I visited a Rt Hon Lady who said to Me "You shall prophecy when ever You please, for, the last time I saw You You promis'd Me that Mr Pitt's good Fortune wou'd certainly attract some good News before the Parliat met and You see it is arriv'd - large and ample."
I am quite pleas'd to be an old Sybil and that
Long Experience doth attain
Something like prophetick Strain.
I am fond of these Lines and apt to quote them: But I cou'd not certainly premise that Jourdan's Army wou'd be lessen'd by 28000 Men since it enter'd Germany, as I am assur'd it is.

For four more years the letters of this wonderful correspondent Frances Boscawen continue, with their vitality, humour, awareness of public events, love and interest in (and sometimes gentle criticism of) her now vast number of descendants, unimpaired. She rejoices in her matriarchy, loved and often visited, alone sometimes but never lonely:

Rosedale
the 31st July 1797

What Goodness have I to acknowledge My Dearest Madam. It fills me, I confess with Shame and Confusion, but still it delights me; and I will not make any Excuses, or Apologies, but trust entirely to that Goodness, and at least take care not to abuse It. What is become of Me, You condescend to ask? Why, I have been quietly settled in my Villa ever since the 15th of June, leaving however All my Family in London (except my Son who was marching his Fencibles to Chester.) My 2 Daurs and their Families remain'd and so frequently contriv'd to come and spend the Day with Me (fashionable Hours of meeting and Engagemts in London not beginning till 10 at Night), that for some Time I was chiefly employ'd in receiving them. Still surely I might have wrote a Letter to a most belov'd and respected Friend whom I constantly thought of, and so doubtless I should , if I had not been simple and sanguine enough to say to Myself "We shall have some good

News" - We can hear the Tower Guns at Richmond if the Wind is the East, and thus I waited - but the Good News did not arrive, and now All my Family are gone to their respective Retreats, and I receive Letters from them so often, that to make Response keeps my poor worn out Pen in as much Employmt as it is able to achieve. . .

Retirement however and Richmond are incompatible: and even to Day I am going to dine Abroad. . . The Gayeties of Richmond are surprizing, and I had the Misfortune to be s Spectator of Them (wch I little intended) a few Nights ago but Twice a Week there is Bands of Musick on the Thames, or on the Hill, and all the World assembles on Its Banks, on Saturdays on the Hill, on Tuesday on the D: of Queensberry's Terras. I was going to visit my Niece Mrs Brudenell who lives on the Hill at 8 in the Evening but found such a Crowd of Coaches, that I might have fancy'd my Self at our Ridottos of old. No possibility of moving on, or Arriving; while the Crowds of Walking People of all Ranks and figures was quite astonishing. I shall take care how I go up the Hill of a Saturday again, but then I was a little diverted to hear my Coachman propose very civilly to a Lady who was driving a Gigg that She wou'd be pleas'd to advance a little, for then he might have hopes to get on. She assur'd him it was the least of her intention to Move, for she cou'd not be in a better Station to hear the Musick; so then, we were perforce oblig'd also to hear the Musick, till some more supplicants not quite so civil as my Coachman convinc'd the Lady She had no right to wedge Us All in so perfectly; and at length I arriv'd at Mrs Brudenell's whom I found alone at her Window contemplating with Astonishment the Multitudes beneath It, and wondering how I cou'd arrive.

She has had a visit from Hester Chatham's granddaughter Hester Eliot (aged 12) with her governess:

Audley Street
28th March [1798]

We talk'd of You and there was One Subject on which Miss Eliot gave me great Satisfaction. I ask'd Her particularly after your Eyes and I find They are excellent, wch rejoiced me greatly, for tho' there are many things in these sad Times that to read gives the Pain, yet we have Our Choice and being able to read with ease even by Candlelight, is a great Source of Amusement to Me who passes many Hours Alone, my Daughters Hours and Mine being of necessity so different. Was it not a good old King Alphonso of Spain who desir'd Old Books to read, Old Friends to converse with - old Wood to burn - and Old Wine to drink? How much Wiser he must have been than his Successor who now reigns in that fine Country! reigns! Oh No, serves and is enslav'd to the Monsters who have murder'd All his Family.

The curious episode of William Pitt's duel on Putney Heath with a political rival George Tierney on 27 May caused something of a panic countrywide:

Aud: Str
5th June 98

My Dearest Madam
Sunday the 27th May is a Day I shall not soon forget! Not but I escap'd all Terror; tho' a young Lady burst into my Parlour while I was at Dinner and with trembling Voice ask'd me if I had heard - - - - I answer'd No, nor did I believe what

she utter'd, for it was impossible; it was a vile Report to spread Terror. I beg'd Her to compose herself and be persuaded there was no Truth in what She had heard: and I actually prevail'd to make her doubt at least, tho' not quite convince Her. I was convinc'd however, and remain'd easy, till at Night I want Out and then I heard the Truth, but Thank God that All was safe, and this poor Country not quite undone. . . I have a great mind to fancy that the Touch of Gout in your left Hand may have been rather favourable in absorbing certain effects of Agitation etc. tho' ending most happily in Overflowing of Thankfulness to the Almighty Preserver of Our Sovereign and his Kingdoms.

and though hoping soon to leave London for the summer 'to sit under the Trees of my Garden', Fanny's departure has been delayed

because my Children are All in Town, the Dss of Beaufort and my Son for the Birthday, the former in her Widow'd State for her Lord after having been twice in Wales to see the supplemental Militia sally forth, is now at East Bourn with his own Men of Monmouth as are also Ld and Lady Worcester, long since resident. In short All the World are arm'd Cap a pee and even the Volunteer <u>Tradesmen</u> of this Parish form a most amazing Regiment reaching in files the whole length of this long Street the Earl of Chesterfield on Horseback at their Head - their uniform dress, their feathers, their numbers, their steady March, All quite surprizing! Many such Regimts there are compos'd of Plumbers, Carpenters etc. but the most respectable is That of Gentlemen Volunteer Horse, all mounted, cloath'd and disciplin'd at their own Expense. . . You see my Dearest Madam I cou'd talk of the Glories of Old England, at least of her Powers but Here is a Shower of unpaid Bills just arriv'd wch I must inspect and pay.

Understandably naval victories rank high in Fanny's criterion of the 'good news' she likes to include in her letters to her friend. Admiral Nelson's victory of the Nile of 1 August gives her all she needs:

Rosedale
Richmond
Surry
5 Octr 1798

I have waited and waited at length I am satisfy'd indeed: delighted, triumphant! Last Night I had a great N in brilliant Lamps adorning the Front of my Mansion and All Our royal Village was illuminated. My Walks have been render'd pleasant by the continual Sound of Bells ringing All around, the Fire of Cannon without ceasing. . . God be prais'd that Thus our success extends, and that the Fear of Us, and the Dread of Us is thus impress'd on these Monsters the french who have overturn'd the World, and extended Slavery and Misery to the remotest Parts of It.

In the final year of the correspondence, Fanny Boscawen's powers of description, of delight of reporting, even second-hand, a special event are, if anything, enhanced in this her eightieth year. Her handwriting too is still firm and bold.

The event she now writes of is the coming of age festivities of the fifth Duke of Rutland; but first some weather and family news:

My Dearest Madam

How often I have thought of You during this bitter Winter - how often pleas'd my Self with thinking You were less likely to suffer by It, by Your never going Out. This I have not prov'd by my inflexible Silence for which I will make no Apology... [Her health] which You are so good to desire an account of is wonderfull at my Age. I always find that a volutary Imprisonment is the only way to deal with a <u>true</u> Winter, such as This has been (preceeded indeed by as <u>true</u> a Summer) so that since I came to Town I have liv'd by my own fireside and left it very rarely to go in my Chair as far as my Daughter's who is just by; as She laid down her Coach last Year Mine has been very convenient to Her, and brings Her daily to Me. My Son too, who came up to Parliat and who has hitherto escap'd Gout I thank God is often with Me, and last Week when the Duke of Beaufort came up to present His noble Wards to Their Majesties, I had the Pleasure of His Company every Day while he staid. The Dss I have not seen since She made me a kind Visit at Richmond in Novr and staid a Week. Both their Graces with 4 Sons and 2 Daughters, Men and Women, were at Belvoir Castle 10 days. A most wonderful Festivity of wch the Dss always contriv'd to give me frequent Accts and I doubt if there has been such an One in any of our noble Chateaux since the Days of good Queen Bess. The Dss of Rutland hop'd for the Arrival of Mr Pitt but my correspondent expected rather His Excuse; It came, and no Wonder! When will He have leisure for any Holydays?...

To return to the Festivities at Belvoir. They pass'd off most happily in all respects, no Accident or Contretemps whatever which considering the vast Concourse of People, without as well as within the House, the extreme severe Weather, the bad Roads, was really most fortunate. The Prince arriv'd the Day before the <u>Birthday</u>. On that Day They, the Guests sat down to Dinner at the different Tables abt 300. At His Table, where He sat between the Dsss of Rutland and Beaufort they were 54: the latter wrote me that the Dinner the Plate, the Attendants in short Every thing was worthy of the Guest; and that it was really surprizing how many could be so well taken care of, for She was assur'd that in Every Room the Tables were as well serv'd as Theirs. The P. had promis'd the Dss of R. that He wou'd not sit long at Table, and He kept his Word, and repair'd to the Drawing Room as soon as the Ladies were well ready to receive Him, this He did duly. He staid 6 Days and His whole Behaviour was just what it ought to be (only He brot T: Sheridan with Him, Sheridan's Son wch He had better have let alone says my correspondent.)... When there was not a Ball there was Musick and Cards but no Gaming. The P. walk'd about and convers'd with One and Another with the greatest Ease and Agrément. The Great Ball Night He danc'd 2 dances with Ly Kath Manners. On Sunday He went to Church, and behav'd with the utmost propriety. That Evening there was no Cards, only Musick till the Ladies were All retir'd towards Morning, in short His RH exerted all those Talents wch He posseses to <u>please</u>, whenever He chuses to do so. As to the Hospitality Out of Doors, it was prodigious: yet no Drunkeness at least no Riot. The Duke told Me of a ridiculous Distress for which they were oblig'd to come and fetch Him. In one of the Booths or temporary Buildings the Guests arriv'd so early that they fill'd it entirely up, and when the Good Dinner presented itself, there was no possibility of its getting in for no body wou'd come Out; however the Duke of B at length persuaded Them to make Room for it (less qualify'd Persons having try'd in vain). The Dss told Me She went but Once to see these Out-Doors Festivities (the Descent being not suitable to her Lameness for Most of the Company went frequently.) She arriv'd at a Booth where a great Number of People were enjoying a good Dinner, they told her abt 700. She says the Remains of Magnificence in the House is the

Pictures wch are superior, and the Old Plate, a vast Quantity of old ornamental massive, as well as endless Sets of usefull modern. The Furniture in general Old and delabré but the Dss of Rutland had contriv'd to keep Out the Cold by green Doors, and baize Curtains every where so that the Drawing Room was really warm tho' 100 feet long, and on the Great Fete the whole Chateau, been illuminated must have counteracted the Cold. For my part I thought of Fire, having Here seen a House burnt to the Ground (Lord Essex) in a very short time, hardly suspected by the Master and Mrs in the Eating Room, while the Flames were in the Street. But the Belvoir and Grantham Yeomanry offer'd Themselves as Guards and must have been very usefull, for, all over the House and all <u>day</u> long you met well drest People walking about, self invited, and unknown. I wrote it for Miss Eliot and send my best Complets to Her and Mrs Stapleton. . . No [more] Paper to tell yr Ladyp how truly I am Yours

FB

The last surviving letter (its impeccable timing would have appealed to Mrs Boscawen) passes on her son, Lord Falmouth's description of Christmas and New Year at Badminton:

Audley Street
9th Janry 1800

Now it is Over I may ask the question and I am sure Mrs Stapleton will have the Goodness to answer It - being no less interesting than how our Dearest Lady Chatham has borne the long and very severe Winter We have just pass'd. Just before It set in I had the greatest Satisfaction to be assur'd by My Son that Lord Chatham Himself had told Him that lately return'd from Burton Pynsent he had the Comfort to see Her Ladyp very tolerably Well, and leave Her so - This gave me such Security and was so very pleasant to Me, that I ask'd for no more - left off Writing - and remain'd silent - till the terrible Frost and Siberian Weather grew every day more and more severe, and turn'd my Thoughts often to Burton Pynsent but Then did I write? No indeed: nor have I any better Excuse to make I believe than numb'd fingers. Now, The Thaw is come, and I have been Out in my Coach - Yesterday for the first time since I came to Town 3 Weeks ago, but on thus breaking Prison I shall find more leisure than I had when I never stir'd from my Fireside, when the Walkers on our dry Streets succeeded Each Other in my Room and left me no Writing-Hour. Well my Dearest Lady Chatham - forgive this Neglect (for I aver it was not Forgetfulness or Ingratitude) in not availing myself of the Privilege She is so good to allow me of sending Her some of my Scribble from Time to Time. I can hardly forgive Myself (for by this time I might have had the Pleasure of a Letter from Burton Pynsent) so that the Crime has been the Punishment: and That will plead my Pardon. I have now Nothing to compose a Letter that is worth reading, no News to tell, or Events to relate that are not convey'd in The Times or the Oracle.

My Letters are fill'd with far different Subjects, for my Son is a very good Correspondent and He is keeping his Holydays at the cour Plenière of Badminton wch really resembles That of Longleate in the ballad of Old Times "where the poor are provided, The rich receive Honor, So Great and so Good is the Lord of the Manor" and indeed None can exceed the Duke of Beaufort either in Gifts of Oxen and Woollen Cloathing and fuel to the Poor to a Wide Extent or in superb and delightfull Festivity to His Family within his Chateau. He has now Eleven Children There, with their Wives and Little Ones, of these (his Gr Children) I cannot tell the exact Number, only I know that Ly Eliz Talbot the last marry'd has brot 3. On New Year's Day the Duke wou'd have Them All assemble at Dinner in the Great Hall and they sat down 40. In the Evening there was a Ball: but first the Duke gave New Year Gifts to all his Children and Gr Children desiring the fine Ladies to remember there was no Mr Gray's shop to furnish better Etrennes wch must account for his being <u>ungenteel</u>, for they were no Other than Bank Notes of wch All his Daurs including Ly Worcester and Ly Cha Somerset had one of £25 (his own Dear Lady's of £50), his grown up Sons £100, School Boys £5 - lesser Children 2£ or £1 according to their <u>inches</u>. It was an agreeable Surprise, and Nobody danc'd less light for this addition of Paper in their Pocket. My Son's Eldest Daur (a favourite with Us All) is so happy as to have been invited to This Festivity. It ended with the Twelth Cakes of Monday last, but my Son is not yet return'd; I expect Him before the Birthday. I'm sure if He were Here He shou'd frank This wch is not worth the Postage.

It carries Every Good Wish to Dearest Lady Chatham, to her sweet Grand Daughter and excellent Friend. They will Both plead for my Pardon knowing how truly I remain Her Ladyp's most faithfull and affectionate Servant.

F Boscawen

Chapter 6

LETTERS FROM CATHERINE STAPLETON 1766-1798

But the most ordinary cause of a single life is Liberty;
especially in certain self-pleasing and humerous minds

Francis Bacon (1561-1626), *Of Marriage and Single Life*

Two only of the women who wrote regularly to Hester Chatham were unmarried, Grace Trevor and Catherine Stapleton and of the two it was the latter who played far and away the more important part in Hester's life. Catherine Stapleton's letters, of all the correspondents, were the most numerous (over 300), the least intellectual and political in content but certainly the most practical. She was a great arranger of people's lives. Perhaps because she came eventually to live with Hester Chatham, as a sort of unpaid companion, she was the least dazzled by Chatham's fame. She was of an intensely independent nature; even after she had taken up permanent residence at Burton Pynsent, she in no way felt bound to spend all her time there; she would leave, often abruptly, if a call for her services came from a member of her own family or from one of the daughters of the late George Grenville and his wife, nieces of Hester Chatham, in whom lay the deepest of Catherine's affections. These absences, however, from 1783 of about four years and from 1790 seven years have yielded to our benefit correspondence which would not otherwise have existed.

Catherine Stapleton was one of four sisters, the daughters of Colonel Russell Stapleton, landowner of Bodrhyddan near St Asaph in Flintshire, in the parish of Rhuddlan. Known and addressed principally by the courtesy title of Mrs, she was born in 1733 and was therefore thirteen years younger than Hester. She had many useful gifts and attributes which made her presence invaluable to a wide circle of friends and family members. She was a good nurse with intuitive medical skills; she had energy and vitality and splendid health; she was a good horsewoman and courageous traveller. Those who were fortunate to be loved and cared for by her, not least Hester Chatham herself, became very dependent on her. From 1769 she took charge of the seven motherless children of the statesman George Grenville, Hester's second brother. Their mother, probably Hester's best friend from early girlhood, Elizabeth Wyndham, died in December and Catherine Stapleton remained in the stricken household until the father's death a year later, when the children's maternal uncle, Lord Temple, became their guardian and the family, including Mrs Stapleton moved from the Grenville home at Wotton twelve miles away, to Stowe. Here they stayed, with Mrs Stapleton in day to day charge of the four girls, and later often as chaperone at the Grenville house in London (the three boys having gone to school and passed out of her charge), until Lord Temple's death ten years later. Her many letters from Stowe are of special interest, describing in detail life in a great house at this time and with descriptions of the house itself and its garden.

Lord Temple's death brought to Catherine a great and continuing sorrow, the parting from her beloved girls. The eldest, Charlotte, had married Sir Watkin Williams Wynn in 1771; Elizabeth was grown-up and the two youngest, Hester and Catherine, stayed on at Stowe with their brother George, Lord Temple's heir, later Marquess of Buckingham. She never lost touch with them but for the next three and most of the subsequent years her letters are mainly from North Wales and Cheshire, from the houses of her married sisters, Lady Cotton of Combermere Abbey, Mrs Watkin Williams of Penbedw and Mrs Ellis Yonge of Acton, and from her own home Bodrhyddan, which she inherited in partnership with her sisters.

In letters to Hester Chatham from other correspondents there are many references to Mrs Stapleton. Mrs Boscawen was an admirer: 'the invaluable Mrs Stapleton' and 'the good fairy'. In 1789, when Mrs Stapleton was fifty-six, Mrs Boscawen had noted her unimpaired vitality and observes that 'youth is vastly well bestowed where there is much natural activity'. But there were also jealousies. Writing in 1772, Lady Chatham's cousin, Mrs Molly Hood speaks of 'family intrigues fuelled by Mrs Stapleton'. James Grenville, Hester's third brother, settled near to Burton Pynsent at Butleigh in Somerset, though an admirer, disapproves of her farming plans for Bodrhyddan and feels she has been cheated, probably because he regrets her absence from Burton and from his sister - 'she is one of your only two companions'. In a letter to Lady Chatham of 6 February 1782 John Smart, tenant farmer at Burton, writes of a difficulty he had in finding a sheephand for Bodrhyddan because of a conversation between a neighbour and the man appointed to go, in which 'some disagreeable circumstances. . . concerning her were mentioned'.

Catherine was not solely a nurse-governess-companion figure. She was very sociable and in letters from Bath and London, she writes of card parties, dinners, balls, the opera, race meeting, picnics, attended partly but not wholly in her capacity as chaperone to the Grenville girls. She was also well-off, having inherited a substantial share in the family sugar estates in the West Indies. If her letters lack the subtle wit and scholarship of those of Mrs Boscawen, Mrs Montagu and their set, she had much else to offer: a shrewd mind, a profound knowledge of country matters - the weather and its effect on health - the care of animals and plants, an abiding love of the Grenville family and of Hester Grenville, Lady Chatham, her patron and friend.

The selection from the large correspondence has not been simple. A guiding theme has been to show from her letters that life for a spinster with some money of her own, probably of little formal education and no great intellect, could nevertheless be of social significance even in the days not famous for female dominance. But then Catherine Stapleton had above all else great strength of character allied to a kind nature, an invincible combination in any age.

The first surviving letter, of 1766, when Catherine was thirty-three, describes in the detail so loved of her time, the death of her mother, the poor lady brought on a horrific journey from London to the family home in North Wales, while terribly ill, presumably to die. It is evident from this letter that Catherine had known Hester Chatham at an earlier time in their lives (their families were distantly connected) though probably only slightly and not on regular corresponding terms.

Bodryddan
Sept the 28th 1766

Dear Lady Chatham
      I do not only Return your Lasp and Lord Chatham my Sisters Thanks and Mine for your very obliging and kind acknowledgement of the unhappy event We had to impart to you but my own more particularly for allowing me an opportunity of justifying myself for a Seeming break of Promise to your Lasp which has given me much Concern, at the same time that we are sensible of your Goodness to us in desiring to hear of Us again; thank God We are Perfectly Well and Bless'd with health at our years. We should rong ourselves not to believe that Time will do the Rest tho God Forbid any of Us should be so undeserving if the Blessing We have had in the Tender and Valuable Parent now taken from Us, as not to feel the Blow. I never could Forget your Ladps Request of hearing from Me when you went out of Town, I was too sensible of your Inducemt for desiring to hear, and I never more fully Intended Writing. For sometime I wait'd in Hopes of better accts, disappoint'd in that I Fix'd upon the Accomplishment of our journey to my Sister Yonge at Acton. There was an attack of Fever in Consiquence of it, when Recover'd how to Compass the wish'd for journey here took up our Whole attention; the Gradual decrease of Strength to a Certain degree, had been so Great from our leaving London, the distance [from Acton] is thirty Med. Miles which in three days in a Litter was perform'd without any disadvantage but from being better one day and worse another... I was setting Pen to Paper when all our difficulties of Moving were conquer'd. Flattering Ourselves the change was in our Favor, which in Reality I believe Proceed'd merely from the move than expect'd Satisfaction of Finding herself here, when she was taken with a shivering Fit; Fever ensued, for a Day or Two it had very much the appearance of an Intermitting disorder that is still a good deal about; She kept her Bed a Week, the Fever if accidental was of no material consiquence, Nothing could have sav'd her We know beyond all doubt. It yielded to Medicine, a Drowsiness took Place and I may say she Last'd far beyond her Strength, Patient more than I can describe. Thus was I led on till I could not Write, always intending it, which I flatter Myself you will not only believe, but excuse this long Tresspass upon your Time and allow me to assure your Lasp that I ever Feel Myself Your Much oblig'd and that I am the affectionate and Humble Servt
                  Cath: Stapleton

There are no further letters for the following three years, until the death of Elizabeth Grenville in 1769, which began the association of Catherine Stapleton with the Grenville children, reopens the correspondence between her and their aunt Hester Chatham, leading to a nearly unbroken friendship between the two women until Hester's death thirty-three years later.

Two letters follow Elizabeth Grenville's death on 8th December:

Stowe
Decr the 13th 1769

Dear Lady Chatham

I return'd here yesterday with Lord Thomond [Elizabeth Grenville's brother], making an allowance for your Poor Brothers seeing Him. I think without flattering you I can have the satisfaction to tell you I think He has gain'd Ground during the Time I was absent. The Dear young people are well except some Common Colds and Sore Throats... Your Dear Brother calling Forth His Most Superior understanding, stops at nothing He knows must be right, However painful, [and] Restrains every Sensation He might Counter Act what is so... Mr Grenville is Truly Sensible of the affectionate Part your Ladsp and Lord Chatham have taken in this Cruel Scene, but as He rightly means to stay little longer at Home, then to Settle and to feel Settled, he is too reasonable to wish you to think of such a journey in ye Late and uncertain Season.

Wotton
Decr the 21st 1769

I am hurt by feeling how little right I have at this moment to the praise you so Liberally bestow on me for an affection it I know Myself unalterable, but if my attention had been as Constant you would have been inform'd before this Time how your Poor Brother support'd Himself upon the Return to this place particularly too as it was much better than any of us expect'd. He immediately plung'd into His Business and Morning walks, in Short continues to Force Himself beyond what you can Imagine, to do everything He says He owes to the Family, Friends and Himself, and certainly is better than at Stowe... Your Brother and Sister Henry [Grenville] according to their kind promise came yesterday, which we have certainly found to be better than if They had Come here with us, for the advantage of having an agreeable Event in Expectation far exceeded any benefit that would have arisen from Continuing so much the Same Society we have been in, with only the Change of Place.

But the solace of life at Wotton was soon to be violently shaken, with the illness and death of the father just short of a year later. First however there is a day's visit to Hayes with 'as Numerous a Body as you kindly wish us always to Do' and visitors to be welcomed at home:

Wotton
Sunday Augst the 19 1770

Our feelings, believe me my Dear Lady Chatham upon the Visit I was happy to have in my Power to make, tho little more than a Peep at You, are the same and most sincerely glad I was to find everything going on so much better than from Letters we not Long before had rec'd... Sir Rich: Lyttelton and the Duchess of Bridgewater [his wife] came here on Wednesday... We have had Charming Weather for them, Yesterday I think was the finest Day I ever saw. They were Driven quite Round, and Bump'd in and out of the Ferrys - Wheel'd to the Top of the Grotto, in short were every where, Expressing and shewing great glee and pleasure, delight'd with the Place which without impropriety or Want of Modesty about it I may say I do not Wonder at for Its Present Beauty is indeed Supreme...

I cannot say your Brother advances much, some Days he is better others Worse, but upon the Whole I do hope He rather gains Ground.

Two months later the dying George Grenville is to make the journey to London, accompanied by Dr Ash and Mrs Stapleton.

Packington
Saturday morning
Octr the 20 1770

Miss Grenville [Charlotte] and I return'd out of Wales Wednesday and from the Accounts We had rec'd of your Brother during our absence, are disappoint'd in His Looks and sensible of a Loss of Strength, altho' all his Complaints are decreasing, and Docr Ash is more and more Sanguine in his Hopes of his Recovery, unwilling to Let this fine Weather for His journey Slip. Mr Grenville has determined to get to London as fast as his Strength will let Him without Calling even at Stowe, for within reach of Daily Physical Help it is most undoubtedly absolutely necessary for Him to be. I think there is no uncertainty upon His bearing His journey Well, for He is always Easier and better during the Time of His being in a Carriage than at any other, there is something in the motion that quiets a Restless[ness] He has almost Constantly at other times, very unsupportable to Him. We set out for Daventry this Day, mean to reach Dunstable tomorrow and London on Monday, such is the Plan, but to be kept or not, as his being more or Less Fatigu'd at the End of Every ten miles shall incline Him, for at pretty near such distance almost equal accommodation is to be found. Dr Ash goes with us to Dunstable where we depend upon Meeting with Sir Wm Duncan.

Rather less than two months later and despite being 'within reach of Daily Physical Help' George Grenville is dead. A new life is in prospect for Catherine Stapleton and the orphaned children, whose guardian is now their uncle Lord Temple, and whose home is in future to be with him. Catherine has reservations:

Stowe
Sunday Nov: the 18th 1770

This Place He makes our Home in the Summer, ours I say as He Lets me have the Happiness of remaining with the Children, and in the Winter He will Continue us in the same House I believe, or fix us in another. The not being to a certain degree independent of Him self and Lady Temple in the Winter, as well as having at other Times a Place ready to go to upon Various Occasions which may occur, is the Single Constraint I am Capable of feeling.

With seven lively youngsters and kind uncles, sorrowing can not be long prolonged and a month later:

Stowe
Dec: the 23 1770

Your very acceptable note did Find a very Numerous Party of us Assembled at Lord Thomond's. We adjourn'd Twelve to the Play and All our Young Friends were both Happy and amus'd.

In this letter Catherine makes a rare, almost apologetic reference to her own health:

I have been more disorder'd with a Cold I brought Here, which is yet hardly over, than I have been for Years. I cannot lay it particularly to the Charge of anything; either Friday or Saturday Morning I felt the First of It and Conclud'd the Play journey made the Most of what otherwise would have end'd in Less than the Least of Colds as mine generally do... I was late in getting up, have been at Prayers since and am afraid of Looking at my Watch

Social life with the girls continues through 1771, with letters from Stowe, Bolton Street and Shortgrove, the bachelor uncle, Lord Thomond's seat in Essex. There are meetings with the Pitt family but the great news is sent in an ecstatic, rather more than usually incoherent letter, on return from a visit of Catherine and the two elder girls to her sisters' homes in Cheshire and north Wales.

Stowe
Oct. the 17 1771

My Dear Lady Chatham
It is not yet without Blushing that I can presume upon the Proofs to my Shame I speak it, that I have already given of It being very Possible for me in Perfect Health to maintain an absolute Silence for at least Seven Weeks where in justice too I am Bound by the kindest Ties to know and am truly sensible, There is a most sincere and Affectionate wish to hear from me. But such is the Nature of the Animal, neither ungrateful or unfeeling, or in any Respect Whatever one got behind hand in affection and kindest Sentiment to the kindest of Friends, which even in the Course of this Letter I do not mean to Leave unmark'd but tell in confidence of Friendly intercourse what I think will not be unpleasing, even before I have the usual Authority for telling, or perhaps you will think Ground to go upon but depending upon your Good Ladyship's <u>Superior Prudence</u> and Caution, I will if you do not find out keep my Promise and tell.

But as politeness required, the big news must be kept until the niceties of communication have been complied with and the excursion described:

Now whether Deserv'd or undeserved it is most True that during this Quiet State of my Pen and Perpetual Motion of my Whole Person and my Two Elder Girls by various means, We never have so totally lost Sight of your Numerous body as not to have at Least a very good Guess about you all and that Lord Chatham has had an <u>Agreeable</u> Fit of the gout, and next to Coming here, I shall now rejoice to hear of your being all Safely Lodged at Hayes. Oh! How much shall We all have to tell of the Prosperous Events of this Pleasant Summer... five weeks pass'd in uninterrupt'd Happiness between my Sisters' Houses with joy and Content in all their Faces... In Point of Amusement We Fix'd our Welsh Expedition very much by Chance, but Favouring Fortune Timed it in the midst of everything that could Delight my Girls... Our private parties were Bordering upon the number of 20 Souls, for we mov'd like the Patriarchs of old from Place to Place, with our Hirds and Flocks Rolling from one Sister's House to another by which means, Five and Twenty Miles of Road like a Garden Walk being the Greatest Distance; I in a Manner spent the Whole of my Time with all of them. We had Races, Balls, Stag Hunting, Hare, Otter and Coursing, Shooting in order to see Dogs in the attitudes of Pointing, Coursing; Music, Masquerades not except'd Driving etc. etc.

At last

And now for the Cream: an Ancestor Conquer'd one County in Wales but a female Grenville Has Conquer'd the Whole of North Wales, every Soul who saw her Wishing what (The <u>Prince</u>, for He is absolutely nothing Less Here) He most Wish'd Himself and by the Sisterhood. I am Concern'd if He Does not even to-morrow arrive with Mr Williams My Brother [in law] to ask Lord Temple the Question, which still Remaining very absolutely unask'd I am hardly justified in this Relation. But remaining in full confidence of your Discretion and Satisfaction I could not as my suspicions strengthen'd, Deny myself any Longer the Pleasure of telling your La:p the flattering Prospect of Happiness that seems held out to your Amiable niece.

After sincere and warm-hearted praise of the suitor, Sir Watkin Williams Wynn, Catherine, still in a whirl, ends

Adieu I am a Little, or not a Little Intoxicated, so pray excuse and believe me my Dear Lady Chatham Your Very Affectionate

Catherine Stapleton

For the rest of the year Catherine's time and thoughts are taken up with the forthcoming marriage. They all, including, to Catherine's surprise, the future bride-groom - 'it's very odd but Sir WWW chose to be of our Party-' move to London after visiting Lady Blandford, the girls' much loved step-grandmother:

Bolton Street
Novr the 7th 1771

We Drank our Coffee with Lady Blandford Last Night and Dine with her to-day, it's impossible to describe as well as your La:p can judge, of Her joy upon the Subject that makes us all so Happy, when I tell you her approbation goes intirely with It. I can Hardly stand all she says upon It but as always, one can see Her Heart and Mouth go together, Her Spirits and Strength seem more than Double in proportion to what she had enjoy'd these Two Dreadful years, during which She says she has felt such an indifference to Every thing existing. . . that she did not know There remain'd any Possibility of Her enjoying the Heart Felt Satisfaction this Happy Event affords Her.

After the euphoria, a few misgivings tempered by compensations:

Bolton Street
Decr the 17 1771

Your Brother my Dear Lady Chatham I know gives by this Days Post, the first Certain Intelligence in His Power to Lord Chatham of the Day [December 21st] which I cannot Help a Little Feeling removes Charlotte Further from us, tho to Myself Less Distant, than any other Situation could admit of. . . She is so very young that it is impossible for me Who wish so Much, to wish devoid of Fear, tho Hoping every thing with the Degree of Confidence I do. I have infinite Satisfaction from Her taking Extremely to His Mother, whom Sir Watkin Himself doats upon, and for which He is not to be liked the Less, for Mother never made a Son More their Object and is Herself in All Respects most amiable, so Chearful and Fond of Amusements and Society, that already They are become Easy companions, which is a most Desirable thing. For in the Worst Cases I think it is judging too hardly not to suppose that a Gentle Hint or Check early from Those They have an affection for, might not prevent many Great Evils. But in most modern Cases Boys and Girls marry without almost any attachment to each other. . . launch out into the World of Amusements, and at First perhaps merely from Different Tastes in those amusements, Themselves are led contrary Ways, the consiquences of which almost Every Day presents to us.

[PS] I cannot Express to You the Comfort I should have rec'd from Mid-Night Conversations since I have been in Town, but I will be too Wise to wish for What is out of Reach.

After the wedding there is an understandable flatness and Christmas at Stowe evidently not quite the usual fun:

> Bolton Street
> Feby the 1st 1772
>
> From the moment of our setting out upon our Xmas Excursion to Stowe, where we Rash Mortals had Promis'd ourselves uninterrupt'd Gaiety and Delights, the World has gone Less Smoothly with me than for some Months before, altho Every Day more and more convinces us of your amiable niece's Good Fortune, which makes up no inconsiderable part of my Happiness.

For the next eight years Catherine Stapleton continued to make her home with the Grenvilles at Stowe or in London; as a useful chaperone for the remaining girls, but more as a family friend and mentor than in any other role.

Regular letters to Hester Chatham, immured at Hayes or at Burton with her sick husband keep her posted with Grenville doings, interspersed with little bits of news and gossip of the great world Hester so much enjoyed hearing:

> Bolton St
> Feby the 8th 1772
>
> The Princess [Dowager, of Wales] Really Depart'd at ½ past Six this morning. The Denmark News [imprisonment of Queen Caroline Matilda] put the Finishing Stroke, from the First hearing of it she has Continued Sinking without being better at any Period of Time which has been the case till then, better for a Few Days then almost gone, and recovering again.

There is an undercurrent of worry about Sir Watkin William's health. In an undated letter probably of this time Catherine writes:

> You Guess'd but too nearly right about Sir Watkin, He came to Town quite well and within the Quarter of an Hour had as Severe a Return of pain as ever, which prevent'd his Taking His Seat in the House, and extremely broke into [their] every Scheme.

Always in advance of her time in medical care, Catherine in this letter adds

A Material thing is Diet in which he has not been so Careful, and to which the Physicians here to my great Surprise seem'd to pay little attention, by what Lady Williams and Sir Watkin say.

Catherine will often have found herself in discomfort, which she accepts philosophically, from the rebuilding of parts of Stowe, work which had become an obsession with Lord Temple. After a round of visits with Elizabeth she writes:

> Stowe
> July the 2d 1772
>
> We arriv'd [back] at this Beautiful Scene of Confusion Monday Last by Dinner. Your Brother and Lady Temple are in most perfect Health but as unhappily He is become a Man of much more Private business than before, the Work He is enter'd upon is so immense that the Trouble of Course is so great, that could it have been a smaller The Pleasure would have been Greater in Proportion to the whole than I think it is now. He has Regulated it extremely well in Point of Habitation; They are Themselves established below Stairs and indeed by no means uncomfortably Lodged. The Window of the Grenville Room is undergoing a Change that prevents that Room from being used, but the Rest is inhabited as before, with Little inconvenience from the Magnificent alterations taking Place on the outside.

Lady Temple, a delicate woman, overshadowed by her forceful and flamboyant husband, evidently appreciates Catherine's gardening skills, of which we get a glimpse in a long letter of 20th September:

> . . .and now all that remains for me to tell is that Lady Temple has been Long Waiting for me to set Honey-Suckles but I have sent her Word it was impossible, that I am very Busy, etc till I am quite ashamed. . . but I am still going on, Lady Temple still waiting, one Word more and I will have done.

In September there is another visit to Wales, with Elizabeth and, for the first time, the youngest Grenville, the precociously clever William, the future foreign secretary:

> Stowe
> Octbr the 11th 1772
>
> Mr Dear Lady Chatham
> Your Letter made the Tour of Wales, where it at Last found your unworthy Correspondent, who Blushes to Confess she Return'd Here with two Companions, Elizabeth and William more than Three Weeks ago, the lat[t]er made the Whole expedition with great success on Horseback, which contributed not a little to His pleasure, and is at all times peculiarly beneficial to his Health. . . We broke a Week into his returning to School, which Lord Temple was so good as to excuse and in Reality Mr William deserves, not being extremely behind hand. He is not Thirteen Compleat and Saturday last sennight I should say went into the 5th Form.

She is waiting for a call to London to be present at the birth of Charlotte Williams's first child:

I regret extremely Leaving this Charming Place and Weather so Early, but Hope the Good Cause will soon make me forget it.

[London]
Octr the 29 1772

I have defer'd my Congratulations upon your Niece's safe Delivery, and the Birth of your Great Nephew believeing your La:p would as an Experienced Person have more satisfafction in hearing [how] the Third Day was Pass'd. . . the Labour was neither Short or Easy, but most perfectly safe in all respects. . . With the assistance of his Dear Wife's being so well and a Little joy in being the Father of such a Son, have quite cured Sir Watkin.

The year ends for Catherine with worry from the bad news from the family plantations in St Kitts, damaged by storms:

Decber the 5th 1772

Among the Fifteen Hund. Letters arrived this Week with bad news from the West Indias, Came ours from St Kitts and Nevis. . . The Losses we have sustain'd at both Islands are estimated at not Less than Six Thousand, Six Hund. Pounds Stirlg, a Severe Blow in our Situations. . . However I Comfort myself with Gods will, it is within the Reach of a Ten Years Prudence to Recover, and I am not the Greatest Philosopher of my Family.

Five days later she admits that she may have exaggerated the losses:

Decr the 12th 1772

I was so Possess'd with Black Ideas that I could not deny myself the unkind relief of making my Friends suffer with me. I am far from Calling our News Good from receiving it in a Great Stile, for God knows it Comes very inconveniently upon us, but my not foreseeing any Cause for a Capital Change in my Personal Situation makes a greater degree of Care and Prudence become almost a Pleasure to me.

With respite from the worst of her financial worries, she can now enjoy some of the season's gaities. The letter continues:

Colds we have amongst us, but quite below observation and I do not mean to increase any of the Evils I wish Your La:p had not to Complain of, by your following me in my Tour of Engagements. I have been at one Opera, Part of an Evening at Norfolk House (the Dutchess much better, Duke as well as Ever). Last Thursday at an Assembly at Madame de Wilderens, One Evening Divided between Lady Egremont and Lady Vere and the Rest of my Time has been Intirely Pass'd in Grosvenor Square, never more People so conveniently situated as the Marchioness of Blandford and Dame Charlotte Williams, the latter was at Northumberland House Last Night. Wednesday is Fix'd for our Christening.

Early in the new year Catherine's nursing skills are suddenly in demand:

Boulton Street
Jany the 23rd 1773

My sister Williams's being just arrived, will prevent my Answering the most acceptable Letter I rec: from Your Dear Ladyship yesterday, as much at Length as it was my intention to do, but shall not Hinder my informing you of the Strain Lord Temple has received in his Arm, Least the Papers which ever seem to take Pleasure in Alarming People, should as usual make your Lasp apprehend Danger where Mr Hawkins says there is not any. . . The Accident Happen'd as the Papers say, by Lord Temple's Chair being flung Down with Great violence by another Chair Running against His. He Fell upon his Arm, which is most Exceedingly Strain'd indeed, but Nothing Broke, or other Hurt received by the Fall. . . The Fall Happen'd on Wednesday Night, and very little Ground is gain'd. He can hardly bare the Weight of his Night Gown, and from the Wrist to the Shoulder cannot move his Arm, without the most Extreme Pain, and even then only as much as perfectly satisfies Hawkins that there is not the Least Fracture.

Three days later:

Your Brother mends as Fast as I suppose such a Violent Strain will admit of, is most perfectly well in His Health, and has the Patience of an Angel, which I fear will be fully Try'd before He gets His Liberty, not yet being able to go further than from his bed to a great Chair, where he pass's the Day in his Night Gown. All his Comfort, and ours, is that the Accident was no Worse, for it is a Sad Check both to his Business, and Arrangements.

And the discomforts of the London house for an invalid:

Janry the 30th 1773

I now have the Comfort of telling your Ladyship He has quicken'd the progress of recovery very much within the two or three last days. Yesterday He got into Lady Temple's Dressing Room; sure a House never was so ill calculated as that is for Those who Inhabit it, but as neither of Them seem to be of that opinion it is as Convenient to Them as a better.

With her husband in no danger, Lady Temple has joined the crowds visiting the preview of the sales of the late Princess Dowager of Wales's personal effects. The letter continues:

Viewing the Princess's jewels, China etc which on Monday are to be sold by Auction, are general objects of great arrangement. Will you believe me if I tell you upon my Word I think Lady Temple finds some Pleasure in going every Day to look at the Jewels, and not Least the First Day, being full persuaded She had a Private View. I fear the Numbers she must have met with, who have had that Compliment paid to Them, have by this Time undeceiv'd Her. I fancy she Dreams of a Pair of Pearl Bracelets, which wanting Furnishes a Good deal of Conversation, most of the other things have Flaws etc etc.

Lord Temple now has gout to add to the pain and discomfort of his injuries, but the social round for others continues:

Upon the Whole tho everything goes on safe and well He suffers extremely and the Progress is certainly very Slow, such an accident with Gout add'd to his Natural infirmities, makes this as Painful and almost as helpless a State as a more Active Person would be infinitely more Gout... Lady Temple was Complaining Yesterday, I hope only in consiquence of Fatigue, she had been Tempted to see Masks at Lady Darlington's which proved too Convenient a Situation; Every Mask by what I hear stop'd There in their way to Almacks, besides the Whole Town, with or without Masks who did not go to the Masquerade. I was satisfied with seing your Niece look better than ever I saw her in my Life. She was perfectly well dress'd; as I had no hand in it, I am at Liberty to say so, a true Vandyke, of Pink and Light Brown Sattins, Her Hair charmingly Dress'd, with small Curls upon her Forehead of no small advantage, a profusion of Pearls and Diamonds without being over Load'd, none hir'd, none Borrow'd except of Lady Williams who spared no Pains to adorn Her and really seem'd to think herself Reward'd. As to herself she cared so Little about it, that I Blamed them for going to Lady Darlington's Dress'd like Welsh or English Beggars, if you Please, whose Dresses were Slip'd on over Their Fine ones - Theirs I say, Sir W being Vandyke also, and which They did not Pull off before Supper, by which Means, not half the People saw her who might, which I am really sorry for.

The next five or so years go by without any fundamental change in Catherine Stapleton's life. Her letters of this period, however, throw small shafts of light on the characters of both women, and on Catherine's relations with members of the Grenville family, notably with the difficult Lord Temple. There were visits made and stupendously difficult journeys taken in order to make them; and of course news from Stowe and Bolton Street and inevitably of illnesses and deaths.

I am very Sorry for the unnecessary Concern One of my Epistles occasion'd by the Account it contain'd of Lord Temple. All I have to offer in excuse for myself is the being very apt to write without disguise, just as I Feel, from which at least the Comfort of knowing in my Favourable representations I do not flatter, is to be derived.

The kindness of your Letter deserved my much Earlier Thanks, still kinder would it have been could it be possible for me to Convince your Ladyship that you may depend upon my assigning Every reason you Can have, many as they are, for your not writing, without the most distant suspicion of your Silence being occasion'd by any thing that would give me the Pain of thinking it Mask'd a want of Affection.

Stowe
July the 4th 1773

His Lordship's recovery... has undoubtedly been I suppose as slow as could be expected. Violent as his Strain was, the coldness of the Weather has certainly retarded His regaining Strength... He has got a Horse he is charmed with and very seldom pass's a Day without Riding, and notwithstanding the Weakness still remaining in His Arm, Drives His little Horses with great success. His Glorious Building answers in the Execution far beyond All Expectation and goes on so quick, that were it not for the immense inconvenience of Carriage, the Next Summer would compleat the Building. I have not a wish to see you, but confess great impatience and Longings for your seeing that, as it advances... In the Evening Your Brother Drove me Round the Garden, and I believe the admiration of Strangers seldom surpass'd what ours was. He is a great Prince and Honours us by Turns, with being the Companion in his Body-Chaise...

About Saturday we expect Mr Tom [Grenville] and the end of the Month, Mr William. As Mistress of Their Horse, I have enter'd into the Business of my Office and Trust They will have the pleasure of finding Their Cavalry in good order.

Probably due in the main to Catherine's influence, another journey to her own Welsh country is undertaken; this time both Lord and Lady Temple are in the party, and Catherine is obviously curious to note their, especially his, reaction to it. Two long letters, written on return, describe the tour:

Stowe
Sunday Septr the 19 1773

I now see before my Eyes... the Sweet letter I rec'd from you before We enter'd upon our most Fortunate and Happy Excursion into Wales, of which I think your Brother has made a Favourable Report... Since our Return He has compleately deceived those in the Principality, as well as myself and many out of It, if He did not like Wales as well as Wales liked Him, which is placing His admiration as High as I think I Can. The change of Scene and Constant Exercise have been of Infinite Service to Him, in all respects, notwithstanding the Cruel Drawback of the unexpect'd death of Lord Lyttelton... Lady Temple was in High Delight with the thoughts of going out of England. The idea of being so great a Traveller pleas'd her extremely, and she really did bare the being Carried about most Wonderfully... We were out more than a Month and never pass'd a Night in an Inn.

Catherine, Elizabeth and William rode most of the way:

William, with his Sister and me... Guarded our Coach on Horse-back the Whole journey, upon the same precious little Mare, and except Twenty Miles between Combermere and Packington I went the whole Tour with my own Horses... We stay'd at Packington only until [the Temples] arrived, and went Twenty odd Miles that Evening, Men, Women and Horses, we were Thirty Six in Number, and we had not so much as the Loss of a Shoe to stop for.

Stowe
Octber the 31st 1773

Let me thank you for the satisfaction it gave me to hear [that] my Long Winded Epistle answer'd the purpose I hoped from it of enabling your Ladyship to make the Tour with us in Imagination, which we have often [travelled] in Recollection, by Furnishing You with some of the Smaller Essentials. It must ever be a pleasure to discover one has not been deceived, more particularly in any thing flattering, and I believe I have already Confess'd to [what] was my Fond hope that your Brother saw some of the Inhabitants, as well as our Country, with a Partial eye. . . It is amazing how much better He is than before the journey; His present eagerness for Improvement here is much beyond what can Fairly be call'd an alteration of This Future Palace, very naturally accounts for it.

Boulton Street
March the 10th 1774

Sir Roger Mostyn has broke in upon me, and The Temples, being such Strange Old Fashion'd Folk as to wish to Dine at the very Early Hour of Four, I must again lay down my Pen Long before I wish to do it.

Boulton Street
March the 29th 1774

Never was such a Fortnight of Fine Weather so Early as we have had, and still enjoy. I have made the most of It in my Garden, the Walls of which never can be stretch'd to a Proper size for such Inhabitants as the Peafowle your Ladyship once mention'd to me, Your own American Ones I mean; but when an Abundant Year comes, I shall be Doubly obliged, or rather you will Oblige Doubly when you can Spare me a pair for my Sister, and Mr Williams, who are going to Ruin Themselves by collecting all the Different kinds of Peafowles They Can, having charming Woods for them to Range in. Consider what I am asking by description: Lord Egremont paid Brooks, the Great Menagerie Man, Fifteen Guis. for a Pair of your Sort; but to succeed in this World, surely the best Method is to take People in Their Way, and if I am not deceived Lord Chatham and your Ladyship's Pleasure in giving is increas'd in Proportion to the Value of the thing in your Power to bestow.

On her return to Stowe from a round of fifteen visits, including a short stay at Hayes, Catherine's letter to Hester contains so much more than the conventional expression of thanks

Stowe
Sunday June the 26 1774

I cannot say the Charms I expected at my Return to London turn'd out Less delightful than I had figur'd to myself they would after the Various Sweets I had enjoy'd in the Two Short Days we Pass'd at Hayes. . . I was up with the Larks on Tuesday, to pay away all my Money, and without fear of being Robb'd went to Dine with Lady Blandford at Shene [Sheen], who I found better, but I cannot satisfy myself quite what she was a Month ago. Quite by Accident too, I had the pleasure of meeting Lady Charlotte Edwin; I thought her much better and we Pass'd a very comfortable Day together. Wednesday was fully employ'd with the general Package, which we compleated in time to admit of Miss Grenville's and my staying at the Grove; the three following Days we pass'd very agreeably there. It really is a Sweet Place and the Lord very greatly improved. We Pass'd one Evening at Russells-Farm which as absolute Villa is the Prettiest of Things. On Sunday Morning we met our London Ladies at Breakfast at Aylesbury and overtook the Lord of Majestick Stowe in his Morning Ride. We descend'd from our Stage Coach and attend'd Him on Foot, upon His Favourite Horse, along his New Road, which must Speak for itself: at least I will not attempt to describe its Beauty and Magnificence. . .

We have not had much to boast of our Weather since our arrival here till to Day, which after a True Summer Storm in the Night is quite what one expects so late in June. This week has been pass'd in very Comfortable retirement, not a Neighbour or Stranger has broke in upon us. To Day we are in fearful expectation of prince Galitzin, who George [Grenville] was acquainted with at Geneva. We hope and propose his Visit is not to Reach Twenty Four Hours. . . The Bell for Church Obliges me to Assure your Ladyship, and all our agreeable and kind friends at Hayes, that the more we are with you All, the more we Love you All.

The peace at Stowe was soon to be broken by an accident which took a life and narrowly missed many more. In her letter about the event, stimulated by shock into powerful description, Catherine writes:

Sunday
[Sept 25th 1774]

My Dear Lady Chatham
I am not a Little Thankful for the Divine Providence that has preseved us all except Poor Old Bachelor, the Stone Mason; He suffer'd but Momentary Pain or Fear. Yesterday, between One and Two o'clock, the Whole Stone Cornish [cornice], upwards of Forty-Foot across the End of the Centre of the House, over the Drawing Room we constantly sit in from having no other, Fell in. At once It broke through the Drawing room from the End to the Further side of the Chimney, next the Eating Room Door, Into the Billiard Room, Crushing and Burying Every thing in its Ruins. Most providentially your Nephews and Mr Charles Finch were engag'd in the upacking of a Chimney Piece in the Strong Room; the Three Girls and I were Literally Finishing up our Morning Business, which saved our Lives by the Ten Minutes so employ'd, by preventing our being at Billiards, as we have very Morning for a short Time before Dressing during this Week [when] the incipient Rains have prevented our sitting out of the House. Mr Cleaver [the boys' tutor] was gone to Buckingham upon some Election Business. I mention these Circumstances, Trifling in Themselves, although the Instruments by which our Lives were saved, for in consiquence of the Weather we should all otherwise have been there, whom I have mention'd, and during the Summer I believe hardly a Morning Pass's that some or other are not from One till past Two. The Servant who waits there, when the Room is not engag'd, to answer Lady Temple's Bell, was not return'd from another Part of the House He had been sent to, before it Happen'd. In the Confusion it was some time before He came, and we thought He Had Perish'd. How short the Space you see that would have Assembl'd us all in ye Drawing Room, if not before Certainly after Dinner. . .

The Noise was as Tremendous as You can Possibly Conceive, the First Idea that Struck one was that of an Earthquake but infinitely Stronger than the One Tremor, for the Cornish was not completely Finish'd. The Workmen were not only Beat off many Hours in Each Day from Tuesday, but the Constant and Violent Rain had quite wash'd out the new Laid Mortar. They are at a Loss how otherwise to Account for this sad Accident, every Precaution having been made use of that there has been in all the other Parts. Its happening at the Hour of their Dinner in all Human Probability saved Numbers of the Workmen from being either Kill'd or Hurt. I suppose such an Accident Never occasion'd so Little distress of that Kind, amidst such Numbers of People in and about the House. As the Papers amuse his Friends with the improvements Lord Temple is making here, I think it is possible They may Treat Them with this Event in more Horrid colours than its [need], therefore I write to as many as I can who will not be Sorry to know the Truth from your Ladyship's scrawling but

Truely Affectionate etc.
Cath: Stapleton

[PS] Your Brother is vastly Hurt but that is between us. The Delay and All its Consiquences, if the Poor Man had escaped, would not have cost Him a Second Thought. God knows, I feel so many Escaping so narrowly, so much that an Accidental Death never shock'd me so Little, its without a question too, He suffer'd as Little as Possible and his Family are Grown-up tho', Poor Souls, Two sons saw the Fatal accident. Adieu - Sunday the 25th Sep 1774 may I every remember the 24th as I ought to do.

In the midsummer of the following year, Lord Temple was struck down by a sudden illness which, from Catherine's letters would appear to have been some sort of blood poisoning in one leg, though as ever there is no clear diagnosis other than that of a form of gout. Catherine writes on 5 June that Lord Temple (who despised illness and disliked doctors)

> told me to my infinite Satisfaction no Man was ever as near Lost by folly, which I gladly understood was [due to] going on so long in unskillfull hands, but too soon I began to suspect he meant no more by it than the Frequent use of the Cold Bath.

Possibly due to Catherine's insistence the well-regarded Dr John Parsons, the first professor of anatomy at Oxford, is called to Stowe to attend the patient, and a month later, in a perceptive letter, Catherine on 2 July is able to report that

> Doct Parsons Arrived very Early on Friday Morning and Left us yesterday in high Spirits. The inflammation is over, the discharge from it seem'd to Relieve and to Night the original Watery Swelling is much subsided and he is better, [so] the People about Him say to day, than he has ever yet been; His Nights are become extremely good, his Appetite very well, his Spirits much better and his Strength greatly Inccreased. He is Wheel'd among his Workmen not imprudently, and does business with his Steward discreetly too, and They all say is as quick in his observations, and exact in his directions as ever They knew him, which I Look upon to be as satisfactory a mark of Strength as if the Swelling and Tenderness in his Leg and Foot would admit of his Walking.

The scarcity of letters in the following year is briefly referred to, but not explained (though a quarrel, later repaired, with the jealous Molly Hood may provide a clue) in Catherine's letter from Stowe of 29 July 1776:

> the Bar to our Correspondence being once more restor'd, I know not how to stop my Pen.

In two undated letters, probably written in the summer of 1776, Catherine is involved in a proposed visit of Harriot Pitt to London:

Saturday

I should not address so short a Scrap as this will be, writ after Dinner at Lady Blandford's, but as I know not how it may be Tim'd, I am unwilling should it prove an anxious moment to set pleasure within Lady Harriot's View: full measure as I give to her every Amiable quality, something must be allow'd to the quick feelings of Youth. All my Girls wish as much as I can to contribute our Mite to amuse her, and urge me to mention my having a Box for the New Play on Monday, if that and an Opera should be without an objection. I can accommodate her, with her Servant whom I shall not forget, for without a Hair Dresser we have in the House, a short preparation on her part for so short an excursion will be necessary. But dont Let this have a Moment's weight against your best Consider'd Ideas, for I know enough of Sorrow to doubt whether an Attempt towards Amusement for short Intervals does not sharpen it.

But apparently for no stated reason, Harriot is recalled home early from the visit, to Catherine's puzzled regret:

I was in Fear when I saw Poor Lady Harriot on Monday that she might not escape the Cloud of disappointment spreading over all our Heads. I have no Right to Ask, Why?... I fear We suffer in our Pleasure from your too Delicate feelings upon Imaginary Trouble, or is it Doubt upon the Prudence of some of the Parties. but seriously I am Sorry it did not fit your Laps Schemes as well as it would ours at this Time to have been all together. It is so much my Inclination to do all the Little in my Power for your Dear Girl, and as I think at all Times will please you best in Points of Moderation in Fashion etc etc, that believe me when ever I can catch an opportunity it makes me Happy. I depend upon Her till Sunday morning, Least your uncomfortable State of uncertainty should, notwithstanding your best Intentions towards her, prevent her going to one Opera.

Perhaps the greatest test to date of her medical knowledge and nursing ability comes to Catherine in 1777. We first hear of Elizabeth Grenville's severe and protracted (unnamed) illness in June, but only after reference to the breach in the friendship with Hester, now ended:

Wotton
22 June 1777

My Dearest Lady Chatham
    I Blush to say to you that I have suffer'd any thing, for I can but Taste of the Cup of Anxiety and Fatigue, of which you repeatedly have Drunk much too deeply of, but a Variety of Vexations and distress has surround'd me for the three last Months. I Bless God the Gloom begins to disperse. An account I heard of Yourself in the Midst of all my difficulties unaffectedly nearly over-Power'd me. The Transport I may call it, which on the whole your undeserv'd Letter as far as my not having answer'd a former one, which will like the last and all I may say, remain imprinted on my Heart, can make it so, gave me, you I am sure will easier Comprehend than I can describe, for I cannot tell you what it is a I feel from the hopes of seeing again my long lost and much belov'd Friend...

Your dear Niece is now advancing fast in the Recovery of her Health, this is the Third day of her getting out of her Room, after being Ten Weeks in Bed, and not as many Hours out of it, I think near Five without having her Bed made or being able to bare the being removed from the one side to the other to have it Beat up. . .

Not that all my Anxiety has been on her Acct: I dare at this distance only to say, which with the greatest Truth I can, that I have not a False Heart, and that I flatter myself I shall not be oblig'd to Change my Opinion in thinking that Sooner or Later it's the best Conductor through the greatest difficulties. . .

Believe me to be your Ladyship's most faithful attach'd and affectionate Friend

        Cath. Stapleton

About a month later the invalid, under Catherine's care, is to go to Brighton for convalescence. While there, she has at least one serious relapse and the visit is prolonged until late in November. Catherine's letters, some undated but all of this time, describe in medical detail not only Elizabeth's setbacks, but they also convey her own oppression (and no doubt boredom) arising from confinement in seaside lodgings with a sick, cross, though greatly loved, young girl.

Elizabeth is under the care of the fashionable Dr (later Sir) Lucas Pepys, about whose medical skills Catherine is, by implication, not very enthusiastic. In a letter to Harriot Pitt she writes:

        Brighthelmston
        31 July 1777

We arrived here Monday Evening, succeeding in journey, in House Situation and every other Material Point, but on the first and very cautious attempt, have fail'd in the most essential. Miss Grenville went into a Warm Bath in the morning yesterday, under Docr Pepys's direction, and small as the Body was, the Weight of Water brought on an immediate attack, not what we reckon a Violent one but that continued from upwards of Two hours.

She does not give up hope of the move succeeding in a cure, but the setback

is a very great damp in setting out. . . It will be at least ten days before Miss G will Try the Bath again, therefore if nothing now occurs I may not trouble you sooner.

And sometime later to the elder sister, Hester Mahon she

cannot help regretting extremely the absence of our Docr [Parsons], for though her progress for the Last Three Weeks is equal to any thing I really think that one can wish or expect, whatever we pursue in Failure, I should set out upon with Greater confidence having seen him.

And later still to Hester Chatham

My Dearest Lady Chatham

I cannot express my Feelings of many kinds, your kindness I have no words to thank you for. My Anxiety [and] Wretchedness I may say has been very great indeed [but] my Happiness is now fully Equal to it. Weak you will suppose my Dear Elizabeth must be after Lying a Hund. and Eleven hours without Swallowing, or receiving any Benefit from other Means, which was her situation from Friday Evening to Wednesday morning and the Worst of Returning any thing she Swallow'd continued till last Tuesday night which was bringing us again into alarming apprehension. Pepys says he know not how to account for her juices not becoming Putrid, but from the salt she had absorb'd in the Hot Bath, she now seems I bless God to have only strength to recover. . .

O! Fluctuating World, one Constant Blessing I enjoy in such a superlative degree I feel myself call'd upon to submit with more than Common Resignation to the Rest, tho I fear I do not, I mean the Blessing of Health which without exaggeration I never felt in a higher degree than now at the end of Thirty very Trying Weeks.

At long last the time for leaving Brighton draws close:

9th Nov 1777

As your happy Daughter [Harriot] mentions that she may perhaps set out in a few days from the time of her writing, I am willing to Secure to you the Comfort, which I cannot doubt of your receiving, from hearing that Thursday next is really the Day we look towards for our beginning our journey, not without hopes of reaching London on Friday.

Catherine can now look forward to easier conditions in which to write her letters and at rather less close quarters than in the Brighton lodgings:

I hope the Time is arriving for my having at least more in my power to derive satisfaction from writing to you beyond what it has of late been within my Compass to accomplish; for the rustling of the Paper is very unpleasant to Elizabeth and my being absent from her more so, except she can Drive me out of the House, which is of all things most unpleasant to me. So small a Thing will overset any advantage We may have been weeks obtaining. Upon these various accounts, I know you will pardon all omission. Your most sincerely affectionate
Cath: Stapleton

There is no mention of Lord Chatham's death on 11 May in any of Catherine's five letters of 1778. They contain however indications of minor diagreements and arguments with Lord Temple, who, however, she 'cannot help loving for all his faults' [12 July], and in a letter of 14 February the following year, disliking his plan to take the family to Bath, she writes:

Your Brother and I differ much in Idea upon the disadvantage of Constant dissipation at any period of Life, particularly so Early as sixteen and eighteen, and where from various causes too, there has been always such a Constant intercourse with the World, as in the Case before us, but at the same time I am saying this I must do him the justice to add that he means to be so reasonable and give me such a Voice on Such Subjects. . . [He is] also most anxious to do what he thinks best for the Girls, that my yielding something, when I think it prudent I can, is best for the whole.

All of which counts for nothing when, seven months later the unpredictable, not always admired, undeniably charismatic, distinctly accident-prone Earl Temple falls victim to a mishap which takes his life and alters the course of Catherine Stapleton's.

> Past 12 o'clock Saturday
> [1779 September 11th]

My dearest friend

I am wretched my self but my Heart Bleeds for you, all the consolation that remains to us is that the afflicting accident did not happen as in frequent Instances it might have done, from a Want of Care or attempting what had not the Appearance of Perfect Safety. In going out of a new Riding over a Temporary Passage where the Waggons etc Pass'd, he lent over to see if the Hind Wheels were Clear; at the Moment the Wheel on the Side he lent enter'd the Little dip, by bringing in that Situation he lost his Ballance and Slipped out. How particular the dear Girls may have been in the acctt of the Manner I know not, but I am happy to find I was unfair to doubt of their attention for a Moment, but in their situation what was not to be expected. As to the Event my dear Lady Chatham, it is not to you for me to say 'God's will be done', for myself I say it. . .

The arrival at Stowe of the heir, George Grenville is of importance to Catherine; her future now lies in his hands:

Both Mr Grenvilles came at three o'clock yesterday morning: in justice to your Nephew I must say his manner in general has been extremely amiable, nothing particular to me, but by no means what could give me pain. He wish'd against its being known he was here, indeed there seem'd no Answering running such a Risk, during the Time there certainly was Room at least to hope. . .

I hardly know where I am, and where I am to be still less, not that I have the pain of expecting any thing here unnecessarily distressing; but you who know the inmost recesses of my Heart, can judge of my feelings, exclusive of my concern for the Loss of your dear Brother himself, independent of all its consiquences.

And a generous if mildly qualified tribute to the dead man:

Perfection never dwelt on Earth, but taking People as they are without any thing in particular to hurt or ruffle his Mind, I ever thought him the most pleasing and engaging of men from the first to the last moment of my acquaintance with him, which began with my less so. The Satisfaction however, remains with me that we could never part in more perfect Friendship.

Displaced from Stowe, her home for the past ten years, by the decision that the two youngest Grenville daughters, Hester and Catherine, should make their own home with the new owners, Lord Temple and his wife, and with Elizabeth grown up and under chaperonage of her married sister Charlotte, Catherine, grieving for the loss of her 'Girls', now has to remake her life. She turns to the shelter of her eldest sister's home, from where she is about to visit Burton, making a first stop on the journey south with Lord and Lady Denbigh at Newnham in Leicestershire.

Combermere Abbey
Nantwich
Cheshire
14th Oct: 1779

I mean to stay two nights and as many at Elford, Lady Andover's, to meet poor Lady Suffolk. It will brake my journey and will be pleasanter than passing a night at an Inn, alone, a thing become more now than agreeable to me. After a time I shall reconcile myself to every thing that must be, but still the more the Girls are what I think them to be the Stronger the Conflict at this Moment of separation... I now really suffer from the Loss of that Society, which was and certainly became, more natural and more pleasing to me than any other, but I have a right to hope enough from them to recompence me for all my Anxiety for them.

On her return north:

Combermere Abbey
13th Nov. 1779

You are always right my dear Lady Chatham in thought, word and deed, tho I have not the Vanity to take to myself all you think or would not say of me; its a superior satisfaction and happiness to me that you do so, but nothing can Soften what I feel upon the Separation from those dear and amiable Girls, indeed the Chief reason for my Silence has been the impossibility I find in writing to your Ladyship without getting upon their subject and when I am, the hardening of my Mind to It. Oh! my dear Lady Chatham, had they only common Dangers to Run; they have Stolen my Heart too much from me to let me think of happiness without them, but at least I will stop my Pen.

Catherine's letters for the next year are from Combermere with a visit in January to Wynnstay, home of Charlotte Watkin Williams Wynn. Slowly her natural good spirits return:

Wynnstay
9th Jany 1780

My fruitful mind adapts, and surely I may call it so. Bless'd with a very uncommon share of Health as I am, and naturally strength of Spirits...

In this eventful year the two youngest Grenville girls, so sadly left behind at Stowe, become engaged, Hester Lady Mahon dies and Catherine makes plans to take up part time residence at Bodrhyddan, the property originally owned in partnership with her three married sisters. In a long letter of great affection Catherine writes:

Combermere Abbey
3d Mar:h 1780

My dearest friend

The place of my Birth I have never lost sight of, by purchase from Sir Rob. Cotton some time ago, from necessity more than Choice. Half the Estate belongs to me but from my Sister Yonge's Daughters being grown up, and one already having a family, my wish is to have a Lease of the House and Demesne for my Life. By this you are not to imagine I have at all my Idea the Running from the World, but many things Continue to make me adopt this Plan... I make no excuses for being prolix upon a subject I know you interest yourself, and her who loves you as well as you can love her. Adieu.

For the remainder of the year however, Catherine is based with the Cottons at Combermere, with a visit in late autumn to Burton and with Christmas at Wynnstay. The correspondence reflects once again her ever present concern for the health of those who matter to her:

Combermere Abbey
19 March 1780

I rejoice to hear you consult Warren for yourself, as poor Addington I fear is really too much an Invalid to have the power always of attending, even by letter. Warren is consulted with great satisfaction by several I know, particularly Ladies rather pass'd their Bloom, and [whom] he seems reasonable enough to think, nevertheless, worthy of the Best advice and attention he can give them.

And fears for her hostess:

...the painfull Watching and suspense my Sister Cotton keeps me in, who is again with Child. If patience and care can secure her, we have hopes of her going on.

It is not clear when exactly Catherine Stapleton took up permanent residence at Burton Pynsent. Two letters of early 1781 indicate that she was being urged to do so:

[Wynnstay]
Jany 2d 1781

I thank you extremely for letting me judge, in this instance, for myself... If health and happiness were at my disposal, I am sure you will believe you would not have long to wait but that not being the case I the more ardently desire to be with you at the time you teach me to think I could be of most use, and of use. You have made me believe I am, unless your Ladyship flatters beyond the greatest flatterers.

And to Harriot Pitt, undated but written in the early spring:

I look for the Supreme happiness it would be to me to pass the Summers at Burton and defy the Winter Winds at Bodrhyddan.

For some time yet however Catherine is reluctant to give up the pleasures of life in her sisters' comfortable and sociable homes, and the fun at Wynnstay. There is also work to be done in setting up the home and farm at Bodrhyddan.

Acton
9th Jan 1781

To night my dear friend I am advanced six miles near'r to you. Yesterday I changed my head quarters, Leaving Mirth, Joy and gladness behind me [at Wynnstay] my only fear is that Lady Willliams will be tempted to do too much, she is so well. Saturday, there were nineteen at dinner and for the next fortnight I suppose there will not be so few as twenty. . .

My Troops March to Morrow, provided my General who is gone to Bed ill, is able, and I shall follow on Friday, Haulting the first night at Penbedw, in order to arrive early in the Morning at my Castle of Cold Comfort on Saturday. Tuesday I meditate my return here, where if you are <u>well</u> I shall be happy to receive your Ladyship's next letter, under cover to Watkin Williams Esq, Acton, Wrexham. Our party here is not small; if we take in aid four Dogs, to the two children, Dean, Wife, my Sister Williams besides Grandfather, G.Mother, Aunt Bab and Great Aunt Stapleton.

Bodryddan
13th Jany 1781

Positively here, my dearest Friend. I left Acton yesterday and stopped at Penbedw last night, out of <u>Prudence</u> to arrive here with the Day before me. Think what the cold of these two days must be, that occasion'd my Cloathing so that I put myself in mind of a drawing I have seen of a Laplander. I actually recd your letter after I was in <u>the</u> Chaise yesterday, and I please myself more than it can be told with the Idea of its being an Omen of a Future supreme happiness. . . I find a Servant here who means to please me, I conclude, from his telling me <u>The</u> Mare will make a most excellent Mare and the Sheep are the greatest Beauties he ever saw. I have seventeen Lambs. . .

If you knew exactly the Operations of the day, you would certainly be confirm'd in the opinion of my being of a different Race from your Ladyship's, but dont have an anxious thought about me: the not deferring 'that most desire'd day' secures My taking all necessary care. I am now by a good Welsh coal Fire, in a Warm Room with Six very Easy Arm'd Chairs, tell Lady Harriot and an Excellent writing Table cover'd with Green Cloth, and a Bed Chamber waiting for me as Warm as an Oven. Least my Luxury should shock it may do well to mention an Earthern Candlestick and a Lanthorn Candle with strength of Constitution. I am satisfied [that] even difficulties, as well as occupation, is an assistance; if I came here with every thing in order instead of out of order, I am certain many thoughts would arise which necessities banish now.

After a Burton visit Catherine is back home again. She sees Bodrhyddan through the eyes of Hester Chatham:

Bodryddan
Feby 27th 1781

How easy in thought are your dayly Visits here, not less kind, but where my <u>Golden</u> Dreams upon the Future reality, that once I felt within reach. Still we travel in thought together round every field and I am frequently angry when I think a gate too narrow for the dear little Chaise. I am such a fool to my Birth Place that I frequently look, and look again, and say Sometimes to My Birds 'sure this is pritty, Lady Chatham would think so.' I fancy there is not a [...] that peeps over a Tree, or a Wave Foams upon the Sea, that I dont know your Opinion of. . .

I have always kept to my Plans and at times felt much Comfort, but still a certain Weight and draw back remain'd as to my Schemes and arrangement from them. I can only say the Days are too short for my Occupations, and the nights truely, not long enough to recover the Fatigues of the Day. For this last Weeks and a Month to come set out with me, at ½ past seven to Bear a Yew Tree against Farm Yards, Stables etc, I and a man and a Half which three Horses and eight Men could hardly accomplish. . . its the most Interesting of all works, completely hiding all its design'd to hide and opening a very Pritty Wood to the House, [I am] finding my Nightingale as at Burton, running a Race with my Prayers.

Except for the one visit to Burton in June Catherine continued to live mainly in the north for the next fourteen months, rather more at her sisters' homes than at the farm.

After June 1782 the letters cease and the correspondence is not resumed until April 1787. With no other evidence it must be assumed that Catherine was based at Burton Pynsent for these four and a quarter years, though it is hard to believe that she paid no visits elsewhere; if she did so her letters have not survived. Before the gap however she has much of interest to write about. By the early winter of 1781 it is evident that she has become more closely involved in Burton affairs. Hester Chatham has gone to London and Catherine is staying with the third, now delicate Grenville brother James, a near neighbour:

Butleigh
1st Nov:ber 1781
Sat. 3 Nov. 1781

My dear Lady Chatham

I have slept too sound, a complaint I dare not flatter myself I shall hear from you, most favourable as the weather is. I waked early and regretted the not being able to sleep again, as it would be long before Sally [Lady Chatham's personal maid] arrived to make her report. . . I went to all your Poor People, I received many Blessings to my own account but truely upon yours. I cannot determine whether the Lamentations for your Temporary absence, or the gratefully over flowings of their Hearts, prevail'd the most. Wretchedness still keeps the upper hand of poor Parsons: another Child and herself have now the Ague, the two first ill are worse; the working out disables their hands from doing as much as the making their Gowns. . . I add'd a shilling for each gown, which she told was what they would cost, placing that to my own acct. . . The shepherdess is much better than I expected; I would have gone in but she came, as well as usual to the Chaise. . . I met Mr Keetch [farm manager] towards Dale Head with a Bill-Hook and bundle of Hazel-poles upon his shoulder, I almost believe beyond my strength, going to repair hedges himself.

My Time having lost his Wings, yesterday pass'd for Saturday with me, so much so that I absolutely consented to stay today upon your Brother's pressing it very much, much against my inclination, under the Idea of Missing the Williams's by so doing, and the happy discovery of my Error sets at right and I have the pleasure to tell you Mr Grenville made a most comfortable Dinner upon Boiled Beef yesterday.

Back in Cheshire after an eventful journey which included a carriage accident, dismissed by Catherine as a 'harmless Tip', her thoughts are still, significantly, back at Burton Pynsent.

> Combermere Abbey
> 12th Nov:ber 1781
>
> My sister astonishes me, she is absolutely as well I think as she has ever been. It was only a little Way, but after we came from Chapel in the true Burton Style, which increased my pleasure, she beat me in Walking to a Patient, and when I was here Last year she had not been as far as the Chapel for above a year.

She has brought some ornamental birds, geese of an unspecified breed and peafowl, evidently also unhurt in the 'harmless Tip', with her from Burton: a week later she is awaiting their arrival:

> Combermere Abbey
> 17th Nov 1781
>
> ...my dear Burden, dear Birds, who all came as perfectly safe and well last night to Whitchurch as if they had [not] been overturn'd

and a few days later, writing from Acton, she

> has heard of my Feather'd Folk, safe and well as far as Penbedw, within twelve or fourteen miles of their journey's end.

Meanwhile there is plenty to do for a woman of Catherine's temperament:

> Combermere Abbey
> 20th Nov 1781
>
> Our Hunting party succeeded admirably. We were out from ten to three, the only impediment was from the Number of Hares: we kill'd three Brace and tho' I was of the party, we rid round one, upon her seat, in the Middle of a Field and would not put her up. Sir Rob: was upon a Horse, I am sure you would think a perfect beauty, and his leaping is more like Flying; his Rider is always prudent, but seem'd to have Forgotten his Fall. I mounted my War Horse with the greatest success, with the Dogs full Cry; I had him perfectly in hand to go full speed, from Hunters to Waggon'rs. Dont be alarm'd, you are in very safe hands. If Chance brought perfection in my way, I should not take it upon losing Terms to <u>either</u> of us... Will you believe that Riding like an Old Fool yesterday as I did, and longing to follow Sir Rob. over the Hedges, Hooping until I call'd off the Dogs and oblig'd to ask pardon.

There are now quite often references in the letters to the rise and rise of William Pitt, not simply straight praise but always set within the framework of a little event:

Wynnstay
13th Jany 1782

Sir Rob: Cotton has been here two days and went home this Morning. Next Sunday he begins his London Journey in the year 82, of which he made seven in 81. I overheard him telling some body [that] it was worth going to hear Mr Pitt and yesterday he would have charm'd Lady Harriot; during a Three hours walk, he hardly spoke upon any other subject. When he is very eager he repeats a short sentence several times over and I really think a quarter of a mile was walk'd to the repitition of 'I never hear'd such a Speech in my Life' and 'his Voice, you hear him all over the House, you dont lose a word, not a letter, I never heard such a speech in my Life. . .'

Combermere Abbey
Monday 21st Jan 1782

I am quite well and hearing much more of Mr Pitt, his being indeed infinitely more the constant subject that where I came from, in a great measure keeps me with you. I am sure you can judge better than most people of the infinite satisfaction arising from those one tenderly Loves being of the same opinions with ones self.

In March she is back at Bodrhyddan

Saturday night eight
o'clock 2 March 82

I have not seen a [hare] Course since I came home; I went out often before Xmas, but the Spade now rivals every thing. . . Today I got three Trees down, it really seems to be removing them by faith and such Weather, its absolutely April, Apricots and Peaches in Bloom from Garden to Farm. Being a good Manager I have Seven Cows and seldom Churn, six Calves the Objection. Selling so Early sounds poor but our Wheat fetches a Good Price, and mine as good as any of my neighbours. . . This Week I have Kill'd a Beef, it was the only thing I have bought and I have a good deal to sell, so when the time comes for me to pass an Acct I hope it will be pritty well. . . I am enjoying every Moment of the Seventeen hours I am up, and never waking during the Seven I am in Bed.

In April there is the final proof of Hester Chatham's keen desire for Catherine Stapleton to make her home permanently at Burton Pynsent:

Bodryddan
12 Apr 1782

How shall I ever, my dear Lady Chatham, prove to you the satisfaction and happiness it is to me to know you wish we may meet, not to separate again; nothing could put me in such good humour with myself. That happy day I still hope to come, but not quite yet.

The letter ends

But you may well think my pen and time shall never separate, a mark at least how difficult I ever find it to leave you, for at most writing is but little better than thinking of those we love, and that I still do when my pen rests. How can I ever cease to think of the extent of your Affection, still harder to find a subject that can contribute so much to the happiness of my best loved friend.

The gap in the correspondence [p178] is broken, surprisingly perhaps, by a letter not from one or other of Catherine's Welsh border homes, but from London. Much has happened in the four years of silence: Harriot Pitt has married in 1785 and is dead a year later in childbirth, her motherless child coming to live with grandmother Hester; William Pitt is become prime minister at twenty four in 1783. Catherine is now fifty-four but has lost none of her sociability: she is staying with John Chatham, the second earl and his wife:

[Berkeley Square]
Seven o'clock 23d Apr 1787 morning

My dearest Friend
        Lord Chatham in this moment Stepped into his Chariot, his Coach is waiting which Puzzels me, Lady Chatham wisely intending yesterday to go as a good Woman to St Jermin's Church and keep out of the hurry of the Day. The illumination is defer'd till tomorrow, its said from His Majesty's wish to see It, but more likely I believe to prevent the Consiquences of the Mob's being out such a great number of hours. The Crowd of Carriages and people before exceeding every thing one has heard of.

She has the great pleasure, though marred somewhat by the worry of Charlotte Wynn's poor health, of meeting all four of her 'girls' on this visit. The marriage of Elizabeth, the last to wed, to the widowed Lord Carysfort, had taken place a few days earlier on 12 April.

        Lady Fortescue is least well, Mrs Nevill quite, Lady Carysfort very chearful, very pretty Coach and great air of Spruceness throughout, two sweet Babes [stepchildren] the Eldest very handsome; but the state of St James's Square casts a general gloom, I pass'd the evening there with Ly Carysfort and Cath. [Neville]. Sir W has been less well these three days, whether in Consiquence of his anxiety for her [Charlotte] or an increase of his disorder from the Nature of it only, remains to be known. Her sad case is the total check of Bile in its proper Course, Spasms between her Stomach and Bowels, happily in the center, kept Moderate by Laudanum, yellowness upon her skin. . . Mr Thos Grenville was at Sir Watkins looking very well, and allowing The Ball turn'd out very disagreeable, the Prince so over dress'd it was frightful. The top of all things in my mind the Dutchess of Rutland's Dancing with the Duke of York. . . The good Westminsters and I supp'd together and went like sober people to Bed. Going to dress for breakfast. Before, and after, today, tomorrow and for ever
                                                Your truely Affectionate
                                                Cath Stapleton

From this time onwards Catherine's time was passed mainly, but not wholly at Burton. But the quiet life there, spent mostly alone with her hostess, could not fill all the needs of her energetic temperament (in 1788 she still had twenty-seven years of life ahead of her). She almost enjoyed the difficult journeys to her own Welsh border country, even in midwinter, and the presumably much easier ones to London. Hester Chatham however missed her greatly and Catherine, in her now much shorter letters home is at pains to reassure Hester that she is fit and well, and to tender advice on questions which had arisen, or could arise on everything affecting day to day affairs at Burton. However distant from home, in spirit she was never far away:

[Bristol]
14th Jan: 1788

The road from Wells to this Place, Bristol, truely better than in Summer. The finest and the brightest of Evenings, Tea at the usual hour but not the company. . . I have order'd Supper a quarter before Nine. Depend upon my care of myself being as great tomorrow, but keep in your mind that if you fail in yours, I shall feel it all lost labour. The journey, trust me I tell you truely, is nothing; I am now as untir'd as if I had stopp'd at Langport and upon my Word most perfectly well [and] have not been sensible of the smallest degree of Tremor in my legs when I get out of the Chaise which I should not have wonder'd at. Your message to Davis [her maid] is not lost upon her, she has been pleasant in timing well her speaking and her silence upon the road. William [coachman] is voted out of Livery which will secure him a good Fire and better Mess, and her a Conversable Companion and messenger at hand.
This account will reach you to-morrow. God in Heaven Bless you.

Monday 28th Jan:y 1788

Setting out for Penbedw, perfectly well, the finest of days. . . Frost seems to be coming, if so pray let the roads Mr Simmons has made be pack'd in and a Roler pass'd over, dont let Mr Cooling [gardener] be against it, as in my Travels I have seen the successful practice.

Berkeley Square
Monday morning 27th Apr 1789

I shall Leave London with a lighter Heart than I did Burton, although I can set forth for dinner at 6 o'clock with as good an Air and better Appetite than most people. Strange, as true, I can hardly satisfy my voracious stomach; I dont mean any abuse of the Good Tables I frequent. Mrs Grenville gave us one of the best dinners I ever saw in the Plain Way, Nine Ladies alas [only] three men.

[Berkeley Square]
First of May, as black as Winter [1789]

Our party, my dear friend, dropped very short of Gentlemen. Lord Chatham went to Windsor with the glad tidings of Prince William's return; Mr Pitt at Holwood. His Lordship dined while we deserted, his Master unmoved and quite well. I shall be short today for I shall not enjoy myself I find while I think of your Lone Sunday.

Two years later Catherine is again in London on what appears to have been a last visit to the capital. She has paid a call on Fanny Boscawen:

[Berkeley Square]
28th Apr 1791

Your Audley Street friend I have pass'd an hour with by Clock, tho' not in thought. Both her Daughters, two Lovely Grand Da:s [daughters] and Lady Bute part of the time. Early Tuesday I shall be as happy to see your dear Ly:p as I have been to see any I have or shall.

Two days later Catherine indulges in a rare outburst of anger against an acquaintance. A fellow guest at dinner with the Fortescues was

Her Grace of Gordon but far from Gracious, cold as Water, not the Name of Pitt utter'd. [She] ask'd after you or I should not have thought she knew me. She look'd liked a Fury Herself, and [her] two Daughters dress'd completely in Black to their Fingers ends, heads not excepted, with strange and enormous projecting ornaments.

Early in 1797 Catherine is called to the bedside of one of her 'girls', Hester Fortescue, ill from a threatened miscarriage. To answer the summons will have been a difficult decision and her letters from north Devon reflect her unease:

Castle Hill
5th Jan 1797

My dearest dear friend,
Without the smallest interruption I reach'd this place within Mr Eliot's eight hours and much to my satisfaction an hour or <u>two</u> before I was expect'd - for expectation you will know does not suit a Weak Frame, and if Please God you do not miss me too much, I must be glad I had resolution to leave you. This poor dear Soul thinks in pleasure she gains so much, the event has not happen'd, she is not worse than I was prepared for, and quite satisfied with the Man who attends her. He is a Woodforde [Lady Chatham's doctor at Burton], comes at eight o'clock and returns in the morning. Now, being only four, I have not seen him, by to morrows post after I have, you shall hear particulars. This [letter] is perform'd by her bedside in the Dark, and like her dear Aunt talking the whole time, tho' hardly above a <u>Whisper</u>, but [with] Spirits beyond my hopes and I forsee nothing thank God to even make me wish to prolong my Stay. Lord F is Charming, so thankfull to us both for my Coming. They desire every thing that is Affectionate to you. More I cannot add than Nurse wanting her Child as much as she can be want'd.
Ever ever in Affection as you would have me.

A letter follows almost every day: Catherine is torn between her heart's desire to nurse one of her girls, and her love and anxiety for the old and frail aunt left behind.

[Castle Hill]
6th Jan 1797

I am overtaken by the Post, but in my Turn, as I shall nearly overtake my <u>Scrap</u> I the less regret its not being a letter, tho' as the last part of my Road is best, and the Niece is not <u>quite</u> such a spoilt Child as the Aunt, I therefore shall not breakfast by her Bed at Six o'clock but come after in stead of before dinner.

[Castle Hill]
8th Jan: 1797
Sunday

Oh my dearest of all friends, the Post ups me Cruelly, only once have I heard of you. . . if you will believe me, it seems almost out of memory since I saw you. . . you cannot miss me, at least I hope not, half as much I do you; the Idea of what the state of the poor dear Neck may be sits heavy on me. My full purpose was to return to day, but your poor dear likeness was so very Ill yesterday, it was impossible without I had known you particularly wanted me.

[Castle Hill]
10th Jan:y 1797

I look towards Friday for the happiness of seeing you, but remember any 14 hours brings me to you. . . No Creature ever suffer'd more than I do, how to absent my self from my first Object, or to leave precipitately such an affectionate, captivating, exhausted being quite overpowers me.

Having heard from Hester Chatham, confirmed by Dr Woodforde, that all was well at Burton, Catherine stays on in Devon a few days longer than intended and ventures, with modesty, a reason for so doing:

Castle Hill
12th Jan:y 1797

While I can hear of you, I can as little express my thankfullness to providence for your standing this extreme severe Weather as these dear people can for thinking of them before yourself. Its impossible for them to be more sensible of your kindness than they are; while I am saying this, I must forget my own is the subject in question, but the Fact is that any friend of my description at present must be essential to her comfort poor thing. Surround'd with Blessings as God be praised she is, still at her distance from her family there is that want. A Man cannot I think be a better Nurse than Lord Fortescue is, but there is the great draw back from his additional suffering, not only from seeing hers too constatly but close confinement dont suit men.

Catherine makes one more northern journey in the late autumn and early winter of 1798, staying as usual at Combermere Abbey and Penbedw, and paying a short, rather nostalgic visit to Bodrhyddan. Family illness detains her but as ever her thoughts are back at Burton:

[Combermere Abbey]
5th Dec:r 1798

I am happy in Mr Woodforde's 'liking you very well'; pray God I may [also] a few days now [and] that being the case will, in defiance of every Pull my Heart is far from insensible to, be most happy. When have I been a month and day absent from you before?

Shevington
[near Nantwich]
8th Dec:r 1798

My dearest dear friend

Before the House is up I am sat down, first to congratulate you on the Great and good News the Sun yesterday abound'd with, Minorca, Malta etc; next best to me my steady hope of surrendering to you on Tuesday late evening, not Night. A Neck or Loin of Mutton in Chops in Broth mine and fellow Travellers delights, and nothing else. . .

Your Ever Ever Affectionate
Cath. Stapleton

There is no evidence that Catherine ever again left Burton until after Hester's death in April 1803. If she did so, no letters survive but we catch glimpses now and again of her presence there in the correspondence of others; William Pitt in his letters to his mother rarely fails to send his greetings to her. And so it is safe to think that this loving and generous-hearted woman remained at the side of her friend until she was needed no longer. We deserve the friends we get and some tribute must go to Hester Lady Chatham for keeping to her end the loyalty and love of a noble soul.

Catherine was living in Shropshire when she died; she was brought to her ancestral church at Rhuddlan for burial. An obituary in the church register reads:

1815. Catherine Stapleton, Manor House, Woore Shropshire Sept 4 [aged] 82. Ceremony the Dean of St Asaph officiated.

Chapter 7

SOCIAL FRIENDS

Equal Society with them to hold

Abraham Cowley (1618-1667), *On the Death of Mr Crashaw*

i. LETTERS FROM GRACE TREVOR 1766-1796

The main interest in this lady's correspondence with Lady Chatham lies in her long residence in Bath at a time of that city's greatest fame as a social centre and spa. Grace Trevor was the second of the nine daughters of John Morley Trevor of Trevallyn Plasteg, Denbigh and Glynde, Sussex. She was born in 1706 and died in May 1797, two months before her ninety-first birthday. The correspondence begins in 1766 when she was sixty; although she never married she enjoyed, as was then customary for older women, the courtesy title of Mrs. Of the 130 letters from her, only 8, an unusually small number for women correspondents, are undated.

Mrs Trevor's letters do not compare in intellectual content with those of Fanny Boscawen, or in the vitality and independence of spirit of Catherine Stapleton's. The earlier letters are over sycophantic, and it was only as she grew older and after Chatham's death in 1778, that the incessant and indiscriminate praise of the Chatham and Stanhope families gives way, to some extent, to more entertaining descriptions of life in Bath, of its residents and visitors.

Her connection with the Stanhopes, to whom she was not related, came through her close friendship with Lady Lucy Stanhope, the unmarried sister of Philip, second Earl Stanhope. The two spinsters shared a house in the Circus and nearly all the letters, though penned by Mrs Trevor, are written in the third person as from both ladies until Lady Lucy's death in 1785. The many references to the Stanhope family give interesting glimpses of life at Chevening, and news of family members from Grizel, Countess Stanhope and passed on by Grace Trevor in letters to Hester Chatham. The eldest child of Hester Pitt who married Lord Mahon, later third earl Stanhope, was Hester, famed later as the eccentric middle-eastern traveller, Lady Hester Stanhope. She appears to have been a most precocious child and Mrs Trevor's letters give breathless descriptions of the cleverness of this granddaughter of Lady Chatham and Lady Stanhope.

Grace Trevor was sociable and her letters give accounts of Bath events and her own entertaining. She was a keen card player: cribbage was her main diversion in old age, but she disliked high stakes and detested gaming. She was not averse to a bit of gossip, of which Bath must have had plenty; nor in fact was Hester Chatham, and Grace Trevor, as with most of the correspondents, felt encouraged to pass on the titbits which came her way.

She was very conscious of growing so old and nearly all the letters written in her last five or six years mention the many infirmities, including failing sight, with which she was troubled. In an age of appalling medical treatment, some credit for her longevity must be given to her physician, the noted Dr Caleb Hillier Parry, and Grace Trevor expresses her gratitude to him in a number of her later letters. Though frail in body she kept her wits about her to the end.

After a visit of Hester Chatham and all the children to Bath, Chatham being already there, she writes:

[Bath]
Saturday Novr 1st [1766]

Lady Lucy Stanhope and Mrs Trevor return many thanks to Lady Chatham for the great pleasure she was so good to give them last night [and] hope the young people did not catch any colds. Lady Lucy and Mrs Trevor could not talk last night of any thing but those delightful children. [They] hope Lord and Lady Chatham, Lord Pitt, Lady Hester, Lady Harriot, Mr William and little Mr James will all enjoy perfect Health, have a pleasant and safe journey and return to Bath quite well before Xmas [and] that my Lord Chatham will not forget the care of his own Health, from his kind concern for the publick.

Mrs Trevor does not attempt waiting on Lady Chatham again to take leave, imagining it could only be troublesome the last day.

Two or three annual letters continue on these lines for the next three years, but by 1770 have begun to increase in number and length. While written still partly in the third person from Lady Lucy and herself, Grace Trevor now breaks out on news of her own.

Bath
Sep: the 30th 1770

... I was much pleased at Mr Hoare's where I went with Lady Frances Burgoyne to see his Pictures. The Bishop of Derry has set, the picture is large, there is a table covered with Green-paper, pens etc. At the end sits the Bishop, by him stands his son, a Beautiful youth; the Bishop's Countenance expresses his anxiety for his Sons welfare and with great earnestness directs his attention to the Noble man who sits at the other end of the table and is strikingly like My Lord Chatham.

After hoping that her dear Lady Chatham will visit Bath and see the pictures, she continues with a description of changes in the city:

The Buildings Here are much encreased since you saw it, the New [Assembly] Rooms covered in and several houses in the Crescent finished as is the Queen's parade. Gentlefolks start up to inhabit all these and many more new Buildings that are every day raised; there is quite a pretty new Town going up the Hill to Lansdown. It far exceeds my understanding to discover where all these fine people lived Thirty years ago. However here they now are and make Living very expensive to those they found here.

The following year the two friends anxiously scan the newspapers for news of Chatham's protracted lawsuit against the heirs at law of the late Sir William Pynsent. At last

Circus
Friday May the 10: 1771

the Bath journal assured us His Lordship had carried it by the Opinion of all the judges. . . We beg dear Lady Chatham will receive our congratulations and make them acceptable to his Lordship. Our little family are this night to rejoyce over a Bowl of punch, the Old English fashion.

From their annual summer visit to the country, she writes

Hampton
July the 28 1772

Lady Lucy and I make constant use of our new chaise and are pleased with the pretty views we see. We go 12 or 14 miles every evening; considering how long we have disused such exercise, we have bore it amazingly well. Whether it does us good I cant tell, but that it pleases us is certain. We have a good neighbour: Lady Trevor has taken a Cottage in the village just by us.

And some recent Bath news:

We hear last Saturday Mr Houghton the Mayor went round the Market to examine their weights; the consequence of which was every Baker (except one, a Widow named Allen) had all their Bread taken from them and given to the poor. Several Butchers proved to have false weights. I admire the Mayor and hope it will be productive of some good.

In December there is an explanation of why letters, written only by Mrs Trevor, have been scance:

Bath
Dec the 18 1772

The same unlucky accident that prevented Lady Lucy and Mrs Trevor for some time from making enquiry after the Health of Lord and Lady Chatham and their sweet family has prevented us from sooner returning our most grateful thanks to dear Lady Chatham for her most obliging letters. The only Hand we have long had between us to guide a pen was disabled by the sting of a wasp on the joint of the forefinger of Mrs Trevor's right hand, which sting (it is thought) opened an artery . . . When we returned to Bath the beginning of October Mr Wright found [it] in a very doubtful state. Three weeks it was every day burnt with a corstik after which he found the bone not hurt as he feared; he healed it. Mrs Trevor hoped soon to be quite well, however that is by no means the case, the joint is very stiff. . .

She is glad the recent floods in Somerset

have only added to the Beauty of the prospect. Having passed two summers at Hampton has reconciled us to Damps, as we had very good health there, and our family.

Lady Lucy is obviously delicate. While at Hampton they

> made great tryal of the exercise of a carriage; the whole time we remained there it agreed perfectly well with Lady Lucy till the days grew too short to go out after dinner. The morning drives did not do, she was cold when she returned tho' the weather was very warm. Since we came to Bath [she] is always at Home, has her acquaintance and plays some times at Tredril. . . Bath is far from empty, Balls and Concerts every night. The Duchess of Newcastle has only her one table of Tredril; Mrs Trevor has the honour some time to make one there, but goes often to her Grace in the morning, not liking to leave Lady Lucy in the evening when she can help it.

For the next five years the third person letters continue, their contents confined mostly to comment on the members of the Stanhope and Chatham families:

> Dear friends at Chevening are well in health; we hope when all the work is finished the improvements will make amends for the fatigue and inconvenience they have suffered (Bath, April 20th 1777)

There is one conventional letter of condolence on the death of Chatham in 1778, written in June, two months after the event; in November of that year the exceptional talents of William Pitt are noticed and his steady rise to early and subsequent fame is a theme of admiration which continues in almost every letter to the last.

Grace Trevor fortunately was gregarious and two letters from Bath in 1779 describe her social doings interlaced with gossip, often amusing, about people she met or heard of, at parties.

> Bath
> Feb: the 3rd 1779

> I don't think good manners abound here and very little of course can be learned here. The Town is much enlarged, the inhabitants so much increased your Ladyship would hardly know Bath. There are two people here however I hope you would not find changed, at least their sincere esteem for Lady Chatham continues the same. . . We at present have my sister Boscawen and her daughter Charlotte here. Lady Lucy is so good, they live with us and Lady Trevor dines here. Every day we play a whist for 6 pence a game; my Lady Malpas and a few more come and conform to our low play, but quite otherwise is the Ton here, card parties and concerts on Sunday evenings. However Lady Lucy's Drawing room is very full notwithstanding; some I believe take us in their way, but Lady Malpas, Lady Trevor and a few more make a point of previewing the Circus. . .

She has news of the orphaned daughter of her late friends, Lord and Lady Lothian:

> Lady Amelia Kerr keeps up a constant correspondence with me. She writes most sensibly and feelingly, seems to dread slipping again into company. I am glad dear Lady Lothian had it in her power to leave her so good a fortune; a Thousand pound a year on the post office left by Lady Fitzwalter; eight thousand

when she marrys, 2100 a year till then left by the late marquis her father, four thousand pound Lady Lothian left her of the five Ld Holderness's legacy and one thousand to Lady Louisa Lenox and Lady Amelia sole executrix. . . I am anxious for Lady Amelia's happiness; Princess Amelia has made her Lady of her Bedchamber and taken her under her protection, to say nothing on that.

[Bath]
Sep the 29 1779

Bath news is curious: Lady Camilla Fleming is going to be married to Mr Wake our apothecary. He is near sixty, she forfeits 1200 a year, house in London, jewels, plate etc etc all for Mr Wake £1000 a year. . . He is to keep on his Shop. She is more than 50, people are never to old to be foolish.

She has observations on the No Popery riots of early in June 1780:

[Bath]
June the 17 1780

We had yesterday the pleasure (by letter from dear Lord Mahon) to hear dear Lady Mahon is well. We felt much for them on account of the Riots in London: they are, I find, as we are, under the care of the Military, a new Scene in Bath. The R. Catholicks are still afraid to sleep in their houses; they should I think avoid exceeding the liberty our Laws allow them, but my thoughts are very old fashiond and must be kept to myself.

Hester Mahon's death in August has left her three little Stanhope daughters in the care of their grandmother, Lady Stanhope. From Chevening a year later Mrs Trevor writes with news of them. The eldest, 'Miss Stanhope' is five years old.

Chevening
Aug the 13 1781

Lady Lucy and I join in assuring dear Lady Chatham we received a great pleasure from hearing by a letter Lady Stanhope received that dear Lady Chatham is well. We are impatient to tell your Ladyship how much we are charmed by the three sweetest children we ever beheld. In Miss Stanhope we see the picture of what we dearly loved and admired: her sense is astonishing, her wit, in short the whole exceeds description. Miss Griselda appears like the representation of Beauty, Health, Happiness and Sweet Temper. Her countenance contains every thing that is pleasing; Miss Lucy is very pretty. Lady Stanhope's fondness to them and theirs to her is charming.

Letters from Mrs Trevor over the next three years are scanty; she modestly provides an explanation in one of 1784:

[Bath]
Sep the 26 1784

Lady Lucy and I have long since wished to make enquiry after dear Lady Chatham's health but a fear of being troublesome, conscious a letter from one of my age must at best be dull, has prevailed with me to deny my self that pleasure.

This day by a letter from Mrs [Henry] Grenville we hear dear Lady Harriot is at Brighthelmston with Mr Pitt. I never know from the papers where Mr Pitt is, but we hope he is in perfect good health and Dear Lady Harriot too, tho' at that place that country will be quite a new scene to them. I am partial to those Downs, having passed my early days there. . .

Early in 1785 Lady Lucy's health is giving cause for worry. In thanking Hester Chatham for her kind enquiries about the invalid, Mrs Trevor writes apologising for the delay in replying:

[Bath]
Jan: the 29 1785

I hoped to answer more satisfactorarily [which] made me defer from day to day taking up my Pen. It is four weeks today since my dear Lady Lucy was taken ill with a cramp and pains on her breast and a bad cough. I thank God she is now much better; I hope to see her able to venture down [on] Thursday.

In this letter she has news of Lady Amelia Kerr, now married to an army officer, Captain Macleod and with a baby. She is evidently considered to have married beneath her; Grace Trevor has observations on such a union:

I have had a letter from Lady Amelia Macleod at the end of a fortnight since she was safely delivered of a son. Cap: Macleod was so good to write to me to say she was safe and when she was asleep went to London to catch the post. Lady Lucy and I like him, which is a great comfort, as we could not forbear feeling some regret when she married. Psse Amelia's anger [about the marriage] continues as violent as ever. I sorrow to see a person I love descend in their situation [but] I feel . . . anger belongs to parents only.

In July Lady Lucy has died.

[Bath]
July the 7 1785

I am very gratefully sensible of the honour dear Lady Chatham does me and the compassionate goodness her Ladyship's kind concern for me shows she possesses. I am very unwilling to say . . . what I suffer. I have felt very severe affliction from the loss of friends I loved before, but alas, what I have now lost is irreparable. Every day, every hour shews me what I've lost. I do as I think I ought to do, strive to submit to my fate, but hitherto all I have obtained is silently to keep it to myself.

But her vitality and interest in others surmounts her sorrow and in this same letter she gives news received from Lady Stanhope of the little girls and is touched to be asked to be a godmother to Mahon's son by his second wife. She is pleased about Harriot's engagement to Edward Eliot:

I am told by many people Dear Lady Harriot has made a conquest of the heart of a very amiable Young Man, of a very extraordinary good character, Lord

Eliot's son. I shall be glad if her Ladyship accepts him, I have heard so much in his favour.

There is one further reference to her sorrow in a letter of 3rd November:

> . . . I don't find my Grief lessens from Time, it if possible increases, as I miss her more every day than before. Dear Lady Stanhope charged me, when we parted, to get rid of that indifference I have for every thing (my friends excepted), her kindness I am sure I never can forget.

Yet time does heal and Grace Trevor's liveliness of mind overcomes he apathy. She agrees, with reluctance, to approach Lady Chatham (in a somewhat confused letter) on behalf of a son of apothecary Wake, he whose second marriage in 1779 to Lady Camilla Fleming, was described by Grace Trevor as 'curious':

[Bath]
Feb the 21 1786

> I am intreated to give your Ladyship this trouble very much against my inclination, as I am very sensible very few people have any scruple of giving trouble, I dont like to view my self amidst them; the only excuse I can make is the knowledge I have of your Ladyship's compassion. The case is this, Mr Wake has a son who when at Oxford entered too far into a love affair and was expelled. Lady Camilla Wake procured him a commission in the army but he has always wished I find to be in Orders. The Bishop of Bath and Wells thought three years should be passed more, and if his sober way of life continued, he was ready to ordain him. It is now five years since the Bishop named that, and his conduct approved if a small living could be obtained. I told Mr Wake I did not believe Mr Pitt interfered with the disposal of church preferments and also told him I did not ever mean to trouble him with any application. Your Ladyship's compassion, Mr Wake thought, for a young married man with children might be of great service. I beg a thousand pardons for complying with Mr Wake's request if it should appear impertinent. I know dear Lady Lucy thought and so did I my self [that] he was misrepresented at Oxford.

Six months later she is in good heart:

[Bath]
Augt the 14 1786

> We have had here the hottest weather I ever remember. I have been at some card partys and really found them too hot, but when I had been at one could not well excuse my self.
> We have had a great Lady at Bath, Mrs Fitzherbert. Her father Mr Smith was given over and she came down to see him. Many people think she did him great honour; I said it was no more than her duty. Mrs Macartney said how few people do their Duty. I wished to say was she my Daughter I would not admit her, but I suppress'd it. . .

and some observations on a cause celèbre, the attempted stabbing of the king by a deranged housemaid:

I cannot persuade my self that Margt Nicholson is mad; I always attend to what appears at first, its easy to make up things after. I think it was wise to send her to Bedlam, whether real or feigned she ought to be confined. I think his Majesty shewed great Humanity.

Mrs Trevor wrote only twice in 1787. There is a passing reference in her letter in June to the death of Harriot Eliot (in September of the previous year) 'who I so tenderly loved'. She had had the 'honour of several visits from the great Earl of Mansfield. He is much shrunk but his conversation charming'. In November she writes that there was much illness in Bath due to the damp weather but 'as to my self my <u>Bodyly</u> complaints are very slight, I am constantly out in my chaise which as I now dont walk does me good'. She 'receives great civilities from many people' and names her chief women friends. She has sent a wax doll to her goddaughter Griselda Stanhope; her companion Mrs Ellis dressed it. She is conscious of getting old but life continues along pleasant lines:

[Bath]
May the 27 1788

Your very kind letter put me to shame, to reflect how long it has been since I endeavour with my Pen to tell dear Lady Chatham how much she employs my thoughts; it is not to be wondered at, at my great age [82] that I should be unable to do many things I wish to do . . . I go out every morning in the carriage, when the road is watered its pleasant. Last Monday we had a Concert, Rouzzini performed. Wed: I made chiefly for my old acquaintance the Duke of Newcastle, who was so kind to pass several evenings with me and expressed great pleasure to see such an old friend and near relation so well as I appeared to him to be. One evening Lord Guilford and Lord Nugent met his Grace here; we told our ages but we thought Lord Nugent sunk 5 or 6 years. He went the next day for Ireland. I hear there are several foreigners of great Rank here; I decline their being introduced to me as I dont speak french.

She is philosophic about happiness in relation to wealth:

Bath
Sep 21 1788

Dear Madam
.. By your not naming it I fancy you may not have heard my nephew Rice's eldest Daughter Cecilia Rice is going to be married to a Mr Dorrien. Lady Dynevor wrote to tell it me. She says his fortune at present is moderate, but that her Daughter thinks she can live comfortably with a person she loves. The young man (I find) travelled with them thro' Switzerland, has a very good character and is pleasing and agreeable. An estate is entailed on him that is not yet come. I hope she will be happy. I dont think fortune ever bestows Happiness. So long as I have lived I never could see where happiness lived: in friendship she dwells for some time, but alas, not to the end of life.

and pays a small tribute to her companion, who was to die five months later

I have been very lucky in the society of a very sensible agreeable women, Mrs Ellis who is very good to me but she is in very indifferent health which gives me much concern.

and on the same themes of age and friendship:

[Bath]
July the 15 1789

Bath is at present much deserted; as I dont go out of evenings it is dull. I dont venture to work or read; I have one Table at Cribbage and seldom miss of a party. I find my self weak tho' not ill enough to nurse. If I live till the 25th I shall be 83. The loss of friends is the sad certainty of so long [a] life. I have suffered severely that way, and have one comfort that I feel all the joy of my friends sincerely.

There are seven short letters of 1790 and six of 1791. Their interest lies mainly in the life led by a very old woman at a time when to live into advanced old age was uncommon. On 14th April she thanks God she is

amazingly well, considering I entered this World in July 1706. When I reflect on the great affliction I have suffered I am astonished to find my self here, but I consider God knows best and I most patiently wait his Time.

Despite failing sight she still entertains:

Bath
Augt the 11 1790

Your Ladyship will see by this that my sight is not perfect as I cant write even, but I am very thankful I can read by candlelight. . . I have a party every night Friday, we make two cribbage Tables.

[Bath]
March the 7 1791

I have begun again my airing and think it agrees very well with me. My party is always full and I am better in the evening. I hear what pleases me when the political conversation begins. The dismal subject of gaming shocks me: I must pity Lady Spencer; sure[ly] there must have been great neglect in their education [for] two Daughters to turn out so.

She has met Edward Eliot, Harriot's widower, Hester Chatham's son-in-law.

Bath
July the 28 1791

I was Madam much pleased with Mr Eliot, he is a pretty man [with] the airs and behaviour of a man of fashion, which is seldom seen now. I was happy to see him yet it affected me extremely. I long to know if his dear little Daughter resembles what I loved so much.

and more philosophising, though not now so clearly expressed:

> Could we know my Dear Madam when we enter into Life what Shocks, what pains we are to suffer, should we Dance and take so many delights. Certainly No, but the veil intercepts our view. My Life tho' very long has been clouded by the loss of those I tenderly loved; all my own family have left me [but] the next generation behave very well to me. . . and express a regard for me.

She welcomes the autumn with its promise of better health:

Bath
Oct the 16 1791

> The weather here is much cooler, which I hope will make all my friends recover Health, as I never remember so sickly a season. Every creature here had a complaint in their Bowels which left a great Weakness. Doctor Parry soon cured me and I am now very well; I have some friends in my House.

Inevitably much of the content of her letters from this time onwards is concerned with health, Lady Chatham's, her own and that of other friends. Good or bad health is invariably linked to the weather.

To Mrs Stapleton:

Bath
March the 28 1792

> Your obliging letter gave me sincere satisfaction to know Dear Lady Chatham is so much better and I flatter my self as the Spring advances her Ladyship will grow better and better. My cough which you so kindly enquire after has I really think taken its leave of me. Dr Parry ordered me a draught to take at noon, which I believe has proved so effectual. If he can do such miracles by recovering an old Woman, sure his skill must be great.
>
> Bath is I believe full but not many of my acquaintance. . . I make no visits but every Evening have a Table at Cribbage. Tomorrow I find Her Majesty is to have a ball, 40 couple, no woman below the rank of Earl's daughter. I am vexed my dear Lady Hester [Stanhope] has not been presented; I hope that wont hinder her from being there.

She would love to pay visits, especially to Chevening but, ever thoughtful of others:

Bath
May the 6 1792

> at my age I scruple making visits as it makes people uneasy where you go, tho' I dont believe the journey would hurt me. Those dear young things I long to see; I wish Lord and Lady Stanhope would come to Bath and bring two or three, how happy should I be. Doctor Parry has just called on me; he has examined my newspapers, having took a fright least the Lords should not pass the Bill we are so anxious for, but my paper has nothing alarming in it.

In October she has a dramatic piece of news:

Lady Middleton and Miss Broderick were with me last night as was Lady Bute and Lady Louisa Stuart; we played at Cribbage.

Mrs Macartney was here, she has had a great escape. She dined with the Prince of Wales at Briton, went to her Lodging to dress [for] the Ball where she was to go with Mrs Fitzherbert. Her cap took fire, all her hair is burnt off and some Holes are in her head. She says she feels great pain but she is better than could be expected.

The weather here Madam is very wet and dark; most people have colds, I have a troublesome cough but Doctor Parry says I am well.

In the two years that follow, Grace Trevor is courageously struggling to keep the correspondence going. She is now eighty-seven rising eighty-eight and her poor sight makes writing difficult. The letters are short and concerned mainly with the ever present topics of health, the weather, William Pitt's triumphs and the Stanhope family. In April 1794 she writes that

My sight is so imperfect I am sensible my letters must be worthless. I am trying a recipe, Linseed Tea, to dissolve the cataraque in my Eye. . . Its melancholy not to read and work but I submit without complaining. I am happy when I hear my friends are well.

In June she writes of worries about the war:

I have a mind very susceptable of apprehensions and feeling for others when I read of so many killed. . . I am very much afraid for our Princes; the papers today say Prince Ernest is wounded. These are dismal times, there was last night a Riot here, no body killed but windows broke. I hear the Mayor has sent for soldiers. God grant we may soon have peace.

In May 1795, approaching her eighty-ninth birthday, ever sociable she still has

our Table at cribbage every evening, chiefly females

though she has

suffered much pain from the gravel, but Dr Parry has ordered me a medicine that seems to have cured me.

Her last letter says it all. Written at all angles on the page but properly dated, she yet is able to cast her mind away from her own troubles to congratulate Hester Chatham on a family success:

[Bath]
Sep: the 24 1796

My dear Madam

My great age and weak state of health, with a great defect in my sight, has prevented me from troubling your Ladyship but I cant forbear a letter trying to express the pleasure it has gave me to hear dear Lord Chatham is placed at the Head of the Council.

I only wish every member of the board may possess his [. . .] and ability, happy should we be. [I] hope your Ladyship enjoys health and Mrs Stapleton, to whom compliments.

I am dear Madam

Your Ladyship's obedt humble

G Trevor

ii. LETTERS FROM MRS ELIZABETH MONTAGU c 1770-1775

This lady, famous in her day as a literary hostess, a centre of the intellectual life in London, whose fame has lingered on from the publication of four volumes of her letters and other writings, was not really a friend of Hester Chatham in the truest sense. Though less than a year younger, it is probable that Lady Chatham was a little daunted by the thought of meeting this so different a woman, and it was only through the persistence of her cousin Molly Hood that any contact was established; visits to Hayes and Burton Pynsent were arranged, but not in reverse. She did however yield to Mrs Hood's desire to allow the socially restricted and over-protected Pitt children, when they were aged from about nine to sixteen, to be entertained by Mrs Montagu under the eye of Mrs Hood.

Exactly why Elizabeth Montagu, probably one of the busiest and most sought after women of her day, was so keen to meet the Chathams is not clear; possibly, along with many others she was simply dazzled by Chatham's fame. Whatever the reason she was extremely kind and generous to the children and several of her letters to their mother are concerned with their amusement, a task she appears to have entered into with relish.

Unfortunately only three of the twenty-one existing letters are dated, but it can be deduced from the texts that nearly all were written between 1770 and 1775.

Hillstreet

Thursday night

Madam

The status of an invalid is in itself full of mortifications, for which even prudent valetudinarium has a stock of patience ready on demand: the headach and a violent pain in my stomach found me very well prepared, but the cruel incident of Lady Hester Pitts calling the very moment after I went to bed, I was unprepared for, and I did not submit to it as a person ought to do, whose best friend has for the benefit of english readers translated the doctrines of Epicticus. If I had not been much indisposed this morning I had intended begging to have the honour of waiting on your Ladyship to know if I might be permitted to ask Lord Pitt, the Ladies and Mr Pitts to let me have the honour of carrying them to a Concert breakfast at Mr Anson's. I imagine Mrs Hood would mention the proposal to your Ladyship; and I hope you will pardon the liberty I took in soliciting this favour, as Mr Ansons house and pictures are well worth seeing, his Concerts very fine. In elegance of taste and manners he is an Athenian and as this concert would be private and in the morning, I thought it might fall in with your

Ladyship's plan; but this I submit entirely [and] only hope you will forgive my taking the liberty to propose it. If it is wrong, you must take as little blame to yourself, for they are the only very young persons to whom I should have thought fine painting, statuary and musick a perfectly suitable entertainment. I will have the honour to wait on your Ladyship tomorrow morning if I am able, but that is a point quite uncertain, for these disorders in my stomach are sometimes followd by a slight fever, sometimes only by a little langour. I have at present shivering fits with intervals of heat, but I hope they are only the effect of pain on a weak system, and that they will go off in a few hours, as is very usual, but I could not defer making my apologies to Lord Chatham and your Ladyship for my daring project. I have the honour to be Madam, your Ladyship's most obedt and most Hble servant

    E Montagu

There are arrangements for a further outing to Mr Anson's, this time in the afternoon. As usual, Mrs Montagu's invitation includes mention of her ailments; she was a delicate woman, as all contemporary reports confirm.

Hillstreet
Wednesday

I have been in so uncertain a state of health ever since I had the honour of your Ladyships most obliging letter, that I was much afraid of not being able to profit by all your kind indulgence to me for Thursday; but I was so much relieved by being blooded yesterday that I flatter myself I shall be in perfect health tomorrow . . . I will order dinner to be ready by three o'clock, that your Ladyship may not feel an anxious half hour before the return of the valuable treasure your goodness entrusts to me. I know Mr Ansons sentiments so well as to be assured he will be very proud of Lord Chathams expressions of regard for him. I shall be as fortunate tomorrow as a Person who shd have the command of two fine gardens . . .

In a postscript to this letter she adds:

I will attend the Ladies in Pall Mall at the hour Mr Anson shall appoint. I believe it will be between twelve and one.

Elizabeth Montagu was a close friend of the actor-manager David Garrick and so able not only to get good seats at his theatre, but also apparently to ensure that the plays to which she took her important guests were of her choosing.

Hillstreet
Monday morn:

Mrs Montagu presents her compts to Lord and Lady Chatham with many thanks for the great favours she received at Hayes. She imparted to Mr Garrick yesterday Lord and Lady Chathams intention of honouring his representation on the stage with their presence and their preference to the Comedy of Every Man in his Humour, which at once determined him to make choice of it for the only day he is to act this season. Mrs M: made a blunder as to the day, which is to be the 24. She has a stage box for that night which will be entirely at Lord and Lady Chathams command. If they have room for her, and will permit her the honour to be of the party,, she will be very happy, but is more solicitous that all the young Ladies and Gentlemen who entertain'd her with a Ball at Hayes should partake of this amusement . . . Mrs M: will send the tickets according to Lady Chathams order when her Ladyship has determined the number she will want.

But Chatham's gout was, as ever, an excuse for the parents to cry off the invitation. Undaunted, Mrs Montagu enlists the Shelburnes to take the Chathams' place and offers every inducement for the children to participate.

> . . . I am afraid your Ladyship will think I abuse your indulgence but I must beg that Lady Hester and Lady Harriot, Lord Pitt and the young Gentlemen would do me the honour to dine with me on Thursday, and I can with the better grace enforce my request, as it will be more convenient to them as well as infinitely more agreeable to me for I will take care the dinner shall be on the table by four o'clock, and I shall have the honour and pleasure of carrying them safe from hence to the Play, and will also attend them home at night. Our carriages shall attend, so that your Ladyships horses, which will have travell'd, need not do it.
>
> I saw Mr Garrick yesterday much out of spirits at being likely to lose the honour of Lord Chathams presence at the play, but I hope he will exert himself so as to give Lord Pitt and the Ladies a great deal of amusement. I will send immediately to Lord and Lady Shelburne; it is possible they may not be at home, but Lady Shelburne has promised to spend the evening here. I will do myself the honour to write to your Ladyship as soon as I hear from them.

And probably a day or two later:

> Mrs Montagu presents her most respectfull compliments to Lord and Lady Chatham, and is infinitely obliged to them for the honour of their letter, which completes the happiness they conferred on her on Thursday, as it assures her that the Ladies and Lord Pitt did not receive any harm from the play. If she could measure the pleasure they received that day from the delight they gave here, she would be very happy in being the means of their enjoying so much pleasure. If there is much satisfaction in seeing assumed characters perform'd with propriety, how much greater is that of seeing real ones appear with propriety, politeness, elegance, and grace. Lord and Lady Chatham must be sensible the company they had [the] goodness to send her give this pleasure in the highest degree. She is rejoyced to hear Lord Chatham is so much recover'd and hopes this attack of the gout which did he so much mischief will make her amends by doing his Lordships future health great service. Mrs M: begs leave to present her most affectionate respects and compts to Lord Pitt and the Ladies. As Lady Chatham may be a good deal confined to the fireside by this North East wind, she takes the liberty to send her Ladyship a new play of Voltaires; she does not make herself answerable for the contents of the leaves which are uncut, and by her unread. It is melancholy to think a man of great and universal genius should have addicted himself to such a manner of writing that one cannot venture to read any of his works like one has been assured by some person of daring curiousity, that they are not shocking to religion or morals.

She has been on a visit to Hayes and takes the opportunity of the thank-you letter to extol the virtues of the way of life she found there and the advantages of the home education of the young Pitts.

I am very glad to find the good account I had heard of Lord Chathams and your Ladyships health so well confirmed. My mind often adverts with great delight to the domestick scene at Burton Pynsent; Virtues and Wisdom giving lessons to ingenuous youth is a sight for angels to rejoice at. I have always thought the Ancients more superior to the Moderns in the virtue and dignity of private life than in any other respect. It is shocking to observe that our Statesmen and Legislators, and even the Prelates of a Christian Church, seem conscious that their children, educated under their inspection, and the hourly influences of their example, would be more qualified to serve God and their Country than if committed to the care of a Pedagogue from whom, at best, nothing can be expected but to admit them to a familiar acquaintance with the characters and doctrines of the great and good men who adorned the Grecian and Roman Republicks. Does virtue then exist with more vigour and efficacy in the dead letter of Platos philosophy, and the shadow of Aristides's life than in the living conversation and actions of men who aspire to the first rank and authority in a Country, in all publick respects and relations not inferior to any of the states of Greece?

I left Tunbridge the very day that your Ladyship set out for Somersetshire. I was much pleased with the effect of the waters, but very weary of the place. It is very charitable in your Ladyship to give by your enquiries a greater importance to my health, as I am obliged to sacrifice all my true and favourite amusements to the care of it. After three years continual suffering I now enjoy a very good state of health, but still on the condition of being indolent and idle; however, finding a sauntering life agrees so well with me, I am become a convert to la Bruyère's maxim, qu'il vaut mieux passer sa vie a ne rien faire, qu'a faire des riens. It was long before I was convinced of this, but to make amends I practise my new adopted doctrine with all the zeal of a convert. The summer season is the festival of a saunterer, there is something sublime in the Reverie of a rural walk that one is apt to fancy oneself more nobly occupied than those engaged in the actual business and useful employments of human life.

News of Hester Pitt's engagement to Lord Mahon calls forth Elizabeth Montagu's longest and perhaps most typical letter to Hester Chatham. It is hard to believe that simple congratulations could be enclosed in such tortuous verbiage. But she means well; her anxieties about possible defects of character in the fiancé are engendered only by admiration for the girl he is to marry.

Dear Madam

It is impossible to express with what sentiments of gratitude and joy I received the honour your Ladyship did me in communicating the certain news of an approaching event, which promises the most perfect happiness where I wish the greatest degree of felicity this World can afford. I will confess to your Ladyship, that a letter from Lady Chatham, and such a mark of her goodness to me, added to my joy on this occasion, tho in the first report I heard of it I imagined my satisfaction had been as compleat as possible. Some of our modern Philosophers, who like other foolish sons, are the reproach of their Mother, would observe here to the dishonour of human nature, that even when the publick joy, and the happiness of those Persons one most admires, esteems and loves unites, still a little point of Personal interest can add to ones exaltation; but I hope neither human nature nor my nature neither suffer from a confession that there is not any event which would not receive additional lustre and force by passing through Lady Chathams pen.

I hope your Ladyship will permit me to say that this intended alliance, the moment I was informed of it, relieved me of many anxieties I had felt for Lady Hester Pitt whenever she was to quit Lord and Lady Chatham to carry honour and happiness into another family. As often as the thought occurred to me, I suffered all the apprehensions one should do for a Person one loved, who was to change the pure air of Paradise for the rank atmosphere of this Sin worn World; but in the transition to Chevening, she still keeps in the regions of uncorrupted Virtue I was well assured that in every situation her Ladyship would preserve the angelic purity of her mind, her noble elevation of sentiment and elegant simplicity of manners; but tho' her virtues would not be contaminated they might be discouraged, they might be mortified in unfit society. With all our boasted refinement of manners in this polite age, there is so little dignity preserved in domestick life, the true guide of character is so lost in an attention to and a confidence in the influence of external things, that in whom but Lord and Lady Stanhope could she have found those virtues that invite her to transfer any of that filial affection and reverence she has paid to Lord Chatham and your Ladyship.

Lord Mahon's character, with which from his earliest infancy I had the pleasure of being very particularly acquainted, by Lord and Lady Stanhopes earliest connection with some of my friends, made me long ago incline to this alliance, but I durst not form the perfect wish till I knew him personally. I was convinced that his Lordship had distinguished talents and a great deal of acquired knowledge, but these things are sometimes accompanied by self sufficiency and superciliousness. I knew he had great virtues, but he might have unpleasing manners. Having been a considerable part of his life abroad and conversant with persons of the first merit of various nations, he would be free from the insularities which often render the English, with all their sense, less agreeable than men of other countries. But then he might be too exotick; his appearance, language, manner might have too many gallicisms mixed in them. All these things occurred to me so strongly that as I could not find any other nobleman so distinguishd by all the essentials of a character till I was convinced the whole was perfect, I was sometimes enclined to fancy I could never consent that Lady Hester Pitt should marry at all. From every one I heard Lord Mahons praises, but where my heart was so interested I would not trust to any eyes or ears but my own, and I continued in uneasy suspense, call'd by the vulgar a sad quandary, when lo, I had the good fortune to meet him by accident, away went my doubts and hesitations and my delicate apprehensions. He won my heart immediately, and what was much more I pronounced him worthy of Lady Hester.. My imagination began immediately to weave chaplets of mistles and roses and to pray to the Venus Urania to tye the true love knott.

Your Ladyship will excuse the freedom with which I have spoken on this subject, but some french writer observes that joy is babillarde and indiscreet.

I was extremely concernd to find that your Ladyship had been so much indisposed; I would fain hope your illness was owing to such weather as one never saw before, and therefore one has reason to hope will never return again. Your Ladyship is very good in enquiring after my health; I was much indisposed by a cold at my first leaving Tunbridge but have been more than commonly well since I came hither, till I caught cold on Sunday and by a violent fit of the tooth ach have been sleepless these two nights and am almost blind of one eye. In such circumstances I am ashamed to write to your Ladyship, but I waited in vain a whole day in hopes of being more capable of returning thanks for the honour of your Ladyships letter which I received on Sunday evening. I beg of your Ladyship to present my most respectful compliments and sincere congratulations to Lord Chatham. To Lady Hester my best compliments, wishes and thanks for making the best deserving the happiest man in the World. I beg my compliments to Lady Harriot and the young Gentlemen.

With the most perfect regard I have the honour to be dear Madam,
Yours Ladyship's most obliged most obedient
Humble Servant
Eliz: Montagu

We know from the observations of other letter writers and in this collection those of her great admirer Mrs Hood, that Elizabeth Montagu was a very witty woman. Alas, there is not evidence in her letters to Hester Chatham of this admired characteristic. Perhaps she felt that frivolous topics and ideas, jeux d'esprit, would not be appropriate, especially at a time when Chatham's serious and chronic illnesses were causing much heartache in the family. Or it may be that like many another witty and amusing person the gift did not extend to the pen.

Whatever the reason, it is easy to agree with Sir Sidney Lee, an editor of the Dictionary of National Biography that 'Mrs Montagu was a voluminous correspondent, writing with vivacity, but with too much prolixity to be altogether readable'.

iii. LETTERS FROM MRS WILLIAM BECKFORD, 1758-1773

William Pitt, Earl of Chatham was generally recognised as having many admirers but few personal friends; William Beckford was both. Though not a giant politically, he has earned a respectable niche in the annals of his time, partly because of his varied interests and his great wealth; his ownership of a famous house, Fonthill Giffard in Wiltshire; his prominence in City affairs; his lord mayoralties of London, in 1762 and 1769 - 'memorable for [their] luxurious character'[1]; his support of the radical MP John Wilkes and his courageous stand against the king in the matter of the Middlesex election. And perhaps not least for his unbroken political loyalty to Chatham.

All these, and particularly the last, were good reasons for Hester Chatham to become and remain friends with Beckford's wife Maria. The two women were not close but their friendship was on an easy and congenial basis, cemented by the nearness in age of William, the Beckford's only son, and William Pitt.

Maria Beckford was the daughter of the Hon George Hamilton, second surviving son of James, sixth earl of Abercorn and so a first cousin of Jane, Lady Cathcart, a friend of Hester's from girlhood. The correspondence between Hester and Maria has already begun by 1758 when, in reply to Hester's thanks for the gift of an unnamed fish, Mrs Beckford writes:

Fonthill
June the 17th 1758

As my dear Lady Hester is so indulgent as even to desire to see some of my scrawl, I will plead no more my incapacity, but take the first opportunity of returning my thanks for her very kind letter. Mr Beckford and my self are very happy the Fish was liked, but at the same time must allow it was a very odd thing to think of sending; but I find we are both partial to what Fonthill produces and fancy our Friends must be so to.

William Beckford's many interests kept him much away from his Wiltshire home, where building and landscaping improvements, almost to rival those of Stowe, were in progress. After congratulations on 'the many Glorious Events that has happened this year', his wife, writing to Hester continues:

Fonthill
Septr the 15 1759

I have been very busy this Summer endeavouring to prevent as much as possible Fonthill from suffering by the frequent absence of Mr Beckford, but I find I have not succeeded; for the Works goes on but very slowly, but I hope he will come and mind them him self soon. I am sure it will make him as happy as it does me that we had it in our power to send you a Turtle, as you and Mr Pitt is fond of it.
I am perfectly well now, but have had very frequent returns of the disorder I complain'd of last year in my stomach, but can assure you it is not what you suspected.

The following letter, however, reveals that it was what Hester had suspected:

Fonthill
June the 28th 1760

I am much better since I came here, for added to all the Complaints one generally has in my Situation, I had the gravel to a most violent degree, but by using gentle exericse I am much better than I was; I believe sometime in Sepber you will hear that my family is increased, for I shall desire they will let you know as soon as possible, as you have always been so good to interest yourself in what concerns me.

There were exchanges of visits. Writing to her husband in 1760, Hester passes on an opinion which will have gratified him. Mrs Beckford thought parts of Hayes had 'much more grace and beauty with less expense of trees than at Fonthill'. The Beckfords are in a temporary home while work at Fonthill proceeds. She assures her

Witham
August the 9th [1764]

Dear Lady Chatham, how much I shall think myself obliged to her and Mr Pitt for their very kind visit, which wou'd have made me inexpressibly happy had I not had the mortification of seeing you both suffer; you were so Polite as to be pleased with everything, but am certain you must have met with many inconveniences in our Thatched Habitation. . .
My little boy is very well, often talks of Mr Pitt's flannen legs, and looks for him and Lady Chatten that he may put them in the Hole they were so often threatened with.

Many years pass without surviving correspondence; Mrs Beckford is now a widow of two years standing and much concerned, to the exclusion of nearly everything else, with the education and upbringing of her son William. Chatham has shown interest in the clever boy who was to become a great eccentric of his time. His mother writes to Hester Chatham:

> Fonthill
> Augst 21 1772
>
> How shall I express my gratitude to My Lord for his exceptional goodness in having once thought of honouring myself and Son with such a peculiar mark of regard, as offering to give his opinion of my son's Education. Doubtless his Lordship's testimony would have had a great weight. The affair is yet undecided, but as it is too long to trouble your Ladyship with at present, shall defer entering into particulars till I have the pleasure of seeing you.

Young William Beckford, a lonely boy, has been to stay at Burton:

> Fonthill
> Sepr 19 1772
>
> I take this earliest opportunity to thank your Ladyship for your kind letter which I found here. I believe I may venture to say that the time William spent at Burton Pynsent was the happiest time of his Life; tho' he expressed great joy and happiness at seeing me again yet he severely regretted the loss of those he left behind, for after dinner his Heart was so full, that not being able to contain himself any longer, a violent flood of tears ensued.

Maria Beckford had, through Chatham, enlisted the help and opinion on the subject of William's education of George, Lord Lyttelton who in turn had consulted the boy's chief guardian, the Lord Chancellor, Henry Bathurst, Lord Apsley. In this same long two part letter of September 19th she expresses gratitude for the unanimous view of all three eminent men that William should be educated at home, and she transcribes and encloses the letter from the Lord Chancellor to Lyttelton and forwarded to her by him. Apsley's mind has been influenced by Chatham's views:

> "I am sincerely glad. . . that I got Lord Chatham's sentiments in regard to the Education of young Mr Beckford; I shall for the present implicitly govern myself by them and reject the application of Sir T.G. and another of his guardians for taking him from home, and sending him to a Publick School. . . I do not entirely subscribe to his [Chatham's] opinion of preferring in general a private to a publick Education, but it is sufficient for my Guidance that his Lordship from the knowledge he has of the young Gentleman, and of the care his Mother will take of him, thinks a private Education more particularly proper for him. . . It may likewise be a satisfaction to Mrs Beckford to know that her Son will be educated for some time longer under her Eye."

Mrs Beckford ends her solemn letter, with its enclosure, on a lighter note:

We have usually a Thing called a hop, on William's birthday (Michaelmas Day).

She names the invited guests and adds:

> I believe Lord Pitt is fond of dancing, if it would be agreeable to His Lordship to make one, I should be exceedingly happy to see him, but if this shd not perfectly meet with your Ladyship's and My Lord's approbation, it need not be mentioned.

In a postscript she adds (thus throwing a light on a small social convention):

> I have just discover'd that I have left a blank side in this letter but I have wrote so much this morning that I have not time to rectify this mistake which I hope your Ladyship will excuse.

In November the decision for William Beckford to be educated at home is confirmed:

Fonthill
Novr 21st 1772

Dear Madam
> If I had not been indisposed I should sooner have troubled your Ladyship with a few lines to have acquainted you and my Lord that I have gained the point I had at Heart, and thanks to Lord Chatham and Lord Lyttelton, shall have at least for some time, my son continued under my care. . . William is in good health, and studies hard at the Mathematicks, in hope of gaining Lord Chatham's approbation.

And with a story about two Persian cats:

> You have heard that a Friend had two blue Cats, very much at your service but I find you did not wish to have them. Now I must beg leave to unravel the mystery. They belonged to poor Mrs Hamilton of Painshill who is lately dead, they were sent her from abroad, and they tell me they are great curiosities, but I never saw them, so that it was I who desired Mrs Mary Pitt to write about them recollecting that formerly your Ladyship loved Cats, but you give so many good reasons for refusing them, that I have nothing more to add upon that head.

The following year and another 'hop' is planned:

Fonthill
Sept 13 1773

> Could I flatter myself with the pleasure of seeing your Ladyship etc at our little Hop the 29th Inst: it wd make me very happy. William would be delighted to see his young Friends, and wd do all in his power to amuse them, and endeavour to render Fonthill as agreeable to them, as they kindly made Burton Pynsent to him.

William's visits to Burton continue, attended by his clerical tutor, John Lettice. In an undated letter answered by Hester on November 3rd, Maria Beckford writes:

Will you My Dear Madam be kind enough to be my Proxy and to offer My Lord my most grateful thanks, and to assure him all that I possibly can say will fall short of what I feel. As for Mr Lettice, he absolutely adores My Lord, and firmly resolved to pursue the Method that Ld Chatham so judiciously points out. . . I must say it wd give me great pleasure if I cd hear that Ld Chatham approved of the Plan that Mr Lettice has layed down for my son's education.

Eight years on and William Beckford, now eighteen, has taken on the duties of host at Fonthill:

> Fonthill
> Sept 15 1781

My dear Madam
    Your Ladyship would make my Mother and myself extremely happy if you allow us to expect you and Lady Harriot at Fonthill the 28th.
    Many of our Friends will be assembled and I cannot express with what pleasure I should see your Ladyship amongst the number. If my Lord Chatham or Mr Pitt would be of the party - it would be adding greatly to my satisfaction.
    Nothing but the hurry of the present moment would prevent my trying personally to persuade your Ladyship to grant our request.
    With our best compts to Lady Harriot I have the Honour to remain ever my dear Madam, Your Ladyship's most faithful and affectionate humble Sert
                                                                William Beckford

With this conventional letter from her son, which gives no hint of his undoubted genius, the kindly, well-intentioned but misguided Maria Beckford passes from the correspondence. His subsequent strange career does not belong to this study. The future author of 'Vatek' went neither to school nor to English university; the latter part of his long life was spent in lonely exclusion at Fonthill, where 'he launched out on . . . architectural and artistic extravagance'[2] to an extent that even his great fortune became depleted and he had to move to Bath. So much promise, so wasted a life.

1 *DNB*
2 *DNB*

Chapter 8

PROFESSIONAL MEN WHO BECAME FRIENDS

i. LETTERS FROM CANON EDWARD WILSON 1766-1800

an acute and intelligent man

John Ehrman, *The Younger Pitt*, New York 1966, vol 1, p 6

It would generally be said that Canon Wilson owed his good fortune and church preferment to the happy chance that he was tutor to William Pitt the Younger for eight years. But it could also be said that Wilson's professional success endured as much because of his acumen and sagacity, his charm and good nature as it did to the powerful patronage he enjoyed until his death in 1804, less than two years before that of his famous pupil.

Edward Wilson was born in 1730 and after leaving his tutorship ministered for thirty-nine years as rector of Binfield in Berkshire. In 1769 he was installed as prebendary of Gloucester and in 1784 appointed canon of Windsor. All the 122 letters from Wilson in these papers are to Lady Chatham and cover a span of thirty-four years. The first group, written while still a resident tutor, not only to William but also to John Pitt and the sisters Hester and Harriot, are from Weymouth in 1766 and from Brighton the following year, to which resorts the children were sent for prolonged holidays in his and the family nurse, Mrs Sparry's charge. The Chathams were devoted parents and these long stays away for their children, two or more days journey time for them, is evidence of the trust they placed in these truly faithful servants.

An even greater responsibility was to fall to them when William became seriously ill soon after arriving at Cambridge as an undergraduate at Pembroke Hall aged fourteen. His entry to that college, Wilson's own alma mater, is evidence of the regard Chatham had for the tutor, who indeed was aware of the future advantage to himself. The historian J. Holland Rose in his two volume life of the younger Pitt (1911), quotes from a letter Wilson wrote to his wife in December 1772: 'I could not have acted with more prudence than I have done in the affair of Pembroke Hall. Mr Pitt . . . will be my steady friend for life'. The boy was devotedly nursed by the tutor and by Mrs Sparry who was sent to help (thus giving rise to the rumour that William entered Cambridge with a nurse). Under the care of a noted Cambridge physician, Dr Robert Glynn, he slowly recovered.

The remaining correspondence, from 1775, is from Binfield parsonage, or from Gloucester when in residence as prebendary and in the same capacity from Windsor, and occasionally from London.

Edward Wilson had attributes on which he could draw to enliven his letters. His was a descriptive pen. In particular the correspondence from 1785 gives in detail and in concise, readable prose, descriptions of life in a rural parsonage; the grand transition to Windsor Castle for his periods as Canon in Residence, and at Gloucester likewise, where he became involved in a parliamentary election. The family consisted of his wife Selina, mentioned in almost every letter but never of course by her name, and their two sons Giffin and Gloster, both of whom benefited from William Pitt's patronage. He was also something of an inventor, with the energy to put his schemes and ideas into practice.

By the end of 1787 the glamour of Windsor is beginning to wear thin - the 'imprisonment' of his obligatory residences of three weeks at a stretch - but still inspires description. At the king's birthday celebrations of June 1791 he notes the difference between King George's ugly brown coat and the Duke of Bedford's finery. He has much to say about the king's illness and slow recovery in 1789, the bad behaviour of the Prince of Wales and so forth; all extensively chronicled elsewhere, but Wilson's letters often transmit an out of the way detail of court life and pertinent observations on the characters of the leading players around him.

This remarkable correspondence of more than thirty years throws a special light not only on the mind of a gifted and witty man, but also on the wide and lively interests of the recipient of the letters. Above all it underlines the enduring admiration, perhaps a kind of love, for the mother of William Pitt.

Weymouth
July the 21st 1766

Madam

I have the pleasure to inform you that we got to Weymouth very well; the day was hot but on the whole we had an agreeable journey. My little Charges are well, in exceeding good spirits, except Mr William, but he poor Gentleman is in great affliction. Ever since we parted from your Ladyship he has secretly intended to surprise his Papa with a Latin letter; and yesterday morning with all the attention peculiar to his character, he had got his pen, ink and paper and Dictionary all ready for the purpose, but at the earnest intreaty of his friends (owing to the horrible misfortune of a bloodshot eye) he was prevail'd on to postpone that pleasure till another post, upon my promise to inform your Ladyship that his silence is not his fault but his infirmity. Lesson has gone on this morning perfectly well, we have had nothing but Optimes since we left Burton. I desire my most respectful Compliments to Mr Pitt; I shall be very glad to hear of his recovery and also that your Ladyship got well to Hampstead.

I have the honour to be
Your Ladyship's most obliged and obedient
servant
E. Wilson

Weymouth
July the 26th 1766

Yesterday afternoon we were entertained with a visit from the Chiefs of the Mohicannuck and Wappinger tribes of Indians from the back of New York who landed here on Thursday; that evening they were entertain'd by the Duke of Kingston, and yesterday morning Lady Mary Forbes was here before breakfast to inform the Young Ladies and Gentlemen that the Admiral, the Governor of Portland, and Capt. Arbuthnot hop'd to have the Company of the Chiefs in the Evening, and as she suppos'd it wou'd be an agreeable entertainment to them, she came to invite them to it... There are four men and three women, the men appear all to be above six foot high, and look warrior like. At their coming into the room, the Chief of the Mohicannuck Tribe made a speech to Master Pitt [John] in the Indian tongue, and at the conclusion presented him with a written translation of it in English.

While at Weymouth there is the excitement of the news of the father, William Pitt's earldom, with the consequent changes in the designations of the children. Whatever doubt the 'Great Commoner' may have entertained in accepting the peerage will have been mitigated by the delighted reaction of his offspring. The dramatic arrival of the news which Wilson describes gives emphasis to the high moral principles underlying the upbringing of the Pitt children.

> Weymouth
> August the 4th 1766
>
> To answer your request in the fullest manner as well as to give you an idea of the very great encomiums that are due to my little Pupils, I shall faithfully and exactly present your Ladyship with the first scene of the drama. At nine in the morning (earlier by two or three hours than the postman generally comes) a letter from Mrs Betty to Lady Hester Pitt was brought in by the Coachman. She instantly broke the seal, but in opening the letter the superscription accidentally caught her eye; upon which she was in the greatest distress imaginable and ran directly to Mrs Sparry to know what she should do, supposing that it belong'd to your Ladyship. Mrs Sparry... as yet uninform'd naturally received the account as it was represented, only with somewhat less concern, said it was an accident, that it could not be help'd, desir'd her to lay it down and said she wou'd take care of it... By this time the Maids, who had all receiv'd letters and read them with greater dispatch, alarm'd the whole house, and congratulations were so thick from every quarter that it is not easy to say how any one behav'd, but on the whole I am fully persuaded that the congratulated were much more compos'd than the congratulators. Lady Hester was a perfect pattern of the most improv'd under-standing and Lady Harriot was <u>very</u> <u>little</u> behind her I assure you. His Lordship was somewhat more elevated but by no means to any improper degree and Mr William was not less animated than any one on being complimented as the only surviving Mr William Pitt.

Five days later it is back to study:

> Weymouth
> August the 9th 1766
>
> Yesterday morning Mr Wm begun to translate from Latin into English, with which he is not a little pleas'd. Lady Hester, my Lord, Mr William and Mr James are all exceedingly diligent and perfectly good; the exact journal that we keep and the <u>supposition</u> that I constantly transmit a <u>copy</u> of it to your Ladyship has put an end to all driving and coughing and sitting crosslegg'd, is a great spur to diligence.

A year later the party is at Brighton after a tedious wet journey from London but enlivened by the receptions met with en route.

Brighthelmstone
July the 21st 1767

We were very unlucky as it rained the greatest part of the way. We now and then were entertain'd with a sight of some beautiful hills and vallies but for the most part our prospect was extremely narrow so that variety of horses was almost all the variety we had . . . The house appears to be well air'd and every way fit to receive us, so that I have not the least doubt of continuing to give your Ladyship a satisfactory account of every thing that respects our health. The Ladies and Gentlemen commission me to send their Duty to Papa and Mamma and propose writing very soon. Their way was strew'd with flowers and they were welcom'd with ringing of bells both at East Grinsted and at Brighthelmstone.

Chatham's protracted nervous illness was at its most intractable at this time and Lady Chatham was deeply worried; even so she finds time to recommend books she wishes Hester Pitt, not quite twelve years old, to read. On 20th July the tutor writes:

Lady Hester has not yet seen Sévigné's letters; I ordered a set to be bound on purpose for her Ladyship and expect them here this evening.

Outdoor activity has to be arranged for the eldest son John, now Lord Pitt, aged eleven, and the young friends he has met:

Brighthelmston
August Tuesday the 11th 1767

Yesterday my Lord Pitt rode out with Master Clinton to a place call'd the Devil's Dike, about six miles off, from whence there is a very extensive prospect of a large tract of naked Downs on one hand, and what is call'd the Wilds of Sussex on the other. . . My Lord Pitt is now acquainted with Lord Kilwarlin who is constantly walking with Master Clinton. Lord Kilwarlin is about 14, and Master Clinton almost twelve. . . Next week there are to be some horse races at Lewes, at which a great deal of Company is expected. I take the liberty of troubling you with this previous notice of it, as we shou'd not like to make such an excursion without your Ladyship's approbation.

And back to reading matter for Hester:

Brighthelmston
Thursday August 20th 1767

Lady Hester is highly delighted with the expectation of reading Madame Sévigné's letters with your Ladyship, and has laid them by for that purpose. I wish I cou'd think of any book that wou'd merit your Ladyship's approbation, but I am afraid it is too difficult a task. The Spectator, Guardian and Adventurer are in some degree amusing, as well as remarkable for their purity of stile - a few particular papers may perhaps be too abstruse, but I am persuaded Lady Hester wou'd read most of them with much more ease than many Ladies of twice her age.

Voyages and Travels are generally entertaining but their stile very indifferent. We have no Letters that I know of except Lady Wortley-Montague's and they are quite as exceptionable as the first Volume of Madam Sevigné . . . Novels I think are wholly precluded, and yet there is one little Tale of Dr Johnson's which I shall beg leave to mention, as it is pretty, innocent, amusing and instructing; and as it is perhaps the only Novel that ever existed without the assistance of a love-story. The title of it is Rasselas or the Prince of Abyssinia. It wou'd be arrogance in me to recommend any of these to a person of your Ladyship's superior reading and understanding, and therefore to name them is all I pretend to, and even that in obedience to your Ladyship's commands.

There is the first mention of his presentation to the Binfield living in a letter of this time, and which also gives his reason (doubtless not the only one) for writing always to Lady Chatham:

> Brighthelmston
> August the 24th 1767
>
> I embrace the earliest opportunity to return you my most grateful acknowledgements for the very agreeable information communicated by your letter of last night. The honour of a Living thro' the Patronage of my Lord Chatham is a circumstance that wou'd have made me happy in almost any situation, but Berkshire is a most delightful Country. At a time when even the tender expressions of filial affection are irksome to his Lordship, a letter from me might justly be deem'd impertinent tho' sent from motives of the warmest gratitude, otherwise I shou'd necessarily have done myself the honour of writing to thank him on this occasion.

But before taking up the Binfield rectorship Edward Wilson still had duties to carry out in his capacity as tutor, including an excursion made in the summer of 1770 with John Pitt to Bocconac in Cornwall, ancient home of the Pitts. Still to come was perhaps the most important duty which fell to him during his time with the family: as cicerone to the fourteen year old William Pitt on his entry to Wilson's old Cambridge college of Pembroke Hall, where an episode full of danger awaited both the man and the boy. First the journey, the only time William had been on his own apart from any member of his family. In an unsigned letter probably composed by them both, Wilson writes:

> Hartford Bridge
> Tuesday Evening
> [October 1773]
>
> Authentick Intelligence for the Western Post
>
> This Evening the Honourable Mr Pitt and his Retinue arrived here in perfect health. The easiness and vivacity with which his Honour converses with persons of all ranks affords the most comfortable assurance that travelling is no fatigue to him. He arrived at Salisbury last night before sunset without any difficulty, and three easy stages brought him this day to Demezzeé. The roads are in most excellent order, and the weather in spight of the Barometer has been uncommonly fine, but one shower yesterday between Hindon and Salisbury and one more today between Basingstoke and this place. To prevent the inconvenience

of arriving at Cambridge on Thursday <u>evening</u> we propose indulging in Bed tomorrow and the morning after. This morning we had desired to be called at six, but our <u>"Dillie John"</u> waked us at three to inform us "we had three hours more to sleep". The interruption was only momentary, John laid the blame on the Cathedral Chimes, and went to bed again.

It is hoped that Somerton fields was as fortunate in weather and entertainment as the journey to the East. The particulars of the latter are sent by an abler pen.

Postscript
Wednesday morning 8 o'clock

Just up, above an hour after the Sun, a fine frosty morning, excellent bread and butter and better appetites.

The 'abler pen' Wilson refers to is found in a lively and amusing letter from William to his mother, written from the same stop (Chap. 10, p 314.)

Very soon after arriving at Cambridge, William was taken ill with a serious chest illness and for the next six weeks Wilson's letters are concerned only with the illness and its aftermath. His responsibility, with neither parent or any senior member of the family at hand, was onerous indeed as the following extracts from some dozen letters will show:

Pembroke Hall
Cambridge
Friday October the 22d 1773

I must have the pain of informing you that he had last night a return of his old complaint. As I was never <u>present</u> with him on any former attack, I cannot judge properly either of its violence or continuance. Yesterday morning while we were at Breakfast his looks were not quite satisfactory but on his assuring me he was very well he went to his Lecture in Thuycides, and after that we took a walk in the Garden, and I did not observe any thing wrong. He dined in the Hall upon roast fowl and eat two Wings with I thought his usual appetite, but his spirits I thought were rather flatter than usual. . . I ordered a little Chicken broth for his supper and meant him to go to bed early. But before the broth came he waked from a sort of Doze in the Confusion that Mrs Sparry has described to me. I gave him immediately the drops and had him put to bed. . . I have called in Dr Glynn to feel his pulse.

Two letters describe the onset of the illness and a temporary rally, a double letter of the same date explained:

Mr Pitt is anxious to know what I write to Burton. I must write <u>another</u> letter for his perusal. You will be kind enough to pardon all the faults of this <u>stolen hasty scrawl</u> for tho' my mind is more at ease, my fingers have not yet recover'd their steadiness.

The illness continued, with rallies and setbacks, diet and treatment described in great detail by the tutor in letters written every other day, sometimes partly in duplicate. Mrs Sparry has been sent to help.

Cambridge
Friday Octr the 29th 73

I think I <u>now</u> have <u>authority</u> to assure your Ladyship that Mr Pitt is in as good a way as can be expected; and for my own part I never in my life was more rejoiced than at the arrival of Mrs Sparry, it has effectually eased me of a load that was almost insupportable. It is the general opinion that Mr Pitt's complaint will <u>not</u> be <u>speedily</u> removed, his weakness is very great but in all other respects he is manifestly better every day.

Mrs Sparry's presence has relieved his anxieties and he can write almost jauntily. By November 1st she has

stood her journey amazingly and I flatter myself there is no reason to be afraid of [for] her. As soon as I knew of her arrival I had a bed put up for her in our study, and I mean to <u>keep her</u> there till I grow tired of her. The Master very <u>obligingly</u> and <u>Earnestly</u> pressed us to make use of a part of his Lodge but that would too much divide us. . . Mrs Sparry seems very easy in this new stile of life. She likes her Doctor, she likes her Apothecary, she hopes well of her young friend and appears to be so much in love with the College, that it begins to be a doubt with me whether I must not call in the Proctors' assistance when I shall wish to remove her.

William's slow progress towards convalescence is faithfully chronicled throughout November. The admirable and gifted Dr Glynn is in close attendance:

Cambridge
Nov. the 17th 1773

Yesterday's dinner like its Predecessors has done its duty. Mr Pitt was disposed to engage with it in the dining room but his friends thought he had adventur'd enough for the day and therefore advised his eating it in bed. Yesterday he was up an hour; this morning an hour and three quarters, in short every thing goes on as well as can be expected, except our Doctor - he has not received a fee since the 7th of this month tho' it has been regularly offered to him every day. He comes constantly twice a day, but he says 'it is only to see Mrs Sparry, we have no further use for him as a Doctor and therefore he cannot allow us paying for one but he shall continue to visit us so long as we stay'.

By 1st December arrangements are in hand for the journey to London and thence on to Somerset, and two days later they are on their way.

Chesterfield
Decr the 3d 1773

Your Ladyship will already have learnt from my last letter that our Airing <u>three days ago</u> was more than 12 miles, you will therefore not be surprised to hear that we now sleep 11 from Cambridge. We set out this morning about half after 11, and got hither by ½ after One. Dr Glynn thought that we might very safely venture to go longer Journeys . . . but to be quite on the right side we have resolved to keep to our resolutions of <u>short</u> <u>stages</u>, and <u>four</u> days to London.

With William safely back at Burton, Edward Wilson's tutorship is, for the time being at an end. But not before he writes from Hayes, where he is staying temporarily to carry out certain commissions for the family, to pass on perceptive advice from Dr Glynn:

Hayes
December the 15th 1773

Before this letter comes to hand I flatter myself you will have been made happy by the arrival of the little Great Man of Pembroke whose health I hope continues to advance every day. That every means may be used to promote so great a blessing I now write to inform your Ladyship of the advice which his sincere friend Dr Glynn very earnestly and very frequently desired me to communicate to my Lord and your Ladyship as the only possible chance for his Patient's living to manhood, viz to take every opportunity of exposing him to air and exercise. So slow a recovery he considers as very unnatural at Mr Pitt's time of life and he seems assured that nothing can save him but the taking every opportunity to make him hardy; for this purpose he advises that he should ride and walk and play in the open air as often as the weather will permit, and go out in a carriage, or at least not be confined to his room in bad weather, for he says that being shut up in the same room tenders, and endangers catching cold by every breath of air. For the same purpose he advises that Mr Pitt shou'd lay with his Curtains very open, and rather in a large room than a small one.

In July of the following year, William Pitt returned to Cambridge again accompanied by Wilson, but only for a short time. In September the tutor handed his responsibilities over to George Pretyman, fellow and tutor of Pembroke, later Bishop Tomline, who remained close to William for the rest of the young man's life and whose first biographer he became.

Early in 1775 Edward Wilson is installed with his family in the Berkshire rectory, where he was to remain, bar frequent excursions away, for the rest of his life. Letters at first are scarce:

Binfield
Feb: the 25th 1775

The situation of our Parsonage is extremely pretty, and we have a great house in view which we please ourselves with fancying something like our old favourite prospects but it's barely fancy! We have no news but from the Berkshire Chronicle, and as our neighbours are all in London or at Bath, all the politicks we hear are only what transpires from accidental meetings at the Jack o' Newberry where the school-master or the Parish clerk generally presides.

After a long gap the silence (if indeed it was one) is broken by a letter of 13th June 1783 from Wilson of congratulations on the marriage of John Chatham to Mary Townshend. He observes, perhaps oddly, perhaps with secret knowledge that 'we now consider my Lord Chatham is honourably landed on a safe shore, with every prospect before them of permanent felicity'.

But from this year ever onwards it is the wonderful career of William Pitt (whom he now sometimes calls simply 'the Minister') which receives admiration and comment in almost every letter.

Binfield
Decr the 23rd 1783

My good Madam
        With the most heartfelt satisfaction I now write to congratulate your
Ladyship on the appointment of our new Minister . . . How superlative must be
your happiness to have in so short a space of time so many unparalled Honors fall
to your lot;   and certainly not the least to have Mr Pitt so nobly <u>refuse</u> the
Premiership <u>under 24</u>, and invited to it again by the united voice of both King and
People in the <u>very same year</u>. For our parts, our humble Parsonage never felt itself
so exalted before, since added to the distinguished <u>Honours</u> we derive from this
Event, we have moreover all the <u>Social Comfort</u> of having all our neighbours (one
family alone excepted) <u>unanimous</u> in <u>approving</u> this change.

The following year opens a new door for the country parson. But first the Berkshire
election meeting at Reading and the only letter from Selina Wilson, his wife, added to
one of his own:

Binfield
Feb the 15th 1784

        Will your Ladyship have the goodness to admit <u>me</u> into your presence, just
to say how much I was gratified yesterday by the universal enthusiasm that
prevail'd among all Ranks of people in favour of Mr Pitt (so like <u>past times</u>, how
it made my eyes overflow) . . . Binfield made a very respected figure - a Waggon
load and a cartload were fill'd from our Parish, all honest <u>well judging</u> freeholders,
<u>for</u> Mr Pitt to a Man. Some honest souls as far off as Hungerford had so much zeal
as to accompany their good wishes with a large blue silk flag with Pitt Forever
flaming on it in gold Letters.

Edward Wilson, already for some years a prebendary of Gloucester, takes his new
appointment as Canon of Windsor with sang froid, the royal preferment receiving only
cursory mention in a long letter devoted to political comment:

Binfield
Feb: the 29th 1784

        I intended as promised your Ladyship to have follow'd the notification of
my new Dignity with another letter or two if any matters shou'd arise during my
stay in Town but I was not fortunate enough to pick up anything worth your
Ladyship's notice of which the Newspapers wou'd not equally early give you a
more circumstantial account. On the whole I think I may now congratulate your
Ladyship on the firmness of Mr Pitt's situation. . . I am inexpressibly gratified by
your Ladyship's approbation of the part I took at Reading, I felt no small
satisfaction in the consciousness that I was doing my duty and that it so
opportunely fell to my lot to testify my zeal, where it was so justly due; but to find
the <u>execution</u> as well as the <u>intention</u> so happily succeed is almost too too much;
it is equal to another canonry at least and elevates my feelings to the highest
degree.

The new appointment does, however, bring a problem (evidently later resolved).

But by the by amidst all my joy a letter from the Dean of Glocester has a little alarm'd me with a surmise that a Royal Chaplainship may be necessary to the retention of Glocs with Windsor; this I was not at all aware of, neither does he name it as a certainty, but I have sent for a copy of the Statutes that I may be clear in this matter before I proceed a step farther, and in the meantime I think myself very fortunate that the want of a Lord Privy Seal has hitherto delay'd my Grant in its progress, otherwise I might by this time have been install'd and Glocester forfeited.

In October, the first residence brings real enthusiasm, and for a special reason:

Windsor
October the 26th 1784

I and my whole family have been basking in the Royal Sunshine at Windsor. My residence being now over we are returning again to the sequestered shades of Binfield, but I cannot leave this sublime spot without informing your Ladyship that amidst all our enjoyments here, which have neither been few nor inconsiderable, we have neither been nor I trust ever can be unmindful to whom we are indebted for the greatest share of them. And added to all the rest we have this morning had the supreme felicity and honour of our Great Minister's company to breakfast, which was in all respects the highest possible gratification.

From this time on, Canon Wilson's life is calm and untroubled, but never dull. Based mainly at Binfield, he is also often in London, and his two appointments require the customary periods of residence at Gloucester and Windsor. His wonderful powers of observation allow him to note everything and everyone around him, and his lively and humorous, sometimes ironic pen passes on to Hester Chatham what he has seen, heard and noted. The careers of his two sons, Giffin and Glocester naturally take up some of his thoughts and time, and ever in the background is the loving and dutiful wife Selina: on the face of it an idyllic life. Troubles certainly do not figure in his letters; in his correspondent's of course, where there were plenty, but not in his.

Son Giffin, a law student, attends his first levée:

Binfield
March the 12th 1785

Giffin accompanied me [to London] to keep a Term as usual and was highly delighted with his journey, it being the first in which he has figur'd away in the character of a Man. His hair was turn'd up and powder'd and I took him with me to Mr Pitt's Levée to his no small gratification.

There is now a curate to assist at Binfield, the appointment a mark of royal approval:

Binfield
April the 13th 1785

Having given out at Windsor about a fortnight ago that I wanted a Summer Curate at Binfield to give me the opportunity of appearing more frequently in my duty at St George's Chapel, it came almost instantly to the ears of the King and Queen and they immediately determin'd to provide me an assistant in a young man of the name of Blomberg whose father and mother died in America.. [He] was then an infant in arms left to the care of a Sergeant's wife who advertis'd for Relations without success. The King seeing the advertisement and recollecting the Father, the Queen having known him in Germany, sent for the child and his nurse, took him under their own roof and he was educated with the Prince of Wales... They wish to have him employ'd in his Profession in some degree under their own eye; for this purpose they have sent him to me.

Though a sociable man, there were occasions which Canon Wilson patently did not enjoy. His experience at a big reception will strike memory chords with many who have found themselves in similar situations.

> Binfield
> June the 14th 1785
>
> I have waited till after the Birthday in the hope of being furnish'd with more important materials to repay your Ladyship in some degree for the trouble and postage of a letter from Binfield. But the delay has by no means answer'd my expectation, for the Court was so excessively crowded it was all fatigue. The day was so very hot and there was so very much pressing and squeezing it was near six o'clock before I had the honour of being notic'd by the Queen, and being at that time quite worn out, and seeing no hope of getting easily at the King, I went away to spend the evening with Mrs Bijou [a play] at the Little Theatre in the Haymarket. I hope your Ladyship is acquainted with the excellence of that charming woman. It was most delightfully acted but indeed Hayley has hit off the measure so admirably, the actors cou'd not fail speaking it with propriety.

He explains why the absence of a doctorate does not cause him concern:

> Binfield
> August the 2d 1785
>
> Your Ladyship by directing your letters to <u>Doctor</u> Wilson honours me with a title to which I have no pretensions, and to which I feel no inclination to aspire, for when I reflect on the Distinguish'd Rank that <u>Mr</u> W had in your Ladyship's family, that <u>Mr</u> W was the Tutor of Mr Pitt, that <u>Mr</u> W is Canon of Windsor, and that <u>Mr</u> W is also honour'd with the most condescending attentions of the King and Queen, what has <u>Mr</u> done to me to induce me to desert it for <u>the Doctor</u>... I flatter myself I shou'd be able to convince both His Majesty and your Ladyship that <u>Doctor</u> in my case wou'd be really a degradation.

He is happy and pleased about Harriot's engagement to Edward Eliot but writing about the wedding brings a rare note of resentment:

> Windsor Castle
> October the 7th 1785
>
> You will remember that I have spoken of Mr Eliot, from the little I had seen and from all I had heard of him as the most promising family man of all Mr Pitt's College acquaintance... The disposal of the Office of Remembrancer was the first material article of news that the Papers gave us after our return to Binfield, and it was no small share of joy that we all welcom'd so fortunate a circumstance, but I will confess to your Ladyship that we were both <u>chagrin'd and disappointed</u> on

learning from the <u>very</u> <u>next</u> paper, that while we were rejoicing over the former Article, the knot was actually tying without my assistance. I cou'd scarcely believe it possible and the kind enquiries of my neighbour only added embarrassment to pain... I am sure from long and well-grounded experience that Mr Eliot has every thing he cou'd hope for in a Lady. This I have always had a pleasure in saying, and I have not been sparing in my testimony in the Company of even the <u>very</u> <u>highest</u> Personages; and I have consider'd it as the testimony of a man who had many years the best opportunity of observing her from her earliest youth; for tho' I seem to myself at present to be laid by on a shelf as old and obsolete, I can never forget the very honourable connection that fill'd up so large a portion of my life, nor be callous or insensible to the slightest concerns of a family from which I have deriv'd such essential marks and honour and regard.

His sons are growing up and need a London base for the pursuit of their law studies.

Binfield
May the 26th 1786

I was just going to write to your Ladyship to inform you that I have purchased a Double set of Chambers for my sons at Lincolns Inn of the Dean of Windsor... [They] are uncommonly commodious, have every convenience for a family, and are large enough to afford a Lodging for Mrs W and me when we go to Town, which we think of doing pretty frequently at first till our Boys are us'd a little to London, or till we find it more prudent to withdraw.

They are also looking to their own future living space:

We are at present very busy in adding to Lady Lucy's Cottage, which I have repurchas'd of her for a Dowager House for Mrs Wilson. The K. has done me the honour to survey it and to rally me not a little about the Plan as well as the Intention.

In this letter there is first time mention of teaching activity, though at its close.

We all went last Sunday upon the [Castle] Terrace for the first time... and their Majesties did me the honour to notice my whole Party, distinguishing little Robert as a new acquaintance. All my Pupils are dispos'd to make the most of this last year [and] I am anxious to devote as much of my time as possible to them... till the breaking up of the Academy.

Edward Wilson was a knowledgeable farmer, a keen gardener and an inventor. He brought his active mind to bear upon all his activities. At fifty-six his energy is unimpaired.

Binfield
near Bracknell, Berks
Novr the 5th 1786

I have been the whole month digging and planting. I am about trying a new kind of gardening invented by a Mr Le Brocq, viz to raise wall fruit at a less expense and in higher perfection than any hitherto known. This is to be effected by digging a Trench eight feet wide or more at the bottom, and sloping the sides as high as conveniently may be. The best of the mould is to be reserv'd for the bottom of the trenches as a bed to plant the trees in, and the worst for the Banks against which a Trellis is to be laid to tye the branches to, if the soil happens to be sand or chalk or gravel etc. but if of a more vegetable nature it will require a coating of tile or brick. These Trenches are to run North and South and to have more Sun and less Blight than any Wall that ever was built. I think it is a promising Plan, and as I have a small piece of Land of a sandy soil, I mean to give it a fair trial.

The rich daughter of the late Peter Jouvencel, one time Privy Council clerk, Chatham's creditor and free tenant of Hayes is with them. Marriage to the eldest son Giffin is in mind; the father is not less than frank in his assessment of her:

London
Feb: the 5th 1787

Miss Jouvencel has been a good deal with us since her father's death both at Binfield and Windsor. Her nerves were very much shaken by that event; but we hope the change of scene and particularly the amusements of Windsor have been of service to her. Tho' she has neither the advantages of Person, nor Conversation, she is very worthy and uncommonly sensible and extremely ingenious. Her Flower pieces both in painting and needlework have been much admir'd at Windsor by the first Masters tho' she never had the benefit of any. . . She has happily the power of gratifying herself in every indulgence she can wish for, as her father by a skilful management of his money during the late War has provided for her near a thousand pounds per annum.

Two months later, the engagement:

No. 10 Lincolns Inn
April the 13th 1787

As your frequent intercourse with Mr Eliot assur'd me of your being much better acquainted with all publick news than you cou'd possibly be from any information of mine, I have not troubled you with any letters from this Place. But I have now a piece of secret intelligence to communicate which has not yet been whisper'd either to the Opposition or Treasury Benches, that will I am sure give pleasure to your Ladyship, as it gives the greatest satisfaction to all my family. . . Know then that a Commercial Treaty much less complex than that under the consideration of Parliament, and form'd on the purest Basis of amity and good faith, is finally agreed on between Miss Jouvencel and Giffin. . . I cou'd have wish'd Giffin to have remain'd single a few years longer in the hope that he might then have met a Wife on more equal Terms. But happily for them they will have a sufficiency to begin with, and to wait that fortunate coincidence of times and circumstances that his Talents and Dispositions [deserve] will, I flatter myself, not fail to improve to the benefit and honour of himself and his connections.

From Windsor in the late autumn Wilson writes on a somewhat low note possibly because he has not been very well.

Windsor
Nov: the 10th 1787

> Before I left Binfield I was not without my apprehensions that I should not be equal to the task of Residence, but I am now, thank God perfectly well again, and this day fortnight my imprisonment will be over, which is a circumstance of no small comfort tho' no confinement can be more agreeable, but even sleeping, eating and going to Chapel, when it is a matter of <u>indispensible</u> necessity for One and twenty days <u>without intermission,</u> may as I have experienc'd be a burthensome duty, however gilded, as I have always found it with Royal honours.

His natural good spirits, however, with interest all around him, soon revive. The letter continues:

> A few days ago as I was (by way of novelty) preparing to mount my horse for a Morning's ride, I had the honour of a Message from his Majesty to meet him at the Chapel to receive the Prince and Princess of Nassau. . . They had been to see the fam'd present of China from the King of Naples and the Pictures that West is painting in the Canopy room. . . The China is a Desert Service, and the Centre consists of several long stands of White figures most elegantly finish'd representing the ancient roman Chariot race with carriages overturn'd and broken in pieces, and this part is most delightfully executed, but the plates, dishes and baskets that surround it, are such as I should pass by in a China shop as not worth notice. I take it for granted they are equally well done and every piece has <u>different</u> figures painted upon it, but the nasty brown Etruscan hue of the whole is to my eye very disgusting. The value of the whole is 30 thousand pounds. As the Canopy room is that in which all the State Visitors were entertain'd on the Prince of Wales's and the Duke of York's birthdays, you have probably had a minute account of it, but for fear you shou'd not, I will as concisely as I can inform you that the Hangings are of Garter Blue with a <u>most rich</u> border of natural flowers in Needlework done under the Queen's Patronage by necessitous young women that she keeps constantly employ'd, and the hangings are farther ornamented with very large paintings of the Victories of Cressy etc. and the whole History of the Institution of the Garter.

Five months on the Wilsons are embarked on building alterations to their house with all the attendant discomforts. By 13th April they have been

> tempted by the offer of a hundred thousand second hand bricks to engage again in building. We are about to add one room to our ground Plan to raise the old part to the same height with the new, and to cover the whole with paper. . . Tomorrow we are to have twenty men at work. Our house is to be laid open on all sides, two stacks of old Chimnies that are smoky and unsound are to be taken down and rebuilt and the whole house rendered completely uninhabitable.

By November of the year, 1788, and for the succeeding three months, Edward Wilson in common with the whole population is deeply affected by King George's serious illness. Though close to the scene, he is no more aware of its medical cause (porphyria) than anyone else, including the attendant physicians, and like them can only note in his letters the alarming symptoms which characterised the illness. He has much to say on aspects of the treatment:

Windsor
Jany the 18th 1789

Lest you shou'd be too much affected at the Saturday's report of his Majesty, I write with pleasure to inform your Ladyship from undoubted authority that the present irritation is owing <u>entirely</u> to an Emetick that did not succeed as was expected and hoped. And to this I will add from the result of our intelligence since we came hither, that every degree of violence since the commencement of the disorder has <u>more</u> <u>than</u> <u>probably</u> had its cause in the ignorance or wickedness of those that have been about his Majesty's Person. The first considerable irritation was on the being prevented speaking to the Princess Royal when he saw her in the Garden.

As a postscript to this letter, with a switch from the monarch to the muck heap, he tells Lady Chatham

On my leaving Binfield I order'd a Model of a Dung Cart, with Ladder and Shambles for Hay or Corn occasionally, to be made for your Ladyship. I hope by this time it is near finish'd, but mean to go over some day if I possibly can before we remove to Glocester and then I will see further about it.

The letter following, of 25th January, contains instructions for the use of the cart:

By tomorrow's Taunton Coach your Ladyship will receive the model of the Cart. . . It is in exact proportion with one I think the perfection of shape and utility. By the directions that I have written upon the several parts of it I hope your Ladyship and Mrs Stapleton will be able to understand the Whole of it. The dung stick is only to be us'd to prevent the Cart's letting out too large a heap at once, and the Ladder and Shambles only to be us'd when Hay or Straw are carried in it. You will observe a stick with iron ends that confines the Cart to the Shafts; by turning up and taking out that stick the Cart is unloaded, and above that stick, where I have wrote <u>your Ladyship's name</u> is a flat bar or brace left square for that purpose.

And so to Gloucester, accompanied by his wife, for the obligatory two months canonical residence, and where Edward Wilson with his essential energy is at once caught up in electioneering. His first letter sets the scene:

Glocester
Feb: the 5th 1789

On our arrival here we found the whole City in the bustle of a contested Election between the Duke of Norfolk [s' candidate] an <u>Alderman here</u>, and a Mr John Pitt, a native of this City who, for the twenty years that I have been acquainted with his name has been held out to me as one of the most disagreeable characters in the place, a low pettifogging litigious man, constantly at war with the Dean and Chapter, the Bishop, the Corporation and almost every body, tho' a man of liberal education and some fortune. Of late with a view to an opportunity like this he has purchas'd above 400 shabby Houses at different times, and let them out to Freemen; he has also defended the cause of Lower Tradesmen against the oppressions of the Corporation and reduc'd the poor rates to nearly one half.

Wilson evidently did not share the Gloucester establishment's dislike of John Pitt and backed his candidature, enthusiastically supported by Selina:

> Mrs W has shewn herself so warm in it, that two days ago when Mr Pitt received something like a Challenge from His <u>Young</u>, <u>Effeminate Opponent</u>, came to show it us and to ask Mrs Wilson to be his Second, assuring her there was no danger.

Also in this letter he is able to tell Lady Chatham that John Pitt won by one vote (in a poll of 1,693).

Back to domestic life after the unexpected excitements and exertions of Gloucester, 'I concluded we should really have nothing to do but read ourselves asleep', they are once again amidst the frustrations of refurbishing:

> Binfield
> June the 23d 1789

> At our return from Glocester we promis'd ourselves the pleasure of seeing your Ladyship again the latter end of May... but the tormenting delays of papering and painting have kept us Prisoners till now. I made my escape twice to London, to the Treasury and Admiralty and had promised myself the felicity of a Trip with the Minister and his Brother to Hollwood during the Whitsuntide Holidays, but the <u>Galas</u> of the French and Spanish Ambassadors and the Changes etc. in the Cabinet kept Mr Pitt in Town the whole time.

In this letter Wilson allows himself a rare criticism of William Pitt, but one born of affection and concern:

> The late Convulsion has shewn us that the best and ablest Ministers are still subject to the Caprices of fortune, and that the Old proverb of providing for a rainy day is still a useful adage. Our great Minister seems to have this lesson still to learn. I have discharg'd my conscience in hinting it to him again and again, but he has not yet profited by it to my satisfaction.

Edward Wilson's letters are never dull and much of their charm lies in his ability to combine description of local, mainly domestic happenings with views on political and international events without interrupting the flow of his pen. He is apologising for a further postponement of their Burton visit:

> Binfield
> July the 18th 1789

> The weather has hitherto interrupted us so much, I have not yet got thro' half my Hay Harvest. I am at present without a Coachman, and one of my House unequal to so long a journey; and added to all this the Bankruptcy of one considerable Farmer and the probable ejectment of another presses me to take their Tithes in kind. This is by no means a pleasant business, but it is I fear indispensable... We had last week the honour of Mr Eliot's company for a couple of days... and also the additional pleasure [of learning] that Mr Pitt is likely to be in <u>his</u> <u>Place</u> <u>again</u> in a few days. I fear the commotions in France will confine him and my Lord Chatham a great deal in town.

By the autumn they have still been unable to visit Burton. They are 'neither of us equal to cold Inns and strange beds at so late a season of the year, being both at all times extremely susceptible to cold' and they 'consider it most prudent to postpone our Burton Journey till the beginning of next summer'.

Age, particularly that of a woman, is a subject almost never referred to in correspondence of the period; but Hester Chatham having entered her seventieth year and doubtless remarking on this fact, calls forth from Wilson rather trite observations on old age:

Glocester
Feb: the 19th 1790

We are both sufficiently sensible, considerably short of the age of Seventy, that frequent exertions wear out both Body and Mind, and that what may appear trifles [e.g. letter writing] to the young and alert are fatiguing exertions in more advanced years.

Rather less tritely Selina Wilson is quoted in her husband's letter of 7th April on the weather:

Mrs Wilson never remembers a sharper North East wind than it has been ever since we got hither [Binfield], and the sun has been equally bright. She says the weather smiles in your face and cuts your throat.

He adds astonishing news of King George's stamina:

I have been too much engag'd in Parochial business to be much expos'd to it [the weather], and therefore I know not yet what mischief it has done, but I have learnt that it did not prevent our good King from taking his diversion of hunting on Monday and riding a chase of near fifty miles.

An undated letter of June indicates that the Burton visit has at last taken place, but first, ever observant of fashion, there is comment on Lady [John] Chatham's headgear:

London
Saturday morning
[June 1790]

Lady Chatham looks better than I have seen her for some time past, notwithstanding a change of head dress that will require some time to reconcile me to, viz: a little small Cap close to her face. I may possibly acquire a liking to it from time, but I cannot give it my hearty approbation at present.

And views on a recent portrait of William Pitt by Gainsborough Dupont:

I have been to see it at the Exhibition. He has wholly taken off the disagreeable look we objected to at Burton, and it is a characteristick likeness, but it is not yet a pleasing one to my eye, there is still a haughty air about it and the leaning against the Couch, neither sitting nor standing, is not what I shou'd have chosen.

A year later they have again been to Burton and on their return there is news of a practical device for the estate:

Binfield
June the 7th 1791

That your Ladyship and Mrs Stapleton may not think me remiss in the matter of the Iron fence, I write to inform you that I have not yet been able to see Mr Grant, but hope I shall in the course of this week, and tho' a suggestion of Mr Pitt's, I flatter myself I shall improve upon my first Plan. Instead of sending you the measure and value, I shall try to procure you a portion of the actual fence as a guide for some Blacksmith near you.

Ever appreciative of his happy domestic life, Edward continues:

I returned home yesterday [from Windsor] to dinner and did not feel regret on removing from all that was splendid, and great and distinguish'd to this sequester'd spot. It was a change from tumult and heat and dust, to quiet and shade and comfort, tho' perhaps these usual enjoyments were considerably heighten'd by the pleasure I had in recounting to Mrs Wilson all that I had to tell her of Majesty and Ministers. Your Ladyship will have heard from better pens than mine of the King's very ugly brown coat and the Duke of Bedford's most splendid equipage and Retinue. The first was most ordinarily plain and the last all that wou'd be expensively magnificent at the cost it was said of between three and four thousand pounds.

Surprisingly in the light of events in France in 1791, Wilson takes the occasion of the Birmingham riots to compare English and French mobs to the detriment of the former.

Binfield
July the 22d 1791

That tumult [at Birmingham] is now thank God by the assistance of the Military awed into peace, but it kept us in constant agitation while it lasted. . . We cannot at all account for it, but it furnishes a fresh proof of the danger of an English Mob. Whatever be the moving cause it is always sure to run into drunkenness and then devastation and plunder are certain consequences. In France the peaceable Inhabitants seem to me to be much less expos'd to danger. Their Mobs may be inflam'd by Enthusiasm, but they are not driven to madness by drunkenness. What strange events has that Country produced since we return'd from Burton.

And from comment on the French revolution, he comes back to home:

[The weather] with us has neither been too hot nor too cold, but it has been much too dry. . . for want of Water my meadows and Grass Plot are burnt up, the vegetation of my shrubs and flowers very much checked, my Gold and silver fishes dying, and what is almost more intolerable than all the rest my Strawberry beds which us'd to surpass all others exhibit a most deplorable spectacle both for this year and the next, as the plants are wholly destroyed.

Early in the year he has an item or two of Windsor news:

Windsor
Jan: the 25th 1792

I finish'd my strict residence yesterday but as I have a Sermon to preach on Sunday next we cannot leave Windsor till Monday or Tuesday. Our new Dean, the Bishop of Lichfield leaves us this morning. We have found them very agreeable neighbours, he is completely a man of business in all Chapter matters and Mrs and Miss Cornwallis unaffected, good temper'd women, but after the two late very hospitable Deans they have not succeeded so as to be popular at all. They neither like card Parties, nor Dining Parties, nor Assemblies, the food essential to the lives of all at Windsor. He tells me this morning that there is no news yet from Lord Cornwallis. . . By our Political Barometer the Stocks, no bad news seem to be expected from any Quarter, <u>they</u> are rising on above all conception!

In a postscript of Thursday 26th January he has

> just heard that Lord Grenville has bought Dropmore Hill. It is a Cottage about 10 miles from hence between Clifden and Beaconsfield, in very high ground with about 25 Acres of land to it, an admir'd picturesque spot, but the House is much inferior to Hollwood. Price between two and three thousand pounds.

At the end of July there is family rejoicing at Giffin's appointment, through William Pitt's patronage, as a commissioner in bankruptcy. Mrs Wilson is laid up for three weeks with a broken shin from 'another slip downstairs', exacerbated by her insistence on driving out to say goodbye to a friend: 'the motion of the Carriage inflamed her leg afresh'. This accident has prevented her

> from trying a new Carriage that I have been amusing myself with building to jolt her about in. It is not on the model of Mrs Stapleton's Gig, nor of any other Vehicle I ever saw, but I flatter myself it will be equally tax free as I think no Country Collector can see any thing in it like Coach, Chaise, Waggon or Cart.

There is only one short letter in 1793, but the following year, Edward Wilson's descriptive powers are in full play about an exciting return journey home from Gloucester:

Binfield
April the 9th 1794

> We are not strangers to the storm of Thunder and Hail that your Ladyship speaks of, we were in the very worst of it, in a most exposed situation, on the high Ground between Glocester and Cirencester, and it beat with so much violence on the right of the Horses and Men, that in spight of all the drivers cou'd do, the Horses turned to the left several times. The lightening, the darkness and the immense force with which the Hail poured down upon us, was tremendous beyond anything I ever saw. Mrs Wilson's countenance exhibited such marks of fright and terror in it as I never observed before, and I myself expected for full two miles that we shou'd have been overturned into a Stone Quarry, for the road was too narrow and too convex to turn about upon, and for two miles together during the whole continuance of the storm abounded with great holes all along the side of it. The Postboy's hand was so cut with the hail it bled all over, old William's hand was not so tender, but he declares he never was in such a storm before in <u>all</u>

<u>his life</u>. To add to the terror of the Scene we expected all the while a Collision with a Mail Coach, which I concluded wou'd be less manageable than ours from being driven with four in hand.

First the drive in the storm and now, two months later, a carriage accident, dramatically described:

Binfield
June the 27th 1794

I was last Monday in some degree of peril that might have incapacitated me, as well as been fatal to old William. I know not how particularly to blame him for it, except for suffering the Horses, that were troubled with flies, to rub their noses together till the Bit of one got entangled in the Curb of the other. But this inattention to where his Horses heads are has been an incurable complaint from my first knowledge of him, as well as his want of activity to get out of a scrape. The Horses back'd, locked the wheels, broke the Pole, reared, and William fell and the Coach upon him with me in it, and nobody in sight. My eyes were upon him all the time and consequently I had sufficient time to prepare myself for my fall. I also let off the Horses, but that as it happened as they were pushing backwards did more harm than good, as it gave them the opportunity of breaking me a Couple of Lamps. I tried first to get thro' the Window of the Door, but had not spring enough in my arms to raise the Weight of my body. I then put aside one of the front glasses, and crept out there between Snap and the Coach, whose Harness had caught hold of a Lamp. He fortunately stood quietly, otherwise the least drag of the Carriage must have mangled William, for he lay completely under the body, and I was obliged to exert all my strength for him to crawl out. He was by this time come to himself enough to cry out Oh! and I had the pleasure of seeing him get up with all his bones whole. He was a good deal bruised, and could not breathe without pain, but on being bled immediately and having all other proper attention paid him he is doing very well again, and says he shall in future keep one eye to the position of the Horses Heads, but if we can meet with any good active driver in his room I believe he will not be [. . .]. Has Mrs Stapleton any good man to recommend? But enough of this subject.

A year later, ever sociable, Edward Wilson is in London taking part in some seasonal events.

London
June the 5th 1795

I have usually made a point of writing from hence to Burton on the Birthday, but your Ladyship will I am sure think I had a sufficient apology for not writing yesterday, when I tell you I was invited to dine with Mr Pitt. This was the first time I had the honour of dining with him, as the Speaker expresses it, <u>on so solemn a day</u>, and was highly gratifying to me, as indeed the whole of my journey to London has been. . .

He has also seen John Chatham who has lost his Admiralty post:

I am sorry to observe that he still feels hurt at his removal, but I had no small satisfaction in perceiving that he throws the blame not so much on Mr Pitt as upon others whom he was conscious of having displeased by his unwillingness to fall in with their Plans. He is anxious to know what you say about it. . .

The newspapers will tell you more of the Gala show at St James's than I can pretend to do. As I begun to grow hot I came away at half after three, before the Princess of Wales, Lady Chatham or Mr Pitt arrived, for the sake of getting cool before dinner. The Princess came with a Train of Attendants but the Prince in a very private manner, as I understand having yet no establishment to make a show with. He is at present very unpopular both in Town and Country. . .

There was a strong report yesterday of a great Victory obtained by the Austrians in crossing the Rhine to relieve Luxemburgh, it came in a private letter to Mr Crawford, late Consul at Amsterdam, and was supposed to arrive thro' a very good Channel. The disarming at Brest and Toulon are also matters of considerable hope as well as the Tumults at Paris. Indeed Publick news promises at present a good deal in every Quarter.

In August it is the turn of the younger son Glocester Wilson to be a beneficiary of William Pitt's patronage:

Binfield
August the 26th 1795

I cannot delay the great gratification that I am sure your Ladyship will share with us on receiving the news that Mr Pitt has most kindly and honourably provided for my son Glocester, in making him Post Master General of the Island of Jamaica, said to be worth £1500 per ann:

But the parents have misgivings:

On the first information of it were none of us so joyful as we ought to have been. The idea of a final separation, the risks of a West Indian Climate to a constitution not the strongest, and the cutting him off wholly from that society and those pursuits to which for some years past he has devoted his time . . . gave a considerable damp to the appointment.

However, with Pitt's assurance that if a home service appointment should arise he will offer it to the young man, and by Glocester's eagerness to accept the West Indian post, Wilson comforts himself with thought of certain advantages to himself arising from the offer:

Your Ladyship is prepared to reflect that this is also a Preferment to me as well as to Glocester that will not a little contribute to ease the Burthens with which I have lately been oppressed by the increase of Taxes and accumulation of expenses at the Bar, and in the Light Horse Volunteers, tho' I have the comfort of assuring myself that no young man ever comported himself with more prudence and sound judgement, with more credit to himself and consideration for his family than Glocester has done.

The thirty year correspondence between the mother and the tutor is nearing its end but Canon Wilson still has bits and pieces of interest to pass on to his beloved friend. The story he now relates has points of social interest, though a little hard to follow because he is filling in gaps in the main story already known to his correspondent from newspaper reports:

After a very pleasant fortnight at Burton Pynsent we had a very pleasant journey to Binfield. The first day was rainy, but the other three were just as we cou'd have wish'd them. We had the opportunity of walking about Bath, and of enjoying all the rest of the road, free from dust and dirt. We got home on Saturday by two o'clock, when we heard the sad news that you will have read in the papers, that Binfield is as full of danger as Belfast. Our poor Turnpike Man was the most inoffensive good temper'd Creature living. He has left a Widow and one Son, an apprentice at Oakingham, who had walked home that evening with his Mother from Market, and all three wou'd undoubtedly have been murdered, but for the arrival of a Cart with a drunken man in it. On the report of the Pistol, the Woman and her Son both jump'd out of bed and ran to the door naked, and in the dark she tumbl'd over her husband calling out Murder. The neighbourhood are all very active in their endeavours to discover the Murderer, have offered a hundred pounds reward, and taken up every person that is of suspicious appearance, but hitherto without effect.

By contrast to the sad local story, he has much to relate of the marriage of the Princess Royal and the Hereditary Prince of Württemberg. The letter continues:

On Sunday morning we came hither, and never saw so crowded a Terrace as on that evening. Report says there were ten thousand people there, the Streets and roads were full of Carriages, and five guineas wou'd not purchase a bed within five miles. On Monday I staid here to address the King and Queen and the new married Couple on their marriage, the two first separately, and the last together at the lower Lodge. As the Prince does not speak English, the Princess thank'd us for both, and held out her hand to be kissed, which he did not; this we thought perfectly right. After all that has been said of his bulk I was disappointed at the sight. He has to be sure an extraordinary large belly and of an extraordinary shape, as the prominency is perfectly globular, but as the K. said of somebody whose name I did not catch, 'he wanted nothing but a large Cheshire Cheese button'd into his waistcoat, to be exactly like him'. I have seen many larger Men, and except in the part abovementioned he is a tolerably well proportion'd good looking Man, and seems active and cheerful.

Yesterday we had what was called a grand Fete at Frogmore. As mourning was not admissable, Mrs Wilson had to return to Binfield for white Muslins. The entertainments were in a Tent of Gipsies and their Children riding about in Panniers upon Asses, a stage for spouting, much dancing, Chimney sweepers riding races upon Asses, and a circular enclosure for feats of horsemanship and tumbling, including the Taylor's ride to Brentford. All of which was well enough, and foolish enough, but everybody seem'd amused. . . The entertainment commenced at five, and lasted till 8, and I believe nobody thought of leaving the Gardens till all was over.

There is the visit of William Pitt to Binfield and that of Wilson to Walmer Castle to record, with particular reference to William's health, already giving evidence of deterioration. Wilson's mention of 'temperence' is significant. The letter will have brought comfort to Lady Chatham.

Binfield
August the 18th 1798

As I learned from Mrs Wilson that she had written to inform your Ladyship and Mrs Stapleton of the supreme gratification afforded us in seeing Mr Pitt perfectly well, and moreover at <u>Binfield</u>, and also that I was revelling in the delight of living with him at Walmer Castle. . . I now seize the first moment after my return to assure you that I left Mr Pitt perfectly well, and exercising that degree of temperence and prudence, every day, all the day, that his best friends can wish, and which must I think insure a continuance of health and strength that will not only carry him thro' all the difficulties he has to cope with, but enable him to display powers superior to everything that has yet been conceived of him. For notwithstanding the Company he occasionally has at his Table, he there finds leisure to devise Plans, and arrange measures, that will in time astonish the World, and remove all the Burthens that the Country now labours under.

And the last dated letter (if it was indeed the last), embraces all the best and most entertaining qualities of this delightful man:

London
June the 5th 1800

My Dear Madam
        As Mrs Wilson is writing under a Cover to Mrs Stapleton I avail myself of the same conveyance to say we were most highly gratified, in spight of weather, with our sojournment at Burton. Your Ladyship's society, uninterrupted by indisposition, Lady Hester [Stanhope's] most enlivening company, and the never failing friendly animation of Mrs Stapleton, were altogether a most delightful feast, the remembrance of which will not be easily done away. The fine weather that accompanied us to Burton seemed to say 'you had no occasion for me there, you had enjoyments enow without me, but I will attend you home again' and indeed nothing cou'd be finer all the way from Burton to Binfield, but before we got out of the Coach it begun raining most heavily and has not been fair since for above an hour at a time. Giffin return'd yesterday from the Park, just as I was going to Court, with his Regimentals so sopped with rain and dirt, he would rather have moved the commiseration of an Enemy, than impress'd him with any idea of his military prowess, and so many white petticoats beflounced with mire were I believe never seen in London before, for the rain seemed not to have interrupted the Spectators, any more than it did his Majesty, and his Military Bands. He cou'd scarce leave the Park till one, and at two he was in the Drawing room looking as well as I ever saw him, and apparently not at all fatigued, but I fancy he was, for at five he whirled short about and walked off to the disappointment of half the room, as well of immense numbers who were then only coming in. I had the pleasure of seeing Mr Pitt at Court and breakfasting with him quite alone yesterday morning, and I further hope before I return to Binfield to spend a day with him at Hollwood. I never saw him in better health.
        June the 6th. I intended to have accompanied Mrs Wilson's letter to Mrs Stapleton yesterday, but was interrupted before I had got thro' the first page, and had no opportunity to return to it again till the Bellman made his appearance. . .
                I am my Dear Madam
                        your most obliged and obedt Humble Servant
                                E Wilson
P.S. I found my Books in so much disorder in consequence of their being brush'd, dusted, and displaced in my absence, that I cou'd not lay my hands on Robinson's History of Jacobinism, but I will not fail to send it before I leave London.

Hester Chatham had less than three more years to live, Edward Wilson about four and William Pitt, the cherished object of them both, just over five. The letters stand as a lasting record of a wonderful friendship.

ii. LETTERS FROM DR ANTHONY ADDINGTON 1767-1786

Physicians of all men are most happy

Francis Quarles (1592-1644), *Hieroglyphics: Nicocles*

The story that emerges from the 304 letters Dr Addington wrote to Lady Chatham must surely stand as a unique record of the total dependence of an anxious wife and mother on the family physician, one who in no way betrayed the trust placed in him, and who did his best to calm her fears and to treat her family, and herself, with only the pathetic resources of eighteenth century medicine for his tools   .

Dr Anthony Addington, MD, FRCP was a fashionable physician with a practice among noted and wealthy patients. His correspondence with Hester Chatham begins in 1767 at the onset of Chatham's long illness, lasting, with occasional respites until the patient's death in 1778. Thereafter the letters continue but with lengthening intervals between the exchanges until 1786, four years before the doctor's death in 1790 at the age of seventy-seven.

The bulk of the correspondence is concerned with Chatham's health: the years from 1775 to 1778, when the statesman had become a hopeless invalid, and during these last three years of her husband's life it is evident that Lady Chatham wrote every day, for long periods to the doctor; on her description of Chatham's symptoms Addington would prescribe for the patient by letter. And not only for the chief patient; all five children, some servants and Hester Chatham herself, also received, through her, written instructions on medicines to take, on food and drink, exercise and total care. Dr Addington certainly visited Hayes; but while there is no exact record of the visits, the impression is that they were infrequent. He also stayed occasionally at Burton Pynsent, accompanied by his wife, really in the capacity of a friend, en route to his property at Upottery in Devon; but these visits too tended to be followed by letters giving medical advice for members of the family,more especially for the two daughters, Hester and Harriot, prone it seems to adolescent disorders   .

It is of course impossible to equate Dr Addington's care and treatment of the Chatham family with any aspect of modern medicine, clinical or ethical. In the latter category, it surprises the modern eye that a physician of Addington's repute and integrity should embellish his letters with details of other patients' illnesses, not only those of Chatham relations but also of friends and acquaintances. Clinically Addington shared wholeheartedly in the contempory belief that gout in the hands and feet, 'a regular fit' was a cure-all. His repertoire of drugs remained virtually unchanged in the nineteen years of the correspondence; his treatment can be compared to that of a musician composing variations on a central theme. Among the favourite remedies, prescribed over and over again, for each member of the family for a variety of illnesses and disorders were: valerian, contrayerva root, spirit of lavender, bark infusion, myrrh, salt of hartshorn, camphor, saffron, tincture of snakeroot, spermalete, tincture of soot, nutmeg, a scruple of Castile soap, syrup of marshmallows, sweet almond oil, acid elixir of vitriol, antimony. For constipation, apparently a great bugbear, he relied on rhubarb, senna, with occasional purging by clysters (enemas) of aloes and, surprisingly, of broth. The draughts were mixed in a variety of 'alexterial' waters, of which peppermint water was the most favoured. Very precise dosages and time to be taken were laid down, both for the administration of medicines and also for wine, tea, asses milk, and for daily foods. These latter consisted mostly of meat in various forms; vegetables were sometimes favoured, more often not.

Without doubt the most important aspect of Addington's treatment lay in the doctor's conviction that the statesman was suffering from clinical depression. He had special knowledge to support this diagnosis: his early reputation had been partly built on treatment of mental diseases and he is stated to have established a 'mad house' next to, or in part of his home in Reading, for the treatment of patients. The Chathams' refusal of King George's offer in 1767 of his court physician to 'assist Dr Addington', gave rise to the rumour that the statesman was insane, with all the political implications flowing from that rumour. Chatham was not of course mad, but there are many references in Addington's letters to his neurotic state, his 'lowness'. By 1775 the physician had begun to write freely to Hester Chatham on the subject; part of the frequent anxiety he expressed for the onset of a 'proper' attack of gout was because it would lift Chatham, at least temporarily, from his mental depths.

Not all Addington's letters refer exclusively to the treatment of illness. He was more to the family than just their doctor: he helped them with the repurchase of their house at Hayes; he kept them posted with political events, notably the progress, or lack of it, of the American war. He wrote about his own family, particularly about his eldest son Henry, the future Speaker of the House of Commons and prime minister on William Pitt's resignation from 1801-1804, when he was created Viscount Sidmouth.

There are two letters only in the collection addressed directly to Chatham and the first perhaps throws light on the prevailing mores of the day. This letter is dated 17th December 1771 and advises him, Chatham, how his wife should cope with 'those changes of her constitution... to be expected in the present stage of her life' (she was 52). There are two letters to 'Mr' Reed, the Hayes family practitioner - a surgeon apothecary - who was in constant attendance under Addington's direction; these contain prescriptions couched in pharmaceutical formulae.

After the death of his wife in October 1778, Dr Addington spent more time visiting his children and his estate in Devon. He was quite happy: 'the ebb of life is neither uneasy, nor uncomfortable'. Alas, the same could not be said for his correspondent: her own life in this period of eight years was beset about with the sorrow of losing three of her five young adult children, her daughters Hester and Harriot and her youngest son, James Pitt.

Dr Addington has left Burton and gone to Cheam where one son is ill:

Cheam
Septr 10th 1767

Madam

I most earnestly pray that this may find Lord Chatham easy, and in the plain Fact leading to Health, and Your Ladyship quite well.

After waiting an Hour and Half at Wells for a Post Chaise, and three hours at Froome, and being obliged after all to go round by Bath in a return'd Chaise, I held out to reach Cheam last night. My poor Child was transported to see me, and the Sight of Him almost broke my Heart. He is rather better this morning; and Dr Lawrence (who is now Here and thinks it possible for Him to recover) is an inexpressible comfort to his dispirited Parents.

I must beg the Favour of Your Ladyship to send all the Letters, with which you may be troubled on my Account, to Clifford Street in London; and with Compliments to Lord Chatham and Mr Jouvencel, am, Madam

Your ever obliged and ever Faithfull

A Addington

PS.   My poor Wife desires me to join her most fervent wishes for Lord Chatham's Recovery, and her best Compliments to Your Ladyship and my Lord with mine.

I will trouble Your Ladyship with another Letter on Saturday, and will expect the Favour of a Line from Burton concerning Lord Chatham as often as Your Ladyship or Mr Jouvencel may be able to oblige me with one.

Thank God I am not the worse for my journey.

From this time begins nearly twenty years, with intervals, of prescribing by post:

Cheam
Septr 12th in the
Morning 1767

I have not yet had the satisfaction of a Letter from Your Ladyship, and therefore am sure you will not be surprised to hear that I grow impatient to know how Lord Chatham has gone on, since I was forced to leave Burton. I hope his Lordship begins to feel some good from his Return to the use of Wine, and from daily Exercise and Amusement in the balmy air, which he resides in. But if he does not, in my opinion He ought to have recourse to the additional aid of Valerian, and take twenty Grains three times every day in an ounce or an Ounce and Half of Milk-Water.

Ten days later, the doctor finds it

not very surprising that Lord Chatham should have profited so little, since I had the Honour of seeing Him, when we consider how unfavourable the weather has been to All Valetudinarians for the last fortnight. . .

Just after I wrote to Your Ladyship on Saturday, there was another thick crop of Rash thrown out upon my Son, which is attended with very profuse sweats almost continually. . . Your Ladyship will understand from hence that I cannot find in my Heart to leave these Parts so soon as I intended.

On 16th October he is

mortified to the greatest degree by hearing from such Hands that Lord Chatham is growing worse.

He approves the Chathams' visit to Bath and has advice for the patient while at the spa:

Clifford Street
Octr 29th 1767

I hope Lord Chatham is exercised in the Air at least three hours every day, and has his Natural Appetite and Relish for Food, and Books and pleasant conversation, and presume that by the time this reaches Bath, each dose of the Confection will be increased to fifteen Grains.

He has news about Chatham's obsession to repurchase Hayes and, with other correspondents, refrains from any hint of criticism. It is such restraint in this, and other unwise and improvident decisions born partly of Chatham's temperament and partly of his mental state, that endears the doctor to the wife. The letter continues:

Since my Return Home, Mr John Pitt [a cousin] has favour'd me with several visits concerning Hayes, and I still flatter myself that Lord Chatham will be re-possessed of it before Christmas, as Mr Walpole [the new owner] has not had the Heart to give him a Refusal, tho' he still appears much enamour'd with the place. But least I shou'd be mistaken, I will take this opportunity of informing Your Ladyship, that I heard this day from good Authority, that the late Sir Ellis Cunliff's House at Wimbledon and also that in Grosvenor Square, are to be lett or sold. . . I am satisfied that your Ladyship will not impute these Communications to officiousness.

The return to Hayes from Bath is delayed, with the consequent frustration resulting in further deterioration in Chatham's state of health, all reported to the doctor.

Novr 11th 1767

It is a great Mortification to me to hear that Lord Chatham continues so ill. I hope, however, He goes on with 15 Grains of the Cordial Confection twice every day and will be soon able to bid Adieu to Bath. I hear there are three Rooms at Hayes very habitable, and no more.

There is no correspondence in 1768 - it is unlikely that Dr Addington's services were not required, more likely that he visited Hayes when needed. But Chatham's health in 1769 had undoubtedly improved:

Honiton
Sepr 30th 1769

Ten thousand thanks to good Lady Chatham and my Lord for their most obliging Remembrance of their old and Faithfull Servant, who has but just time enough by this Post to acknowledge their Goodness to Him, and to let them know how Happy he feels himself in receiving at this Time an Assurance of their Health and that of Lord Pitt and Lady Hester; and that Lady Harriot, Master Pitt and Master James are in his humble opinion on the high Road to Health.

Ten days later he writes from his Devon home with even greater fervour at the continuing good news of Chatham's health:

Upottery
Sepr 30th 1769

The Pleasure I felt at the Sight of Lord Chatham's Hand-writing on the Cover of your Ladyship's last obliging letter, and on the Perusal of that Letter is not, I assure you, to be described. It was nothing less than that divine Sensation which soars above common Joys, and charms the Reason and Understanding.

But for the children's ailments some down to earth advice:

I hope Master Pitt has by this time received good Effects from the little Blister, and that his manly Patience and Resolution will endure the continuance of it, so long as he profits by it. Lady Harriot and Master James have suffered from the Hooping Cough longer than usual. If your Ladyship pleases, I wou'd now lay aside the Bark, if it is not done already, and give them only a Scruple of Gascoigne Powder in a Spoonful of common Water every night at Bedtime with five Grains of Rhubarb mixt with the Powder every 3d or 4th night.

Calmness is the keynote for the following year. An Addington daughter is married - and mother came too:

Clifford Street
Jany 4th 1770

Dr Addington presents his best compliments to Lord and Lady Chatham, with the most grateful Acknowledgements for the Honour of their very obliging Card and Present yesterday. Just after the Ceremony, Mrs Addington set out for Oxford with the Bride and Bridegroom.

In August, Hester Chatham has been on a visit to Chevening, home of the Stanhopes, in a few years time to be linked in marriage to the Pitts. The doctor approves:

The Flight to Chevening is but a Prelude I hope to other Excursions. Such Excursions, often enough repeated, have the virtue of a thousand Medicines.

The untroubled waters of 1770 are soon to be disturbed:

Apr 12th 1771

Tho' I am very glad to hear the Severity of Lord Chatham's Head=Ach is abated, yet I wish'd that Gout might have come before this time, which I think wou'd carry away every Sensation of Head=Ach, and as Your Ladyship says nothing of the anodyne Axeterial Liquor of Hoffman, it may be presum'd that no material Good has been done by it. . . I beg leave to advise Lord Chatham to continue taking twenty Grains of the Confection in three large Spoonfuls of simple Pepper Mint-Water three Times every [day] and to add four Grains of the volatile Salt of Hartshorn to each Draught, in Lieu of the Anodyne Liquor.

In the autumn Dr Addington has returned from a west country tour, visiting patients and including a stay at Burton. At his return on 17th October he writes from Clifford Street, with unusual irony that

> I can give no account of my Sons, from whence it may be concluded that they are not yet in want of money.

This year also records the first of the only two letters he addressed directly to Chatham. Lady Chatham is fifty-two:

> Clifford Street
> Decr 17th 1771
>
> My Good Lord
> Your most obliging and most friendly letter to me ought to have been acknowledged long before this Time. . . The great object with her Ladyship at this Time is to attend to those Changes in her Constitution, which are to be expected in the present stage of her Life. If her Ladyship therefore shou'd be subject to Flushings in her Face, or to unusual Glows of Heat in any Other parts of her Body, or to Head-Ach, Giddiness, or considerable oppression, I think she shou'd lose some Blood, and take three or four gentle Purges.

The daughter Hester's health needs the doctor's advice. Hester is sixteen:

> Jany 21st 1772
>
> The Pains which Lady Hester has felt in her Neck, Shoulders, Collar-Bone and Side, have been all muscular. But as they have not yielded altogether to Bleeding, Purging and James's Powder; as her Ladyship's Blood and Pulse have not mark'd Inflammation, and the Strokes of the Pulse are at present rather weak and unequal, I think She ought to enter on a new Plan. Something lightly cordial and persporative I believe is indicated, and therefore if Your Ladyship has no objection to it, I wou'd advise Lady Hester to take a Scruple of Gascoigne's Powder with five Grains of English Saffron, finely powder'd, in an ounce and Half of simple Alexeterial Water, warm'd with a dram of Nutmeg-water, and sweeten'd with 25 Grains of double refined Sugar every Night or Morning or oftener till she is better.

Hester's ailment is however proving troublesome. There is now a rash:

> Feb. 1st 1772
>
> I am entirely of Your Ladyship's opinion that Lady Hester's present illness will be of great Service to her future Health. But that it may be so, I find it necessary for Her to have Patience, with her Bed, not only till the Eruption disappears, but till there are certain symptoms, that every Impurity is separated from her Blood. We ought to be particularly cautious in this Case, because Chrystallines are an infallible Mark of Malignity, and the Sort which Lady Hester has, is rather rank and was in some measure check'd at the Beginning. I believe Your Ladyship and Lord Chatham are satisfied with me, that it is necessary to support Lady Hester with light and nutriceous diet. . . For this Reason it must be right to allow Her Chicken, or Turkey or Rabbit for Dinner with Wine and warm water; to give Tea

258

with toasted or untoasted Bread and very little Butter for Breakfast only; to use Broth or Sago or Panada for Supper; and thin jellies or Gruel between Meals. . . In slow Fever of this Kind I have often experienced very good effects from Camphor; I must therefore advise Your Ladyship's Apothecary to mix half an ounce of the compound Spirit of Lavender with six ounces of the Camphor Julep, and must recommend it to Lady Hester to take two Table Spoonfuls of the mixture twice at least every day, provided it agrees.

Dr Addington's treatment combined nursing as well as medical advice and he is never averse to adopting Lady Chatham's suggestions, especially in the care of the children:

Feb. 8th 1772

By your Account dated the 5th, I find her Ladyship had on that day the 3rd some transient Pain in her Sides, and a fresh appearance of christalline and other Eruptions. These symptoms were clear indications that at that time the Malignity was not so near spent as was expected. And indeed I can hardly believe it will be spent before this day sennight, if so soon. In the most favourable way it frequently requires full three weeks. I must therefore commend the Prudence of Lady Hester for laying in her Bed all Tuesday, except while the maids were making it.

Hester recovers and now it is William who must receive postal attention from the doctor. There is a hint of the illness which was to threaten his life the following year:

Clifford Street
March 21st 1772

Tho' the attack on Master Pitt was evidently the effect of a Cold, and tho' from its slightness and the long continued discharge of his Back after the Dressing had been disused, I believe He will soon do well again without much trouble, yet I cannot but wish his Colds in the Spring wou'd not produce such an effect. I have no doubt but Your Ladyship and Lord Chatham will judge it right to prolong the drain by refreshing the Plaister with Flies, when there is occasion. At the same time I think it will be proper to give Master Pitt the following draught three times every day viz. Morning, Noon and Night. Mrs Sparry will please to mix a Scruple of Spermalete with a drop of the yolk of a new-laid Egg, and then to add to it of Gascoigne Powder, a Scruple of simple Alexeterial Water an ounce and a half, and Syrup of Balsam Half a Tea-Spoonful for one draught. If there is no Mark of Malignity in Master Pitt's throat, or elsewhere, such as white Specks, or Ulcers, Eruptions, Copius Sweats, flying rheumatick Pains or a quick flow Pulse. . . I wou'd add ten or twelve Grains of Rhubarb to the Night draught on Monday.

Finally Harriot:

May 7th 1772

Your Ladyship, I think, has chosen the right Plan for Lady Harriot. Fifteen Grains of the cordial Confection twice a day, and two spoonfulls of the Camphor Julep as often, are likely to dissipate the Eruption in a few days.

Beset about with children's illnesses and with the ever present worry of her husband's health, it will have come as something of a distraction to Hester Chatham to hear from Addington, through a letter addressed to Chatham, of the death of a mutual very rich friend, John Calcraft and the provisions of his Will in favour of two mistresses both actresses, and their children:

> Clifford Street
> 25th Augt 1772
>
> He has left Mrs Bride £2000 a year for her Life, her Eldest Son his Real Estate, her four younger children £10000 apiece, his two children by Mrs Bellamy £5000 apiece, his own Brother £300 a year and his Sister a Legacy by me unknown.

But this information was only an amusing diversion. For the rest of the year and most of the next, the doctor's letters are a never ending stream of advice and prescriptions for members of the family until

> July 4th 1773
>
> You are infinitely good in inviting us so repeatedly and politely to Burton Pynsent. I am likely to be confined to Town a Fortnight or three weeks longer. My destination must then be into Oxfordshire, then to Berks, then to Somerset and then to Devon.

He has news of his own children, the eldest son Henry showing early evidence of qualities which would be needed for his future role as Speaker.

> The two Girls are settled with their [married] Sister Goodenough for the Summer, and the Boys with Dr [Samuel] Goodenough at Ealing near London. The Doctor was one of the Under-masters at Westminster School many years, and has the care at present of only four Boys. We left Winchester with Credit, in a strain of Virtue and Jubilie Spirit exerted by Harry in his great Zeal to put a Stop to some Irregularities, a Course of which, he thought, would ruin a few Individuals, and hurt the School.

Chatham is on a long visit to Lyme Regis, accompanied initially by his two elder sons. Dr Addington, ever instructive, has some advice on sea bathing to impart:

> July 15th 1773
>
> I am very Happy to hear, my Good Madam, that the Powders have been of Service... the young officer [John Pitt] seems to make no Complaint of Pain or Uneasiness in the Region of his Stomach; and therefore I shou'd hope the Sal Polychest may be laid aside and that Bathing in the Sea every Morning, fasting, may be used very profitably in its Stead. Not that Bathing and the Salt are incompatible; for they may be safely used together provided the latter is taken by his Lordship after he comes out of the Water... The only thing to be found is that the young Gentlemen, from the Pleasure and Luxury of Bathing, may be tempted to bathe too frequently or to continue in the water too long at a time.

A month later he has much to relate about the illness of a patient, and humbly to reveal his bafflement with the case:

Richmond
Augt 19th 1773

The Duchess of Montagu, being very ill, I went to Richmond. And here I am still, with almost everything to make me happy except the consciousness that I have not been of service to my Noble Patient. God Alone knows what the Issue of this Illness will be. I cannot help being alarm'd, as her Grace is never clear of Fever, and reduced in Strength to the greatest Degree. The only Dawn of Hope is, that I think there has not yet appear'd any certain mark of inward decay.

By the autumn, the patient has improved in his absence:

Clifford Street
Octr 12th 1773

In obedience, my Good Lady, to your very obliging Command, I sit down to acquaint your Ladyship that I arrived yesterday in Clifford Street, much the better for my long absence from Hurry and Business. I had the pleasure of finding my Noble Patient at Richmond in a more hopeful way rather than [when] I left Her. Your Ladyship and Lord Chatham will likewise be glad to hear that my daughter's Business is nearly concluded with Mr Goodenough to the satisfaction of both Parties.

At the end of the month he has been to Cambridge, presumably at the parents' request, to see the sick William Pitt. In a letter of 30th October he sends a detailed report of William's condition and pays tribute to the skill of Dr Robert Glynn, the Cambridge physician, in charge, fortunately for William, of the case.

For the next four years, the last of Chatham's life, the statesman's health slowly went downhill, with occasional short respites. Both husband and wife appear at no time to have lost faith in their physician, and during especially fraught periods, Hester Chatham and Dr Addington seemingly exchanged daily letters about Chatham's illness. More and more in Dr Addington's letters, there is evidence that he thought Chatham's troubles were of nervous origin and due to depression:

Mar 11th 1775

Your good account of Lord Chatham encouraged me to eat my dinner before I return'd an Answer to your obliging Letter. Lord Chatham, I think, is in the right Course, and undoubtedly we ought to persist in it. Our particular care must be to guard against Lowness; and therefore in the case of Lowness after the Effects of the Clyster, or at any other Time, a glass of wine, mull'd with Spices or Spt of Lavender on Sugar, or some other Cordial, will be proper once, twice or oftener. . . Tomorrow, give me Leave to ask the favour of another Letter from you.

And later in the year:

Octr 31st [1775]

The Noise, which my Lord heard last Night was, I believe accidental and not likely to return. But shou'd it return it is not to be regarded, as it is a Sympton of the nervous Kind.

Later still:

Decr 18th 1775

I am very glad to hear Lord Chatham's Cough is so much better. This being the case, surely his Lordship ought to go abroad again every fine day in his Coach. The grand Cause cannot be removed without a Return of good Gout, according to my judgement. But I hope the subordinate causes may be greatly mitigated, if not wholly removed, by the active virtue of my Lord Himself. The publick stage is out of the Question at present, but if his Lordship cou'd force himself to bear, and learn to enjoy again, a little domestic Society, it wou'd be a great Step, and tend to break the charm. The medicine wou'd be the more effectual, cou'd this Point be once gain'd.

Lady Chatham has been unwell and in the immediate care of the local doctor, Mr Reed, under Addington's direction:

Apr 6th 1776

The sight of your obliging Letter, my Good Lady, was a real Cordial to me; and I beg you to accept my best Thanks for it. I much approve of Mr Reed's Proposal and advise your Ladyship to take the Bark twice or thrice every day, especially if you are disposed to profuse sweats, or have any other Mark of great Relaxation. The best Form, in my opinion, will be an ounce and Half of the decoction with two drams of the Simple Tincture for one dose, unless there are Reasons of which I am not aware, for giving the Bark in substance.

He then takes the opportunity in this letter to restate his views on a subject near to his true understanding:

I am much the Happier to hear Your Ladyship is recover'd, because it restores you to Lord Chatham; and will, I believe, hasten the Restoration of his Lordship to his Family and the Publick. Wou'd He cou'd taste the same Pleasure in the Society of his Family, that every Body else does! Cou'd his Nerves bear the Balm of such conversation, the Advantage wou'd be inexpressible. Gout cou'd come the sooner; and air, Exercise, and the Cordial wou'd act with their proper vigour. But where am I straying?

All through that year, and the next the postal prescribing for Chatham continues, though perhaps henceforward with a slightly greater emphasis on diet:

May 27th 1776

As there is No reason to believe that the present Medicine disagrees with Lord Chatham, I wou'd go on with it by all means. . . My Lord, I hope, will persist in his airings and his present course of Eating and drinking, adopting Pease, Beans and Colly-flouer, as they come in Season; and while Fever continues, seasoning them with Salt rather than Pepper.

But a week later he is against vegetables. In a letter to Mr Reed he writes:

June 2d 1776

Let us go on therefore with the draughts, Emulsion, Julep and Wine, as they were directed yesterday, till the Pulse comes right; and then give them seldomer. Good spicey Broths, and Sago enrich'd with Wine and Nutmeg are, in my opinion, the most eligible Food for my Lord at present. Notwithstanding which, I wou'd recommend a dinner of roast or boil'd Chicken, without vegetables, if his Lordship's Stomach points that Way. With such a dinner a free glass of pure Madeira will not, I believe, disagree at this juncture.

In August he is jubilant at the arrival of a severe attack of gout, for the usual reason:

Clifford Street
Augt 19th 1776

My Good Lady

Gout in the degree, and in the Parts where my Lord Chatham has it is, in my opinion, a Blessing; as I really believe it will be a perfect Crisis of his nervous Complaints. Such violent, frequent, shooting Pains in the Tendons of the Feet must needs make his Lordship's Pulse very strong and quick. . . I am sure my Lord ought to go on with the Camphor Julep and Stomachic Tincture every six Hours, notwithstanding the Heat and Fever. But unless his Appetite inclines more to Chicken than Spoon-Meals, I own I prefer a diet of Spoon-Meals for the next 24 hours: viz. Sago with Wine, Gruel or Panada with Wine, the Almond Broth, Tea with Bread and Butter, Wine and Seltzer Water with a slip of Bread toasted to eat with it, or one or two more Glasses of pure Wine in the 24 hours, if Sickness or Lowness makes it necessary. We are at present to regard the want of an Evacuation by Seige. Nature has Business in Hand of greater Importance.

With extraordinary resilience and, it must be said, despite his treatment, Chatham is temporarily better. But as always, and probably rightly, Addington is strong on the psychological aspect of the illness:

Sunday Septr 29th 1776

I am very glad to hear, my Good Lady, that Lord Chatham has been on his Horse Again, and hope He will be able to use the same Exercise every fine day for the next month. . . I cannot for the life of me see any Reason why Mr Reed shou'd be desired to sleep every night at Hayes. I wou'd by all means have Him wait on my Lord once every day. If he does it oftener (unless there shou'd be more occasion than there is at present) I think it may be the means of nourishing and prolonging the hypochondriacal Part of the disorder and can do no good. I hope Your Ladyship and my Lord and Mr Reed will have the Goodness to excuse the Freedom with which I write.

From about this time, with Chatham's condition moderately stable, Dr Addington feels able to include in his letters occasional comment on political and international affairs:

Decr 4th 1776
near six o'clock

I was very glad to see your Hand-writing, My Good Lady, before I open'd your Letter; and am sure there is nothing in the Letter to make me sorry, except that it will not be possible for me, without the greatest Inconvenience in the World, to wait on Lord Chatham before Friday morning. . . In the meanwhile I am sure He ought to proceed in the present Course of Medicine, diet and Excericse unless there shou'd arise a reasonable and clear disability to any Part of it.

On Friday morning I had the Honour and Pleasure of passing an Hour and Half with Lord Temple. . . Ticonderoga, it seems, has not been invested or annoy'd by Genl Carlton. We have heard of no action between Genl Howe and the Provincials. The indiscreet Conduct of Governor Toning has made a sad Piece of Work in Florida. Your Ladyship's Family, I am afraid, is in danger of losing £16,600 by it. The Governor had no wise Reason to provoke the Georgians to lay waste his Colony. I own I have not the same Expectation of a speedy Reconciliation with the Colonies which some other People have. I think America is against it; and all Europe too, except England.

And so, a little recovered but still subject to periods of pain from gout, and a hernia - the 'protrusion' for which Dr Addington has difficulty in finding a truss - Chatham enters the last full year of his life. Addington, while continuing to prescribe from his limited medicine chest, is as much convinced as ever that the statesman's illness is in part psychological in its nature:

Jany 4th 1777

I have considered the Contents of your Ladyship's Letter again and again, and can see no good Reason for making any Alteration in our present Medicine. . . I wish my Lord wou'd please me to try once more the Effect of Tea every afternoon about seven. It may help his Digestion, promote the Secretions, especially those by the Skin, and by these means be a Remedy against the present Cause of his principal Complaints. There is one Remedy more I wou'd recommend to Lord Chatham, were it possible for Him to take it, I mean the Balm of friendly Society, which is an Antidote to the Poison of Solitude.

As the Medicine we are now using has by no means allay'd the Irritations, I own I am for laying it aside and adopting a new one. The Medicine I wish to recommend is the Confectio Damocratis, the good effects of which, in gouty and nervous cases, have been experienced for Ages. As a Sedative in hypochondriacal Affections, it is certainly preferable to the Confectio cardiaca.

Feb. 1st 1777

I am persuaded it is right for us to go on with the Cordial Confection four Times every day in the present dose, whether there is Gout or not, or Fever or not. We ought likewise to proceed in our present Course of diet, and therefore I am recommending either Chicken or Calves Feet, or Sweet Bread for dinner, with two or three Glasses of pure Wine after Dinner. There is no doubt but my Lord will be the better for getting up. . . If possible I wou'd turn the Stream of his Lordship's Thoughts into a new Channel. Let him banish Despair, and resolve to be well, if we can and as soon as we can.

Dr Addington was not present when Chatham collapsed while attempting to speak on 7th April 1778 in a House of Lords debate on America. He was however summoned to the sick man's bedside in a London house to which he had been taken from the House, within the hour. That evening he writes optimistically, in a scrawled note, to Lady Chatham at Hayes:

Apr 7th [1778]
Half after 6

I am happy to assure you, my Good Lady, that Lord Chatham is as much recover'd as possible in so short a Time. I am almost persuaded that his Lordship will do very well again.

I am afraid, and so is Dr Brocklesberry [Brocklesby] to advise his Lordship to return to Harley Street this Evening. We have therefore provided a Bed at Mr Strutt's and wish my Lord to rest there this Night. Your Ladyship, I hope, will banish Fear, and have Resolution to come to Mr Strutt's as soon as you can conveniently.

When Chatham died on 11th May it fell to Dr Addington to convey to the widow, in a graceful note addressed to William Pitt, the nephew, Thomas Pitt's wish, which was granted, for a death mask to be taken of the statesman by the sculptor Joseph Wilton:

Clifford Street
May 11th 1778

Mr Thomas Pitt is extremely anxious to preserve to Posterity some Idea of the Features of poor Lord Chatham. He thinks the Pictures He has seen have but a very indifferent Resemblance of Him. Wou'd it be very improper to ask the Favour of Lady Chatham to suffer a plaister Mould to be taken of his Lordship's Face? Were this done, it wou'd serve as the Model of a Bust or Statue. And the doctor thinks it might be done by a skillful Hand in a few minutes. Such a Hand is the Bearer of this Note. But if Mr Pitt wou'd be hurt Himself, or believes it wou'd hurt Lady Chatham, to have such a Model taken, the Doctor implores Mr Pitt to burn this Paper, and say Nothing of its Contents being assured that Mr Thoms Pitt wou'd not willfully do any Thing which might wound Lady Chatham or either of her Children.

With the death of the patient, it might well have been expected that the friendship between Dr Addington and Hester Chatham would have waned; he was old and she was very tired. But it ran too deep for such an expectation. Certainly Dr Addington's professional attendance lessened, but never entirely ceased while he was active, and other physicians attended members of the family; the correspondence, however, continued at approximately quarterly intervals until the doctor's death in 1786.

First the delicate matter of the fee. There seems to have been some confusion in its transmission:

Clifford Street
Augt 29th 1778

I have but just Time to return my best Thanks to your Ladyship for your most obliging Letter in which was inclosed your very ample draft on Mr Coutts & Co. for eight Hund<u>d</u> Pounds, a Noble gratuity for my poor Endeavours to serve the most perfect man I ever knew. Where I have laid your Ladyship's friendly note for Payment of 500£, I really cannot tell at present. But wherever it is, be assured, my Good Lady, it will never rise against the Executors of my late Lord Chatham, and shall when found, be transmitted to Your Ladyship.

That autumn Dr Addington's wife died. So typical of the courtesy of the age, the letter announcing her impending death first deals with Hester Chatham's problems of her late husband's estate, then about her health and only in a final sentence:

Clifford Street
Novr 3d 1778

Your Ladyship had heard from me yesterday, had it been in my Power to write on Saturday. My Poor Wife! I expect to lose her in 24 Hours. The Loss to me and my children will be irreparable.
With All due Compliments, I am, My Good Madam,
Your ever obliged and Faithful Humble Servt
A Addington

After his wife's death, Dr Addington's life, though still a busy one, is naturally and increasingly centred in the affairs of his children; but his interest in Hester Chatham's family remains keen:

Clifford Street
May 1st 1779

It was a great Mortification to me, that it was not in my Power to wait on Lady Harriot, when your Ladyship desired it. But when I heard that her Ladyship and Lady Mahon were under the Care of Dr Lawrence, I was perfectly easy; being fully assured that they could not be in better Hands. It is very true that I have been much engaged this whole Spring, and often obliged by prior Appointments to follow Business in Town when old Attachments wou'd have carried me out of it. But this is a misfortune which every Man of my Profession must expect and submit to. . .
Thank God, we have All rubb'd on tolerably well. My two youngest daughters are with me; my Sons at Oxford.

Upottery Farm
Honiton
Devon
July 14th 1779

I have many Compliments to pay to Your Ladyship from Lord Temple, who honour'd with his Presence [at] the late entertainment in the Theatre at Oxford. Accept, My Good Madam, the warmest congratulations of my Heart on the glorious appearance of your youngest nephew [William Grenville] on that occasion, before an audience of about three Thousand Gentlemen and Ladies.

The death of Hester Mahon, aged 25, in July 1780, some months after the birth of her third child elicits a restrained and touching reference from Dr Addington:

Malvern
Augt 15th 1780

I can forbear writing to you no longer tho' I know not what to say. There are some Subjects too tender to be named, at least for a time. Let me therefore only enquire How your Ladyship and Lady Harriot Pitt do; and how Lord Chatham, Mr Pitt and Mr James Pitt were, when you heard from them. It is unnecessary to add, that our best wishes ever attend the whole family.

We are arrived at Malvern Wells, near Worcester on Thursday last. The Air and Water are, I believe, as pure as any in England. We all drink the water, and think ourselves the better for it.

From his son Henry's house near Devizes, his Wiltshire constituency, a letter from Dr Addington is an example of advice given on total care to a favourite patient:

New Park
Sepr 26th 1781

I am happy to find by Your Ladyship's kind Letter yesterday morning, that some Progress at least has been made towards a Recovery: Indeed I think as great a one as cou'd be expected in the Time. But tho' you are better, it is best for us to lay aside the oily Mixture and have recourse to the cephalic Plaister, and the other Medicine. I shall be much disappointed if they do not strengthen Your Ladyship's Stomach in particular, and your Constitution in general. They are also intended to check the defluxation, and relieve the Langour. I own, I am afraid of cold North Winds in Your Ladyship's case.

It must be certainly right to encourage that disposition to Eruptions on your Fingers. For which Purpose I know nothing better than to hold them over the vapour of water for 20 minutes or longer, twice or three Times every day. Immediately after each Operation of this kind, Your Ladyship, I dare say, will judge it right, as soon as your Hands are wiped dry, to put on a Pair of soft warm Gloves, and to wear them almost continually, till the Heat, Itching, Redness and Puffiness are intirely gone. You will please to wash your hands in warm water. . . I believe the disposition to Giddiness will be caused by the Plaisters etc, especially if they occasion considerable Appearances to the Eye or any Parts of the Body. . . In the mean while you will please to moderate the Laudanum according to your Feelings, taking greater or less doses, as the Symptoms may require. . .

My little Grand-daughter has so interrupted me while I was writing this Letter, that I fear it is hardly intelligible.

In October Dr Addington moves back to his home town of Reading, and his letters for the last five years of the correspondence are mainly from that town, with some from his son's homes in Southampton Street and at Devizes, or from Upottery. He still has plenty of medical advice, with all the old remedies, for Hester Chatham and some for members of her family. Harriot is now living in London with brother William at 10 Downing Street, and 'Mr Reed' is evidently still in attendance:

Reading
Feb 16th 1785

Lady Harriot Pitt is rather thinner than usual, but no Body that sees Her Ladyship, wou'd guess that she has been, or is, at all indisposed. Perhaps the

267

vermifuge medicines, which Her Ladyship has had occasion to take, and has taken with success, may have reduced and lower'd Her in some degree. Be that as it will, Lady Harriot has some nervous complaints which, in my opinion, require the assistance of light persperative Cordials. Her Ladyship has accordingly taken seven or eight Grains of the Confection with two Grains of Contrayerva three Times a day in three Table Spoonfuls of Simple Alexterial water warm'd with thirty drops of the Compound Spirit of Lavender. I have had the Pleasure of Learning that the Medicine agrees. It is prepared by Mr Reed, who met me at the Treasury. Lord Chatham says he is quite well, but He looks as if He wanted Exercise in the Air. I had not the Pleasure of seeing Mr Pitt. . . but am Happy to say that His Friends report Him to be completely well in every Respect.

Later that year it is the physician himself who has been ill, probably from the after effects of a stroke, but insists on writing (in a smaller but still firm hand)

Reading
Nov. 26th 1785

I cannot express how gratifi'd I was and am, with the two polite and charming Letters which I had the Honour to receive from your Ladyship, soon after we return'd to Reading. Tho' my Companion was ready to lend me her Hand to thank your Ladyship for them, I neglected to accept of her Kindness, believing it right to thank you myself, and that I was equal to an Undertaking so pleasant and so easy. But how was I mistaken? A Failure in my Faculties came over me, by which I was disabled from speaking, writing or thinking on common subjects without Confusion. The Complaint is not yet gone: but by Rest and Time is so abated, as to allow me to transmit my best Thanks to Your Ladyship and your Good Friend [Mrs Stapleton] for the very Cordial Congratulations on the marriage of my youngest Son.

Recovery, at least in part was on the way, and with his daughter Charlotte he visits Burton Pynsent, presumably enroute to or from Devon:

North Perrott
June 16th 1786

We got safe Home about eight o'clock on Monday, unfatigued and equally delighted with the charms of our Expedition. . . The late seasonable Rains seem to have been extended far and wide. They can hardly fail to make the Country smile, and the Farmers sing for Joy.

On this happy note the correspondence ends. The doctor lived on for another four years, dying in 1790, doubtless as a very disabled man, else why no more letters?

Dr Addington was a physician of his age; his limited portfolio of remedies, the same for every type of disease, was probably of little use but also may have caused little harm. He certainly had knowledge of neurotic illness. It can be noted in his professional favour that only Chatham himself died while under his care: the rest of the family, most of whom outlived him, all died while under other medical hands. Whatever his shortcomings as a doctor, there can be no doubt that Anthony Addington was a man who inspired confidence and affection in his patients and in those near to him. That must be his epitaph.

Chapter 9

SOMERSET PEOPLE

A time there was ere England's griefs began
When every rood of ground maintain'd its man

Oliver Goldsmith (1728-1774), *The Deserted Village*

Hoc saltem fungar inani Munere[1]

**LETTERS FROM LOCAL FRIENDS AND PROFESSIONAL ADVISERS, AND FROM
TENANTS AND STAFF OF BURTON PYNSENT 1765-1801**

i. FIRSTCOMERS

William Pitt, first Earl of Chatham, famous politician and war leader, was born a
landless younger son at a time when ownership of land was the *sine qua non* of
aristocracy. It was therefore with surprise and joy that he and his wife Hester learned
in 1765 of an unexpected legacy, that of the estate of Burton Pynsent at Curry Rivel in
Somerset together with a smaller property from the same source at Urchfont in
Wiltshire. The owner and benefactor was Sir William Pynsent, a man known to be
eccentric and obsessed with political grievance brought about by the decline of the Whig
party from the end of Queen Anne's reign. Though they had never met, Pynsent
evidently admired William Pitt as a great statesman and at his death left the Burton and
Urchfont estates to him. When Pitt received a peerage the following year he took beside
the title of Earl of Chatham, the secondary title of Viscount Pitt of Burton Pynsent, held
until Pitt's death by his eldest son John.

The Chathams spent some months of each year at Burton. They sold their much
loved small property at Hayes in Kent in 1766 and divided their time between Somerset
and London. But the decline in Chatham's health had begun, and with it his restlessness
and depression, and in the following year, on his whim and in disregard of their
precarious financial state, Chatham sold the Urchfont property in order to buy back
Hayes Place; from then until his death eleven years later it became their most used
residence. Brief intervals each year were, however, spent at Burton, but these visits
were dictated largely by Chatham's state of health and were not linked to particular
seasons. As a result of these frequent moves there is considerable correspondence in
the papers with local people including tenants and employees of the estate.

When Chatham died in 1778 his widow, after periods spend back at Hayes until it
was finally sold in 1784, moved permanently to Burton Pynsent which became her only
home until her death there at the age of eighty-two in 1803.

Below are short biographies based on their letters and local research of some of the Somerset folk whose lives in their various capacities were linked to the Pitt family, but primarily to Hester Chatham in the years of her widowhood. With three of her adult children dead, and her younger and famous son William tied to his responsibilities in London, it was the affairs of her estate, of her country neighbours and the wellbeing of her staff that absorbed her mind and occupied her days.

The Somerset correspondence opens in the year of acquisition of the estate with a letter to Pitt from:

Elias Bampfield, an attorney of Langport. He was born in the same year as Hester Chatham, dying only a few months before her in 1802. It was he who rode to London to tell William Pitt of Sir William Pynsent's bequest. He continued to look after the Chathams' affairs where these concerned the two estates and was for a long period a sort of cashier for the properties, receiving money (in small dollops and after several reminders) for general outgoings and to pay the wages of the employees and, in particular, pensions to Sir William Pysent's annuitants. The tone of his letters is cordial and friendly until right at the end of his and Hester's joint lives, when he is pressing her for repayment of loans he had made to her and sadly but understandably his letters grow short and cold.

Bampfield's letters are not very interesting, being confined to business matters and lacking what could be called the human touch. We can get no intimation from them of what sort of a man he really was; but he was an important person in Hester Chatham's Somerset life and his correspondence with her (and initially with Pitt) cannot be ignored.

Langport
25 July 1765

Hond Sir

Keetch your Burton Bailiff hath lett to one Henry Lye for a Term of 6 years, Moortown Farm with the Lands there to belonging; and about 95 acres of Arrable, 33 Acres of Meadow (mostly lying in common meads) and 79 Acres of Pasture on other parts of your Estate lying near to Moortown Farm (on condition your Honour approves of it) at the price of 200Ls ann., your Honour keeping the Houses and fences in repair (except stoping shards) and paying or allowing out of the Rent all Taxes and other outgoings (Except Tithes and the Window Tax.) And also refering to your Honour all Woods and Timber grown on the precincts and a Way for your Carriages at all times into, through and over Benham and Park Grounds part of ye Demised [premises] during the Term. Lye the tenant is to spend all the Hay and Straw grown on the premises there: to plough no more Ground than is now in Tillage, or have been so for the space of 3 years last past: and he's to Divide the Tillage and Lands in to 4 Allotmentts as near as may be.

The letter continues with details of the lease and states in conclusion that he and Keetch think him (Lye) 'a proper Tenant', ending with particulars of two existing tenancies.

The Keetches. At this point it is appropriate that a note be entered about the Keetch family, William, his brother Robert and an unmarried sister Ann. They were inherited, so to speak, by Chatham with the Pynsent bequest. William and Robert were bailiffs in succession; Ann kept the estate accounts. They were well educated but there is only one letter, from Robert, and that enclosed in one to Hester Chatham from another estate employee. The impression formed from the many references to them in the correspondence of others connected with the estate is that of a certain aloofness from the Chatham family. They were, after all, Pynsent servants, almost certainly for many years, possibly for generations and the switch of loyalties to the new owners may not have come easily, if at all.

The Keetches were a Wiltshire family that had been brought from Urchfont to Burton by Sir William Pynsent. William eventually returned to Urchfont, but Robert and Ann stayed on in Somerset; Ann's death, aged eighty and burial are in the parish records for 1785, as are Robert's ten years later.

Elias Bampfield also, and for much the same reasons, may have found the transfer of his services from the old baronet, steeped in the ideas and customs of the west country, difficult; some of the lack of warmth in his letters may in part be due to this cause. He continued throughout 1766 to address his letters to Pitt (who became Chatham that year) but he gave up doing so on finding that there were long delays in receiving a reply and that when one came it was from Hester. Thereafter, and for the next thirty-four years, his letters, some thirty-six in all, bar one, were to her. There were long unexplained gaps in the correspondence, probably because his services were not needed; there is no evidence that Hester Chatham employed anyone else in his place. For the ten years from 1779 there are no letters at all, and after one only in 1790, another long gap ensues until towards the end of their joint lives, there are two short notes of 1800.

The early letters are cordial enough. There is a dispute in progress between Chatham and the Duke of Queensberry regarding ownership of some land at the second property, Urchfont in Wiltshire:

Langport
19th Jany 1767

My Lady

Last Saturdays post brought me a letter from Mr Wapshare, the Duke of Queensberrys Agent, signifying that his Grace wd leave the matter in dispute (at Urchfont between him and my Lord Chatham) to Mr Wapshare and me; to which I have given answer by this post that my Lord on his part is content to do the same and that at any time after the end of next Term viz 12th of February, I shall be ready upon a Weeks Notice to meet him for this purpose and put a final end to the dispute.

A Quarter's pay is now become due to several of the weekly annuitants (and as I have at this time no money in my hand to discharge it) 'twill be necessary for your Ladyship to make me a remittance as soon as it may be convenient for that purpose, as the people in this very Dear time stand in great need of their money.

My Lady
       The last time I heard from your Bailiff Wm Keetch from Wiltshire was the 28th of last month, when Sainsbury's Account was not quite settled, on account of the Dispute about the field Lands unsown on his Enterance. This man I take to be verry honest but with all verry Ignorant; he seems verry timerous about signing the Bond but says he'l Honestly to pay his Rent at Lady day, as I make no doubt but he will. However I will write to Keetch by Mondays Post to press this affair to an End . . .
       I have discharged all the Burton fee Farm Rents; Mrs Howe's half years Rent up to Mich:, and all the weekly allowances (except Nic: Hoddy's wch is mortgaged and not yet called for) up to this day wch Including my small Bill has exhausted all the money in my hands.
       Herewith I send your Ladyship a copy of Mrs Keetch's account to Xmas last as desired.

And so on. Always more money is needed. In March there is an itemised account:'Some cash is now wanted by me to discharge the particulars, to wit. . .' Poor Hester, even her calculations are wrong, left as she is apparently unaided to cope with the estate accounts. On 5th April:

Your Ladyship seems to have quite mistaken Mrs Keetch's last account sent you. Your Ladyship observed the Ballance in her hands 220 £ 17s whereas in fact the real Bllce due from Mrs Keetch 25th March last is only 61.19.7¾ and this mistake seems to arise from your Ladships adding the bllce of the Farm Acct 158.17.5 to the bllce of the General account.

Two weeks later:

Smith your [Hayes] Bailiff tells me he has no cash in his Hands at present; your Ladyship will therefore be pleased to make me a remittance some other way as soon as it may be convenient, as the poor people (in this time of Dearth) stand in great need of their money, and press me for payment wch I've promised 'em soon.

This was the year, 1768, that Chatham with the utmost improvidence bought back Hayes Place (at a loss) and sold the Urchfont estate in part payment. Money could not have been tighter, Bampfield's letters will have been dreaded. Somehow money owing for Burton was found. On 7th May:

I have recd the Hundred pound Bill of Mrs Keetch and thereon I have discharged all the Weekly and a part of the half yearly Annuities, and will discharge the rest as fast as the people call for or I have an oppertunity of remitting it to them.

There is a mix-up about payments to annuitants with two Keetch ladies involved, the first named being the wife of William Keetch and the second, Ann, thought to be his unmarried sister who kept the books at Burton. In his letter of 20th January 1770 to Hester Chatham, Bampfield shows his annoyance in a postscript:

> PS.   Notwithstanding Mrs Keetch of Urchfont promised me that she wd pay Mrs Swallow's Annuity of 210£ a year and Hannah Giddings's of 3/6 a week, both discharged by me to ye 24th June last, yet this perverse Woman is gone of her Word and will not altho' Mrs Ann Keetch of Curry has wrote her Several Letters on ye occasion, pressing her to it, and promised to allow her the Money in Acct, so that these poor people are in the utmost distress for want of thier Money, and I know of no method how I can pay 'em without sending a special Messenger to Urchfont on purpose, wch is 100 Miles out and home. Your Ladyship will therefore consider this case and give some Direction about it as soon as may be convenient.

Whether or not on Hester's advice a scheme for payment of the Urchfont annuities is proposed by the then bailiff of Burton, one Holder, which Bampfield hopes 'may effectually answer that end'.

From this time, March 1770 onwards, money for the annuitants and other outgoings for which the attorney was responsible, appears to have become regularly available judging by the absence of letters for the next five years. In 1776 however the correspondence resumes and problems arise, possibly due in part to Hester's total absorption in Chatham's illness and also in part to the shortcomings of the unsatisfactory current tenant farmer John Grigg Batten (of which more anon), whose responsibilities appear now to include part management of estate funds. Bampfield writes:

> Langport
> 13th April 1776
>
> My Lady
>   As Ladyday is past, the Annuitants have called on me for payment as usual, wch for want of your Ladyship's Order to receive from Mr Batten, I cd not comply with. I have for several Posts past been in expectation of receiving a Lr from your Ladyship upon the occasion, but having received none, I now take the Liberty of mentioning this business to your Ladyship, and am hopeing to hear soon from you thereon, and that my Lord's health is better.
>   Your Ladyship's much obliged and most obedient humble servant
> E Bampfield
>
> PS.   We have had exceeding dry Weather here and for some time past, and a great likelihood of a very backward Spring.

> Langport
> 9th Novr 1776
>
>   Wednesday last Mr Batten paid into my hands £100 more on Account of Lord Chatham wch I immediately paid over to Mr Whitty in pursuance of your Ladyship's order. Mr Batten was in haste and went off without a receipt, saying he wd call on me at yesterday for it, but did not. If he had, I intended then to have fix'd with him a time for settling his half years account and paying me the ballance. The first time I see him will press him to do this, and when done will send your Ladyship an exact account thereof. I have discharged all the annuities to Mich. last.

Mr Bampfield is busy the following year acting for Chatham in a complex negotiation with a neighbour, Richard Combe of Earnshill about payment of tithes in respect of Burton Parsonage lying in the parish of Drayton adjoining the Burton property. Combe, a sharp Bristol businessman, fought his case with firmness, through his agent, one Donne. On 5th April Bampfield writes to Hester Chatham:

> I am exceedingly sorry Mr Combe sho'd refuse my Lord's offer for the Burton Tithes in Drayton; more especially as I am much persuaded in my own mind Mr Donne and self shall never be able to adjust 'em, having no plan that I know, or can think of, to found our judgments on, save that already proposed to, and rejected by Mr Combe.

The arguments dragged on until Richard Combe comes up with a scheme, obviously greatly to his favour. Bampfield conveys the details to Hester but

> Langport
> 24 Janry 1778
>
> I did not think myself at Liberty to close with the last proposal of his without first acquainting your Ladyship therewith. . . Thus your Ladyship sees how this Gentleman wavers, and how I am from necessity led to trouble your Ladyship again on this disagreeable Business, you so much wish never more to hear of.

With reluctance he has to advise her to accept the new terms, and the question drops from the correspondence. After one further letter of condolence on Chatham's death in May, there is silence from Mr Bampfield until a bombshell arrives more than ten years later:

> Langport
> 3 Febry 1790
>
> My Lady
> I am call'd on for a sum of £400 I some time since borrow'd of a friend to make a sum of £1000 by me lent on Mortgage, which sum of £400 I must now pay off the Second week in May, at wch time and for that purpose, I shall want the £200 lent your Ladyship, of which I take this oppertunity of giving you the earliest Notice, and hope it will be convenient to your Ladyship to pay the £200 and its interest to
> Your much obliged and most obedient humble servant
> E Bampfield

and ten years on, the last sad letter:

> Langport
> 9th June 1800
>
> Wednesday next is the 11th June when the £105 on your Bond to me will become due and be verry much wanted. I have borrowed the principal money once already and paid if off again. But I am in hopes now your Ladyship will be

able to pay it off in one month from this time, or I shall be driven to the necessity of borrowing it a 2nd time and where to apply for this at present is unknown to [me].

Very different to that with Bampfield is the relationship to the Chathams of another early correspondent,

George Speke. Of all their neighbours, he was the closest and most affectionate friend. A son of Dame Jennings Lloyd, his was an influential family of Jordans, Horton Ilminster, and holders of the living of St Andrew's church at Curry Rival. George Speke farmed land adjoining that of Burton; when the Chathams were away he acted as a sort of unofficial guardian of and adviser to the estate. The two families constantly exchanged gifts: in January 1766 he writes to Hester Chatham to report that all is well at Burton Pynsent and thanks her for the 'Pot of Charr' (small trout). In a letter to her the same year he writes:

> Curry Rival
> 17th April 66
>
> I had settled a plan for inquiring weekly after your departure, without giving any trouble, but soon was my friend and corrispondent taken extremely ill, and only just got on his leges again, and to get to B. Pynsent for the best intelligence.

After expressing, through her, gratitude to Pitt for his successful action in regard to the repeal of the cider tax, and stating that he has ordered three or four dozen of white port 'the best of its sort I ever tasted', as a gift to him, Speke ends with modesty:

> If I have over acted without orders, I will do so no more, fearful least it [the supply of port] should be gone. I shall at all times be ready and chearfull to receive any commands from Mr Pitt, your Ladyship and every branch of the Family.

As would be expected there was little that George Speke did not know about farming, but he was no scribe and his spelling is shaky:

> Curry Rivel
> 7th January 69
>
> Madam
> I have had the Honour of receiving too letters from your Ladyship unanswered, wch I assure you has given almost as much Paine as from a Rumatic complaint in my shoulders and armes as hardly able to write, with confused thoughts for want of sleep by night; am now better thank God. . .
> As to my Lords affairs at Burton Pynsent, I think much for the best under present Bailiff Mr Holder. I lately viewed all the Cattle there except 6 Oxen down at the Dary house; the Hay is so very bad, that I dont think the oxen will ever be salable Fatt, or amount to a Praisment except 4 out of the 18 wch are pritty good meat now. If we have not a considerable advance price by Lady day, this Country must be great sufferers. Its a general complaint and the Cattle bought toodeys and those of Smith out of sight, so, am tender in saying more Gutts than Brains. . . Mr Holder tells me he is to send a 100 weather sheep to Hayes, a <u>very good thing</u>. If

more could be taken from hence and the sooner the better, and likely to be sold at a better price and no questions asked, for to say all sound are to hard words.

I am afraid we shall not be able to buy many ships this spring, for the eyews will be late with their Lambs and consequently late before they can be sold at any advantage. I have altered my thoughts in letting Owl Street or Vaggs this year, to get at a stock of Hay beforehand for all on the premises little worth. Mr Holder and I have agreed to lett 50 Cows, 30 at the Dary house and 20 at Moor Town. and I hope greatly increase them the next year and then wee shall be able to determine what stock we can keep. There must be ground reserved for Fatting of the Cows that are dry and those that prove faulty in there milks. . . the meadows to be made better with no great expense, by applying to the water showers, wch shall be taken care, of, every thing else I can think on for your service and interest. . . What is wanting in ability you have in an Honest and Faithful Hart.

George Speke's letters do not do justice to him and it is from the pens of others, in particular the exchanges between Chatham and his wife, that his charm and kindness come alive. In an early letter Hester writes:

> Burton Pynsent
> Friday Night
> past Ten o'clock

> I met Mr Speke this morning in my walk coming to see me. He was very solicitous about your Health, and in conversation he gave me advice to have enlarged one of the Coppers in the Brew House, for he woud take upon him to say it would be necessary. I answer'd very reservedly and discretely.

And later from Hayes, with Chatham at Burton:

> Hayes
> August 2nd Thursday
> 1770

> I figure you all at Burton P. and am persuaded every thing round wears a Face of Joy upon seeing you, and his young Lordship [John]. . . Mr Speke I am sure is delighted, but I hope he has some regrets that my Lady is not of the Party, as I really am <u>very sorry not to see him</u>.

On her return from Lyme Regis where she spent a few days with Chatham, in residence there with the two elder sons, she writes from Burton:

> Burton Pynsent
> July 1st 1773
> past Ten

> I felt (as I was sure I shou'd) our separation as bad as at the First, and did not know how to compose my self with a proper disposition. Happily Mr Speke came to breakfast, with the impatience of true friendship, to be inform'd of the State of the Absentees. This did very well, as Lyme was uppermost in mind, and we cou'd never talk too much about it for Him.

Having promised to send Mr Speke word [of] what news Podge brought of the health of all, I cou'd not resist the temptation of sending him William's correspondence to amuse Him. He brought me back his letters this morning, with which he was so struck, that the Tears came into his eyes when he was praising Them. One of his expressions was that he wish'd to be young again (not that he wish'd to live his Life over again) to have the pleasure of travelling with Him from Penzance in Cornwall to, I don't exactly remember where, but a long Tract.

In fact, Mr Speke had early recognised the special qualities of William Pitt, at that time a boy in his pre-adolescent years, and his obvious affection is shown in a long letter written to William, then aged eleven:

Curry Rivel
the 8th December 70

My beloved Friend
Master Wm Pitt
I set down with great pleasure to acknowlige the favour of both your obligeing letters, wch I confess should have been answered long since. But truly old age and indolence joyn hands. I was truly sorry to find you was not one of the party with Ld Pitt in the Trip to Burton Pynsent. I trust you'l make us quite happy by amends by your long continuace with us the next summer.

William has evidently asked for news of hunting and shooting in the neighbourhood:

As for Partridge, we had but two Coveys, those bording on B —ton Pynsent, and altho I had too London Friends with me, who would have been glad to be thought shots men, we not so much as afrighten them, and believe they are living to this day. Wee picked up our share at a distance, but far from a Plenty.
I have saranaded the Hares around the [. . .?] to or three times, but not kild one, who pt off after a round or two, but so afrighted them that I believe if the Doors of the House [had] been open, they would have ran in for shelter . . .
The first morning we got to Somerton Hedge Corner, the first inclosiers going down to the Town, and the first Inclosier found an old Corsed Hare, who would not venter her self into the open Field but ran up and down the Inclosiers til she was puled out of a Thick Hedge in less than half an hour. The Hounds puled off one of her fore legs, Is [eyes] open in revenge for not useing it as she ought. In less than half an Hour, found an other in the same Inclosier not far from [the first]. . . She with great resolution ran near the same ground, went home again and then dyed.

And so on to the letter's end. It is difficult for us to believe that the subject of the letter, and the crude descriptions, was from a sensitive man to a sensitive boy but so it was then. And always there are the gifts as we learn from further letters of 1773 from Hester at Burton Pynsent to Chatham at Lyme. On 29th June

You are (if you please) to keep a Mare with a beautiful Colt, chestnut, silver tail and mane till Michess [Michaelmas] and then give anything you please for the colt. Mr Speke will keep it if you want, but we cannot keep our grass down, so there seems no objection.

and at the end of the year, 23rd December:

> By the last return of the London Coach came a new piece of the White Beaver for the waistcoat. Mr Atwood will know nothing of any Price, and only desired to have his compliments join'd with Mr Spekes to your Lordship. I was forced to be satisfied for you, and what is still more, am today forced to be so for myself. The original piece Mr Speke has this morning brought back again, with an humble suit from the same Mr Atwood, and Himself, that it may be accepted by me. I cannot see that I can refuse it without hurting Mr Speke. I suppose he thought we shou'd not look as if we had belongd to one another, unless I was cloath'd with it too.

And at Christmas time:

> I dispatch'd a Christmas compliment yesterday to Mr Speke, in which I included your thanks as you desird. They were so well taken that they produced a fresh Present, which arrived towards eleven last night, with a request to have it forwarded. The Contents, a Quarter of Lamb and some Collar'd Pig, of the manufacture I believe of Mr Atwoods cook, as his compliments were joined.

George Speke was a delicate man, and seems to have had premonitions of early death. He writes to Hester on 21st May 1774 that he regrets not writing sooner:

> but its old man wch I am obliged to give way to, for this fortnight back I have been in my old sleepey way, forsed out of my [bed?] very early in the morning and about 10 into an Easy Chair for two or three hours. I am not dejected for I bless God I have had a good share of Health, but the old man must be indulged.

He goes on to say that

> Thursday last I was roused by a story convey'd me overnight of an old Roage imployed at BP, whether by my Lord or Batten, in the Garden. I saw him only give a hint to Mr Jermin to keep a good look out as the sailor says. The man I mean is John Wethey the younger. . . You know me well, that I hate flying storeys and have as little conveyed me and as little regard for them as any man, [but] a Roage in any shape is my aversion, and more particularly those that are every day fed on your most generous Bounty.

George Speke died three years later at the early age of forty-one, two years before Chatham. His loss to Hester in her long widowhood, spent mainly at Burton, will have been irreplaceable.

Among those already employed on the Burton estate, when William Pitt and his family took up residence there, was a small builder and general craftsman who could turn his hand to many tasks both indoors and outside. His name was **Philip Pear** and it is from his letters that we learn something about the interior of the house and its decoration. We first hear of him in an early letter from Hester to Pitt. On 11th July 1766, after deploring Pitt's absence she finds the Dear Children's society, and business with Mr Pear and Madam Keetch the best remedies.

The 'business with Mr Pear' appears to have been discussion on the preliminary work to be carried out on the memorial column to Sir William Pynsent. He writes to Pitt (the only letter not addressed to Hester):

Burton Pynsent
8 Feby 1766

Sir

I recd your Hons and according to your Honrs order have begun a Quarry in the Barley field... I have Dug for the Foundation of the Coulmn on Troy hill 7 feet Downe and no Appearance of a rock nor nothing but Clay for which Reason thought Proper to boar the Ground to feel for the Rock, which lays 10 feet under that, and which makes 17 feet from the surface, as the Ground is soft. I think there will not be sure Foundation without going Downe to that Rock for the Purpose, for which Reason must Waight for your Honrs aperbation... [I] have got a quantity of Stones for the foundation on Troy hill. The Bricklayers cannot work at all as the Frost is so excessive, and all our In Door jobs are Done in Bricklayers worke, but [they] will all be here as soon as weather Permits. If your Honr approves I should recommend the Picture of Prince Ferdinand to be had [sent] to towne to be Repaired as it cannot be well done here.

From your Honrs most obedt Servant
P Pear

Very soon the mounting cost of maintaining the estate is causing Hester worry. Signing himself from now onwards 'Philip Pear' he writes to her:

Burton Pynsent
27 July 1767

According to your Ladyships desire I have here in sent an acct of all the Bills in regard to the Building accept Mr Streets and for some deals at Bristol... I prepose according to his Lordships order to Part from more of the workemen next week.

The letter ends with a statement of costs of labour and materials amount to £337.16.5. More expenses are detailed in his letter of 24th October of the following year, with a reminder of several bills of 1767 still unpaid:

I find by Mrs Keetch she has not money to Pay Mr Evans of Bristol, from whome I have had a Letter since I came to Burton about his Bill...

He has

examd abt Moortown the Dairy etc. what Repairs is wanting... Mr Jermins Hot House want the most... the glass is verry much out of Repair and wants painting verry much, the whole of which will come to abt 14 or 15 Pounds, and the Chinese Railing against the Turnpike Roade wants a little Reparing and Painting verry bad. I am at Present about the Coradore and things as was left undone as I informed your Ladyship before. As to the new appartments the cealing etc wants white washing and stopping verry much.

Doubtless because of his special skills, the Chathams, after its repurchase, bring Pear to Hayes Place to advise on refurbishment. In this same letter of 24th October he sets out the sums, amounting to more than £2000, which will be needed for this purpose. This year, 1768, Pear has moved his base to Curry Rivel, possibly to act in a free lance capacity. In his penultimate letter from Burton of 9th December he reports on work completed:

> I have got the Coradore done, the Chinese Railings Painted and other odd jobs that was needful to be done, and am abt the garden seats as was ordered. . .

but he has also

> lay'd by Everything Relating to the hot houses etc and shall do nothing but necessary Jobbs which may keep a man on some time Longer.

The change appears to have been accepted amicably and, though now operating from Curry, work for the Chathams continues:

> Curry Rivel
> 23 May 1769

> Your Ladyship takes notice my Lord wants to know the further state the great Room is in, as to the walls, Windows, floor, Dado etc. The Walls are Plaisterd nearly in there Principal Morters, or all but the last Morter which will be verry thin, the Dado is all set round the Room, the Windows are all Boxt for shutters. . . in short every thing will be quite done before the Cornice, which shall if Possible be done sooner than I mentioned in my Last.

He has been called back to Hayes:

> Burton Pynsent
> 20 June 1769

> I Recd your Ladyships Letter dated the 14 instant, with Regard to being Prepaird for coming to Hayes and leaving every thing here in proper order to take no Dammage the time I shall be away, which I shall be sure to do as the Great Room will nearly be finish'd by the time I presume I may Receive my Lords orders for coming to Hayes.

Five years on, and he has had a damaging fall while in Langport:

> Curry Rivel
> 16 April 1774

> I recd a violent Bruse on my Heep which continues down to my ankle Bone on which is a verry Cociderable Cutt, as is on my Elbow and Hand. My arm is Pretty much Brused and a violent Crick in my Neck. I took your Ladyships good

advice [and] at Somerton got Blood[ed] etc. from which I am certain I recd great Benefit.

Even so, he has

been too and from Burton Pynsent every Day since on Horse-Back and now thank God am able to walk a little.

Funds for work on the estate grow short again:

Curry Rivel
13 December 1774

I take the Liberty of troubling your Ladyship to beg the favour of a little money, for what with Packing Cases, alteration in Mr Battens stable, necessary jobs on the Farm [and] almost always some thing or other, have run me quite aground; as your Ladyship knows, I was not very strong when I left Hayes. Trade People here have been enquiring abt there Bills. . .

He also wants a loan for himself:

I must beg lieve further to trouble your Ladyship, that is for want of more Employ I have taken a little farm and to enter in to it at Candlemiss Next, at which time, if it will be agreeable to your Ladyship to advance me a Hunderd Pounds, I shall be much oblig'd to your Ladyship and it will be of service to me. . .
All is well at Burton where I have constantly had an eye to, with regard to the house and furniture.

He reports on 17th April the following year that local tradesmen are getting restive - 'troublesome' - about their unpaid accounts, but three months later he acknowledges (with relief no doubt) a draft for £200 'to apply as your Ladyship Directs'.

This is Mr Pear's last surviving letter. We do not know what happened to him in the three years he still had to live. His death on 5th September 1778, another to follow Chatham so closely, is entered in the parish records. At Burton he does not appear to have been replaced; as a master craftsman he was perhaps too expensive for his chronically impecunious employers.

During her absences from Burton, Hester Chatham received reports on estate matters from men who, over the years came and went, and whose duties while there were manifold. Three at least were certainly tenant farmers of the home farm, Burton, and among the first to come to notice in this category is:

John Grigg Batten. He was a well educated man, not local, probably Devonian. His initial letter finds him seeking advice from the helpful and kindly neighbour, George Speke in two local matters in both of which the astute Richard Combe was in dispute with Chatham and others. All his letters are to Hester.

My Lady

Agreeable to Mr Spekes direction I have sent your Ladyship inclosed a copy of an Order lately obtained by Mr Coombe at a meeting of the Trustees of the Somerton turnpike. . . I shall take the liberty of troubling your Ladyship with his observations. He seems displeased that Mr Coombe, who has but a small property in the Parish in comparison to my Lord or himself, shoud wish to burden the Parish by raising so large a sum as Eighty Pounds, which I believe would amount to at least a Shilling in the Pound; this money together with the aid from the Trustees to be laid out on the Road from the Bool Inn to Westmoor. If my Lord has no objection, Mr Speke would resort to a sixpenny rate, which he thinks would be sufficient for the purpose of repairing the Roads, as he says they are by no means bad or [?foundatious], tho not so smooth as Mr Coombes might wish. Mr Coombe not having consulted any Person of the Parish, and his confining the whole sum to be laid out on the Road leading to his own House, and under his own direction, seems to Hurt Mr Speke much.

As an answer is soon to be given to Mr Coombes proposal, Mr Speke would wish to know my Lords Sentiments on the matter that he might act accordingly.

And the question of the Drayton tithes, an on-going dispute between the Chathams and Combe (and featured in many letters from attorney Bampfield, acting for the former):

Your Ladyships goodness will I hope excuse my mentioning the Tythes claymed by Mr Coombe from my Lords Estate in the Parish of Drayton. I find by Mr Speke that what Mr Coombe asks is quite unreasonable, which is fifteen Pounds a year. Mr Speke says it cant amount to more than five Pounds annually or thereabouts. I shoud [be] happy to have your Ladyships direction relative thereto, as my paying more than I ought would in my opinion be a dangerous precedent, and possibly bring a perpetual burden on my Lords Estate.

I am with the greatest respect your Ladyships dutiful and most obedient

J Grigg Batten

Batten remained with the Chathams for the next fifteen months. He wrote frequently to Hester, mainly on farming matters, aware of her need to make Burton farm pay. His reports cannot have been cheerful reading:

Burton Pynsent
Sept: 15th 1776

I have now two Hundred and fifty sheep for Sale. As yett I have had no person to offer to buy them, owing to the great Fall that is expected 'em. As the great Sheep Fairs are not tomorrow, I'm apprehensive I may not be able to [?meet] the half years Rent by the time it becomes due. I must therefore beg your Ladyships indulgence. . .in case I should not sell them before till the latter end of October, by which time there will be many Fairs, as some or other of which I will dispose of them for certain, tho it should be under their value. . . Im sorry to say that the allowance of Hedge Wood, which I was in hopes would have been sufficient for me and my Dairy Tenants, does not prove to be so. All the Wood I [got] last year was not sufficient for the Dairy Men, notwithstanding they burnt a vast deal of Furze. As for my self I have burnt Coal entirely.

Things are not as they should be between the landlady and her tenant. He is hurt at her attitude to the non-payment of his rent, and imagined aspersions on his farming skill. He is

> very ready to resign my Lease into my Lords hands or to assign it in favour of anyone who my Lord shall think on proper Terms as soon as your Ladyship pleases. Your Ladyship I recollect was pleased to mention something of the cheapness of the Farm in a Former letter, on my application for wood. I must beg leave to say that I find it hard to be obliged to buy Coal on such a farm as this. . . I am sorry to have given your Ladyship any disagreeable impressions of my going on as a Farmer and hope it does not altogether proceed from my omission of Payment; I imagine it to proceed from the efforts of designing People who may wish to injure me. As to my conduct as a Farmer. . . I am conscious of having discharged my Duty. I have, my Lady, done by my Lords farm as if it had been my own, and have endeavoured to improve it to the utmost of my Ability.

The correspondence continues through most of the following year on a fairly even course:

> Burton Pynsent
> Jany 27th 1777

> By my Lords permission I shoud be glad by way of experiment to vary the present method of husbandry on Burton Farm. At present, by Lease I am allowed to till about eighty acres for wheat and the like quantity for Lent Grain. I have found by experience that the Lands round Moortown, as well as the generality of Lands round Curry to be very unfit for the culture of both Beans, Pease and Barley, for unless we have the most favourable Seasons, attended with frequent showers, the land is of so stiff a nature that the Crops are of very little value. I therefore propose to sow no Lent Grain at all (except for a few Oats for my Horses) but to sow a much larger Quantity of [?. .] and Turneps and to lay down a larger quantity of Land in Artificial grass, and to have the more Wheat which I find the worst of the Ground will bear, with a good dressing.

He wants Hester's approval to the new scheme:

> Your Ladyship will perceive that I dont mean to increase the quantity of acres by Tillage but rather to lessen it. I hope it will appear that my proposal is by no means a selfish one, as it must be attended with the undoubted improvements of the Farm, for of course the more artificial Food, the better it must be for the Lands. Your Ladyships answer as soon as possible will be esteemd as a particular Honour, as the Season for sowing spring corn advances. . . and I shall act accordingly. ⋅

But before the year is out, the ugly spectre of the rent is once again the subject of a letter:

> Burton Pynsent
> Oct 4th 1777

> As the Fair at weigh Hill is reported to be very Bad, I'm rather fearful I may not be able to sell my Sheep soon enought to enable me to pay the whole half year

directly, as it will in some measure depend on the spirit of the Dealers after the Fair. I shall be able with inconvenience to pay Mr Bampfield on your Ladyships order two hundred pounds immediately. If not disagreeable I shoud be much obliged to your Ladyship for your indulgence for the remainder for a month.

And again five months later:

Burton Pynsent
March 20th 1778

As the Half years Rent is now due, I have taken the Liberty to beg your Ladyships directions as to the payment of it. . . and as soon as ever the Several Tax gatherers have called on me (which will be very shortly) I shall call on Mr Bampfield and Ballance the half years account. Your Ladyships goodness will I hope excuse my mentioning the absolute want of Timber for the necessary repairs of [. . ?] Waggons.

A few weeks after this letter was written, Chatham is dead. Batten's letter, after expressing appropriate condolences, is back once more to the rent. Hester Chatham's domestic financial affairs are now partly in the hand of a trusted accountant, William Johnson (who a few years later was to oversee the sale of Hayes Place):

Burton Pynsent
May 19th 78

I rather understood by Mr Johnson that your Ladyship expected an answer to your last letter but as it was in Order for me to observe as to the Payment of Rent, which order as well as all others I may ever receive from your Ladyship, I shall soon readily obey, I apprehend it did not require an answer from me. I find likewise from Mr Johnson I have now the Honour of being your Ladyships tenant and that you wish me to attend to the Care of the Farm. Had I not the strongest of all motives (that of self interest to fix my attention to it) your Ladyship expressing a wish on that Head, would be sufficient to induce me to do every thing in my Power for the advantage and improvement of the Lands under my care.

Despite his loyal sentiments, Batten did not last much longer at Burton. We do not know when he left, or why, but from the evidence of a letter written four years later, it seems that the departure was not necessarily made in acrimony. In fact, of all Hester Chatham's estate employees who left her service, Batten is unique in one respect in keeping in touch with her (almost certainly because he was aware of the political rise of William Pitt and its possibilities for his own welfare). His move back to Devon has not been a success:

Wear
Novr 20th 1782

After a most painful struggle in my own Breast as to the propriety of my present attempts, recollecting the many proofs of your Ladyships great condescension, and universal Benevolence, I have ventured to lay before your Ladyship the state of my affairs.
On my leaving Burton I was in hopes that I should have found Wear an

advantageous situation from the very flattering picture held up to me by present Landlord. I'm sorry to say that all his promises and assurances have failed, and instead of finding myself comfortable and happy, I have been on the most disagreeable terms with him ever since I have been here, and I'm afraid shall be forced to have recourse to law in my own defence. . .

So it comes:

My present situation being rather embarrassed, and I fear like to be attended with further difficulties, I have ventured to solicitt your Ladyship and humbly request that you will be pleased (provided there be no impropriety in the request) to interest yourself with the present Chancellor of the Exchequer in my favour, as I humbly apprehend there may be many subordinate places that must be filled by some one or other.

This request predictably was not complied with, but Batten was a tenacious man. Two years later he is still at Wear, and trying a new approach in his search for William Pitt's patronage. There has been some previous correspondence which has not survived:

Wear
March 20 1782

The very kind reception with which my letters have been honourd by your Ladyship incourages me to take the liberty of giving you an Account of the County meeting intended to have been held yesterday in the Castle at Exon, but the judges being friends to Mr Fox, availed themselves of the opportunity of saying as the Assizes were not finished, that it would impede the Business, and therefore refused to permitt the meeting to be held in the Castle. The Sheriff therefore desired the Gentlemen and Freeholders present to attend him to an eminence in the Castle Yard, a place far more convenient than the Castle would have been.

Batten then describes the meeting in detail, including the content of the speeches, and encloses a copy obtained apparently with difficulty of the loyal address, and ends with a tribute to William Pitt and the words:

May your Ladyship long live to enjoy the inestimable blessing of such a son.

Three years later he has moved to London and has received, it seems by Pitt's influence, a Treasury appointment as a Port of London gauger. Tenacity has paid off for this possibly over-educated farmer, now in a post in a coveted department, the Customs. But, as always, short of money, he writes after six years asking for government employment for his wife; in his final letter to Hester Chatham of 20th March 1797, he asks her to use her influence to effect a transfer for him to a post with 'something equivalent to my present income' but which makes less physical demands upon him.

ii THE GARDENERS

Of all the outdoor staff it was those described in the parish records and in the estate accounts as 'gardeners' who were closest to Lady Chatham and, initially, before he became chronically ill, to Chatham, whose passion for garden design was known to and appreciated by his relations and friends, notably the Lytteltons and Lord Temple, from a time long before his marriage. The designation 'gardener' could be misleading in modern terms: the four men whose correspondence is noticed here were literate (in varying degrees) and facile letter writers and in particular their work embraced much beyond that which would be associated with gardening today.

The first of the gardeners whose letters have survived is **Edward Tapp.** He was already in post when Chatham inherited, but his health was poor and he retired soon after. The four letters he wrote are all to Chatham except the last which was addressed to both, and they cover only the months of July and August 1766. As such they are of interest as an early record of the horticulture employed on a Somerset estate.

Mr Tapp has been visiting and inspecting the stock on offer from different nurserymen:

> Burton
> July 26th 1766

> Hond Sr
> I have sent Mr Broadrips Letter that your Honr may see what he say He have. I was at Pollards this week, the Oakes there will not do, nor but few plants beside.
> This same day I was at Mr Whitelys at [?Meare] where are fine strait Oaks from Eight to tenpence Each and on to Eighteenpence for two and all very cheap at the above prices. He have also Five Hundred Laurells near your Honrs size, Bays and some Laurestinus and Siringas. The work is finished through Mr Keetchs Orchard and the Bank and Dicke at the East end of the above orchard is done, and the road into the Quarry pitt is smooth Down and from the end of the orchard along to the bars that are put up across is finished. . .
> I shall send one or more Pineapples by the Coach Monday morning to be left at Mr Wulbier's in Bond Street, Pickadilly.
> I hope your Honr and her Ladyship enjoy good Health.
> From your Honrs Dutyfull Servant.
> Edward Tapp

The letter from the nurseryman John Broderip enclosed in Tapp's letter warrants a place here if only as an example of the wide range of stock carried by a local supplier:

> July 9th 1766

> Mr Tapp
> I am but just now returned from a long journey, otherwise shoud have answerd your Letter before. I have five or six hunderd Cypresses from three to four feet, have two thousand Scotch and Spruce firr of your size and five hundred

of Larches of the same growth, and have a hundred of the true black Spruce fir a foot high and a hundred of a less size. I have about sixty cockspur Thorns and a few of the jerusalem thorns, fine plants. I have five parcel of Acacias, ash leaved maple, Lilacs, Laburnums, Cedar, China aubor vitaes, Swedish junipers, one hundred of Laurels of a proper size, and some hundred of an under size, a great variety of Roses and other Shrubs, with an infinite number of perennial flower plants. I have above of a hundred of the broadleaved lime and many other things. Be pleased to let me know what size Baskets I must have, that I may bespeak them in time.

There is a useful note added to Tapp's letter:

> Mr German came here Fryday evening

thus revealing the date of joining of his successor.

George Jermin (always spelt Jermyn by Hester Chatham) was very much a local man, and married a local girl, Ann Podger in 1772. His father-in-law, 'old Harry Podger' from peasant stock, was something of a mystery man, largely because it was rumoured that he was rich - a figure of £300 is mentioned in the correspondence. Surprisingly, there is evidence in her accounts that Hester Chatham had borrowed money from him.

A curious feature of Jermin's twenty-four surviving letters to Lady Chatham is that all were written in the same year, 1775. The explanation may lie in his holding temporary charge of the home farm between tenancies; his second letter of 1st April, with its emphasis on farm matters, bears this out. His first letter however finds him coping with the results of bad weather, out of doors and within the house:

> Burton Pynsent
> Febry 4 1775
>
> My Lady
> If it is agreeable to my Lord and your Ladyship, Crosland I intend to lay up for Hay, for [the] walk of trees and the field by John Thomas's will be enough to keep the stock in sumer with the advantage of the Moor; as to Lime kill Field, there have been no stock in it since the oats have been cari'd, sum places the Grass seed Came with a little Clover, but not half Crop. . . I ask your Ladyship's pardon, I must tell my mind that Lime Kill Field will never pay half yr rent as let. . . it would answer better to Corn than Grass. If my Lord choses to part with it, Mr Marwood says that he will plow it up and put it into wheat, but none of the ride[s] round it shall be Plow'd up.

This letter contains two pages of well set out statements of income and expenditure, including entries of payments made to outdoor, and indoor, staff and with a note of his own wages for one year and a quarter: £37.10.0 with board wages of £24.3.0 for nineteen months.

On 1st April he lists the barnyard stock; this includes poultry of all kinds, chicken, turkeys, ducks, guinea fowl, geese. He has hired a team of horses to 'draw down sum Hot Dung'. A day earlier he has drawn from attorney Bampfield a sum of £134 to pay, among others, Mr Pear for Elizabeth Wood's schooling. He is also collecting rent and trying to sell a horse. He reports the death of an annuitant which will save the estate her ten pounds, ten shillings a year.

All this activity, together with livestock management would seem to have left him little time for gardening:

Burton Pynsent
April 17th 1775

I have not offered the Bay Horse to sale as yet, for I think it will be proper to have him ridd Furst to prove whether hee is sound or not. . . If your Ladyship approves of it I think it will be proper to wen the Calfes now, for they are Higher than the Cows, for by their sucking so long, keeps the Cows very Low. The Black and White cow have taken the Bull some time before Christmas but the other not at all, tho I have had her tried several times. All the little Horses is well and [the] Birds.

But the helpful George Speke has other ideas about the calves. A month later:

Burton Pynsent
May the 13th 1775

I went to Mr Speke as ordered, Mr Speke will have [buy] four Turkey Hens, one Cock, then will be three hens one cock left. Also Mr Speke will have 4 Hens one Cock of those at Burton, the others I will part with as soon as posible. . . [He] desier'd me not to wen the Calfes till I hard from your Ladyship again, for Mr Speke want to have them kill'd. I think it is a pitty for they will make too very pritty Cows.

A hot summer has brought water problems and frayed tempers:

Burton Pynsent
July the 17 1775

There is sum of the last plant'd Trees gone off round the Colum, for when wee had that hot Burning weather heare, I keep'd the water cart going every Day, for I was oblig'd to water the new plant'd Trees in the Kitchen garden, [and] as the Horsleas pond was handy I thought no harme. I sent my men for sum water, but Madam Batten came and forbid them to take any from there. Had it been water fit for any use, I should not have taken any of it. I will leave it to your Ladyships judgmen wheather I acted right.

And a snippet of local news on 20th July:

Mrs Powel[l] gave one Hogshead of Cyder, cash one pound one, to the [bell] Ringers on account of Esq Collins of Hatch having a son Bornd.

A visit to empty Burton noted by Jermin on 3rd August (and by several other correspondents) was that of the Pouletts:

Lord and Lady Poulett with sum Gentlemen and Ladys had a could Dinner heare Last Monday, in the portigo and was very must Delit'd in the vues of B:

Pynsent. Lady Poulett went up on top of the Colum. I gave them Grapes and Mellons.

There was no end to the variety of tasks that George Jermin carried out for the family. In an undated letter of 1773 to Chatham at Lyme Regis, which throws a beam of light on Jermin's character, Hester writes that Mr Speke has invited James (then aged 12) to a hunt in the forest, an invitation she would like to accept for him:

> but I believe the riding is bad, and I have no soberer Governor than Jermyn to send with him and I fear he is a man of too much spirit for such a charge, so I have told James <u>Papa</u>'s not being Here, I did not venture to consent.

After Chatham left Lyme for good, it was Jermin who was sent to pack the contents and close the rented house:

> Burton Pynsent
> Septr 28th 1775
>
> My Lady
> I recev'd Mr Wulbier's Letter the 18 past and went to Lyme the 20. I pack'd up all my Lords goods, return'd to Burton Friday evening, sould all as mention'd in the Inventory except the Kitchen Iron range and too forms [and] one stepladder. Could have [got] no more for the iron range than Two pounds which I thought was to little for it. I have left [it] with the two forms and steps for Mr White to sill, then your Ladyship can settle the balance with Mr White the Carpenter, as hee have a bill for work done about five pounds. . . I left the Bedsted Compleat at Chard for Mrs Hood, as I had orders from Mrs Hood. I paid the maide that took charge of the Hous five pounds one shilling.

After detailing further payments, and breakages, Jermin ends with news of the burial of the landlord's wife and remains

> Your Ladyships Dutyfull Servant to Command
> Geo: Jermin

None of George Jermin's remaining letters mentions gardening, but there is much in them about payments received and, more often, paid out on Hester's behalf. There is also a personal matter to report:

> Burton Pynsent
> Octr the 16 1775
>
> I canot say but it have given a good deal of uneasyness to me that your Ladyship should have such Reports of me that there should bee too much Drinking at Burton; let the informers be who they will, it is a very great falshood, for it is very easy Prov'd by the Inventory. But I know that there is sum round Burton that dont like me, for no other Reason for what I know, Except it is that I will not suffer them to plunder and do what they please.

If gardening is not a feature of Jermin's letters to Hester, his skill in that art has been borrowed by the Hoods, now Somerset neighbours. Mrs Hood writes to Hester:

South Cricket
Septr 30th 1775

Mr Jermin will be here next Tuesday to give Mr Hood his advice about planting. The Bed was dropd at Chard when he sent the things from Lyme.

and two years later:

Cricket Lodge
Septr 20 1777

[the fine weather] had so good an effect on me that on Thursday I ordered my chaise and made an excursion to Burton, met Mr Jermyn, who conducted me through the grounds, and up the pillar.

This was the year that George Jermin's young wife died. His own death, still a young man not yet thirty five, followed seven years later.

Richard Cooling was the longest serving member of the Burton Pynsent staff. As with the other 'gardeners' his duties embraced all and every task which could fall to a trusted employee, and like Jermin he often acted as messenger between Burton and the current residence of his employers. We first hear of him in this capacity in a letter from Hester Chatham to Pitt (as he then was) at Bath:

Burton Pynsent
Nov 17 1765

I hope you have approved of the Dispatching of Richard Cooling which appears still to me to have been a right measure, circumstances considered, of positive information, and also that having one letter at Bath, there might be more, proper to enquire after.

Cooling was born in 1735 in Curry Rivel and lived most of his life in his native village and is buried there. Cooling and Jermin were in employment at Burton at the same time and it is difficult to determine how the work was shared. Jermin was certainly in charge of the home farm in 1775, but so apparently was Cooling in 1781-82; all Cooling's twenty-four letters to the now widowed Lady Chatham belong to this short period of stewardship. He was a lesser scribe than Jermin; his letters lack all punctuation and his spelling is largely phonetic. In his first letter of 28th February 1781 he hopes

your Ladeyship will be abel to under stand my scribe; If I must troubel your Ladeyship with my letters, you will be so good to Lett me know.

Hester evidently told him that she welcomed his letters, for the following month he writes:

Burton
Novber the 10 1781

By the Desier of the Cook I take this Leberty to troubel your Ladeyship with this few Liens to aquent your Ladeyship that there will be a Basket at the Black Bare [Bear] on Tuesday the 13 Instent at the usual time we hope. The Basket concest of one goos and giblets, one turkey, three Ducks, 6 Chickens. The Cook desier hir Humbel Duty to your Ladeyship and Ladey Harriot and hope that your Ladeyships are Boath well. The Cook has the ague still. The Coachmans Duty to aquent your Ladeyship that we are as Bissey as we can be a sowing; we have sown all fifteen ackers this Day in Burton field, and a veary good Season.

Richard Cooling continues for the next few months to write regularly about farming and estate matters (but nothing about gardening other than tree lopping), calm letters from an even tempered man. Not all the news is good:

Burton Pynsent
Febry the 25 82

I had the honor to recv your Ladeyships letter and I will indever to let your Ladeyship know concerning the sheep. There is teen dead, one of them was a Ram. . . They purge themselves so much that it was the Caus of there Death. Two yoas [ewes] died with what they call the Readwater and two weather sheep in some thing of the same Disorder. The Ram was Dead before your Ladeyship left Burton. I was goin to write to your Ladeyship about six weeks or two months ago but Mr Keetch desierd me not, his Reason I cant say waht but he said he thought it would freat your Ladeyship if you know of it, that was my Reason in not aquenting your Ladeyship of these matters before.

He reports on the tasks in progress of the garden workers:

they are a shrouding som ash trees, one hear and there. . . but the trees that I wroat to your Ladeyship about is not quite finished. There has been a lettel triming from a few of the trees wich I hope your Ladeyship will not mislike.

And so on. He ends modestly

I could only wish myself a better letter writer that I may be able to inform your Ladeyship of things in a better maner wich I lay under a lettel dout that your Ladeyship cant make out my scribe.

The health and diseases of the farm animals, and of the horses, so vital for transport and farm work, figure largely in the letters of March and April. A favourite horse 'Captain' has been ill and Cooling has given him a 'Drink for the yallows'.

Burton Pynsent
April the 15 82

I write with pleasure [to] tell your Ladeyship the hors is Better and will I hope quite Recover. The Rest is very well and the horses at the Barn is well. The Cows, oxen and young Cattel all well. We can do nothing to the Barley ground to prepare it for a Crop, the Land is so weat, the horses inploy[ed] Droying of hedging stuf and Dung from the Stabel and hay from park.

And always the baskets for Hayes to be sent:

A Basket with one turckey to com as usal

Hester disapproves of his intention to pay sixpence for each crow or magpie to be destroyed. In this same letter Cooling accepts her order to desist but makes his annoyance clear:

There has bin 4 Crows and one magpy keeld. Your Ladeyship may depend on me that there shall not be no more Crows nor Magpys keeld by my order. Your Ladeyship is the sufferer not me. I thought I may be right in so doing.

Perhaps more than those of the other outdoor staff, Cooling's letters show the emphasis Hester placed on the need to succeed in her farming activities; and though absent from Burton during this time for at least six months of the year, her influence is paramount; no action is taken without her approval.

Richard Cooling left Lady Chatham's service in 1795 and died, aged seventy, at nearby Somerton ten years later.

John Smart is described as a gardener in the estate accounts but, as with the others so designated, his duties ranged beyond the garden. The date of his appointment is not clear. There is in the correspondence a letter from William Woodward, a surveyor of Axminster who, on the advice of the Hoods, was consulted in 1779; in his report to Lady Chatham of 22nd October, Woodward states that he took 'a slight view of the estate, which in general is very good land but very badly managed' and goes on to advise that it should be split into five or six farms at least. Smart's appointment may have resulted from this report or he may simply have been engaged in place of Jermin who had probably left the estate sometime before his early death in 1783.

Smart was a better educated man than Tapp, Jermin or Cooling; he was a copious correspondent and though in service at Burton for only seventeen months, there are over thirty letters from him to Hester Chatham, mostly long, written during her absences at Hayes. His first three letters cover the familiar ground of those of his predecessors:

Burton Pynsent
Novr 12th 1781

My Lady
I received your Ladyship's note and the Books you mentioned was sent by the Waggon on the 5th of the month with other articles. . . Since your Ladyship's absence from Burton, we have a very seasonable rain and on Friday last I made a beginning to the planting. I also have been at a Nursery. . . where I have procured for your Ladyship 100 Beeches, 20 Oaks, 20 Elms, 20 Ash, 30 Spruce firr, 14 evergreens of sorts, and with the hunred Oaks which we can take up from among your Ladyship's own plantation, will plant the vacancys in the wood, the firr

plantation by Sedgemoor and all other places where your Ladyship have shewed me. . . There will be 22 Spruce Firrs more wanted to place round the Woodyard, but could not get them in the Nursery already mentioned, there being none tall enough for that purpose.

He ends by proposing to leave this planting to the spring and then to use those from the garden. He is

My Lady with all due respect your Ladyship's Humble and obedient servant
John Smart

Burton Pynsent
Novr 26th 1781

Since my last Letter to your Ladyship I have got the Trees from the Nursery and they are all planted. [I] have filled up the vacancys every where but the bottom of the Wood. . . The Underhill Pond that was in hand reparing is no nearer a finish than when your Ladyship left Burton though Lime and all other materials is ready. Baker have promised me time after time but [I] find there is no dependence on his word.

Burton Pynsent
Novr 28th 1781

I have not got any Baking Apples which your Ladyship wishes for, but there is about a Bushel of the Nonpareils which I wait for orders when to send. Kitchen apples here can be bought for Seven Shillings pr Bushell, if the above price together with the conveyance be cheaper than your Ladyship can have them in or about London will, if approved of, Buy some and send up, but shall leave this to your Ladyship's consideration and wait further orders in your next.

Smart's letters were not exclusively about his work. He adds little items of local news, as now:

Last Saturday Henry Northover [an employee at Hayes] came to Curry, and through the willing consent of Jane Garland, was publish'd in Church for the first time. I believe she intends keeping fast hold of him, untill the whole of the ecclesiastical ceremony be performed.

In a following letter, there is the first hint of Smart's inability to get on with the bailiff Robert Keetch, division of labour the cause:

Burton Pynsent
Dec 5th 1781

I have finished the Planting and I had John Weathey and Thomas Atkins two weeks and three days to help me, for which time Mr Keetch refused to pay them, in consequence of which I have done it and placed it to an account. I return'd them again to the Farm service this day. . . It would be very requisite to open the gutters at the Bottom of the Wood for the benefit of the new plantation of trees as well as for draining the ground and I should wish to know whether I am to employ John Weathey and the other man in it, or get some other body. The garden men have already been more than a month absent from doing any work in the garden, therefore cannot be spared, that work being needful to attend to as well as any other.

Early in 1782 we meet a man with whom John Smart was later to have a violent quarrel, leading to the man's arrest and appearance before the justices. He was William Hillard, described as a baker, sometimes as a maltster. On January 7th Smart writes that

> Hillard the Baker has paid Twenty Pound in part payment to Mr Keetch for the Wood we had last year.

In this letter he reports also that

> Henry Northover and Jean Garlin [Jane Garland] was married the last day of the old year, and about three Hours after set out from Curry to their new residence.

A month on, in the letter of February 6th, there is a small piece of village gossip:

> Sometimes ago Mrs Stapleton sent to your Ladyship's tenant at Moortown to get her a sheephand, which he did and upon terms agreed to go, but unluckily being at Burton, and getting in company and conversation with Henry Northover, being here at the time, the latter mentioned some disagreeable circumstances to him concerning her which I think dont deserve, and immediately upon the same [he] refused to go.

Catherine Stapleton and Hester Chatham were close friends; doubtless both will have found amusement in the anecdote.

In March there is continuing hostility between himself and Robert Keetch, this time regarding replacement of a fence which Smart considers necessary:

> I spoke to Mr Keetch conerning it, and also the other Fences which want very much to be renewed. . . but his answer being so full of indifference gives me little incouragement about the matter.

There is curious little story to report in April:

> Burton Pynsent
> Apr 6th 1782
>
> Your Ladyship's Under Hill tenant has been very unlucky this winter with his Stock, he has los'd betwixt 40 and 50 pounds worth and last Thursday one of his yearling Bullocks fell into the new repair'd Pond in Cowleas, and being full of water was drown'd. Therefore its really necessary that Posts and a single Rail should be put round them to prevent further damage. The Tenant and his wife is of the opinion that some Evil-Eyed Person or Persons, have over look'd their Stock (if such a thing be) which is the cause of them loosing so much. He has been Twice 8 or 10 miles below Taunton, to a man who professeth to put a stop to such bad consequences, and goes by the name of a Conjuror, but his reall name is Baker. It is at present very much talk'd of heare.

Hester Chatham returned to Burton in May for the summer, and Smart's next letter after her departure six months later is to Hayes:

> Burton Pynsent
> Novr 4th 1782
>
> I write to acquaint your Ladyship of there being three Pine Apples, a Dozen of Brown Brewery Pears and a dozen of Cressons all pack'd into one Box, and this day sent to Hatch Inn to go by Tuesday's Coach. It is directed to be left at the Black Bear in Piccadilly till call'd for. Your Ladyship will give further directions for its being conveyed to Hayes. I have got home the Apples that was contracted for on your Ladyship's account, and this day made a beginning to make them ripe into Syder.

If Hester ever hoped to make farming at Burton pay, she will by now have surely become disillusioned. Smart, like the other gardeners, is the communicator of the setbacks:

> Burton Pynsent
> Novr 27th 1782
>
> Mr Keetch has not yet sold the Sheep, they being so much hurt by the foot-rot that I am afraid they will be winter'd at Burton, the loss of which will be considerable. The Horse 'Captain' was sent to Chiselborough Fair, and to Langport Fair, but could not be sold. . .

But work on the estate goes on reasonably well:

> Tomorrow, if a good day, Mr Keetch will finish Wheat sowing. . . The Syder is all made up, the produce of which, Ten Hogsheads, all safe and well in the Cellar and also the account discharged. . . The look [view] from Pan's House is much mended by taking away the Hedge; I have deepened the Ditch against the Pleasure Ground to make it fenceable.

There is criticism of the neighbour, the sport loving Dr Farr, in a letter of 9th December:

> Last Friday I meet Dr Farr's man a little below Moortown, with three Brace of Spaniels, two Grey Hounds, and a Gun. I think the Doctor behaves very much unlike a Gentleman, particularly in your Ladyship's absence, allowing his servant to go about with such a parcle of Dogs, to Hunt, Shoot and destroy all before him. Your Ladyship ever denys your self the produce of game on your own Estate in order to increase it, and other people reapes the Benefit.

A bankrupt farmer has absconded owing money to creditors 'of which I am sorrow to say your Ladyship is one'. But a far more serious case is that of Hillard's debt to the estate. Smart at Keetch's request has been to see the attorney Bampfield twice about the debts. At the second meeting he, Smart stated the case betwixt your Ladyship and Baker Hillard, and advises your Ladyship to arrest him as soon as possible, thinking that the sum not being great, he may find some wayes or means to discharge it. . . I meet with him last Monday, at the Sandpitt in the Park, where he had two Waggons and several workmen loading them, he had ordered one of the men to cut down a Thorn Tree and had a Ladder plac'd against an Oak tree and cut several Limbs of it. Seeing the whole my self, I observ'd to him that of his conduct not being right, not having the liberty, and also mention'd to him of his not having fullfil'd his promise respecting the Wood account. . . The first and last put him in such a passion that one would [have] thought he was destitute of Common Sense, for I never heard a man speak more unreasonable language in my Life. The matter respecting him being arrested is left to your Ladyship's immediate consideration. . . that nothing may be done without your Ladyship's orders.

Hester Chatham agreed to the arrest and Hillard duly appeared before the justices. The judgement states that he 'in a most unjust and unwarrantable manner. . . made use of the most abusive. . . language towards Lady Chatham and threatened to set fire to the mansion. . . and also to burn the said Lady Chatham in her bed'. On a later expression of sorrow and apology, Hester Chatham agreed not to proceed further and Hillard was let off against a surety of £200 from his brother Thomas for good behaviour.

Thus was John Smart's action against 'the Baker' justified but it is failure to get on with Robert Keetch which spells the ending of his employment at Burton Pynsent. The letters of the first few months of 1783 indicate a less than good relationship between the two men due in part, it must be said, to the lack of a proper division of responsibilities.

Burton Pynsent
Feb 5th 1783

Mr Keetch has been at me five or six weeks to have the Fence fresh done by the Moor side, but there being so much of it and in such bad repair that I can not think of doing any thing to it, without particular orders from your ladyship. I spoke of the same fence to him last year. . . but he said there was so much of it, and would be so expensive that he should not do it, but now when the care is taken from him, he wants it done. This matter betwixt him and me respecting its being done or not done, is now left to your Ladyship's determination.

Burton Pynsent
March 26th 1783

Since my last letter to your Ladyship their has nothing particular occur'd. Mr Keetch has recal'd back his word respecting the money which your Ladyship desired me to receive and I have had none from him. I thought he had forgot what I to him before mentioned. . . therefore I mentioned it to him again yesterday as I intended writing to your Ladyship by this days Post. His answer now is that your Ladyship's order is not sufficient for the sum required, nor my note of hand to be accountable; and if he delivers any money, your Ladyship must direct the order to him your self. . . Now I beg if your Ladyship approves of it, and without any disrespect to him, that I may be indulged with the following request which is, that I may not receive any money from him, and that all transactions of Business occurring respecting the Farm may be required of himself to communicate to your Ladyship, and also, that your Ladyship may writ to him your self on the money subject.

There is also trouble about the use of wagons. Smart is unable to complete a hedge for lack of plant material:

> but when I spoke to Mr Keetch to let the Waggon go down to Dungell to bring up the Stuff for that purpose, he gave me such an indifferent answer that I dont like to say any more to him on the subject, because he thinks I order without your Ladyship's commission.

The differences between the two men apparently irreconciable, Smart will have left his post sometime after this letter was written. But we get a glimpse of him four years after his departure from Burton:

> Broad St Giles
> April 28th 1787
>
> My Lady
> I went yesterday to Mr Coutts and received Cash for the draft which I had of your Ladyship, the same being settled and placed to account, and I thank your Ladyship for my character to Sir Robert Cotton, but my application being too late prevented my having it. . . [the post]
> Your Ladyship has got two Canada Geese, believe them to be both Cocks, I was in Oxford Street yesterday and saw a Hen of the same sort, which is much smaller than the Cocks. If your Ladyship wishes to breed from the sort, and give an order to be bought I will do it and send her down. I enquired the price from the owner, which is two guineas; by this your Ladyship will judge whether it will suit you.
> My Lady, I am your Ladyship's humble and obedient servant.
> John Smart

iii FRIENDS AND OTHERS

Hester Chatham was a charming woman, loved by her family and by her old friends, respected by those who served her, esteemed by her neighbours (and revered by one). And then in her long widowhood there was the rise and rise of her devoted son William to be noted by those in need of favours: a heady mixture indeed of charm and power. It is regrettable therefore that such a potion should have been weakened by the corroding and corruptive influence of chronic indebtedness, of relentless borrowings, of failure to redeem loans.

One such creditor was the old nurse, **Elizabeth Sparry**. Though not a Somerset woman (she was born at Hagley, home of the Lyttelton cousins) she nevertheless spent many years at Burton, on and off since the children grew up, and died there. There is correspondence between mistress and nurse throughout the papers and affectionate mention of her in the letters of many others; but a single letter from an old lady of eighty to one of ninety, living not at Burton but in Curry Rivel, and anxious to get her affairs in order, is sad evidence of Hester Chatham's money problems:

Burton Pynsent
Janry 5th 1800

My Dear Dear Mrs Sparry
I feel it almost impossible to express to you the real and sincere Gratitude with which my mind is filled towards you for the many obligations I owe to you for the abundant attentions of unceasing care extended to myself and all those you so truly loved. I cannot without the Greatest Regret think how much pain it is to be renderd incapable of coming to you, from doing of which I shoud receive infinite Happiness. I lament unfeignedly the being unable, from the distress of my present state, to acquit myself as I ought of what I am indebted, but I beg you will order where and to whom it shall be repaid, in any case. . . Be assured I will perform everything agreeable to your wishes in the most exact manner. I doubt I must not enlarge my letter, so my dear Friend of <u>so many years</u>, I finish this with ardent Hopes for your future comfort and happiness.
Hester Chatham

Twelve days later Mrs Sparry is dead. There is a memorial tablet to her in Curry Rivel church, which reads in part:

This small tablet was put up by me, Hester Countess of Chatham in memory of Elizabeth Sparry. Born of a good family at Hagley, Worcestershire, she died at the advanced age of 90 years and attached herself to me and proved a most excellent servant. . . and twas my satisfaction to show her my unfeigned respect. Her infirmities increased with her age and she died perfectly calm the 17th January 1800.

Before we leave Mrs Sparry, there is a letter from Catherine Stapleton to William Pitt, who was devoted to both women, which should be recorded here:

Burton Pysent
18th Jany 1800

My dear Mr Pitt
Poor Pam left this World without a Sigh or Groan at Ten O'clock last Night. From eight o'clock in the morning she was in a Continued Dose; once about noon said 'Oh Molly' and that was all. Lady Cha:m has long had her Instructions for her Funeral written Down, and a Deposite to defray the expence; where she Died there to Remain except within a short distance of Hagley. Her Pockets [to be] Seal'd by long and repeated Orders brought to Lady Chatham. . . The Pockets contain all her Keys, some Cash, Bills, and one of 50£, the half only [but] without the smallest shadow of direction to find a Will if one exists.
Your dear Mother is pretty well, but its impossible for her not to Feel the Event, tho' it can only be seen in the Light of a release. . .
I am my dear Sir your Affectionate and Obedient
Cath. Stapleton

But the old nurse was shrewd. In a postscript to her letter Catherine Stapleton writes:

The Two Cancelled Wills found, both in Favour of her own Family. More Box's still to open - £800 in Bank Bills.

Hester Chatham's nearest neighbours were the Alford family of Heale House. Their respective parks adjoined and the two houses were only about a mile apart. The **Reverend Samuel Alford** the elder was vicar of Curry Rivel to his retirement in 1779, and it is with him that Hester corresponded. His surviving letters, all written in the eight years from 1790, tell a story of affectionate neighbourliness, interspersed with anxious desire for promotion for his naval son Thomas and for the placement of his third son Henry; and with a watchful eye on the wellbeing of that possible source of patronage, William Pitt. In an undated letter, probably of 1797, he writes:

> It gives the Family at Heal infinite Pleasure to find by Mr Wilson's letter that the reports in the News-Papers in regard to Mr Pitt's health are unfounded.

The motive for the preservation of these mainly short notes (there must have been countless others that preceded them) would seem to lie in the record they present of referrals by his mother to William for patronage for the Alford sons. But they also contain touches here and there of gentle charm and friendship between country neighbours:

> Heal-House
> Thursday Eveng
> Febry 25 1790
>
> My Lady
> I am exceedingly obliged by your kind attention to my Health and return you my sincerest Thanks for the assistance of the Poney: after having rode a Favourite Horse for fourteen years, without having any reason to find a single fault, the loss of such a valuable Creature cannot but be very sensibly felt. I have employed People to make all the enquiry they can to get me an easy Poney and I hope I shall not long intrude on your Ladyship's present particular kindness of assistance, and in the meantime the Poney which is now in Heal Stable shall be taken particular care of. . .
> Mrs Alford begs leave to join with me in our respectful Compliments to your Ladyship and Mrs Stapleton. I have the honour of subscribing myself to your Ladyship's most obedient and obliged Humble Servant.
> S Alford

Four years later, and son Thomas's future naval career is the reason for a letter. There is no dissimulation or beating about the bush in the request for help:

> Heal House
> Saturday June 21st 1794
>
> I was at Chard yesterday where I heard that Sir Alexander Hood was daily expected at Crickett, when he will without doubt come to Burton. I shall esteem it as an additional favour if your Ladyship will be so good to recommend my son Thomas to him, whose future conduct in his Profession I hope will gain his good Will.

It is not only the welfare of his family that is important to the retired vicar, he also shares Hester Chatham's wish to help the local poor people. He has attended a vestry meeting and begs leave

Heal-House
Tuesday morng
Sept 23d 1794

to inform your Ladyship that on my representation yesterday of the hardships the Poor Labourers laid under, on being compelled to pay their Compositions to the High-Way, and giving my hearty Vote that they should be all excused this year. It passed unanimously in their behalf; so that this business, which we were apprehensive might have proved disagreeable, is entirely done away.

There is neighbourly exchange of items of food, a domestic matter to which Mrs Alford's thanks are joined:

Heal-House
December 10 1794

Mr and Mrs Alford are much obliged to Lady Chatham for her kind offer of a Roaster, and beg permission not to have it till Tuesday next; all their young Folks being expected to Dinner at Heal Wednesday, when it will prove a great treat to them.
Mr Alford begs Lady Chatham's acceptance of some Cauliflowers, and shall be obliged for the sight of the last night's Papers.

New Year greetings bring another request for the loan of the newspapers. At this last period of Hester Chatham's life, she enjoyed the boon of the near constant companionship of Catherine Stapleton. Mr Alford, in common with other correspondents, including William, reflects her presence in his letters:

Heal-House
January 1st 1795

Mr and Mrs Alford present their respectful compliments to Lady Chatham and Mrs Stapleton and most sincerely wish them many happy returns of this present day. They hope to hear that Lord Chatham is better and shall be obliged for the sight of last night's Papers.

The years pass, and now there is a third son to be started in a career; Mrs Alford also has a say in this question:

Heal House
November 9th 1798

The Confidence with which I rely on the goodness of your Ladyship, and the many Favours I have received from you makes me take the Liberty of troubling you with this letter. I mentioned to your Ladyship, not long ago, my really not knowing what to do with my son Henry, and it's now high time to fix on some way of life to pursue. I once thought of bringing him up to the Church, but his Elder Brother being of that Profession, I fear there are great doubts of his being provided for in that line. To the Law, Mrs Alford and myself have both an objection, and as to Physick it may be a long time before he could get his Bread. If your Ladyship could contrive to get him Clerk, through Mr Pitt's influence into any of the Publick Offices, the Treasury, Admiralty or any other of them, I would take him away at Christmas from the Latin School, in the head form of which he is at present. . . It would be necessary to know whether there is a probability of success between this time and Christmas, because of removing him from his present school.

The letter ends with 'many thanks for the roasting Pig'.

There is some evidence from his letters that William, disliking patronage but loving his mother, did help the Alford sons, though none rose to any eminence. Life at Heale House may have been too comfortable to provide the spur.

There is however ample evidence of William's help, over a long period and in response to his mother's urgings, to **William Hoyte**, rich local farmer, prominent in Curry Rivel affairs. Hoyte regularly attended vestry meetings and was a churchwarden for fifteen years from 1766. He was also a major creditor of Hester Chatham.

As far back as 1782, at the very outset of his career, William writes to his mother:

Nov 2 1782

I will certainly not forget Hoyte's Business and have told Pretyman that I would answer your letter to Him. I believe however that value of the Place is (from Fees) considerably more than we imagined. But I will take care that it shall not be disposed of to any one else without your knowledge. It is certainly in my Gift.

The unspecified place is accepted by Hoyte:

Curry Rivel
26th Novr 1782

My Lady
I embrace this earliest opportunity of returning my most grateful and sincere thanks to your Ladyship and to the Rt: Hon: Mr Pitt for the Appointment which he has been Pleased to Honr me with. If any thing could add to this very great and (hitherto) unmerited Favour, it is the very kind manner in which your Ladyship was Pleased to acquaint me of it.

A year later, William Hoyte's letter indicates that Hester has taken a loan from parish funds:

Curry Rivel
26th January 83

In consequence of a letter I receiv'd a fiew Days since from Mr Parsloe I trouble your Ladyship with the Inclosed Discharge from the Overseer of the Poor of this Parish, which your Ladyship will be Pleased to deliver to Mr Parsloe upon his executing a Bond for one Hundred Pounds payable one Year after Date to your Ladyship. . .

A Hare, a Brace of Cocks, and 2 Couple of Teal accompanies this Letter, which I beg your Ladyships acceptance of.

He has also been consulted by Hester in the complicated matter of the mental state of Henry Podger, the gardener George Jermin's father-in-law, and her creditor:

Curry Rivel
26th Febry [1783]

I was Honrd with your Ladyships letter of the 8th instant with the Inclosure in due course and shoud by the return of that Post, have informed your Ladyship of what had been done for Old Harry Podger, had not your Ladyship informed met that you had Wrote to Mr Smart for a full Account of it. . .

As soon as I heared of Harry Podgers being Insane (which was long before I recd your Ladyships letter) I sent for Mr Sanders who Bled him and sent him some Medicines but they not having the desired effect, I desired Dr Farr to visit him, who thought it wd be proper to have a Man to take care of him. Mr and Mrs Keetch being of the same Opinion, Geo: Mounter has attended him ever since. . . Dr Farr still attends him and has hope of his recovery. Soon after he was first seized he carried part of his Money to Mrs Keetch and in his lucid Intervals since, he has carried other sums of money to her, amounting in the whole to 94£.8.0 and desired in Case of his Death that all he is worth may be divided between German's Children, except a note of Hand for 4£ which he desired may be given to his Sister. I have been to Mr Bampfield, who says that the Law has made a better Will for him than he can at present make, for by the Statute of Distributions his Effects must be divided as he wished them to be. If your Ladyship is pleased to give any directions about this unhappy Man, they shall be carried into immediate Execution.

William Hoyte died in June 1793. But before then debts have to be paid in still more patronage. In two letters from the now workworn William Pitt to his mother, we find Mr Hoyte still in need of placement:

Downing Street
[Sept 13 1787]

I have been in some hopes that I should be able immediately to make good my Promise to Mr Hoyte very satisfactorily. An office is vacant of Messenger to the Order of the Bath, which has been held by Gentlemen and may be done by Deputy. But I am disappointed in the value, as I understand it is not above Fifty or Sixty Pounds a yr, which by paying a Deputy is reduced to below forty. If however It would be an object to Him, I should be very glad to let him have it en attendant, and it shall not at all diminish his prospect of something better.

Downing Street
June 19 1788

As to Hoyte, he has certainly a claim to the very first thing I can find that will suit him, and you may most safely assure him He shall not be forgotten whenever there is an opening

And finally, from Hollwood on November the 21st the following year:

I have reproached myself very often for not having sooner enabled you to relieve Hoyte from his suspense. It turns out as I imagined that the appointment had been delayed only by mistake, and he will have the Benefit of the Office from the time of the Vacancy, which is some months ago.

A sort of blackmail? Perhaps.

So **Dr Samuel Farr** of Curry Rivel was called in by Mr Hoyte to attend Henry Podger, but there is no evidence that he ever attended Hester Chatham or members of her family. He had sporting tastes and it is in this capacity that we first hear of him early in 1782 in a letter from John Smart complaining of the trespass by the doctor's servant with dogs and a gun on the Burton estate. Dr Farr is apologetic:

Curry Rivel
Decr 26. 1782

Madam
It was with great concern that I received a message from your Ladyship... concerning my Servants coursing in this neighbourhood, and I hope I shall be excused for the liberty I take in writing to your Ladyship to vindicate my Intentions and my Servants actions which I fear have been misrepresentated. A Greyhound was given him about two years since, and thinking that this would afford me an opportunity to oblige a friend, I suffered him to hunt upon Mr Spekes and Mr Hoytes estates, for which I obtained leave and gave him the strictest Injunctions not to trespass upon any other persons Land (unless by leave) and especially at Burton, because I knew your Ladyship wished to preserve the Game there inviolate.

The doctor goes on to explain that although he 'could never attempt to justify a servant at the expense of Truth' he has 'upon a strict enquiry' found that there was no trespass. He 'cannot conclude without assuring your Ladyship how sorry I should be to give the least umbrage to a person for whom I have so great and real respect'.

At a later date the doctor has moved to Taunton and with good relations apparently restored (if in fact they were ever jeopardised), he writes from

Taunton
Sunday Jany 1st 1789

Dr Farr presents his best repects to Lady Chatham and Mrs Stapleton and is happy to hear of their health. [He] is much obliged for their kind present which arrived safe but a little wet [and] hopes it will not be disagreeable to them to hear that Dr. F. is very comfortably settled in this town

In March he describes in a long letter a gala day of rejoicing at the King's recovery and including a tribute to William Pitt which will have brought joy to Hester's heart:

Taunton
March 14. 1789

The Day was not only ushered in by ringing of Bells etc. but concluded by the most elegant Illuminations throughout the whole Town, by some Quakers only excepted who object to such Marks of Thanksgiving, but are by no means disloyal.

The day had ended with a dinner at the Castle Tavern attended by

> all the Country Gentlemen and every person of Note in the Town. . . Many Loyal Toasts were drank and Mr Pitt was by no means forgotten. His Spirit and Resolution were highly commended and his regard to the Constitution applauded by a general Huzza of three times three. . . The <u>heart</u> must now rejoice of every one who loves Virtue and who loves Mr Pitt, amongst whom I beg your Ladyship will allow me to include
> Your much obliged and ever devoted humble servant
> Samuel Farr

In a postscript he adds that 'your Ladyship's present (never specified) is well and in good spirits'.

Hester Chatham was a charitable and, curtailed only by her financial straits, a generous woman to those in hardship around her. Now, with her family responsibilities reduced, she was able to throw herself into a cause which mattered to her, that of opposition to the threatened enclosure of West Sedgemoor. In this she was supported by William Hoyte and others, including a neighbouring landowner, John Collins of Hatch Court and it was he who introduced her to a 'man of judgement and reliability' to help forward the campaign, **Mr John Mountstephens How** of Chard in south Somerset. J.M. How (as he always signed himself) appears to have been a man of wide interests, locally in Somerset, in London and in the neighbouring county of Devon. The friendship with Hester takes root quickly:

> Chard
> Sunday afternoon
> [February 1785]

> My Lady
> I have taken the liberty of sending a Brace of Pheasants and another of Woodcocks, of which I wou'd intreat your Ladyship's favourable acceptance. . .
> I expect to be call'd to London in a few days where if I could render your Ladyship the least service it wou'd make me very happy. As soon as I return (and I hope to do this in the course of ten days) I promise myself the pleasure of paying my respects to your Ladyship and bringing with me the further Opinion of Mr Hardinge relative to the Action depending against Meade. This Opinion seem'd to me to be necessary in this Case, as too much caution can't well be us'd where we have so many Friends to please and Enemies to guard against.

Some seventeen letters follow covering the period of the next four years. As a means of introduction, Hester has sent a message to her son William in London to be delivered in person by Mr How, but without success:

Chard
13th Jany 1786

Tho' I had not the honor of a personal Interview with Mr Pitt, for that Gentleman was too much engag'd to admit of it at one time, and at another had retir'd into the Country for the Holidays, I learnt with the greatest pleasure that he enjoyed very good health. I took the liberty of troubling him with a line expressive of the Errand your Ladyship was so good as to honor [me] with but as I heard nothing in answer to it I took it for granted there was nothing just then for me to convey to your Ladyship.

He has summoned a meeting of what may be called the anti-enclosure committee:

I have taken the liberty of requesting Mr Hooper, Mr Cozens and Mr Hoyte to meet me Tuesday, for as I have at last Mr Hardinge's further Opinion relative to the Moor, it will be right to consider what is to be done.

The exchange of produce continues, to which is added some reading matter:

Chard
29th March 1786

I beg to return your Ladyship my most grateful thanks for your obliging present of a Turkey - it prov'd a very good one. The Book your Ladyship mentions I will take the liberty of borrowing when I have next the pleasure of paying my respects at Burton Pynsent.
Inclos'd I have troubled your Ladyship with Kent's hints to Gentlemen of landed Property, and as Ladies are equally interested in the subject matter of them, it will make me very happy to hear of their affording your Ladyship amusement and satisfaction.

Not all the content of How's letters is personal or local, several contain political news from London and comment thereon. But a year on the request that was ultimately to break the friendship has been made:

Chard
9th Feby 1787

At the same time that I acknowledge the Honor of your Ladyship's letter of yesterday I beg to return your Ladyship my most grateful thanks for this additional mark of your confidence. I will with the greatest pleasure set about procuring the sum mention'd by your Ladyship and trust it will soon be in my power to give your Ladyship satisfaction on this Head.

The enclosure question drags on:

The Business of West Sedgemoor being so interesting to your Ladyship and the Association, I cannot but feel the greatest anxiety for the Event. It seems strange that We have not yet been able to ascertain whether the Moore or any part of it lies within the limits of any or either of the surrounding parishes or hamlets. . .

and after arguing the merits of various views, he agrees with those of Mr Hoyte, Mr Hooper and 'some others of our Friends' that it is extra-parochial.

The matter of the loan has become urgent:

Chard
19th March 1787

To prevent any little anxiety that may be felt by your Ladyship in negotiating the loan wish'd for with any other person, I have partly procur'd and in the course of next Week shall I flatter myself have completed the whole sum, with which I propose paying my respects at Burton Pynsent to morrow fortnight.

There is a setback:

Chard
3rd April 1787

It is a most severe mortification to me that I am depriv'd of the pleasure of attending your Ladyship today. . . but having been unexpectedly disappointed of receiving the cash which was promised me yesterday, I am under the disagreeable necessity of solliciting your Ladyship's indulgence for a few days only.

At last:

Chard
5th April 1787

Inclos'd I trouble your Ladyship with two Bills value £400 each and it gives me no small degree of anxiety that they will hardly reach your Ladyship so early as I cou'd have wish'd.

There enters a new contestant in the enclosure question:

[Chard]
14th May 1788

A few days since, Mr Andrews, steward to the Dean and Chapter of Wells, call'd on me to say his Clients have it in contemplation to inclose a considerable part of West-Sedgemore as belonging to the Manor of North-Curry, and that they hope your Ladyship will not be unfavourable to their intentions.

Hester's reply can be guessed and three days later:

It will afford me the most grateful pleasure to render your Ladyship every assistance in my power against the intended inclosure by the Dean and Chapter of Wells.

By 30th June he has received the support of John Collins to oppose the cathedral establishment and from thenceforward the subject drops from the correspondence.
In a letter of 6th April 1789 he sends Hester a receipt for the year's interest on the loan and on the cover of the letter she gives the sum - £40 - but five years later after apparent silence:

[?Wis]combe Park
near Honiton
12th July 1794

Madam

My removal from the Town of Chard where I have left in my late house a Mr Bawden, a most deserving young man in partnership, and several Engagements I have enter'd into for the purchase of lands in this Neighbourhood, lay me under the necessity (and sorry I shall be if my doing it will be productive of the least inconvenience to your Ladyship) of solliciting your payment of my £800 at Michaelmas.

I have the Honor to be Your Ladyship's most oblig'd and faithful Servant

JM How

Hester Chatham got on well with her doctors, in the case of Dr Addington supremely so. Her relations with her Taunton physician, **Dr Thomas Woodforde** were no exception; he attended her for many years, probably to the end of her life. He was her doctor and friend but also a long-standing creditor. From a source outside these papers it is learnt that she borrowed money from him and in a letter asks that 'the matter' be not mentioned to her husband. This debt may have weighed on her mind; what certainly troubled her were the services he gave her free of charge and which she felt were harming his practice. However, Dr Woodforde, a first cousin of the diarest Parson James Woodforde, though undoubtedly a kind man and attentive physician, was not a saint. He was aware of the power of William Pitt to advance not only his own career but also those of his sons. We have the evidence in two letters from Hester to her son William:

Burton Pynsent
April 25th 1796

You will have recd a letter from Mrs Stapleton of a few lines written at a late hour, when I was just got into Bed, to state my serious Request to you, at the earnest Petition of Woodforde, that you wou'd have the Great Goodness to appoint him successor to Haviland, who indeed appears to be a man of the basest and most ungrateful character that can exist... Woodforde's unwearied Attendance upon me, which engrossd so much of his time that he certainly sufferd with his Patients, makes me much interested in his success.

Burton Pynsent
Septr 15th 1798

I feel how much I have teas'd you already by my application for the two Parties I named to you. [Charles] Woodforde is one... as indeed I am most extremely obliged to his Father, and have made him the happiest of men by letting him know I had recommended his son to you.

Dr Woodforde's surviving letters to his patient - and patron - are few and not of much interest, written always formally in the third person. There is the customary exchange of gifts:

Taunton
Febry 27th [1790]

Mr Woodforde begs permission to present his most respectful compliments to Lady Chatham and requests her Ladyship will have the goodness to accept his grateful thanks for Her Ladyship's handsome Present of Mr Pitts Picture, and for Her Ladyship's condescending kind Card.

and in an undated note, probably of this time:

Taunton
Saturday afternoon

Mr Woodforde presents his most respectful compliments to Lady Chatham and requests Her Ladyship will do him the honor to accept a small Turbot, which he met with this morning. . . he trusts a little Fish of the above description, cannot disagree

Catherine Stapleton with her nursing skills is a useful intermediary between Hester and the doctor. He thanks her for forwarding a letter and continues:

Taunton
Friday night
Oct 21 1796

Mr W. is extremely glad to find that Lady Chatham pass'd yesterday as well as expected, and that last night prov'd a good one. . . and that Her Ladyship may have no return of complaints, but if unfortunately the pain so often of late expended shou'd recur, she will than have the goodness to return to the Nephritic Draughts she has by her, which have generally afforded relief.

Taunton
Wednesday night
Augt 29 1798

Mr Woodforde presents his respectful compliments to Mrs Stapleton. . . He has to request she will have the goodness to make to Lady Chatham every possible acknowledgement of gratitude for the kind interference with Mr Pitt in favour of his son. He has also to intreat Mrs Stapleton will be pleas'd to be the bearer of his best thanks to Her Ladyship for a fine haunch of venison which arriv'd safe by post this evening.

Williams 'interference' in respect of the Woodforde son Charles was successful beyond anything that the son of a country physician could have hoped for. To his mother William writes:

Downing Street
Saturday
Feb 9 1799

I am happy to tell you that some Arrangements of the Treasury will afford an immediate opening for two of your Proteges. Woodforde I understand of course stands first, and I only wish to know whom you would place next of the two you mentioned.

Not only Charles, but James Woodforde is also successfully placed, at the Exchequer 'in consequence of your Ladyship's kind interference with Lord Grenville' as the young man writes to her 1801.

Immediately after her death, the estate of Burton Pynsent was put up for sale by John, Lord Chatham. Regrettable perhaps but he had no choice [Appendix 1]. That it financially survived Hester's lifetime is the wonder. And yet the power of love can work a miracle: only Hester's love for Burton and her children's love for her (and that of a few generous friends) somehow ensured that despite all the difficulties she remained there, and died there.

1 Inscription placed by Pitt on the pillar erected in memory of Sir William Pynsent

Chapter 10

WILLIAM PITT AND HIS MOTHER

1759-1803

. . . a grave and premature sense of responsibility

J Holland Rose, *William Pitt and National Revival*, London 1911, p 41

At Chatham's death on 11th May 1778, his second son William was just seventeen days short of his nineteenth birthday. The elder brother John, now the second earl, was serving in Gibraltar with his regiment, having reluctantly left his dying father's bedside to answer the call to duty. It therefore fell to this very young man to represent the family in all the many and complex arrangements to be made for the state burial in Westminster Abbey on 9th June. Letters to his mother in the three days before the interment give early evidence of his grasp of detailed planning, a gift which was to be fully needed in his long tenure of the headship of state.

Harley Street
Saturday morning
[June 6th 1778]

My dear Mother

The Solemnity is to take Place at 10 o'clock on Tuesday <u>morning</u>. My principal Purpose in sending is to let you know that 70 Poor Men are to attend the Procession, and by doing so will gain a black Cloak. You are at Liberty to name all of them, or as many as you please. They are call'd Old Men, and therefore shou'd not be Persons looking younger than 40. The object of these 70 men is by their number to denote the Age. You will be so good as to send us any names you fix upon, as soon as possible. It is not however necessary for you to name any unless you chuse it.

Lord Mahon is not to see the Herald till this evening; but we imagine Mr Pell cannot be to attend in particular Character, unless as a pretended Chaplain; and in that I shou'd think there wou'd be no Impropriety as there will be no real Chaplain there except Mr Wilson, who probably will come.

I have enclosed from this morning's Paper, the City Petition, and the Answer, as ungracious I think as possible. Doctor Addington has freed himself from his engagements, and will be at Hayes soon after this Note. He has had some Transactions on a certain Subject, and therefore of his own accord told me he shou'd carry you his Papers. We are desirous you shou'd receive this as soon as possible, which make me write in so much Haste.

Your dutiful and affectionate son
W Pitt

This letter has on the facing page a note from Lord Mahon, husband of Hester Pitt, son-in-law of Lady Chatham. At this time he was close to the family but drifted apart after the death of his wife and his increasing eccentricity. He was of help and support to William in the funeral arrangements.

My dear Madame

I took care of your two letters as you desired. . . Inclosed is the City Petition, and most <u>Gracious</u> Answer. I send a Pamphlet just published. Pray read the 85th page of it.

The good Esculapius, who will be with you today, will tell you something about a <u>Certain</u> <u>Letter</u> to a <u>Mr Martin</u>; if he should not pray ask him about it.

Believe me ever my dear Lady Chatham

Your most dutiful and affectionate son

Mahon

Harley Street, Sunday
[June 7th 1778]

Everything is settled for the Solemnity on Tuesday, and the Procession is to assemble at Ten o'clock in the morning. The city does not attend but they have come to some very strong resolutions (as we are told) expressive of their grave respect for my Father's Memory, and masking their Resentment of the Manner in which they have been treated. Their sense being thus publish'd to the World the Honor of the day (which is all I am anxious for) will not be diminish'd by their Absence. We find upon Enquiry that none of the three offices I mention'd will be proper for Mr Jouvencel. We have fixed upon Wulbier and Johnson for two of them and will find some third Person of the same kind. I have today sent to Mr Jouvencel to desire him to carry one of the Standard, which gives a considerable Place in the Procession and expect the Answer every moment. Cresswell and James Croft appear under the same Characters as they have at present and twelve other persons in the general description of servants. There is a place destin'd for Physicians, Dr. Addington will attend if He can venture. At all Events, I have secured Dr. Lawrence, I hope. . . I believe we shall have a very respectable Attendance at the Ceremony, but it will not be from the encouragement of the Court, who do every thing with an ill Grace. . . We think it will be highly improper to go to St James's on Wednesday, especially as we have no reason for particular empressement in our Loyalty and Gratitude at present. . . There is not the least occasion for your sending more Servants than you can conveniently spare, as the number necessary can with equal propriety be supplied here.

Harley Street
June 9th [1778]

I can not let the Servants return without letting you know that the sad Solemnity has been celebrated so as to answer every important wish we cou'd form on the Subject. The Court did not honor us with their Countenance, nor did they suffer the Procession to be as magnificant as it ought; but it had notwithstanding every thing essential to the great object, the Attendance being most respectable, and the Crowd of interested Spectators immense. The Duke of Gloucester was in the Abbey. Lord Rockingham, the Duke of Northumberland, and all the minority who are in Town were present. The Pall Bearers were Sir G[eorge] Saville, Mr Townsend, Dunning and Burke. The eight assistant Mourners were

Lord Abingdon, Ld Cholmondeley, Ld Harcourt, Ld Effingham, Ld Townshend, Lord Fortescue, Lord Shelburne and Lord Camden. All our Relations made their Appearance. You will excuse my not sending you a more particular Account as I think of being at Hayes tomorrow morning.   I will not tell you what I felt on this occasion, to which no Words are equal, but I know you will have a satisfaction in hearing that Ld Mahon as well as myself supported the Tryal perfectly well, and have not at all suffer'd from the Fatigue. The Procession did not separate till four o'clock. .

I hope the additional Melancholy of the day will not have been too overcoming to you and that I shall have the Comfort of finding you pretty well tomorrow. I shall be able to give you an Account of what is thought as to our going to Court. Adieu my Dear Mother.

William Pitt the Younger was a child prodigy, a phenomenon fully recognised by his parents at an early age. He never went to school. His tutor from the age of six was Edward Wilson, later rector of Binfield and canon of Windsor, whose teaching services he shared with his elder brother and sisters until he left for Cambridge at fourteen, entering Pembroke Hall under Wilson's care, himself an old Pembroke man. Some early letters to both father and mother survive, including the often quoted Latin letter, undated but certainly written from Weymouth when William was seven. The children had been sent to the seaside under the care of the tutor Wilson and the family nurse Mrs Sparry, known always as 'Pam', to leave their mother free to be in London with Chatham, whose long mental breakdown had begun. In this letter William describes the visit to Weymouth of the Indian chiefs:

Mi Charissime Pater
Gaudoe audire te rersum benevalere. Vidimus Premates Mohecaunnuck et Wappinger, Tribuum Indicorum a Septentrionali America, qui veniunt in Angliam supplicare regem obquosdam agros. Gulielmus Johnson eques Auratus desiderabat auxiluum corum in bello, et illi omnes abierunt ut pugnarent contra Gallos sed cum, domum rediebant sentiebant Batavos arripuisse omnes suos agros. Volgus apud Portland illog parum commode tractabat
Sum mi charissime Pater tibi devinctissimus
Gulielmus Pitt

Five letters from Brighton the following year, all to his mother, express anxiety about Chatham's health: 'I am very sorry that I had not the satisfaction of hearing by Hester's letter of Papa's being better'. He is missing his parents:

Brighthelmston
Sept 6th [1767]

Dear Mama
It gives me great pleasure to hear that Papa is well enough to undertake a journey. I think that as he is moved from North End for change of air, he might as well come here or we come to you.
I am Dear Mama, your most duitful and most affectionate son
William Pitt

With approaching adolescence, William's letters to his mother reflect the self-conciousness, with its attendant stiffness so much a bane, then as now, in the growing-up years. In 1772, one day before his thirteenth birthday, he writes:

> Hayes
> May 27th 1772

> As I cannot rest satisfied without making the best apology in my power for what has pass'd and not being able to have the pleasure of offering my excuses in Person, I trust you will allow me by letter to express how truly I am sorry for my having done improperly and how sincerely I beg your pardon. . .
> P.S. James begs his Duty to you and desires to express that he feels exceedingly sorry for what he has done and hopes you will have the goodness to pardon him.

It is hard to believe that William could have committed a serious misdemeanour. Whatever it was that occasioned a scolding from their mother, it is likely that James, from later evidence not free of minor wrongdoings, was the leader.

Chatham's influence over William's early years and during adolescence, fostered by the adoring wife, is undeniable. Though a man of presence and great national fame, he was a gentle, tender and affectionate father and his children showed no fear of him. Wiliiam's letters were written to one parent or the other (but never to both at once) according to the family's moves and divisions. In the summer and autumn of 1773, ever in search of health, Chatham rented a house at Lyme Regis, taking with him the two elder sons, later exchanged for Hester and James. This visit with his father was something of a high peak in their relationship. William was fascinated by Lyme and the letters flow to his mother:

> Lyme Regis
> June 7th 1773

> Dear Mama
> A prosperous Journey; arrived safe (with ringing of Bells) at Seven o'Clock; a neat House, a sweet Garden, and a Summer-House divine. A King's Lieutenant has just passed under the Window, and a King's Cutter lies here. Players are just arrived in Town. . .
> Papa bore his journey very well. Love and duty to all.

And on 11th June

> The Journalist, flatter'd by your kind expression, takes up his pen with pleasure to say how much he rejoices at the welcome account of all at Burton Pynsent. The Messenger reached before the younger part of the Society were well up, which was occasion'd by attending the Ladies last night to the play-house alias Barn, where we saw Zara, an exceeding pretty and affecting Tragedy; especially as we saw it represented, part for laughing part for crying. The Farce afterwards was the Lying Valet, one of Garrick's, really performed to admiration and laughing from beginning to end. It altogether so took up the Evening, that we did not <u>walk</u> Home till towards Eleven. I mark <u>walk</u> <u>Home</u>, as I am not a little proud of being in the Streets at that Hour. This was the evening entertainment. In the Morning, I was honor'd with accompanying Mr Hollis and Papa a most noble drive. We saw a

prodigious Slide which one of the clifts has lately taken and carried with it part of the Bridport Road. The whole is poetically terrible. Those who had leisure and abilities might likewise find innumerable scenes for the pencil. Uplime, a Village within two miles is a sweet picture, and there is a Hayes near us too, which from what I have heard of its Beauties, I believe deserves its name. The Hills are some of them rather steep but when ascended seem to call for Baby and Poppet etc. with their much wish'd for Charioteers. Indeed the Beauties of Lyme join with our wishes in inviting you here. If they could contrive to place Burton Pynsent here for the Present they wou'd appear with double and treble Charms in the eyes of Dear Mama, Your most dutiful and affectionate son.

William Pitt

May I trouble you with distributing love to the Ladies and their Squire not forgetting the sage Duenna Mrs Sparry.

This letter carried a note on the back in Chatham's handwriting: 'The Contents are inimitably charming. I cannot help this exclamation on reading them'.

In October of that year William, now fourteen, left with Wilson, his tutor, to enter his Cambridge college, Pembroke Hall. This was the first time he had left home alone, without any member of his family. In his first letter home, written from a journey stop, he expresses no apprehension and describes the journey with satirical humour:

Hartford Bridge. Tuesday
Evening 5 o'clock
[1773 October]

The Post being to set out westward from this Place tomorrow Morning, an opportunity offers of informing you that we arriv'd here after a journey of the most prosperous kind, tho it has not produced any very striking Materials for a letter. We reach'd Salisbury last night with the greatest ease before six o'clock, and after a good Night's Repose set out again this Morning about Seven. For the sake of variety we followed the Stockbridge Guide-Post which points to the shortest great Turnpike Road to London, at which the Andover Guide Post, which as you perhaps remember stands in difiance at the opposite side of the Way, and directs to the best Post Road etc. seem'd not a little incens'd. In numberless Places boards are set up contending for the Honor of the different Roads. The Stockbridge is certainly shorter and in my opinion not the least agreeable. There is a very good Inn (as far as we saw) in the Town, and an excellent Tapster, who informed us that it is a very considerable Place, and that a Market is held there every Wednesday, only somehow or other they have had none for some years. From this <u>Market</u> Town we proceeded to Popham-Lane where we had some excellent Mutton-Cutletts and a Chicken that might perhaps have prov'd the same had we had the courage to taste it, but fancying (for the mildest of Landladies assured us it was nothing but a Fancy) that it was intolerably stinking we desir'd it might be remov'd out of the Limits of smell. Thus ended for this day everything that can in any degree deserve the name of adventure, our drive here being without any enlivening incident whatever that can give it any little to more notice. And now we are sitting by a comfortable Fireside at Mr Demezys, where we shall before long drink to all the Society at Burton Pynsent, hoping that all Sensations of gout are fled, and that yourself and every one else are perfectly well and that no cold remains either with my Dear Hester or my kind Benefactrice Harriot, out of whose endeared and precious ink-Stand come all good wishes, love, and duty to yourself, Papa, and Brothers and Sisters.

Shortly after their arrival at Cambridge, William was struck down with a severe illness, probably pneumonia; he was devotedly nursed by Wilson, and by Mrs Sparry, sent by Lady Chatham to help out in the crisis. Her presence in the college gave rise to the legend that William Pitt entered Cambridge with his personal tutor and a nurse. 30th December finds him convalescent back at Burton writing to Chatham at Lyme:

> ... Every Thought is employ'd in wishing You every Joy and Comfort with approacing 74. May it shortly compleat the work of Recovery 73 has so happily begun.

Returning to Cambridge with his tutor in July of the following year, William is again writing to his mother about his journey:

Pembroke Hall
July 13th 1774

My dear Mother
    The first Thing I undertake in my new Quarters is to discharge myself of my promise, by informing you that after a dull and prosperous journey, I am once more within the Walls of Pembroke. . . We breakfasted this morning at Chesterford, which when I was there last, was a day's journey from this Place, but is now diminish'd into a short Drive and follow'd the Footsteps of many Gentlemen of the Turf who were flying to Newmarket, Today being sacred to the Grosvenor Sweepstake. I fear I am too late to obtain a Place in the <u>Coach and Four</u>, so that I must defer being initiated. .
    I am with the sincerest affection, my Dear Mother,

your most Dutiful son
William Pitt

From this time onwards for the next three years, William's letters, all but one to his mother, are mainly from Cambridge. They give little news of his daily life at the university, but in each letter (about two or three a month, sometimes more frequently) he comments at length on the home news she has given him in her letters. He never fails to express concern on the course of Chatham's long illness; his brothers John and James, and his favourite sister Harriot are mentioned throughout, and in nearly every letter he sends his love to 'Pam'. It is plainly evident where his heart lies at this time.

Pembroke Hall
July 20th 1774

    Part of this Morning has been taken up with Riding, and a <u>small</u> share dedicated to the Muses, and as Dinner is at an early Hour, after I had pull'd off my Boots it was too late to write, so that I have only a few Minutes before the going out of the Post. I regret this Constraint of Time the Less because I have scarce any Thing to tell you but that I was made very happy by your Last letter, and that yesterdays Post gave me the additional Pleasure of one from my Father. . . My Father's Letter was doubly agreeable as it gave me an ocular Demonstration that his Hands were quite recover'd from the Weakness of the Gout. I delivered his Message to the Master, who was much flatter'd by It.

In September his tutor from childhood, Edward Wilson, left Cambridge and handed over his charge to George Pretyman (later Tomline), fellow and tutor of the college, whose life was to remain close to William's until the latter's death in 1806. William had been well prepared for the change: his letter of 17th September merely records that 'My friend Mr Wilson left me this morning and you will, I imagine, have seen him before you receive this letter'.

His ego is constantly buoyed but never inflated by his mother's praise:

Hayes
Sept 21st 1774

I was extremely pleas'd with your amiable Letter, my dear William but since the contents would not admit of your having any doubts of that being the consequence, I should not write <u>only</u> to assure you of it. My present view is to send you the enclos'd Paper, the original of which came accidently into my hands. We think that certainly it belongs to you <u>of Right</u> and are great Admirers of the fine things it records. We know of your great Modesty, and therefore dont wonder you never have arrogated them to yourself. Tho for my part I own I think you must sometimes have boasted of them.. It is true that when People are so superior (as it is proved the Person must be) who performd all these Wonders, that they are never apt to talk of their own Doings; and that accounts for our not having heard you make any Brags upon the Subject; for otherwise nobody acquainted with you, but wou'd agree that you was naturally born to such high Deeds. Let your Modesty be so great as it will, I am sure you will have infinite satisfaction and Pride in it, and entirely forgive the generous Panegrist for having taken such Liberties with the <u>Name of William Pitt</u>. I think your Cousin Candidate with all his freshly blown Honors full upon Him wou'd feel his vanity still increas'd by the sense of having a claim in Blood with such an Extraordinary Person. . .

I am to tell you that Miss Chapman, urged by the Ambition of enjoying the honour of having the Work of her skilfull hand worn by the celebrated Mr. Pitt, has already finish'd your Waistcoat, and sent it to Hayes. It is very much approved by those Ladies of Taste, your sisters. . .

Love in full measure from all

Your most affectionate mother
HCh:

The following year 1775 finds him back at Cambridge, and writing a day or two after his sixteenth birthday, ever worried about his father's health:

Pembroke Hall
May 31st 1775

I am much obliged to you for your kind Letter of the 29th, which contained much pleasing and flattering marks of your goodness to me. . . I regret infinitely that the Pleasure it brought was not unmixed with what was far from being satisfactory. At the same Time as some degree of Gout has been felt, I hope I may flatter myself that it is likely in a short Time to operate effectually. I fear I must expect this as the only Step to amendment, tho' it is painful to be obliged to wish for so severe a remedy. It gave me great Comfort to learn, as I did by means of a Letter from Wulbier, that you continued well, notwithstanding all the fatigue you undergo, which indeed I was not a little anxious to be assur'd of. The Papers are full of the bad News from Boston which you mention, and perhaps have magnified the Event. Here I do not recollect a single Word of News which can be in any degree interesting to you and therefore will not trouble you any thing more, except as you have desired, informing you that I am perfectly well.

Adieu my dear Mother.

Pembroke Hall
June 5th 1775

Your letter of the 3rd, my dear Mother, as it gives an account of a small amendment allows me, I trust, a comfortable Hope that the happy period of recovery begins to draw nearer. How much slower the Pace is than my wishes, I think I need not tell you, because I am certain that you know perfectly what I feel on this distressing Subject, and how afflicting the repeated disappointments. I am happy that our kind Friend the Doctor is established with you, which must be a great relief to you, and necessary indeed in so much anxiety and fatigue... I am perfectly well, and employ this delightfull Weather in constant rides which are very agreeable.

Three days later there is a rare reference to the academic side of his university life:

When you send me the Ethnics, I should be much obliged to you, if you wou'd order Davenant on Peace, War and Alliances to be sent at the same Time, if the London Booksellers can supply me with it, since I cannot procure it from any of the Libraries here.

and in his letter of 6 July there is an equally rare reference to university affairs, written more in the tone of an onlooker than of a participant:

Cambridge has been much enlivened lately by the Amusement of the Commencement, which is now over, at which there was a great deal of Company. Lord Granby undertook procuring the Music which was, as you will imagine, exceedingly fine. He staid but two or three days, being obliged to return on business to London.

The mention of Lord Granby evidently alarmed Lady Chatham, who feared that William might be drawn into the rich self-indulgent life in the Rutland house, Chevely Park, three miles from Newmarket, as his elder brother John had been. William reassures her:

Pembroke Hall
Monday July 10th 1775

You are exceedingly good to think so much of me in the midst of your occupations. I shall certainly observe your Caution in respect to any Visit in this Neighbourhood. The Owner of the Place you probably allude to is, I believe, not at present in the Country, as I know he was obliged to go to London as soon as Commencement was over, and I have heard nothing of Him since, so that I have no particular View that way at present.

Our Society begins to diminish at this time of year, but notwithstanding I continue to find my Residence perfectly agreeable, and productive both of Health and Pleasure as much as ever. Yet I begin to think it long that I have been at this Distance from you and cannot help wishing, if you see no objection, to make a short visit to Hayes, for a <u>very few days</u>, merely to enquire after you, either towards the End of this month or the beginning of next. I know your goodness, and indulgence to my wishes, but I must beg that if the Idea creates a moment of difficulty, or inconvenience, you will give yourself no further trouble but to inform me of it, that I may entirely lay it aside; and I assure you if I did not trust that you wou'd do this, I shou'd not have mention'd it at all.

To this tentative and humble suggestion that he should visit his own home, Lady Chatham replies in words that must have cost her dear. Chatham's nervous state now dominates all her thinking and all her actions:

Hayes
Tuesday July 18th 1775

You will have been able but too well, my dear William, to have accounted for my having suffer'd your amiable Letters to remain without being answer'd to this Time. Wou'd to God that I cou'd send you news in this, that might be compensation for my silence, but Heaven does not yet think fit to grant our Prayers, and send the Blessing of Health where it is so much wanted. Your Father for some time past has certainly had no marks of Amendment, nor is there at present any signs of Gout being in Motion towards the Extremities. This throws our hopes of recovery to a greater distance and offers the prospect of a distressing interval. . .

I shou'd have the greatest Joy possible in having you with me for a few days, but having weighed it, I think difficulties may arise in consequence which makes it wise to forego for the Present your purpose of coming. You may trust to my reasons being good against it, for you have a strong Friend in my Inclination to persuade me to agree to your Plan, but it is certainly better to decide against it. Shou'd any favourable change of circumstances happen to make it eligible, you shall hear from me. I own I wish you cou'd make some little Excursion, as change of Air and Place are good undoubtedly for health, and dissipate the mind properly. Cou'd not you get Mr Pretyman, your Friend Doctor Glynn, or some other Person, for I name at Random, to go a Party with you for Four or Five days to see Places that have something worth seeing?. . . If any agreeable Idea, that is not <u>too</u> expensive, occurs, follow it, that is all I can say further.

William's reply to this letter (which took only a day to reach him) was to be expected. No shadow of disappointment he will have felt is expressed. The maturity of his sentiments is breathtaking, given his age of sixteen and two months:

Pembroke Hall
Wednesday July 19th 1775

I have this instant received your most kind letter of Yesterday, and will not lose a minute in thanking you for it. . . It wou'd have given me real pleasure, you will I am sure believe, to have seen you for a short time, but I can easily imagine, and partly apprehended when I mentioned it, that Circumstances might make it better to suspend the Idea. I assure you that the Accounts I have given of myself are quite honest, and that I am in the fullest Extent of the Words, perfectly well. Cambridge being so propitious to Health, and agreeable in every Circumstance, I am by no means impatient to quit it with any other view than that of seeing absent

Friends, and shall by no means be in pain if no opportunity for any considerable Excursion shou'd offer. . . There are some places however in the Neighbourhood, which will make a very good object for a day's Expedition, and which my good Friend Dr Glynn has proposed to me to make a party to see, and I accepted.

William returned home in mid-September. Back at Cambridge the following May, he writes on the 10th, after the usual concerns about Chatham's illness:

> the only thing I have to add of myself is, that I have acquir'd the important Title in this Place of Master of Arts, which the Time I have spent at the University gives one [as a matter] of Course.

His letters from Cambridge for the remainder of the year 1776 continue on the same lines as those of the previous two years, with the same emphasis on the news about which his mother or Harriot write from home but now perhaps with a little bit more about his own affairs:

Pemb. Hall
May 27th 1776

My Dear Mother
You will easily judge, that I was much concerned to find from Harriot's Letter, that the Negligence of the Post had given you uneasiness on my account, and in consequence will naturally imagine that I had great pleasure in hearing from you Yesterday that you had received my last, which had removed all anxiety. How much I grieve that your letter was not equally satisfactory in your account of my Father, is a Subject I need not dwell upon and indeed that I have unhappily had too much occasion to dwell on already. I say no more on that, than that I am most truly impatient to hear, how far Doctor Addington's hopes are realis'd by the effect of the new medicine, and leave the subject to repeat the same good account of myself, that I have before given you. It is impossible to enjoy more the Comfort of perfect Health than I do, and if my satisfaction depended only on Circumstances here, it wou'd be as impossible to enjoy more Pleasure. In the Article of riding, so connected with both, I hope my Wishes are likely to be successfull, as I have had the good fortune to see a horse which I think will answer my Purpose, and of which I have a very good Character. His height is I believe rather above fourteen hands and a half, and his appearance genteel. The age is six years old, and the Price 20 guineas, so that if upon strict Examination and Trial, he should turn out what he seems I shall think myself very happy in making the purchase.
Your most dutiful and affectionate son
W Pitt

Pembroke Hall
September 4th 1776

I arriv'd here yesterday, as I intended, after a journey of which I have nothing to say but that the continued rain gave me reason every moment to rejoice that I perform'd it in a Post-Chaise. I find the University very empty, as expected, but not quite solitary. Besides Mr. Pretyman, who arrived here the day before me, I have two or three Acquaintance still here, which is sufficient to make it by no means dull. The only melancholy Circumstance is the Weather, which still continues unfavourable to every thing but the Partridges.

> Pemb. Hall
> Oct 2nd 1776

> The Particular Motive for my writing to you arises from the approach of the Time in which it is necessary for me to pay the annual Sum to my Tutors and discharge College Bills for the Summer, the amount of which you will I know wish to be inform'd of some time before, and I shou'd be glad to be enabl'd to do it about the Tenth of this Month, I wou'd defer applying to you any longer. I am afraid a less Sum than £100 will not be sufficient for the Purpose, tho' that is greater than I wish, and rather more than I expected.

> Pembroke Hall
> Wednesday Nov 27th 1776

> I am very much concern'd to find from the letter I have this moment receiv'd from you that you have had so much uneasiness on the subject on which you write. I wish I could give you any satisfactory information on the subject but as I have not seen my Brother, nor heard anything of him since I receiv'd the letter before mention'd, It is altogether out of my power. You will see from this that I do not know where to direct a letter to reach him, but I will certainly write to him tomorrow and address the letter to Belvoir to your direction.

Thus begins the reliance his mother placed in the willing and capable hands of her second son, and which lasted until her death; a burden born by him with no hint of resentment but which will have added to the punishing load of his years as head of state.

The Pitts were a united family and Hester Chatham's treatment of her five children was even-handed. But devoted mother as she was, her love for her eldest and youngest sons did not blind her to their defects as they grew towards manhood, minor though these were. John's tendency to enjoy overmuch the rakish life of the Rutland household at Cheveley, worried her; the house was too near Newmarket for her comfort. Contrast the tone of her letters to William with the draft of one to John, written to him on his first military assignment to North America in 1775. The letter begins 'My dear Pitt' and contains this admonition:

> ... Where this letter may find you is absolutely impossible for me to have any idea about. I can therefore venture upon no advice to you, but that of entreating you to be sure in every part of you to take care that your actions shou'd be consistent with your Honor. That They may be so, determine nothing without the Advice of those persons whose knowledge, whose Honor and whose Heart are chiefly to be trusted.

Whatever his mother's private thoughts on the character of her eldest son, all the evidence shows that William deeply loved him, and fostered his career when he certainly knew that John was not capable of the public roles he later accorded him. And he turned to John when his own political career was in some disarray, at the time of his resignation in 1801; their friendship through the years never wavered.

For the first time William now writes to his mother at length and with enthusiasm on an academic subject:

Pemb. Hall
Novr 10th 1776

I wish to mention a Subject to you on which I shall be impatient to know your Decision. . . a Course of Lectures is to be begun in a few days on Civil Law, which I shou'd be very happy to attend, if I thought you wou'd have no objection to my remaining Here during the time they are to continue, that is, till the 16th of next month. What makes me very anxious to attend them, is that I recollect my Father was some time ago very desirous that I shoud if I coud be at Cambridge at the time of these being read, as Lord Camden had recommended it to him as a proper introduction to the study of English Law. I am the more eager to do it because I apprehend it may be right for me before long to enter upon the latter, and consequently if I omit this opportunity of laying the Foundation, the Purpose of it may be entirely defeated. The Sum to be given to the Professor of Civil Law is five Guineas, which I believe you will agree with me in thinking will not be ill employd, if you shoud approve of the proposal in other respects.

This letter, perhaps more than most, illustrates the total degree of control which Hester Chatham now exercised over William's life. Chatham, though frail and depressed, had not lost his mind; at times he recovered enough to ride out, and some three weeks before his death eighteen months later, was attempting to speak in a House of Lord's debate when he collapsed. How was it then that this essentially submissive woman of no outstanding intellect was able to find the moral and physical strength to take on this commanding role in the lives and fortunes of those members of her family, including her husband, who had not moved out of her immediate sphere? The full answer to this question may never be known. It rests in the mysterious element in some natures called courage.

William spent a fourth university year, 1777, with gaps, at Cambridge. He began also to keep terms at Lincoln's Inn as a student barrister; his first letter of the year is from Nerot's Hotel in King Street, St James's, an address which was to head most of his letters from London for the next year or two.

Hotel, King Street
[1777 Feb 30th]

I found yesterday on going to Lincoln's Inn at the usual time, that the Hall was empty, as they dine at two o'clock on Sunday, of which I was not appris'd. This makes it necessary for me to appear today and tomorrow, on which account I must beg you to defer sending the Carriage till Wednesday morning, early in which we shall be able to leave London.

With the return of brother John from America, he and William were often together and many letters of this time, as that above, make use of the pronoun 'we'. John's continued stay at Cheveley so near to Cambridge made frequent contact between the brothers possible: 'Pitt's being weather bound at Cheveley' he writes a few days earlier.

This year saw an improvement in Chatham's health; he was able to ride again and to attend the House of Lords. He could also tolerate visitors at Hayes: the Mahons, John Pitt who had based himself at home, and others. William however was reluctant to leave Cambridge.

Pembroke Hall
March 19th 1777

Probably you continue to approve of my Idea of not leaving my Station here this Vacation, as I think it will in every respect answer better than any other Plan. Every circumstance here is agreeable to my inclinations, as it always has been, and the change of my Lodging, tho' it has placed me in one less magnificent, I am easily reconcil'd to, as it is attended with no real Inconvenience. . . As the end of the quarter approaches, I propose to send you an account of my Finances, as I know you would wish to see what is necessary, but as I have not yet been able to get the Bill for the furniture of my new Rooms, which will have a principal share, I have not [been] able to execute my intention today, but will trouble you with a Letter, as soon as I am able to make my Computation. . . I know your kind Feelings upon [this subject] and trust you are prepared that I endeavour to make the only Return I can for them, by incurring no unnecessary expense. I will trouble you to give my love to Pitt and Harriot, not forgetting my Friend Pam.

William's expenses at Cambridge were rising and much of his correspondence with his mother is about the need for money to pay his quarterly bills. By now he knew well the terrible state of the Chatham finances, and it cost him dear to have to ask her constantly for funds.

Pemb. Hall
June 30th 1777

I take the first moment I can to resume the subject. . . and to inform you of the state of my account. I can not help feeling the Subject very unpleasant, because I fear my demands may be attended with difficulty and inconvenience, but trusting that you must be convinc'd how much I wish to avoid that, as well as how careful I shall always be in consequence, to incur no unnecessary Expense, I will not detain you by saying anything superfluous. If I discharge all my bills at present it will require an Addition not less I fear than 60£, which will make the whole of my expense this Quarter, amount to something greatly more than it ought. This proceeds partly from my having to pay somewhat beside the current expenses of a Quarter's Residence, both for the furniture of my Rooms and for my Taylor's bill. . . The Commencement day is tomorrow, after which the Vacation begins, and the Commencement Ball tonight. I expect Pitt from Cheveley this Afternoon, to take his place there, among the Beaus of the University.

Later in the year, William has been lured, presumably by John, to Cheveley, and hastens to tell his mother of his host, Lord Granby's pleased reaction to a message from Chatham:

Pemb. Hall
Nov 4th 1777

If it is not inconvenient, I believe I must trouble you before my Departure to favour me with the sum of £40, for the Purpose of discharging my Bills.

I return'd from a visit of a couple of days to Ld Granby about a week ago and exchang'd the nocturnal occupations of the Card Table, for the sober Hours and Studies of College. Lord Granby seem'd highly pleas'd with a Message from my Father, and was full of the hopes of seeing Him. . . before his intended Expedition to Belvoir.

If Hester Chatham was alarmed at this news, she need not have been. The short life ahead of her seventeen year old son was to be spent far, far from card tables. His host, who succeeded as fourth duke of Rutland in 1779, became lord lieutenant of Ireland five years later, dying, it is thought of drink and overeating, in Dublin three years after his appointment, aged thirty-three.

Towards the end of the year and in the first two months of 1778, William took every opportunity of visits to London to keep his terms at Lincoln's Inn and to listen to debates in the Commons, confirming his direction towards a political career. He was frustrated when debarred by distance from attendance.

Pembroke Hall
Tuesday Feb. 17th 1778

I have nothing interesting of any kind from Hence, and expect every thing of that kind from London. Among many other subjects, the Debate in the House of Commons to Day has occur'd to me frequently. On the supposition that Lord North was to produce his Plan (for I know not what Epithet it is to take) I have wish'd much to transport myself into the gallery of the House of Commons. I am condemn'd however. . . to know nothing of it, but as it is transform'd in the News Paper.

After Chatham's death, William returned in due course to his Cambridge college, where he remained based, but often away, for the next twenty months. He is still dependent on his mother for funds and has, additionally, now to ask her for the substantial sum of £1,100 to buy the lease of a set of rooms in Stone Buildings in Lincoln's Inn, (later paid by his uncle, Lord Temple):

[Nerot's] Hotel
King Street
Thursday Dec 31st 1778

I am much concern'd if your Goodness in furnishing me with the necessary supply is productive of inconvenience to you; and still more so if, from not being acquaint'd with all the Circumstances, you imagine I was precipitate in closing the Bargain, before I heard from you a Second Time on the subject. The Truth was, that I was desired to give a final answer immediately, which I cou'd no longer defer doing, as as it therefore became necessary either to relinquish the Scheme entirely or to secure Purchase without loss of Time, I [therefore] did not hesitate to prefer the latter, after receiving your first Letter, which brought me your full Concurrence and Approbation. . .

In this same letter he writes at length about his brother James, now aged seventeen, on leave from Portsmouth.

James is himself writing to you and from Him you will learn that his leave is expiring and that there is no possibility of his absenting Himself any longer. I regret most truly, and I am sure he does, that he cannot now make another Visit to you at Burton; but I know Captain Hood seem'd to think He cou'd by no means defer returning to Portsmouth longer than tomorrow. The scene which will be opening there is indeed in many respects a most distressful one, but I do not suppose any thing is to be apprehended from his being mix'd in it. As far as my judgment can go, I think I may answer for his conducting himself in his Situation with perfect propriety, and in the way of his Profession. . . I am sure he will have all the Caution and Delicacy you recommend to Him, both from his own feelings, and out of Attention to your Admonitions. I can not say how much pleasure and Satisfaction I have had in meeting Him, and finding in Him every thing I cou'd wish.

And continues about his quarterly allowance:

I am sorry also to say that the end of the Quarter will make me in want of money before I can leave Cambridge. The large Demands which I have just been obliged to make, and what you tell me of the State of Affairs, renders me very unwilling to trouble you on this subject; but I trust entirely to your Goodness on this occasion. If you can favour me with a Draft for £50, it will be sufficient for the purpose. . .

He expects within a short time after his return from Cambridge that she

may depend upon my setting out for Burton. It will give me very real Satisfaction if I contribute at all to yours, and I shall be very happy to continue with you as long as I am able. The Term at Lincoln's Inn, which will be in the Beginning of February is the only Call that is at all likely to interfere. I need not say that I shall be very glad to escort Harriot either in her Village Airings, or in her Progress to London, but in the latter, I shall not easily reconcile my mind to the Idea of leaving you the only Inhabitant of Burton.

Responsibility for the much loved sister Harriot arises on her next London visit in the following spring: 'I slept last night for Harriot's Protection in Harley Street [the Mahon's London house] but have now removed to my former Habitation' (Nerot's Hotel, 8th Mar 1779). In this same year a letter from London encapsulates all the many family responsibilities, including his mother's entitlement to a pension or grant voted by Parliament at Chatham's death, which now fell upon a young man not yet twenty years old, but yet cannot swamp his burgeoning interest in public affairs.

[Nerot's] Hotel
King Street
Thursday Feb 11th [1779]

My dear Mother
I flatter myself a letter from me may not be unwelcome, tho it can not have the merit of much news to recommend it, neither of a public or private Sort. To begin with the second, which I believe pretty generally claims Precedence, nothing has, I am afraid yet been obtain'd on the subject of the Arrears [of the grant]. I saw Mr Coutts on Tuesday, who told me that Mr Craufurd had been ill, which had delay'd the presenting of the Memorial but that he now expected to hear of its effect every day. I shall renew my Enquiry in a short Time, and wish I may receive a favourable Account of the Seven Quarters [in arrears]. Since I wrote last I have had a letter from my Brother [John, in Gibraltar] dated Jan 9th, still hoping to set out in about Three Weeks from that Time. I have heard nothing fresh on the Subject of Lord and Lady Mahon's moving but I have no doubt of its not being long Postponed. I am to meet my Sister [Hester Mahon] at Hayes on the Subject of your

Commission, as soon as she can find a leisure moment. Her great Business is that of Secretary to Lord Mahon, whose Electricity is almost ready for the Press, and will rank Him I suppose with Dr. Franklin. I have just been dining with a Brother Philosopher of his, Dr. Priestley, at Shelburne House. His Lordship is very cordial with his Enquiries after you and if you continue in the West till next Summer, will think it his Duty to make them in Person at Burton. He is very obliging to me. Lord Camden I have not yet seen, but will call at his Door again in a day or two.

The Sentence of the Court martial is already anticipated Here, and the actual Account expected every Hour. Great Preparations for Illuminations and every Mark of Joy - Keppel's Triumph is indeed complete. All seems agreed that Lord Sandwich is to leave the Admiralty. Lord G[eorge] Germain and Lord Suffolk are also it is imagined going with their Laurels about them, to honourable Retirement. But I mention none of this as at all certain. Lord Howe has been talked of for the Admiralty, but it seems pretty clear that he will never accept while Lord George continues. Keppel himself is mentioned for this Post, and if the Change begins it cannot be said where it will stop. At present I believe things are totally unfix'd in every Quarter. The call of the House is today and when People's minds are no long confin'd to Portsmouth, Business will probably return again to its Channel. The Clamour against our Friend [Capt Alexander Hood] is I fear very general and the Affair is not yet fully explained. Till the Thing is more clear'd his Friends have I think nothing to do but to avoid Particulars, and rest on the general Conviction of his Honor and integrity. I have seen Mrs Hood who seems composed and tolerably well.

Pray give my kindest Love to Harriot. The Sadler at Sherborne or Salisbury has I hope done his duty. You will have the goodness to excuse the Haste of a letter written on my way to the Opera.

I am, my Dear Mother, your most dutiful
and affectionate
W Pitt

I must not forget my Friend Pam

A month later, 9th March, he is writing at length on actions he has taken 'in consequence of your directions' mainly about, some would say, the regrettable and unkind decision to remove James from their good friend Captain Alexander Hood's ship *Robust* following that officer's evidence given at the Keppel court martial, when he admitted to altering the logbook before appearing at court. While advocating this course of action, William obviously felt some unhappiness:

> The Measure which seems to us absolutely requisite is that of removing <u>my Brother immediately from the Robust</u>: and tho it seems at first a disagreeable step to take, I am fully persuaded that when you have considered every Circumstance, you will not see one possible objection. I own I had from my own Feelings, the greatest Reluctance to bring my Friends to this Idea, and you know how much in the earlier stage of the Business, my Opinion and Inclination was against it: but as the Matter now stands I am firmly convinc'd after consulting all the Opinions I cou'd, and viewing it in all its Lights, that there is <u>actually no Choice left</u>, without involving ourselves and James in endless difficulties. . .
>
> The Grounds on which I rest my opinion are various; the first is a point in which we shall agree with you is that of the <u>Necessity of putting a Final Stop to James's Indiscretions in Conversation and Behaviour</u>. On this it occurs [to me], that it will be very difficult to remove his prejudices and to make him continue in a proper Disposition, while he remains in a Ship, which (whatever it professes) must always be hostile to Admiral Keppel.

But even in this difficulty William is already confident that he can sort things out and does not shrink from a difficult task:

> The best mode perhaps might be if you approve of it, for you to write what you think proper in a Letter to me which I might communicate myself to Capt. Hood. I think it clear that if you take this determination, it cannot be executed <u>but</u> on the Spot: and I am very confident that by going there, I could both reconcile James's mind entirely to what he may be prejudic'd against, and state it to C. Hood in such a manner as not to leave him dissatisfi'd with the Proceeding.

In the event, James was removed from *Robust*, Hood and his wife were deeply hurt and the friendship lapsed for many years.

Hester Chatham's letters to James are missing, but two from him to his mother are significant and reveal a disticly severe approach absent from her letters to the impeccable William at about the same age. She is concerned with James's excessive, at times embarrassing ambition for naval promotion, overlooking perhaps his whole upbringing under the shadow of financial problems. He was born in 1761 towards the end of his father's golden years of fame, and at the beginning of the decline of the family into chronic debt. In a letter from his ship *Greyhound* at Spithead dated 18th November 1779, he writes in obvious agitation and with little regard for grammar and punctuation:

> I am extremely sorry that you do not imagine that I have entered into the Idea of my Friends wishing every thing that was best for me, and being ready to exert themselves for my advantage, when they cou'd do it with Propriety, as I assure you I am thoroughly convinc'd that they have at all times my Interest perfectly at heart... I am extremely grieved that the situation of affairs at these times is such as to prevent, at present, their using their interest for me which I do not in least fear they otherwise wou'd, very readily have made use of in my Favour; as it obliges me to lay aside all Idea of Promotion, which I confess I do not think it extraordinary the Degree of ambition I am possess's of, had made my great and indeed first Object ever since I return'd home.

One month later, shortly before sailing to the West Indies, he writes:

> Dear Mother
> I did not receive your Letter of the 5th till yesterday, it not having reach'd London before my Departure from thence; which I now take the first opportunity of answering, being extremely hurt at the Contents of it; and being determined not to lose a moment in endeavouring to clear my Conduct to you, which you have judged so wrong; and to convince you that the Duty and Affection which I owe you and which I ever have felt for you, has not nor ever can be diminish'd...

He then goes on to say that he is

> shocked and mortifyed beyond measure in perceiving your whole Letter to contain disapprobation of my conduct and even doubts of my Affection. I am not concious in what I have acted with so much impropriety; and I am positively certain that <u>no one of your Family</u> possesses a more firm and sincere affection for you than I do... You make me also I assure you extremely unhappy in doubting that my wishes to see you were real which you seem to do by telling me that it is

<u>Actions</u> and not a few tender expressions that are the Proofs of Affection and duty. I did not conceive that you cou'd have imagined that I cou'd have been so totally devoid of every good Principle, and so unnatural as to have my affection consist in mere words and not in Actions. God knows the sincere and ardent affection of my heart for you.

The long letter continues with protests and explanations: 'The reason of my not writing to you till the later part of my stay in London was that I had nothing particular to communicate to you' and ends, as do all his letters 'Your affectionate and dutiful son, Charles James Pitt.' He sailed for the West Indies at the end of October, and several letters were to follow in 1780 from St. Lucia to St. Kitts. His last letter written from his sloop *Hornet*, to the command of which he had been appointed shortly after arrival is dated English Harbour, Antigua, 1st November 1780. They have taken two prizes and he has received 'seven hundred pounds which is no bad beginning'. He is avid for further promotion and he 'trusts it may possibly take place in some Line of Battle of ship, as that woud enable me to have a share in any contest'.

But the greatest contest of all was to come that same month: he died of fever aged only nineteen. It is probable that his mother received this last letter after his death.

William continued as a frequent and dutiful letter writer during his final year and a half at Cambridge. In the month of July 1779 alone, he wrote to his mother five times. He loved the university and was reluctant finally to cease the connection.

Pembroke Hall
April 19th 1779

I shall be very glad to have the Interruption of my Residence here at this Time, as short as possible, being excessively happy in finding myself return'd at Leisure to the Pursuits of a Cambridge life.

Apart from a few interesting sidelights on university post-graduate life, a clear picture emerges from these letters of the blossoming politician. He had hoped for selection for the university seat itself, and having obtained his mother's consent entered his candidature. He came bottom of the poll, but was philosophical about his failure to be chosen. He is still painfully dependent on his mother for funds, and the need to have to ask for money every quarter, or more frequently if unusual expenses arose, and the consequent inability to plan his expenditure in advance, give rise to a situation hard to imagine today.

Pembroke Hall
June 28th 1779

. . . one other Subject indeed I have to mention which without any Vanity with regard to the former [his good health] must I believe be the less welcome of the two. I mean that which is produc'd by the arrival of Quarter Day. It becomes necessary to me to apply to you for a further supply, and if you can have the Goodness to furnish me with a Draft for a Hundred Pounds, it will not be much more than will in a little time be requisite. I am afraid this may appear a large Sum, but the economical Summer Months will I hope make up for the expense of the five or six last. . .

> This Place has so many Advantages for study, and I have unavoidably lost so much Time lately, and can spare so little in the Future, that I cannot help wishing to continue here a considerable Part of the Summer.

William's long student years at Cambridge were ending but not his association with the university: four years after leaving he became its parliamentary member and it remained his seat for the rest of his life.

With an eye to his future career, he writes on December 27th that he has hurried back to college from London

> as Christmas Day is here the Beginning of a sort of Publick Time, at which in my Capacity it is proper for me to be present. College Feasts are the principle Business just now attended to in the University, which I so far like as they give me an opportunity of cultivating Acquaintance which I may find useful. The Time too passes not unpleasantly as there is a good deal of Society, and yet a good deal of Leisure.

Urged no doubt by his mother, he has had some sort of medical examination:

> Pembroke Hall
> Jan 3rd 1780

> The Charge of looking slender and thin when the Doctor saw me, I do not entirely deny: but if it was in a greater Degree than usual, It may fairly be attributed to the hurry of London and an accidental Cold at the time. Both these Causes have equally ceased on my Removal hither, and as my Way of Life has ever since been as fattening as any one could desire, I believe I now possess as much Embonpoint as I have naturally any right to. I had followed the doctor's Advice by drinking Asses Milk before I received your Letter; and so easy a Prescription I have no objection to obeying, though I believe it unnecessary, for some time longer. The use of the Horse, I assure [you] I do not neglect, is the properest Medium; and a sufficient number of idle Avocations secure me quite enough from the danger of too much study. . . Among the principal Occupations of Cambridge at this Season of Christmas, are perpetual College Feasts; a species of exercise in which, above all others I shall not forget your Rule of Moderation.

In his last letter from Cambridge of 24th January, William is once again where his heart perpetually lies, in family affairs. His brother John's regiment had been unexpectedly ordered on foreign service and William therefore felt obliged to take a

> rapid flight to London that I might have a Chance of catching him before he set out. . . I had on my first Intelligence left Cambridge so hastily, that I have been obliged to return, tho' but for a few days, in order to wind up my Business here.

At the age of twenty-one, William Pitt was intellectually mature. He still had much to learn and being essentially a modest man, he took any opportunity which presented to avail himself of knowledge and training, always with the single object in view, that of political competence. So much for his mind. Of the development of his spirit, of his emotions, the story differs. We look in vain to the continuous correspondence with his mother for a clue to his inner nature, to his deepest feelings, to his life's philosophy. In essence his letters to her after leaving Cambridge differ little from those he wrote during his university years. There is less comment on the news she writes from home, partly perhaps because Harriot was also in London in the early part of 1780 and she would have shared with him the news from their mother. William divided his time between Grafton Street, where Harriot lodged with her cousin Charlotte Williams Wynn, and his rooms in Lincoln's Inn. For the first time he is evidently enjoying some social life of the town, but essentially as an onlooker rather than as participant.

Lincoln's Inn
Feb 9th [1780]

My dear Mother
It is so long since I wrote to you [Jan 24th] that I am determin'd not to let this Post go without a Letter from me, tho I have not time to trouble it with a very voluminous one. You will I hope have excused my trusting intirely to your most constant Correspondent Harriot for your knowing that I was established in Town. I have really been a good deal engaged, and in some Measure necessarily, having begun to attend as a Lawyer in Westminster Hall, to which I confess has also been added occasionally the less professional Pursuit of Opera, Pantheon etc, etc. so that my time between Business and Pleasure may be fully accounted for. I am now going to a Scene where both are united, I mean the House of Lords who are to enter today on the Consideration of Lord Shelburne's Motion. The Pleasure of it would be a good deal heighten'd, if there were any present prospect of its having a considerable Effect. The Ground is certainly very strong; and some Accessions to the minority are expected; but I fear there is little Chance of their being for some time numerous enough to turn into a majority.
I am, my dear Mother's most dutiful
and affectionate
W Pitt

In this letter the topic of the family's long-running battle with the Treasury is again raised, to pay Lady Chatham the annual grant voted by Parliament to her at her husband's death, the money for which had to be found from the 4½ per cents dependent on the fleet arrivals from the West Indies, receipts from which were initially several quarters in arrears. It naturally fell to William to be the chief negotiator, not always with success; and for many years, until at last the procedure was regularised, few of his letters fail to mention this and other financial worries, hers and his own. The letter continues:

Harriot has shewn me your Letters on the Subject of the Interest etc, which explain the Business very clearly and satisfactorily. Mr Coutts tells me that he had a long letter from you on the subject, and expects a Paper by Wood, which is all he wants further. Having some necessary Bills to pay for my Rooms here, I have received an Advance (according to what we before settled) of £100, to be repaid when Lord Temple [cousin] pays the £1000 [his legacy from his late uncle]. Lord Temple has been a few days in Town, I have call'd upon him but not found him. We hear various Reports of the Destination of my Brother's Regiment, but not to be relied on. I have some hope however that [they] may be exchanged in the

Passage for Regiments already abroad, and be stationed nearer home than the Leeward Islands. I am very sorry to think that the Arrangement for Harriot throws a new obstacle in the way of my seeing you, but when that is removed there can I trust be nothing to delay it longer.

Grafton Street
April 4th 1780

I had not time by the Post to thank you for your kind letter. I hope I need not assure you how much reluctance I have had in again deferring my long intended Visit to Burton, but on the whole, all Circumstances considered, as you consent to my putting it off till May, I think I must postpone it till that Time. Next Thursday will be a most important day. The whole Matter of the Petitions will come to be considered in the House of Commons, and I suppose during the Holidays, both Sides have been preparing for this great question, with Arguments and Numbers. It does not seem yet quite clear in what Points of Political Reform the several Countries who have petitioned, and the different Parties that support them, will be brought to concur. Some as it is expected in such a case, wish to make it more, and some less extensive. . .

Last night was the Masquerade, the Pompous Promises of which the Newspapers must have carried to Burton. Harriot went with Lady Williams to Mrs Weddel's (who is I believe a Sister of Lady Rockingham) to see Masks. She was very much pleased with it, principally I fancy because it was the first thing of its kind she had seen. I was there as well as at a much more numerous Assemblage, at a Magnificent Mrs. Broadhead's which some few Ladies did not like to go, from little Histories relative to the Lady of the House. These did not prevent it being the most crowded Place I ever was in. The Company I was not conversant enough in masks to judge of. I concluded my evening at the Pantheon which I had never seen illuminated, and which is really a glorious Scene. In other respects, as I had hardly the Pleasure of plaguing or being plagued by any body, I was heartily tired of my Domino before it was over.

It was not until towards the end of the year that William is able to tell his mother, almost as an aside, about the firm possibility of a parliamentary seat, Appleby.

Lincoln's Inn
Thursday
[Nov 23rd 1780]

I do not wonder that you seem to consider me rather as an idle Correspondent, which much against my will, I feel I have been. If I had been able to give you any Information worth knowing of what pass'd in Parliament, I certainly would. But really there has been nothing decisive, and all seems to be put off till after Christmas.

I have been out of the Way of hearing Particulars: there have been scarcely any Debates which I have thought worth attending and the general state of Politics seems in absolute Suspense. You will I am sure be ready to excuse a little either of Ignorance or Laziness, when I assure you that ever since Term began, I have been almost every day in Westminster Hall the whole time between Breakfast and Dinner, and that the rest of the day is sufficiently taken up by necessary business and incidental Avocations, which are unavoidable. There is one Piece of News not unconnected with Politics, which I am just enabled to tell you, and which if it turns out as I expect, I think will not be unwelcome. I just [heard] from the Duke of Rutland to whom Sir J Lowther (who is a good deal connected with Him) has expressed a wish of bringing me into Parliament for one of his vacant Buroughs. He has the Command of several, and has returned the same person for more than one, which necessarily creates a Vacancy. He proposes it on the most handsome Terms, and without any expense, merely out of respect for my Father and friendship for the Duke of Rutland. I have not yet seen him, and therefore cannot speak quite positively, but have no doubt of it being perfectly agreeable to my Feelings and Principles.

Lady Chatham's reaction to the news appears to have included a complaint that she was either not told sooner or in greater detail. Her son replies:

Thursday Dec 7th [1780]

I hope you will believe I would not willingly fail mentioning any thing which I thought really worth knowing.

After explanations he continues:

I have not yet received the Notifications of my Election. . . The Parliament adjourned yesterday so I shall not take my Seat until after the Holidays. I shall enter the House with exactly the Ideas you recommend to me, of which I feel the Justness.

The letter ends with a backward look at the constituency he would so dearly have preferred:

I propose before long, in spite of Politics, to make an Excursion for a short Time to Ld Westmorelands, and shall probably look at my Constituents that should have been at Cambridge, in my Way.

And so the 'wonderful boy' was launched. He continued down the years to write to his mother but the letters, though of importance to historians, grow fewer in number and shorter in length as his responsibilities become ever greater and his health less robust. At no point in this unique correspondence is there any hint of deeper feelings, though they would have been present; he was a shy but not a cold man. There is no mention in the surviving letters of the deaths in July 1780 of Hester Mahon, who never recovered from the birth of her last child, Lucy, five months earlier (for whom William stood as godfather), or of James's death in the West Indies at the end of the year. Such omissions are not significant; the letters could have been destroyed or lost. A letter from William early in the following year will have brought more solace to his mother. He writes of his maiden speech:

I know you will have learnt that I heard my own Voice yeaterday; and the Account you have had would be in all respects better than any I can give if it had not come from too partial a Friend. All I can say is that I was able to execute in some measure what I intended, and that I have at least every reason to be happy beyond measure in the reception I met with. You will I dare say wish to know more particulars than I fear I shall be able to tell you, but in the mean time you will I am sure feel somewhat the same Pleasure that I do in the encouragement, however unmerited, which has attended my first Attempt.

And later that year, a three part letter joins his private life with that of his political career, and underlines his continued dependence on his mother for practical help:

Lincoln's Inn
Tuesday Oct 24th [1781]

I went the next morning to Chevening where I had the pleasure to find all extremely well, the little ones looking I think better than I ever saw them and in high Spirits. Lord Mahon has just been in Town for a Couple of days, but is gone back to stay till near the Meetings of Parliament. They continue still in Harley Street...

I somehow or other forgot, when I was at Burton, the East India Treasures in your Possession. I understand it is likely to make a considerable Part of our Business in the Session. If you can conveniently examine, and will have the goodness to bring, any Material Papers on the Subject (especially if there is anything relative to the money which has come to Government) I shall be very much obliged to you. With regard to my Horse, I wish certainly [to] sell Him. If He is pretty well recovered, I should suppose He will fetch much more in this Part of the world; but if he is unsound, probably it may be better to sell Him for whatever He will fetch at Burton. I don't wish to set any Price upon Him, but shall be glad if you will do with Him whatever seems best on the Spot.

Many loves to Harriot...

In the two years before his election as prime minister, William has the time and inclination to write at some length and frequency of his involvement in the cut and thrust of high level politics:

Friday July 5th 1782

You will I am sure be impatient to hear something more from Me. Things appear to be pretty near settled, and on the whole I hope well for the Country, 'tho not precisely as one would have wished. Fox has chosen to resign, on no Ground that I can learn but Lord Shelburnes being placed at the Treasury. Ld J. Cavendish also quits, wch is not surprising as He accepted at first merely on Ld Rockingham's account. Other Inferior Changes will take Place in some Departments, but the Bulk stands firm. My Lot will be either at the Treasury as Chancellor of the Exchequer, or in the Home Department as Secretary of State. The Arrangement cannot be finally settled till tomorrow or next day; but everything promises as well as possible in such Circumstances. Mr Townshend certainly makes part of this fresh Arrangement, and probably in a more forward Post, which is to me an infinite Satisfaction. Lord Shelburne's conduct is everything that could be wish'd. Parliament adjourns in a day or two, and little or nothing can pass there till next Session. The Principal Thing I shall have to regret will be the Probability of this delaying my having the happiness of seeing you, tho' I trust it will not do for the whole Summer.

I am very sorry Mr Coutts has found it necessary to call for his Balance; but the Inconvenience will I trust be remedied. I am excessively obliged to you for the wish of accommodating me, which really was never that I was in any pressing want of, and I shall now be able at <u>least</u> to do perfectly without.

I have written in great haste, and at first with a view to the Post, but I believe it will become more the discretion, which I must now have about me, not to send it by that Conveyance.

The shadow of patronage looms:

Grafton Street
Tuesday July 30th [1782]

I am not able to tell whether I can succeed as I wish for your <u>Welsh</u> <u>Friend</u>. Of all the Secrets of my Office I have in the short time learnt the least about <u>Patronage</u>. I rather believe this Branch belongs almost entirely to the First Lord, tho' certainly Recommendations will have their Weight there. I think I need not say I will try as far as I can with Propriety. Harriot's Request, or rather her Neighbour's (for I certainly do not charge Harriot with being too pressing a Solicitor) is I am afraid of a sort which I cannot much forward; but I will consider whether I can do anything and let her know. In the mean time she may be perfectly assured that I am not yet so tired of being asked, as to take it very ill of Her to have been the Channel of it. . .

[PS.] I expect to be comfortably settled in the Course of this Week, in a <u>Part</u> of my vast, awkward House [10 Downing Street].

And not omitting what she most wants to hear, news of his health and measures to keep fit:

Downing Street
Thusday Sept 12th [1782]

I am much obliged to you for your Letter, which I received yesterday on my Return from Cheveley, where I had been for two days. A short Visit for such a distance; but as my Brother was going there I thought it worth the Exertion, and it was very well repaid by a great deal of Air and Exercise in shooting, and the finest Weather in the World. The finest part of all indeed is a fine East Wind, which as the Fleet is just sailed for Gibraltar is worth everything. I assure you I do not forget the Lessons I have so long followed, of riding in spite of Business, tho' I indeed want it less than ever, as I was never so perfectly well.

Early in 1783, the first of the many great decisions, this one wholly personal, with which William Pitt would be faced for almost all of the remainder of his life, confronted him now. He craves his mother's opinion and advice:

Tuesday morning
½ past nine
[February 25th 1783]

My dear Mother

I wished more than I can express to see you Yesterday. I will if possible find a moment today, to tell you the State of Things and learn your opinion. In the mean Time, the Substance is that our Friends almost universally are eager for our going on, only <u>without</u> Lord Shelburne; and are sanguine in the expectation of success. Lord Shelburne himself most warmly so. The king when I went in yesterday, pressed me in the strongest manner to take Lord Shelburne's Place, and insisted on my not declining it till I had taken Time to consider. You see the Importance of the Decision I must speedily make. I feel all the difficulties of the Undertaking and am by no means in Love with the Object. On the other Hand, I think myself bound not to desert a System in which I am engaged, if probable Means can be shewn of carrying it on with Credit. On this general state of it I should wish anxiously to know <u>what</u> <u>is</u> <u>the</u> <u>Inclination</u> <u>of</u> <u>your</u> <u>mind</u>. I must endeavour to estimate more particularly the probable Issue, by talking with those who know most of the opinions of men in detail. The great Article to decide by, seems that of numbers.

> Yr ever dutiful
> and affectionate
> WP

Hester Chatham's reply is missing, but if what she wrote, or said (she was nearby at Hayes), or if his consultations with those in the know were against acceptance, he refused the offer of the Treasury and bided his time.

An event in this year that could have brought forth letters of outstanding interest, lay in William's first and last excursion abroad, to Rheims and Paris, accompanied by his friend Edward Eliot, later to become his brother-in-law, and William Wilberforce. In all the five letters from France, four to his mother and one to Harriot, he never fails to mention his anxiety to have news from home; the impression is left that only a small part of him was absorbed in his travels, in short that he was homesick.

> Calais
> Sept 12th [1783]

Lest any howling at Burton should have given you the Idea of a Storm, I am impatient to assure you that we are arrived here after a rough but a very prosperous Passage. We shall set out tomorrow, and reach Rheims Sunday night or Monday morning. A letter directed to a Gentilhomme Anglois at La Poste Restante, Rheims, will I find be sure to reach me.

> Rheims
> Sept 18th Thursday [1783]

We arrived here after a Journey, which had little but the Novelty of the country to recommend it. The Travelling was much better than I expected and the appearance of the People more comfortable, but the face of the Country thro' almost all the way from Calais, the dullest I ever saw. . .

The Place is chielfly inhabited by Mercantile People and Ecclesiasticks among whom however I suppose we shall by degrees find some Charitable Persons, who will let us practise our French upon them.

> Hotel de Grande Bretagne
> Paris
> Wednesday Oct 15th [1783]

I am just setting out to Fontainebleau for two or three days, where I shall find the Court and all the Magnificence of France, and with this Expedition I shall finish my Career Here. Since I have been, I had had little to do but to see the Sights, as the King's journey to Fontainebleau has carried all the World from Paris except the English who seem quite in Possession of the Town. I have been in constant Expectation of a Letter from Burton, but the Post has hitherto disappointed me. . . We shall return hither on Sunday and probably set out towards Calais on Tuesday and I hope reach London by the end of the Week. I imagine I shall find the Party assembled at Stowe. . . if so I shall probably join them as soon as I have picked up the News of London.

On 19th December 1783 William became First Lord of the Treasury and Chancellor of the Exchequer, at twenty-four the youngest prime minister in British history. The first letter to his mother following this momentous event characteristically is concerned with her health and ends with an excuse for his brother John's notorious laziness.

Berkeley Square
Dec 30th 1783

I steal at Length one moment from my Business to my Wishes, and employ it in thanking you a thousand times for your letter. I need not tell you how much I am concerned to find that it was written from your Bed. But I trust you will keep the Promise which interests us all so much, of being soon quite well. I hope I shall soon have the satisfaction of hearing from you, tho I cannot be sure when I may be able to write again. You will easily believe it is not from Inclination I have been silent for so long. I enclose you Mrs Boscawen's Letter again which did amply pay for reading. Things are in general more promising than they have been, but in the uncertainty of Effect. The Persuasion of not being wrong is, as you say, the best Circumstance, and Enough, tho' there is a Satisfaction in the Hopes at least of Something More. My Brother would have written to you tonight, if I had not taken the Pen from out of his Hands.
Adieu my dear Mother.

One further tragedy lay in store for Hester Chatham and her son, the death in childbirth of the beloved daughter and sister, Harriot, now the wife of Edward Eliot. She died after five days of illness, faithfully recorded day by day by William to his mother, from his house in Downing Street where the Eliots had come to live with him. And finally:

Downing Street
Tuesday Sept 26th [1786]

I will not suffer myself, at this sad moment, my Dear Mother, to express my own feelings, which I know are but too deeply yours also. My anxious hope is that your strength may enable you to support the Shock with a Fortitude of Mind equal to so trying an Occasion, and to your Sentiments of Tenderness and Affection. Your Goodness to me will Make it a sort of Relief to you, in the interval till we meet, to know that severely as my Mind must be wounded, my Health has not suffered from the Blow we have sustained. I should not lose a Moment, you will believe, in coming to Burton, but I am sure you will approve of my not leaving poor Eliot at this Time, for whom We have all, and I most especially, so many affecting Reasons to interest us. His mind begins to be as composed as could yet be expected; and a few days will I hope bring his Brother from Cornwall, which will make me consider myself more at Liberty. I will add no more now. My earnest Wishes and Prayers are ever with you.

A few letters survive, written in old age, from Hester Chatham to her son. All contain requests for William's help in placements for her local friends, or jobs and promotion for their young relations. Her widowhood, as in the latter years of marriage, was beset about with debt and many, though not all of these Somerset friends, were also her creditors. The survival of these few letters is probably due to William's need to be reminded of her requests. They illustrate, both in the firmness of the handwriting and in their composition, the endurance of her mental poise, at least until her eightieth year when the last letter was written:

Burton Pynsent
Monday June 10th 1799

My dear son

It is by no means my wish to trouble you at this moment of Business with a Letter, but I feel it impossible to secure myself from sending to you <u>one</u> that I have received from your old Friend Doctor Dumaresq. You, I am sure, will be struck with it when you think of his age of 87, and will manage that assistance for him which has become so very necessary to him. Unfortunately, a mistake of my kind secretary [Mrs Stapleton] about the Post, has delay'd its being forwarded the day it ought to have been. The Weather being less oppressive this morning, I insisted upon using my own Pen that I might not interfere with her ride, and farming affairs, which add also to the amusement of your dear niece [Lady Hester Stanhope]. I am charged with an humble petition from poor Alford who is very ill, tho' just now a little better but not likely to last the present summer. His son <u>Thomas</u> the <u>seaman</u> is pass'd for a Lieut. He has been aboard Captain Wolley who is <u>excessivley</u> fond of him, and very sorry to lose him, but he is already provided with Lieuts. The opinion is that there are many Lieuts wanted, and that Woolley, who admires him so much, is to be sure most likely to recommend him to Lord Spencer, who is a relation, and is liked and in great favour with his Lordship. Poor Alford thinks that a <u>Word</u> from you wou'd be the <u>Thing of Things</u> by mention of him on the present occasion, if there was no objection to it. It will rather surprise me that Wolley, who is a constant correspondent of Lord Spencer should not name him <u>with</u> <u>his</u> <u>merits</u> which are certainly very uncommon... You will judge whether it will be agreeable to you. I dont intend to make my Letter longer than just to tell you what a very real and most Flattering Pleasure I have enjoy'd in consequence of the delightful letter I received from Lord Camden, than which nothing cou'd be more expressive towards my Family and my self. Now my Beloved William I add no more than that I remain ever

Your most affectionate Mother
H Chatham

William Pitt was a good son; some might say today that he was over devoted to his mother. He never married. His only tentative advance into suitorship, which finds no reference in the correspondence, was his shortlived friendship with Eleanor Eden from which, according to Stanhope and other biographers, Pitt was the one who retreated, implying though not stating in a tortuous letter to the young woman's father, his neighbour Lord Auckland, his financial difficulties. Another biographer, Rosebery, thought he lacked what would now be called sexual drive. Whatever the reason for his single state (and there is no shred of evidence that he was homosexual), one aspect of his inner life is paramount; his intense love of and preoccupation with his mother, sisters and brothers. From them he derived the deepest emotional dependence; on him, for the most part, they depended for all their needs.

After the death of her husband, Hester Chatham lived on for another twenty-five years. Her widowhood was spent at Burton Pynsent except for half-yearly visits to

Hayes until its sale in 1783. She enjoyed good health and a full life. Her correspondence with friends and relations was enormous. She had terrible sorrows to meet; but she also gained great pleasure, interest and consolation from the marvellous career of her son William - 'William the Great' - as she prophetically called him in a letter written to her husband shortly after his birth. His early death at forty-seven in January 1806 occurred fortunately three years after hers: thus was she spared the supreme sorrow of her old age.

APPENDIX I

BURTON PYNSENT

In February 1803 Hester Chatham was an infirm old lady of 82. Anticipating her death in the near future, her eldest son John, second Earl of Chatham had the estate surveyed and valued. The resulting 'Estimate' runs to several pages of figures. It is extraordinarily detailed: for example each lawn is separately listed and valued. Here is the summary of the valuation:[1]

Febry 1803
Estimate of Purton Pynsent in the County of Somerset with the Lands in Domesne and the Farms thereof belonging, the Property of the Right Honble the Countess of Chatham

RECAPITULATION

			£ s d	£ sd
1	Mansion House part of the Lawn		205.14.0	
2	Home Farm	Mr Bellamy Sen[r]	409.16.6	
3	Moreton Farm	Mr Bellamy Jun[r]	360.10.0	
4	Poelbottom Farm....	Sam[l] Hopkins Ten[t]	227. 5.3	
5	Vaggo Farm	Tho[s] Denham Ten[t]	87.10.0	
6	At Old Street	W[m] Baker Ten[t]	2.12.0	
7	Owl Street		93. 0.0	
8	D[o]		3.10.0	
9	M[rs] Stapleton's Dairy		173 . 5.0	

Total   £1562.12.9

In his book *Social History of Curry Rivel in the 19th Century*, the late Mr A O Mounter gives details of the ensuing sale, extracted from the auctioneers' prospectus:

'Burton Estate Sale,
   Following his mother's death in 1803 Lord Chatham lost little time in putting Burton Estate on the market. The auction sale took place at Garroway's Coffee House, Cornhill, London on 16th October 1804 it was conducted by Messrs Skinner Dyke and Co.
   The property was described as *"a Capital and truly Valuable Freehold Estate in the parishes of Curry Rivel, Drayton, Fivehead and Swell bounded by West Sedgmoor in Somersetshire, Containing about 1100 acres of fertile, Meadow, Grazing, Arable, Wood Land and Orcharding. Forming one of the most Noble Estates in the County, Abundantly stocked with capital Oak,*

[1] PRO 30/8/71/5

Elm, and other timber trees of very large dimensions. The whole estate is capable of the greatest improvement, and upon an inclosure of West Sedgmoor and other moors, containing several thousand acres over which there are many valuable rights, the rental will be very valuably increased and in point of situation no property is more eligible for a residence or farm."

It was offered in thirteen lots:

Lot 1. Burton Pynsent Mansion.
*   described as of modern brick structure, the remainder Ancient Gothic containing,*

A large entrance Hall, Servant's Waiting Room etc.
A Dining Room 34 feet by 31 feet.
A Ballroom 60 feet by 27.
A Second Drawing Room and Grotto room.
A Library 36 feet by 19.
The Bird Room 24 feet by 20.
South Parlour or Morning Sitting Room.
Several Waiting and Passage Rooms.
Two Stone Staircases.
Twenty Chambers Dressing Rooms, a Part of Commodius Dimmensions.
A detached spacious Servant's Hall and Rooms over A Stewards Room etc...
In the Basement a very good arched Vaults and Cellarage.
A Bake House, Brewhouse, Laundry etc.,
A range of buildings consisting of the Mews, containing five coach houses four stables for twenty five horses, Men's Servants rooms and Lofts.

The pleasure grounds shrubbery and walks, hangings, and grounds are formed in a grand scale, also a flower garden walled around and a capital green house and two hothouses.' This lot, was a total of 277 acres, it included the obelisk on Troy Hill and 165 acres, occupied by Mr Samuel Slatter, and 100 acres, Burton Dairy House and two cottages on the edge of West Sedgmoor occupied by Mr William Lomas.

Mr Mounter's list includes also the auctioneers' descriptions of the remaining lots, Moortown, Peel Bottom and Owl Street farms, some pasture and meadowland and village property, in all about 1200 acres.

So ended, after thirty-nine years the Pitt family's occupation of Hester's beloved Burton. Today after more than a century of demolition, alteration and rebuilding there is little left of the original house. But the present owner, Mr John Schroder, has repaired the obelisk on Troy Hill which stands as it was intended to do when erected by William Pitt, Earl of Chatham, as a memorial to Sir William Pynsent, benefactor of Chatham and his wife.

APPENDIX II

THE WEATHER AND HEALTH

Almost none of the women's letters to Hester Chatham and few of those from men, fail to mention the weather prevailing at the time of writing, the state of their health (often related to the weather) and anxiety about their correspondent's health. Everyone it seems was a valetudinarian.

None of this surprises. Houses were unheated other than by open fires and no hot pipes ran through them; for outside, in bad weather, clothing and footwear, in the absence of rubber, was inadequate to say the least. Rubber, or caoutchoue as it was called, a product of the Hevea tree, had been known to the Indians of the Americas for generations but it was not until early in the nineteenth century that a viable method of its manipulation was discovered. The comforts of waterproofed coats and rubber boots were unknown to the Chathams and their friends. The primitive sanitation, mainly outdoor, though taken for granted and never (with one exception)[1] mentioned in the correspondence, will have added to the miseries, especially of women, during the all too frequent bouts of illness and to the results of the first of the two remedies most often prescribed for the treatment of any kind of ill health, namely purging, which together with bleeding were, with the help of a limited pharmacopaeia, all the tools available to physicians for treating everything from a cold to a death-dealing illness. The medicine most mentioned is simply referred to as 'the bark'. This would have been either the bark of the Cinchona tree, known as Peruvian bark from which quinine is derived, or its substitute introduced about 1763, willow bark, from which salicin is obtained; both varieties of bark were useful as febriguges, and salicin in particular was effective (as in its modern form it is today) in the relief of pain.

Remedies to prevent illness were unknown (other than the universally prescribed visits to spas), with one important exception: inoculation of children against smallpox. The memory of this disease, epidemic in the late seventeenth century and still around, was fresh and rightly feared. Edward Jenner, the discoverer of the immunising properties of cowpox, only performed his first vaccination in 1796, too late for the Pitt children and their young friends. It had, however, become customary among the educated classes to have their children *inoculated* with a mild form of the disease, a practice introduced by Lady Mary Wortley Montagu in 1721, copied from the Turkish custom she had noted on her travels. The system was not without danger and the event was rightly treated as a serious illness. At the time the Pitt children were undergoing inoculation, the whole household observed quarantine for the specified time, probably about three weeks.

A detailed study of the weather of that time does not belong here, neither also does

---

[1] See letter undated of 1752 from Elizabeth Grenville p. 136

a close analysis of eighteenth century medicine. Rather are we concerned with the reactions to both of Lady Chatham's correspondents. There is, however, one correspondence, that between Hester Chatham and her physician Dr Anthony Addington, from whose frequent, at periods daily letters to her over a long stretch of time in the seventeen-seventies, contain a raft of prescriptions and dietary advice and from this possibly unique record emerges a list of the remedies with which he treated his chief patient, Chatham and also Lady Chatham and their children. Addington, born in 1713, would have received his training at a time when the views of the influential physician, Thomas Sydenham, were still fashionable. Sydenham had advocated the need for a return to the teachings of Hippocrates, namely a system of straightforward clinical observation uncluttered with intellectual theories: a procedure which in Addington's hands was not very productive of cure but at least could do no great harm. The list given here is extracted from the Addington letters (Chapter 8 ii) and the information about these remedies, where identified, is from the Oxford English Dictionary.

Alexterial water	Alexterial = remedy, alleviation, protection
Aleximpharmic	Remedy against poison. 'The horn of a deer is alexipharmical'
Aloe	Drug of bitter taste and purgative qualities procured from the juice of plants of genus aloe.
Antimony	Bright metallic substance, part of the elementary bodies nitrogen, arsenic etc. Calx of antimony = powdery residue left after burning
Balsam, syrup of	Balm. Substance dissolved in oil or turpentine 'The Bark' Bark of various species of the cinchona tree from which quinine is procured, formerly ground into powder and taken as a febrifuge. '. . . a quartern ague is very apt to be rebellious' 1783. W Stark in Med Common I 383:
Bleeding	'Bleeding is the appropriate remedy for a cough'
Blister	Vesicatory. Anything applied to raise a blister. Addington writes that 'extreme pain in the tendons of the feet is a s overeign antidote against gout in the head. But . . . should such an attack happen . . . a blister on the back is the remedy'
Calomel	Purgative medicine
Camphor	White translucent substance belonging chemically to the vegetable oils
Caraway draughts	Volatile oil distilled from seeds of the caraway plant
Castile soap	Formerly Castle soap from Castile in Spain. Addington prescribed one scruple to be taken internally twice daily
Clyster	Enema or suppository. Addington prescribed 'a pint of warm unsalted broth by way of a clyster', and for bladder stricture he prescribed an enema of 10 grs of camphor dissolved in sweet almond oil, 'when the symptom is pressing'

Confection	Medicinal preparation compounded of various drugs 'Confectio damocratis'. Stated by Addington to be a new sedative for irritation in hypochondriacal affections [not identified]
Cordial	Medicine, food or beverage which invigorates the heart and stimulates the circulation. Cordial confection prescribed by Addington:

aromatic species   )

bitter decoction   )   one draught

nutmeg water   )

tragacanth powder   )

Contrayerva	Stimulant and tonic from the rootstock of species Dorstenia, native of tropical America. Diaphoretic. Addington prescribed compound powder of contrayerva and gum arabic, 15 grs, soluble tartar 10 grs, syrup of marshmallow, all in one draught.
Hartshorn, spirit of	Acqueous solution of ammonia obtained by distilling shavings from the horn of harts
Hernia	Addington's difficulty in finding a proper truss maker for Chatham's 'protrusion'. He considered the patient's increased irritation cannot be due to the bandage but more likely arose from internal gout and hypochondria
Jessop water	or Stoke water from Stoke Common, near Claremont in Surrey
Julep	Liquid sweetened with syrup or sugar used as a vehicle for medicine eg cordial julep, expectorant julep, musk julep
Lavender, spirit of	1751 'Lavender has at all times been famous as a cephalic in nervous and uterine medicine'. Hill. Hist. Mat. Med. 424. Addington prescribed this often for Lady Chatham
Marshmallows, syrup of	Expectorant herb used for relief of cough.
Mitheridate of mithridate [not identified]	Described by Addington as soothing and quickening the vital powers.
Myrrh	Tincture made from gum resin of spiny shrub of Arabia and Ethiopia (Balsa). Addington prescribed 5 scruples of the confection and 1 of myrrh in 24 hours
Peppermint water	Cordial distilled from peppermint

Rhubarb	Medicinal rootstock of Rheum. Purgative.
	1803 Med Journal IX 330 'The following bolus . . . consisting of 5 grs of calomel and 15 of rhubarb'.
	Bolus = medicine of round shape adapted for swallowing, larger than an ordinary pill
Saffron	From dried stigmas of *crocus sativus*. Formerly extensively used in medicine as a cordial and sudorific
Seltzer water	Effercescent mineral water from Hesse Nassau, Prussia. (Also an artificial mineral water of similar composition)
Senna	Dried leaflets of *cassia*, used as a cathartic and emetic
Snakeroot	Dried root of *polygan senega* used in medicine.
	Sudorific or counter poison.
	Sudorific = promoting or causing perspiration, diaphoretic
Spermalete	Probably spermaceti = oil from the sperm whale
Valerian	Herbaceous plant *valeriana*. Stimulant or anti-spasmodic.
	Addington prescribed 60 grs valerian and 4 spoonfuls of alexiterial water every 6 hours
Vitriol, acid elixir	Sulphate of metal, eg iron. Elixir of vitriol = distilled essence of vitriol, aromatic sulphuric acid. Addington prescribed 10 drops of the elexir with warnings about its use.

FOOD AND DRINK

Dr Addington gave detailed advice on dietary regimes, varied according to the patients' (mainly Chatham's) medical state. Example: he prefers meat baked in aromatic flavours and salt rather than butter, with a glass of Cyprus wine after dinner; he thought that Chatham's 'enormous and bilious evacuation' may have been caused by dining on beef; he wants Chatham to take daily 2 glasses of plain hock, over and above the Madeira mixed with water and the port taken in sago; French brandy, one tbs to be taken in every cup of sago or sage tea. For a bad patch he advises a diet of 'spoon meals' for 24 hours, viz sago with wine, gruel or panada with wine, almond broth, tea with bread and butter, wine and seltzer water with a slip of bread toasted to eat with it, one or two more glasses of pure wine, all in the 24 hours if sickness or lowness makes it necessary. The want of an evacuation is not serious: 'Nature has business of greater importance'. He was keen on visual evidence of excretions: 'we must not depend on a sudden . . . change in the complexion of the urine', and on analysis by implication: he wishes Mr James (? the son, aged 15) to save the effects of the purge in separate pots and pans'. Chatham can have animal food but should be sparing, 'temperate', in the use of vegetables.

The good doctor was nothing if not diplomatic. He describes both Chatham and *himself* as valetudinarians, eg a person in weak health, one who is constantly concerned with his own ailments.

APPENDIX III

MONEY

The Chathams were always in debt. They were not poor, except by contrast with some, perhaps most of their relations and friends. But they lived in a style far beyond their means. Even in the long years of her widowhood Hester Chatham, though a simple woman, intelligent and practical, for many complex reasons seemed unable to retrench, and her debts and loans continued as during her profligate husband's lifetime, unabated. Throughout the correspondence the subject of money is seldom far away. The letters of Mrs Molly Hood, whose family were substantial creditors and who, with her husband spent long periods trying on behalf of the Chathams to sell Hayes Place, without success, abound in references to financial matters. The Burton letters from 1765, when the estate was inherited, and especially after Chatham's death in 1778, are heavily laced with figures of expenditure. Though outside the scope of this study there are in the papers two volumes of correspondence with the Chathams' banker, Thomas Coutts, a patient and sympathetic man, genuinely fond of Hester Chatham, but also shrewd in awareness of the political power of William, her son.

It seems appropriate therefore that an attempt should be made here to link the value of money in the second half of the eighteenth century with the value of the present day. This is not an easy task. The American historical writer, J J Mangan, in his book *King's Favour*[1] has attempted to do so; in a brief note or foreword to his book, which he has kindly allowed to be quoted from, he writes:

> Because money is among the most troublesome of human inventions, translating prices of a particular time into present day prices is a risky business. No handy booklet exists. Nor do monetry experts when closely examined, agree on much. . . Writers have used the price of a loaf of bread, or a workman's daily wages to convey 'money's worth'. However most aristocrats of the eighteenth century never purchased a loaf of bread, nor did they have any idea of what a workman might earn. Courtiers and the propertied classes of most periods understood, however the price of gold as do investors today.
> Even the 'golden constant', as it has been called, is only really useful for rough translations of value from century to century. Gold has withstood wars, revolutions, devaluations and revaluations, with greater integrity than most standards, but not perfectly. The author hastens to disavow any claim to precision, therefore, in comparisons of antique and present-day money in this book. They were arrived at with reference to the price of gold, using the following simple formulas: Prices in English pounds of the early 1700s were multiplied by fifty to arrive at prices in pounds sterling and by a hundred for US dollar prices of the late 1900s.

Mr Mangan includes in his note the equivalents in French livres and imperial gold roubles and asks that the reader's indulgence would be appreciated.

---

[1] Allan Sutton Publishing 1991

Using Mr Mangan's formula, we find that the widowed Lady Chatham's annual pension, nominally of £3000 but after deductions about £2000 and generally in arrears of payment, would be worth about £100,000. The refurbishment of Hayes Place in 1766 (while still retaining Burton Pynsent) cost over £2000 or £100,000 at today's prices. On the other hand, in the year after Hester Chatham's death, 1804, Burton Pynsent was sold at auction, in lots, the mansion and 1200 acres, including three productive farms and their buildings, at an estimated return of about £1600. In today's values (using Mr Mangan's formula) this would represent a sum of about £80,000, certainly considerably less than such a property would fetch today.

There is no easy answer to this problem of comparison between the value of money then and now. Historically, some interesting facts emerge: all through the latter part of the eighteenth, and for all of the following century, prices, though subject to short but fairly violent upward movements, and to considerable regional variation, remained in essence stable. For example, Hester Chatham would have found the cost of living in 1895 not much different to her experience in 1780. It is only when we try to equate money values with the state we find them in at this century's end, following the unrelenting inflation of the last thirty years or so, that attempts at comparison make little sense.

APPENDIX IV

THE POST

In a work given to correspondence of the eighteenth century, a note of postal arrangements of that time seems to be called for. There are many references to the post in the letters written to Hester Chatham. One example will suffice. Dr Anthony Addington, writing from his property at Upottery, a Devon village on the river Otter five miles north of Honiton, thanks Lady Chatham on 28th July for her letter of 19th July from Hayes in north-east Kent, two miles south of Bromley. Even for this somewhat complex journey, an interval of nine days for a letter to reach its destination was unusually long and would have drawn comment from the recipient. In a later letter Dr Addington remarks that a letter to Lady Chatham which 'our servant put into the Post Office at Taunton' on 4th August only reached her at Hayes three days later. He goes on to explain 'our situation here [at Upottery] as to Post Letters is unfortunate. The Axminster Boy returns from Honiton with the Western Bag from the East, so that we can never receive and answer a letter the same day'.

In fact the post in the latter half of the century, given the still primitive state of the roads and hand delivery by single riders was surprisingly good. From early in the seventeenth century the rulers of most European states were at pains to maintain a regular service. By 1777, when Dr Addington was writing, improvements in road building had brought corresponding improvements in the postal service on main routes radiating from London. At the end of the century the arrival of the stagecoach, used by the post office, and superceding the mounted postboys on main routes, had already transformed delivery times: by 1830 letters posted in towns more than 120 miles from London could be delivered the morning after posting.

Sending letters was expensive. The cheapest rate was fourpence and the average just over sixpence; charges were assessed by the distance the letter had to travel and were paid for on delivery. But letters were the only way in which friends and relations could communicate one with another and separations were mostly long. Thus it is that no complaint of cost is ever voiced in this correspondence, only of delay. It is, however, noticeable that all the writers were at pains to fill all four pages of the double-fold writing paper in use at that time. Only rich men, Lord Temple being one such, ignored the cost and wrote mainly short notes. (He probably also sent these by private messenger though we have no proof in the correspondence that he did so). Some letters were enclosed in envelopes but the majority were folded down and sealed, not gummed, to reveal the name and address of the intended recipient, not unlike the modern air letter.

Another dodge to save cost was to have your letter franked on the exposed address portion by a member of parliament, a privilege introduced in 1660, and much abused;

such letters were carried free of charge at great loss to the Post Office. Catherine Stapleton's brothers-in-law, all three of whom were MPs, were readily at hand for this service when she was on her round of visits to her sisters' homes and she made frequent use of this cost saving device. A stratagem for the same purpose, used by some of Hester Chatham's correspondents, was to address letters intended for the wife to the husband.

It was not until the publication in 1837, more than thirty years after Lady Chatham's death, of Rowland Hill's 'Post Office Reform' leading to the introduction three years later of the prepaid penny post (and abolishing also the privilege of post-free letters of members of parliament and their friends) brought the revolutionary change in postal arrangements which in principle - though not in cost - continues to this day. How welcome would this change have been to Hester and her correspondents.

INDEX

A

abeles, white poplars, 19

Abercorn, James (Hamilton), 6th earl of, 78

Abingdon, Peregrine (Bertie), 6th earl of, 312

Absentee Landlords (Ireland), bill (1773), 114

Acton Hall, seat, co Denbigh, 180, 200-202

Addington, Dr Anthony MD, 11, 105, 307, 310-311, 319, 341-343, 346

    letters from, 253-268

    Mary, his wife, 255, 257, 266

    Charlotte, their daughter, 268

    relations with Hester Chatham, 253-268 *passim*

    knowledge of mental illness, 254, 261-262

    drugs and treatment prescribed *see* medicinal remedies

    fees, 265-266

    on American war, 254, 264

Addington, Henry MP, from 1804 1st Viscount Sidmouth, 255, 260, 267

Adelaide, Madame, 4th daughter of Louis XV, 89

Admiralty Office, 34

Aix la Chapelle, treaty of (1748), 80-81

Albemarle, George (Keppel), 3rd earl of, 92

Alfonso the wise, King of Castile (1221-1284), 173

Alford, Revd Samuel and wife, Heale House, Som, 299-301, 336

    son Henry, 299-301

    son Thomas, lieut RN, 299, 336

Alfred, HMS, 120

Allen, Ralph, notable of Bath, 6

Almacks, social club, 150, 155, 189

Althorp, Northants, seat, 141

Amelia, Princess, daughter of George II, 213-214

America, North, Anglo-French war in *see* Canada

America, War of Independence in, 10, 30, 49-50, 120, 317

    see also Versailles, Peace of

Amersham, Bucks, Mr Drake's inn at, 154

Ancaster, Mary, Dowager Duchess of, 164

Anci le Franc (? Annency), 169

Andover, Mary (Finch), Viscountess, 198

Andover, Hants, 1, 314

Andrews, Mr (Wells cathederal), 306

Anson, George, adm, 1st baron, 60, 126

Anson, Thomas, 220, 221

Antigua, island, 327

Appleby, Westm, constituency, 330

Apsley, Lord *see* Bathurst,

Arbuthnot, Capt, RN, 232

Argyll, John (Campbell), 5th duke of, 111

    Elizabeth (Gunning), his wife, formerly duchess of Hamilton, 111

    Jane, Dowager duchess of, widow of 2nd duke, 131

Arley or Areley Hall, Staffs, seat, 67, 71-73

    rural sports at, 66, 72

    Xmas festivities at, 73

arqubusade, medicinal water, 110

Ash, Dr John, MD, 182

Ashburnham, John, 4th baron, 80

Ashburton, baron *see* Dunning,

asses'milk, remedy, 17, 82, 86, 254, 328

Attorney General *see* Yorke, Charles,

Atwood, Mr, 278

Auckland, William (Eden), 1st baron, 336

Audley End, Essex, seat, 20

Audley Street, no.14, Boscawen house in, 147-176 *passim*

Augusta, Princess of Wales, 78, 92

    death of, 185

    sales of jewellry and effects, 188

Augusta, HMS, 63

Austrian Succession, war of (1740-48), 80-81

    see also Aix la Chappelle, treaty of; Maastricht

Aylesbury, Bucks, 1, 36

    races at, 26

Aylesford, Heaneage (Finch), 3rd earl of, 41

    Charlotte (Seymour), his wife, 41, 145

Ayling, Stanley, historian, his *The Elder Pitt* (1976), 99, 145

Ayrshire, 93

    St Quivox in, 94

Ayscough, Revd Dr Francis, 65

    Anne (Lyttelton), his wife, 69

B

Baby *see under* horses

backgammon, board game, 34

Badminton House, Glos, seat, 152, 154-159, 162, 168, 170

    Christmas festivities at (1800), 176-177

Bagshot Park, Surrey, seat, 155

Balchen, John, adm, 63

Bale, Mr, 132

Balm of Gilead, medical remedy, 134

Bampfield, Elias, attorney, Langport, Som, 270-275, 282, 287, 295, 302

Bamfylde, Lady, 163

Banks, Margaret (Peggy), from 1757 Mrs Henry Grenville, 36, 58-59, 63, 81, 181, 214

Barbados, island, governership of, 36,58

Bardel *see* Bardwell

Bardwell, Thomas, portrait painter, 130-131

'Bark, the' (chinchona/willow), remedy, 40, 262, 340

Barker, G F R, historian, 33, 65

Barré, Isaac, MP, 31

Barrington, William Wildman, MP, 2nd viscount, 34

Bath, Som, spa, 48-50, 59, 69-70, 79-80, 92, 100, 105, 126, 147, 152, 167-168, 209-220, 256, 290

    Pitt's house at, no. 7 The Circus, 5-6

    Mrs Trevor's house at, nos 5/6 The Circus, 209-220 *passim*

    entertainments at, 152, 212, 216-217

    election at (1775), 49-50

    growth of, 212

    mayor of *see* Horton

Bath and Wells, bishop of (Dr Charles Moss), 215

Bath, Sir William (Pultenay), from 1742 1st earl of, 126

Bathurst, Henry, Lord Apsley, from 1775 2nd earl, 227

348

Combe, Richard, of Earnshill, Som, 101-102, 274, 282
Combermere Abbey, Salop, seat, 179, 190, 198-199
Commerce, gambling game, 163
Condè, Prince de, 85
Constantinople, embassy of, 58
Conway see under Wales
Cookham, near Maidenhead, Berks, Mrs Edwin's house at, 131-132
Cooling, Richard, gardener, Burton Pynsent, 290-292
Copley, John Singleton the Elder, painter,28
Cornwall:
    constituencies, 153
    fencible cavalry of, 167-168, 172
    see also Boconnoc; Truro
Cornwallis, Charles, 1st marquess, gen, 248
Cornwallis, Rt Revd James, bishop, later 4th earl, 248
Cotton, Sir Robert, MP, 199, 202-203, 297
    Frances (Stapleton), his wife, 179, 198-199, 202
Coulanges, M. de, 136
Coutts, Thomas, banker, 29, 265, 297, 324, 329, 332
Coventry, George William, 6th earl of, 88
    Maria (Gunning), his wife, 88
Crauford, George, lawyer, 324
Crawford, ..., consul, Amsterdam, 250
Cresswell, William, manservant, 311
cribbage, card game, 141, 168, 209, 217-219
cricket matches, 97
Cricket St Thomas, estate, Som, 112-113, 117-118
Crillon, Marquis de, 86
Croft, James, manservant, 311
Cröy, Prince de, 21
Cunliffe, Sir Ellis decd, 256
Curragh, races at, 67-68
Curry Rivel, Som, 269-309 passim
    St Andrew's Church in, 275-298

D

Darlington, Margaret (Lowther), countess of, 111, 189
Dash, Johnathan, riding master, Bath, 168
Dauphin and Dauphine see Louis; Maria Josepha
Davenant, Charles (1636-1714), his Essays upon the Balances of Power; The Right of making War, Peace and Alliance etc., 317
Dawson, Nancy, dancer, popular song named for her, 72
Dean, Mr of Warwick, 74
Defiance, HMS, 64-65
de Clifford, Sophia, Dowager lady, 165
Delany, Revd Dr Patrick, 69
Demezys, Mr of Hartford Bridge, Hants, 314
Denbigh, Isabella (de Jonge), countess of, 124, 126, 128, 134, 198
Denbigh, co, 23
Denmark, queen of see Caroline Matilda,
Derry, bishop of see Bristol
de Stael, Madame Germaine, 170
Devizes, Wilts, 113, 267
Devonshire, Georgiana (Spencer), duchess of, 161, 217
Dieppe, port, N France, 151
Doctor James's powder, favorite remedy, 40, 91
dominos, hooded dress, 80, 330

Doneraile, Hayes (St Leger) 4th viscount, estate of, 69
Donne, ..., surveyor, Som, 274
Dorchester, baron see Carleton
Dover Street, Cathcart house in, 97
Downing Street, no. 10, 267, 333-334
Downs, The, seaway, 63
Drayton, parish, Som, tithes dispute in, 282
dress see clothing and dress
Dropmore Lodge, Bucks, seat, 248
Drumlanrig, Henry (Douglas), earl of, death of, 5, 137-138
Dryden, John, writer (1631-1700), his Fables, Ancient and Modern (1700), 82
Dublin:
    Castle, 68
    Merrion Street in, 66, 68
    Stephen's Green in, 70
    see also Blackrock
Dumeresq, Revd Dr Daniel, of Yeovilton, 336
Duncan, Dr Sir William, MD, 22, 40, 134, 182
Dunning, John, MP, from 1782 1st baron Ashburton, 31, 311
Dunstable, Beds, 22, 182
Dupont, Gainsborough, portrait painter, 246
Dynevor or Dinevor, Cecil (Talbot), baroness, 216
    Cecilia (Rice) her daughter, 216

E

Eastbourne, Sussex, Beaufort house at, 156, 174
Eastbury House, Blandford, Dors, seat, 39-40
East India Company, treasures of, 332
Easton Hall, Northants, seat, 141
Eden, Hon Eleanor, 336
Edward, HRH Prince, 163
Edward Augustus, HRH Duke of York, death of, 101
Edwin, Lady Charlotte, 83, 135, 191
Edwin, Mrs of Cookham, Bath, singer, 80-81, 131-132
Effingham, Thomas (Howard), 3rd earl of, 312
Egremont, Sir George (Wyndham), 3rd earl of, 20, 191
    Alicia Maria (Carpenter), wife of 2nd earl, 187
electricity, 325
Elford Hall, Staffs, seat, 198
Eliot, Hon Edward MP (son in law), 123, 163, 214, 217, 240, 245, 334-335
    Harriot, his wife see Pitt
    Hester Harriet, their daughter, 163, 173, 176-177, 204. 217
Elliot, Col, 59
Ellis, Mrs, Mrs Trevor's companion, 216
Emden, regiment of, 17
Enfield, 154
    Enfield Chase, 156
Epsom, Surrey, races at, 163
Ernest, HRH Prince, Duke of Cumberland, 219
Essex, William A H (Capel), 4th earl of, 176
Eton College, Windsor, 37, 39, 40
etrennes, 177
Euston, George Henry (Fitzroy), earl of, MP, 32
    Elizabeth (Wrottesley), his wife, 163
Evelyn, John, diarist (1620-1706), 146
Exeter, Henry (Cecil), 1st marquess of, 157

Wurttenburg, Hereditary Prince Frederick William of, 251
    Princess of *see* Charlotte Augusta Matilda
Wyatt, James, architect, 159

Wyndham, Elizabeth, from 1749 Mrs George Grenville, 1-2, 14,
        35, 41, 79-80, 90, 94, 178
    letters from, 124-145
    parentage, 124
    character, 124
    love of riding and horses, 130, 132-133, 135, 139, 144
    political awareness, 125-126
    supports Protestant causes, 142
    dress, 138
    appearance, 125
    health, 37-38, 103, 124, 143
    on Forty-five rebellion, 128-129
    marriage, 36, 125, 131
    domestic life, 133-134
    death, 22, 38, 103, 125, 144, 178, 180
    brothers of *see* Egremont; Thormond
Wyndham, Sir William, 124
    Lady Catherine (Seymour), 1st wife, 124
    Maria (de Jonge), 2nd wife *see* Blandford
Wynn, Sir Watkin Williams, 23, 26, 106, 111, 179, 184-185, 187,
        189, 204
    Charlotte, his wife *see* Grenville
    Frances (Shakerley), his mother, 23, 106-107, 184
Wynnstay, co. Denbigh, seat, 31, 198-200

Y

Yarmouth, Francis (Seymour Conway), earl of, from 1794 2nd
        marquess of Hertford, 165
    see also Fagnani, Miss
Yonge, Penelope (Stapleton) wife of Ellis Yonge of Acton, 179-
    180
York, dukes *see* Edward Augustus; Frederick
Yorke, Charles, attorney general (1762), 44
Yorke, Lady Elizabeth, 162

Printed in the United Kingdom for HMSO
Dd294245 7/95 C5 G3397 10170